Schwarz on Tax Treaties

Schwarz on Tax Treaties

Jonathan Schwarz

a Wolters Kluwer business

Wolters Kluwer (UK) Limited
145 London Road
Kingston-upon-Thames
Surrey
KT2 6SR
Telephone: +44 (0) 844 561 8166
Facsimile: +44 (0) 208 247 1184
email: customerservices@cch.co.uk
website: www.cch.co.uk

This publication is sold with the understanding that neither the publisher nor the authors, with regard to this publication, are engaged in rendering legal or professional services. The material contained in this publication neither purports, nor is intended to be, advice on any particular matter.

Although this publication incorporates a considerable degree of standardisation, subjective judgement by the user, based on individual circumstances, is indispensable. This publication is an aid and cannot be expected to replace such judgement.

Neither the publisher nor the authors can accept any responsibility or liability to any person, whether a purchaser of this publication or not, in respect of anything done or omitted to be done by any such person in reliance, whether sole or partial, upon the whole or any part of the contents of this publication.

Legislative and other material

While copyright in all statutory and other materials resides in the Crown or other relevant body, copyright in the remaining material in this publication is vested in the publisher.

The publisher advises that any statutory or other materials issued by the Crown or other relevant bodies and reproduced and quoted in this publication are not the authorised official versions of those statutory or other materials. In the preparation, however, the greatest care has been taken to ensure exact conformity with the law as enacted or other material as issued.

Crown copyright legislation is reproduced under the terms of Crown Copyright Policy Guidance issued by HMSO. Other Crown copyright material is reproduced with the permission of the controller of HMSO. European Communities Copyright material is reproduced with permission.

Telephone Helpline Disclaimer Notice

Where purchasers of this publication also have access to any Telephone Helpline Service operated by Wolters Kluwer (UK), then Wolters Kluwer's total liability to contract, tort (including negligence, or breach of statutory duty) misrepresentation, restitution or otherwise with respect to any claim arising out of its acts or alleged omissions in the provision of the Helpline Service shall be limited to the yearly subscription fee paid by the Claimant.

British Library Cataloguing-in-Publication Data

A catalogue record for this book is available from the British Library.

Cover painting © Annette Schwarz 2009
Typeset in-house at Wolters Kluwer (UK) Ltd
Printed and bound in the UK by Hobbs the Printers Ltd

About the author

Jonathan Schwarz

Jonathan Schwarz, BA, LLB, LLM, FTII, is a barrister at Temple Tax Chambers in London. He has extensive practical experience in international tax planning and tax disputes involving international issues, and is a recognised expert in the field. He is a vice president of the International Fiscal Association and Visiting Professorial Fellow at the School of Tax Law, Queen Mary, London University. His unique background, including postgraduate study in the United States, and experience as a South African advocate and Canadian barrister and solicitor, gives him a truly international perspective on the UK system of international taxation.

Preface

You shall have one manner of law, as for the stranger, as for the home born.

Leviticus xxiv, 22.

The primary purpose of this book is to examine tax treaties from a UK perspective. Each jurisdiction views tax treaties by reference to not only international law but also its own tax rules, administrative law and constitutional rules whose variations reflect domestic values of each society. Thus, treaties need to be seen both in their international context and the wider legal systems of contracting states.

Each jurisdiction makes its own contribution to the developing international approach to interpretation and application of treaties. The UK has long had considerable input in the development of tax treaties at an administrative level through its participation in the work of the OECD Committee of Fiscal Affairs, and its antecedents in the Organisation for European Economic Cooperation and the League of Nations. Courts in the UK, for reasons of both history and cogency, carry respect and authority worldwide. Legal systems in the UK intersect with common law countries to share legal traditions, constitutional norms, and approaches to questions of international law. At the same time, in addressing the requirements of Community law, the UK intersects with the civil law traditions of other European Union member states. I hope this book will assist not only readers concerned with the international aspects of taxation in the UK but also all those with an interest in tax treaties.

While the development of law and practice relating to tax treaties has been rapid, it remains unsystematic. Despite an increasing number of judicial decisions each year, there are many unanswered questions where guidance will inevitably be sought from foreign sources, as well as the commentary to the OECD model itself. In order to maintain a UK perspective, I have refrained from referring to foreign sources or excessive reference to the commentary and other works published by the OECD. While they are undoubtedly important sources, their use is still dependent on the cogency of their reasoning. Despite the presence of the OECD models for 50 years, UK treaties are by no means uniform. Each is based on negotiations relating to the state of the UK tax system at the time, the foreign tax system, the negotiating strength of the parties and the overall balance of each specific treaty. As in recent years, the pace of domestic change has become more rapid, and the OECD model and commentary itself is amended and updated more frequently. Its normative quality is eroded as a result. At the end of the day, however, there is no substitute for a close study of individual treaty provisions using the proper interpretative tools.

This book is grouped loosely into several parts, the first dealing with the legal framework both under UK and European law. The second part deals with interpretation of treaties, followed by the third part, which examples the factors qualifying persons for treaty benefits. The fourth part looks at the distributive provisions of typical income tax treaties and the rules relating to credit for foreign tax. A further chapter examines treaty shopping and other avoidance. Finally, chapters deal with the practical administration of treaties, including claiming treaty benefits; and dispute resolution, including the Transfer Pricing Arbitration Convention. Finally, the growing field of administrative cooperation between tax authorities, including exchange of information and cross-border collection of taxes, is considered.

This work builds on my previous book *Tax Treaties: United Kingdom Law and Practice*. Much has changed in the intervening period in which the UK has negotiated over 20 comprehensive income tax treaties, some with countries whose tax systems are very different from the UK or other OECD member countries. The biggest change, however, has been in relation to the conclusion of nearly the same number of treaties devoted entirely to authorising administrative cooperation in the exchange of information and collection of taxes with foreign tax authorities. In the 20th century, administrative cooperation was largely limited to exchange of information in conjunction with the elimination of double taxation. It has taken time for cross-border cooperation to catch up with the mobility of people and resources. In this time, scant regard has been paid to the special concerns and safeguards necessary, particularly now that information may potentially be exchanged with or sought from countries that do not share democratic values or institutions. Peace and order, along with social and economic justice, form the cornerstones of democratic society. These cornerstones do not come cheap, and it is the responsibility of those able to pay to finance their cost. Caution should be exercised lest the machinery of state in the pursuit of democratic objectives at home be used as an instrument of oppression elsewhere.

My thanks go to the CCH team, in particular to Paul Robbins for much encouragement and patience. This book is generally up to date to the beginning of March 2009, and the treaties commented on are generally in force at the time of writing. All comments and suggestions from readers are most welcome.

Jonathan Schwarz
London
March 2009

For

my parents, Annette and Harry,

with love and appreciation.

Contents

The Legal Framework: United Kingdom Law

Chapter 1

10-000   Introduction

Tax treaties are no different, juridically speaking, from any other treaties that may be entered into by the UK. Tax treaties do differ from their counterparts outside the tax area in that, with two exceptions, they are bilateral while the UK is a party to many multilateral treaties. The distinction is of limited significance, although it arguably affects the way in which treaties are interpreted.

10-050   What are tax treaties?

A treaty is 'an international agreement concluded between states in written form and governed by international law, whether embodied in a single instrument, or in two or more related instruments and whatever its particular designation'.[1] Thus, although particular treaties may be labelled as 'agreements', 'conventions', 'arrangements' or otherwise, they are, in effect, treaties under international law.[2] In modern treaty practice, the expression includes, in particular, agreements, conventions, declarations and protocols.

Exchanges of notes by way of letters between the contracting states have become increasingly important, particularly in treaty negotiations with certain developing countries. In some cases, notes are exchanged to clarify or expand the formal treaty document. This has been justified on the basis that certain items are more easily agreed in this way (with the authorities of those contracting states) than by their incorporation into the formal treaty. As a matter of international law, they are either part of the treaty or separate treaties in their own right.

Exchanges of notes are also used to make the updating of treaties more flexible. For example, the Malaysia Treaty[3] excludes from treaty benefits persons entitled to any special tax benefit under a law that has been identified in an exchange of notes of either contracting state. In this case, a note was exchanged contemporaneously with the signing of the treaty. In addition, it leaves the way open for relatively informal and speedy amendment, in order to deal with subsequent developments in the domestic law of member states. To date,

---

[1] Vienna Convention on the Law of Treaties 1969, art. 2, para. 1(a).

[2] See also HMRC, *International Tax Handbook*, para. 501.

[3] 10 December 1996, (SI 1997/2987, art. 25(2)).

exchanges of notes have only appeared contemporaneously with the execution of treaties, but no doubt in the future, notes may be exchanged on other occasions.

Non-treaties

It is a requirement for the existence of a treaty as a matter of public international law that it be concluded between states.[4] The government of a state normally has the authority to conclude treaties on behalf of that state. Until 2002 the implementing provisions of s. 788(1) referred to arrangements 'made with the Government of any territory'. The words 'made in relation to any territory' were substituted by Finance Act (FA) 2002, s. 88(1), on and after 24 July 2002 in relation to arrangements made before that date (as well as in relation to arrangements made on or after that date). The result is that an arrangement within s. 788 need no longer be concluded with a foreign government. This legislative fig leaf was introduced specifically to give effect to an 'arrangement' entered into in respect of Taiwan, which is not recognised by the UK but with whom a treaty was thought desirable. Agreement was reached on 8 April 2002 between the British Trade and Cultural Office, Taipei and the Taipei Representative Office in the UK for the avoidance of double taxation and the prevention of fiscal evasion with respect to taxes on income and capital gains. This agreement is based on the OECD Model and looks much like a treaty. It is, however, doubtful whether it qualifies as a treaty. While it is given effect to in UK domestic law,[5] its legal status and manner of having been entered into will affect the way in which it is interpreted.[6] It also raises questions about mutual agreement procedures and exchange of information.[7] Section 788 should be reserved for treaties and specific legislation ought to be enacted to give effect to such expediencies.

These changes to the scope of a treaty have several consequences. The ability to enter into 'arrangements' that relate to a particular territory are very wide. They may provide an opportunity for arrangements with provincial or state authorities in some federal jurisdiction where, on the one hand, the federal government cannot bind the provincial government by its treaty and, on the other hand, provincial or state governments have no capacity to enter into treaties under their relevant constitutional provisions. The amendments allow arrangements to be entered into with any person with respect to any territory. No limitations are imposed on this and no connecting factors between the persons entering into the arrangements and the territory are identified. The new language cannot, however, convert these arrangements into treaties as a matter of international law. In addition, the changes will have an impact on tax treaties. Since agreements may be made with respect to territories, it is possible that more than one treaty will apply to particular territories where two or more foreign governments both lay claim to that territory.

The implementing legislation in respect of income and corporation tax[8] refers to 'arrangements'. This is an unfortunate expression given that the word is used in other

---

[4] Vienna Convention on the Law of Treaties 1969, art. 1.

[5] SI 2002/3137.

[6] See chapter 3, para. 12-000.

[7] See chapters 18 and 20.

[8] ICTA 1988, s. 788.

contexts to mean something totally different. It is presumably intended to denote a wide variety of agreements between the UK and other contracting states, yet, in reality, it adds nothing to the term treaty as understood by the Vienna Convention. In this book, the word treaty is used throughout as a matter of consistency and to accord with the Vienna Convention.

10-100   Treaty-making

The power to make treaties forms part of the conduct of foreign affairs and the power to make treaties is a function of the Crown. It is a residual power that exists as a matter of Royal prerogative.[9] Authority to negotiate and conclude treaties is given to agents of the Crown. [10]

The procedures involved in negotiating treaties have been well set out by RT Bartlett.[11] Only a few additional observations are appropriate. The negotiation and conclusion of treaties takes place behind closed doors. Although HMRC invites submissions from interested parties, when discussions are to take place with a view to concluding a treaty, the text of the treaty is not revealed until a draft Order is laid before the House of Commons. Thus, unlike domestic legislation including subsidiary legislation, there is no opportunity for interested parties to comment on the terms until the agreement has been concluded. The text of treaty provisions forms part of the work of the HMRC Solicitor's Office staff with formal constitutional and international law aspects addressed by Foreign Office lawyers.

Before any Order in Council proposed to be made is submitted to Her Majesty in Council, a draft of the Order must be laid before the House of Commons, and the Order is not submitted unless an address is presented to Her Majesty by that House praying that the Order be made.[12] Thus, the opportunities for interested parties to comment on the acceptability of treaty provisions is extremely limited. Although the terms of the treaty may be the subject of debate in the House of Commons and in principle the House may decline to submit an address to the Crown for an Order to be made, requiring the treaty to be renegotiated, this has yet to happen.

10-150   Scope of tax treaties

There is no limit on what may be agreed in a treaty in connection with taxation. In the field of taxation, until the 21st century, almost all tax treaties were bilateral and principally aimed at preventing double taxation. The earliest tax treaties to which the UK was a party only addressed the profits of shipping and air transport; a handful of such treaties remain, notably in countries that the UK has been unable to, or simply has not, negotiated a 'comprehensive'

---

[9] See, for example, *Blackburn v Attorney-General* [1971] All ER 1380 per Lord Denning MR at 1040: 'The treaty making power rests … in the Crown; that is, Her Majesty acting on the advice of her Ministers. When her Ministers negotiate and sign a treaty … they act on behalf of the country as a whole. They exercise the prerogative of the Crown'.

[10] See Bartlett, RT, 'The making of double taxation agreements', *British Tax Review* (*BTR*), 76 (1991).

[11] *Ibid.*

[12] ICTA 1988, s. 788(10).

double taxation treaty. These have been followed by broader treaties covering income tax, corporation tax and capital gains tax that aim at preventing double taxation. These comprehensive treaties form the vast majority of UK treaties. The UK is also a party to a limited number of rather old estate and gift tax treaties, which today cover inheritance tax. The first multilateral tax treaty entered into by the UK in 1992 was the EC Arbitration Convention. The essential function of multilateral tax treaties is to avoid double taxation and allocate taxing rights between treaty partners. These treaties have the common effect of conferring specific benefits on particular taxpayers who meet the requirements of the treaty.

A second aim of treaties has been the prevention of fiscal evasion. This has traditionally been addressed by exchange of information provisions in bilateral treaties. The scope of these provisions has broadened over time. Since 2004 a radical departure from the traditional use of treaties to avoid double taxation has take place. The UK has now entered into three new categories of tax treaty that confer no benefits on particular taxpayers but assist HMRC in administering UK taxes and require HMRC to assist foreign tax authorities in the same way. Tax information exchange agreements simply provide, firstly, for the supply of information concerning taxes specified in those agreements; secondly, savings tax agreements provide for the exchange of information in connection with interest payments to UK residents and require the non-UK contracting states to withhold tax on such interest payments in certain circumstances; and, thirdly, in 2007, the UK became a party to another multilateral tax treaty – the OECD/Council of Europe Convention on Mutual Assistance in Tax Matters – which deals, in particular, with cross-border collection of taxes. Cross-border collection of taxes is also now provided for in the 2007 protocol to the New Zealand Treaty. This trend towards the use of treaties to facilitate collaboration between HMRC and other tax administrations is likely to continue.

10-200 Treaty implementation

Although treaties validly concluded are binding on the state without parliamentary sanction, they do not have effect on the laws of the UK until appropriate legislative action has been taken.[13] The precise consequences of this in the taxation context were summed up by Park J in *Boake Allen Ltd & Ors (including NEC Semi-Conductors Ltd) v Revenue and Customs Commissioners*[14] thus:

> '[9]. Double taxation agreements are treaties concluded between sovereign states. Under the law of the United Kingdom they are entered into in exercise of the prerogative power of the Crown. Under our law treaties are not "self-executing": that means that, although they are binding in international law between the United Kingdom and the other State as soon as they are concluded (or ratified, if by their terms they require ratification), they do not then take automatic effect in domestic law as part of the law of the United Kingdom. The intervention of Parliament, either directly by statute or by statutory delegation authorising another person or body to bring the treaty into effect domestically, is needed.'

---

[13] In *McLaine Watson v Department of Trade* [1989] 3 All ER 523, HL, Lord Templeman said at 526: 'A treaty to which Her Majesty's Government is a party does not alter the laws of the United Kingdom. Except to the extent that a treaty becomes incorporated into the laws of the United Kingdom by statute, the courts of the United Kingdom have no power to enforce treaty rights and obligations at the behest of a sovereign government or on behalf of a private individual.'

[14] [2006] BTC 266 [2006] EWCA Civ 25.

This formulation was fully adopted by Lloyd LJ on appeal.[15]

ICTA 1988, s. 788,[16] contains enabling legislation to give effect to tax treaties in domestic law. Section 788(1) specifies that:

'If Her Majesty by Order in Council declares that arrangements specified in the Order have been made in respect of any territory outside the United Kingdom with a view to affording relief from double taxation in relation to:

(a)   income tax;
(b)   corporation tax in respect of income or chargeable gains; an
(c)   any taxes of a similar character to those taxes imposed by the laws of that territory,

and that it is expedient that those arrangements should have effect, then those arrangements shall have effect.'

The section does not provide for authority to conclude treaties, but simply refers to arrangements 'that have been made', the authority to negotiate and conclude treaties being a matter of delegation of the Crown's treaty-making prerogative.

10-250   Extent of treaty implementation

Although there is no limit on what may be agreed in a treaty, the implementing legislation may not give unlimited authority to give effect to treaties. In relation to income tax and corporation tax, for example, s. 788(3) of the Taxes Act 1988 prescribes that treaties shall have effect insofar as they provide for:

'(a)   relief from income tax or from corporation tax in respect of income or chargeable gains;
(b)   charging the income arising from sources or chargeable gains accruing on the disposal of assets in the United Kingdom to persons not resident in the United Kingdom;
(c)   determining the income or chargeable gains to be attributed:

(i)   to persons not resident in the United Kingdom and their agencies, branches or establishments in the United Kingdom; or
(ii)   to persons not resident in the United Kingdom who have special relationships with persons not so resident;

(d)   for conferring on persons not resident in the United Kingdom, the right to a tax credit under section 231 in respect of qualifying distributions made to them by companies which are so resident;
(e)   relief from foreign tax by way of credit is not specifically authorised, although tax sparing as a sub-species of foreign tax credit relief is.[17]'

Insofar as treaties apply to capital gains, authority is extended by reference to the income and corporation tax rules.[18] For capital gains purposes, references to income in Part XVIII of the Taxes Act 1988 are substituted by references to capital gains.

[15] [2006] BTC 266 [2006] EWCA Civ 25, para. 25.

[16] Hereinafter referred to as 'Taxes Act 1988'.

[17] ICTA 1988, s. 788(5).

[18] Taxation of Chargeable Gains Act 1992 (TCGA 1992), s. 277(1).

In the case of petroleum revenue tax, a similar device is used.[19] For the purpose of petroleum revenue tax, references in s. 788 of the Taxes Act 1988 to income tax are treated as references to petroleum revenue tax and references to income are to include references to consideration brought into charge on receipts attributable to UK use of foreign field assets.[20] This only applies where the treaty includes petroleum revenue tax as a tax to which the treaty applies.[21] The petroleum revenue tax provisions are more precisely described in incorporating the references than is the case with capital gains. Thus, references to ss. 788(3)(b), (c) and (d) are not incorporated by reference. Tax treaties have effect for inheritance tax purposes under Inheritance Tax Act 1984, s. 158.

Somewhat surprisingly, the extent to which s. 788(3) gives effect to treaties has given rise to a number of disputes that have come before the courts where the Inland Revenue has sought to rely on non-incorporation in domestic law to refuse treaty benefits.

The process for testing whether a treaty provision is incorporated was described in *UBS AG v Revenue and Customs Commissioners* [2007] BTC 285 [2007] EWCA Civ 119 by Moses LJ thus:

> 'One might expect to be able to look at one of those [treaty] provisions and resolve the statutory question posed by section 788(3), namely does that Article provide for any one of the matters within section 788(3)(a)–(d)? If that substantive provision does so provide, then it has effect in UK law.[22]'

In response to an argument that, in the context of the non-discrimination provisions of the Swiss Treaty, UK treaty negotiators proceed on the basis that the treaty would not be fully in effect, he said:

> '[10] Whilst it is easy to accept that those negotiating the Convention on behalf of the UK will have been aware that not all the provisions of the Convention will have effect by virtue of section 788(3), it is less palatable to conceive that they intended Articles 23(1) and (2) to be mere windy rhetoric, on the basis that they make no substantive provision for anything.
>
> [11] Accordingly, I take the view that there must be some process by which the non-discrimination provision can be given effect in United Kingdom law.'

Similarly, in *Bricom Holdings v IRC*,[23] the Special Commissioners commented, that a conclusion that a treaty is not given effect in domestic law is unsatisfactory because if the conclusion is correct, the UK is in breach of the treaty.

Despite this, in several instances, treaty provisions have not been found to have effect in domestic law. In recent cases, the courts have taken a narrow view of the domestication of treaties. The expression 'to the extent that' in the introductory wording of s. 788(3) indicates

---

[19] FA 1993, s. 174.

[20] Oil Taxation Act 1983, s. 12.

[21] FA 1993, s. 194(2).

[22] At para. 8.

[23] [1997] BTC 471; [1996] STC 228.

selective incorporation of treaty provisions into domestic law. The cases have examined the language of s. 788(3) in detail.

Corporation tax in respect of income or chargeable gains

It is a requirement of s. 788(3)(a) that the relief be from 'income tax' or 'corporation tax in respect of income or chargeable gains' The scope of this requirement was considered by the High Court in *Bricom Holdings v IRC*.[24] The case involved the interaction between the Netherlands Treaty and the UK controlled foreign companies (CFC) legislation. It was argued, amongst other things, by the Inland Revenue that the CFC charge[25] was not 'corporation tax'. It was argued that while the charge under s. 747 of the Taxes Act 1988 is a tax, it is not corporation tax. The sum assessed under s. 747(4)(a) is a sum 'equal to' corporation tax; it is to be assessed on and recoverable from the resident company 'as if' it were an amount of corporation tax chargeable on that company.[26] The Inland Revenue therefore argued that when the taxes that are referred to in art. 2(1) of the treaty as forming the subject matter of the treaty, the CFC charge is not included. Article 2(1) of the treaty, however, referred to not only corporation tax but also taxes 'substantially similar to corporation tax' as being included by art. 2(2). The Inland Revenue argued that corporation tax is tax charged on profits of companies. 'Profits' means income and chargeable gains. The amount chargeable under the CFC rules is not a profit of the company assessed but is a sum equal to the corporation tax on a notional profit of the non-resident CFC. The Inland Revenue argued that the CFC charge is a fiscal *impost sui generis* introduced to cover a specific form of tax avoidance. It has nothing to do with the profits of the company assessed.

The Special Commissioners concluded that the controlled foreign company charge is a tax, but that it is not a corporation tax. On the question of whether the controlled foreign company charge is 'substantially similar' to corporation tax, the Special Commissioners noted that the difference between that charge and corporation tax is principally that the CFC charge is levied only on UK-resident companies having interests in controlled foreign companies. It is not charged on the profits of the UK company itself, but on profits (calculated essentially as for corporation tax) excluding capital gain and on certain assumptions. Only reliefs set out in Sch. 26 of the Taxes Act 1988 are available for setting against it. The Special Commissioners considered that the tax base is the most important factor in determining similarity: a tax computed on the same base as corporation tax, but charged on a specified class of company with some variations appropriate to that class of company, might well be substantially similar to corporation tax. There are differences not only in the class of company charged, but in the computation of profits, the person taxed on those profits and the reliefs available to be set against it. They regarded the matter as one of degree, but inclined to the view that the differences from corporation tax are not so great as to prevent the CFC charge from being substantially similar to corporation tax.

The Special Commissioners recognised, however, that before the taxpayer was entitled to relief, it still had to be the case that relief was available domestically under s. 788 of the

---

[24] (1996) Sp C 76; [1996] STC 228, SCD, and [1997] BTC 471; [1997] STC 1179, CA.

[25] ICTA 1988, s. 747.

[26] (1996) Sp C 76; [1996] STC 228 at 234.

Taxes Act 1988. It was noted by the taxpayer that s. 788(3)(a) refers only to relief 'from corporation tax in respect of income or chargeable gains'. It was argued for the taxpayer that the reference in this subsection should be read as including a reference to the CFC charge. This was on the basis that s. 788(3) is a provision applying generally to corporation tax. It should therefore be read subject to the necessary modification that it should cover the CFC charge as if it were an amount of corporation tax as provided in s. 747(4)(a). Section 754(1) requires the provisions of s. 747(4)(a) to apply to 'all enactments applying generally to corporation tax'. The Special Commissioners, however, regarded s. 754(1) as simply dealing with the machinery provisions as distinct from imposing a charge to tax. They concluded that s. 754(1) did not have the effect of widening the scope of s. 788(3) to cover the CFC charge.

The Court of Appeal recognised that the case raised fundamental questions on the relationship between the treaty and the CFC charge. It found it surprising that the CFC rules had been on the statute book for more than 12 years and no dispute had previously arisen. The Inland Revenue argued that its understanding of the effect of the CFC provisions was so obviously correct that no-one had considered it worthwhile to challenge the view previously. In the Court of Appeal, it was observed[27] that treaties have no direct effect in English law. They are given effect by Part XVIII of the Taxes Act 1988. After certain formalities have been observed, 'the arrangements contained in a double taxation agreement are given effect by section 788(3) of the 1988 Act'. It was also noted that Part XVIII contains no reference to identical or substantially similar taxes.

In framing the issues, the Court of Appeal noted that the final question for determination was whether the relief sought was granted by s. 788, the questions relating to the application of the treaty merely being preparatory to the asking of this question. Lord Justice Millett decided that the CFC charge was not within the relieving provisions of the treaty anyway and that it was unnecessary to consider whether the issues related to substantially similar taxes. He did, however, regard the argument that the CFC charge is not a corporation tax as failing to give full effect to s. 754(2), which provides 'for the purposes of the Taxes Act any sum assessable and recoverable under section 747(4)(a) shall be regarded as corporation tax'. Such a conclusion still avoids the issue as to whether s. 788(3) extends to substantially similar taxes. In this context, substantially similar taxes are those taxes levied pursuant to the Corporation Tax Acts whether or not they are labelled as corporation tax in the narrow sense, as the Inland Revenue contended in *Bricom*.[28] In the context of foreign taxes, s. 788(1)(c) refers to 'any taxes of a similar character to those taxes imposed by the laws of that territory'. The broad wording used to refer to foreign taxes analogous to the principal direct taxes of the UK and the purpose of the section as a whole would suggest an all-embracing interpretation of the term 'corporation tax in respect of income and chargeable gains' rather than a restricted one.

---

[27] At 1190.

[28] See above, n. 24.

Relief

A treaty provision must provide 'relief' from income or corporation tax to meet the requirements of s. 788(3)(a). In *Taylor (HM Inspector of Taxes) v MEPC Holdings Ltd* [2002] UKHL 70, Lord Hoffmann said:

> '[10] The word "relief" is not a term of art but has been used in tax legislation since the earliest statutes to refer to a provision which reduces the tax which would otherwise be payable.'

In *UBS*, this formulation was adopted by Moses J to conclude that the tax credit which UBS claimed did not and could not relieve UBS from any liability to corporation tax because, being in a loss it had none.

Charging the income or gains

A treaty provision must fall within one of the enumerated classes to have effect in domestic law. Section 788(3)(b) provides 'for charging the income arising from sources or charging gains accruing on the disposal of assets in the United Kingdom to persons not resident in the United Kingdom'.

In *R. v Inland Revenue Commissioners, ex parte Commerzbank AG*,[29] the court refused to give effect to non-discrimination provisions of the German Treaty. In that case, the taxpayer, a German resident, claimed the repayment supplement pursuant to what is now s. 825 of the Taxes Act 1988. This was denied on the basis that the section only permitted the repayment supplement on taxes overpaid if the taxpayer was resident in the UK. Article 20(1) of the German Treaty provided that:

> 'The nationals of one contracting state may not be subject in the other state to any taxation or any requirement connected therewith which is over or more burdensome than the taxation or connected requirements to which nationals of that other state in the same circumstances are or may not be subjected.'

The Inland Revenue attempted to argue that the words 'requirement connected with' taxation could not cover entitlement to the repayment supplement. It argued that these words are primarily directed to the amount of tax payable, although not limited to this. The Court rejected this argument and noted that if a German national is not entitled to the repayment supplement on the repayment of tax overpaid, it is subjected to a more burdensome requirement as regards the payment of tax than is a UK counterpart. The legislation was therefore clearly discriminatory within art. 20(1). The Inland Revenue contended, however, that the taxpayer could not rely on the treaty in this respect. This was because treaties are to have effect in domestic law 'insofar as they provide' for the matters set out in ICTA 1988, s. 788(3)(a) to (d). It was held that the repayment supplement rules did not constitute either a charging or a relieving provision. They simply allowed, in effect, for interest on an overdue repayment of tax. Consequently, neither the non-discrimination nor any other provision of the treaty could apply to the repayment supplement. In coming to this conclusion, the court rejected the argument that the repayment supplement fell within the terms of s. 788(3)(b) which provides 'for charging the income arising from sources or charging gains accruing on

---

[29] [1991] BTC 161; [1991] STC 271, QBD.

the disposal of assets in the United Kingdom to persons not resident in the United Kingdom'.

Tax credits

The most difficult aspect of implementation of treaties has arisen in relation to s. 788(3)(d), which addresses the conferring of tax credits on non-residents.

Cases on this have arisen in the context of the imputation system for the taxation of companies and their shareholders introduced in FA 1972 and generally abolished by FA 1999. In *Pirelli Cable Holding NV & Ors v Inland Revenue Commissioners* [2006] BTC 181 [2006] UKHL 4, Lord Walker of Gestingthorpe noted that:

'[104] A thunderbolt from Luxembourg, in the form of the decision in *Hoechst*, has shown that under EU law the statutory scheme was flawed, and has been flawed since its inception in 1973. There is no answer which resolves all the difficulties. But in those circumstances your Lordships should in my opinion adopt a construction which best accords with the original scheme of the 1988 Act, flawed though it is now seen to be, rather than abandoning the attempt to find any sort of purposive construction.'

He further stated that:

'[105] The requirements of justice are not easy to discern in the world of cross-border taxation of multinationals but I think that common sense does point in favour of the Revenue's appeal.'

The implications of the troubled imputation system were not restricted to cross-border shareholdings within the EU; in several cases, taxpayers have sought to persuade the courts that the treatment of non-residents or non-resident-owned companies contravened tax treaties in addition to being breaches of European Community law. It has become apparent that the higher courts, and the House of Lords, in particular, have been uncomfortable with these claims, and HMRC has largely succeeded in seeing them off.[30] The judges have been far from unanimous in their reasons for rejecting the taxpayers' claims. The imputation system was abolished in 1999.[31] In *Boake Allen Ltd & Ors (including NEC Semi-Conductors Ltd) v Revenue and Customs Commissioners* [2007] BTC 414 [2007] UKHL 25, both the High Court and the Court of Appeal agreed that, except for the implied reference to Advance Corporation Tax (ACT) in the provisions about tax credits in para. (d) (which was added when ACT came into force), the section did not give effect in domestic law to any arrangements which a treaty might make about liability to ACT. 'Corporation tax in respect of income or chargeable gains' in para. (a) meant mainstream corporation tax, not ACT. The infringement of the treaties therefore gave rise to no cause of action in English law. In the House of Lords only two out of five Law Lords were of the view that ACT was not within s. 788(3)(a) as it was not 'in respect of income or chargeable gains'.

Lord Mance simply said so without analysis[32] while Lord Neuberger of Abbotsbury accepted that that ACT is 'corporation tax' but is not 'in respect of income or chargeable

---

[30] See below at para. 10-400. *Union Texas Petroleum Corporation v Critchley (HM Inspector of Taxes)* [1988] BTC 405; [1988] STC 691, Ch.D.; [1990] BTC 253; [1990] STC 305, CA.

[31] FA 1998, s. 31 and Sch. 3.

[32] At para. 36.

gains' because it is payable on the making of a distribution, unlike so-called mainstream corporation tax, which is payable on income and chargeable gains.

He also rejected the argument[33] based on what Diplock LJ said in *Salomon v C & E Commrs* [1967] 2 QB 116, 143, to the effect that, where a statutory provision was 'not clear' and was 'reasonably capable of [bearing] more than one meaning', the court should favour 'the meaning which is consonant' with the UK's treaty obligations. In doing so he reasoned that this principle is of less weight in a case such as the one before him, where there is no question, as in *Salomon*, of the legislative provision in issue, namely s. 788 of the 1988 act, having been enacted to give effect to a specific treaty obligation. In this case, he said, s. 788, 'while enacted to enable the UK's treaty obligations under DTCs generally to have effect in domestic law, was plainly not designed to give effect to any specific obligation or even any specific Convention'.

Nonetheless, despite this broad statement, he conceded that the point would have some force had the claimants succeeded on the main issue, namely that they had been discriminated against contrary to the provisions of the treaty.[34] In other words, the rejection of the argument was linked to rejection of the discrimination claim.

In *Pirelli Cable Holding NV & Ors v Inland Revenue Commissioners* [2006] BTC 181 [2006] UKHL 4, Lord Walker of Gestingthorpe said:

'[94] It is a striking feature of section 788(3)(d) that it is expressed in precise and technical language (in contrast to the three preceding paragraphs, which are expressed in more general, and largely non-technical, language).

[102] The Court of Appeal (Peter Gibson and Laws LJJ and Sir Martin Nourse) upheld the judge's conclusion, and again seem to have had little difficulty in doing so. The core reasoning is in paragraphs 46 and 47 of the judgement of the Court delivered by Peter Gibson LJ:

"Given the elaborately detailed nature of the DTAs and their purpose of relieving double taxation, we would find it very surprising if specific provisions limiting the conferring of tax credits in the domestic tax legislation so as to exclude it in particular circumstances were intended to govern the availability of tax credits to a non-resident. Is it really to be supposed that every statutory qualification enacted from time to time in the UK fiscal legislation to the availability of a tax credit under section 231 qualifies the entitlement conferred by the DTA to the limited relief of double taxation by the tax credit as provided for in the DTA? We think not. Moreover, section 247(2), which forms the linchpin of Mr Glick's argument, is not in fact purporting to affect the meaning of "tax credit" in UK tax law. It is merely limiting the circumstances in which a tax credit under section 231 will be granted."

[103] I have found this issue much less easy. It is to my mind a short but very difficult point of statutory construction. The unanimous view of the very experienced judges in the courts below commands great respect. But in the end I have come to the conclusion, differing most reluctantly from the courts below, that they reached the wrong conclusion because they did not give enough weight to two factors. One is that in applying the DTAs it is necessary to look, not only at their terms, but also at the language of section 788(3)(d), which uses a technical

[33] At para. 51.

[34] In relation to the discrimination issue, see chapter 15.

expression of domestic tax law, "qualifying distribution." The other is that the clear scheme of the 1988 Act is that the payment of a dividend should be accompanied by a payment of ACT if a tax credit is to come into existence, and if exceptionally (because of a GIE) the payment of a dividend is not accompanied by a payment of ACT, the dividend would not give rise to a tax credit, because of section 247(2). Section 247(2) does not directly affect the meaning of "tax credit", but it does to my mind affect the meaning of "qualifying distribution"; a dividend paid under a GIE is in terms excluded from section 14(1), and section 231 is in terms made to take effect subject to section 247.'

Section 788 and international law

As has been noted, a conclusion that UK law does not adequately implement a treaty is an unhappy one. The manner in which the tax credit cases have been decided and comments on s. 788(3) suggest that they are exceptional and not necessarily a useful guide to the post–tax credit era. Questions over the construction of these provisions are far from concluded. In distinguishing the tax credit provisions, Lord Walker in *Boake Allen* has left open scope for a broad construction of the more general and less technical elements of the section. The treaty-making authority as a matter of Crown prerogative is generally unfettered. When Parliament wishes to fetter the Crown's treaty-making powers, it must do so in express terms.[35] Section 788(3) should not be viewed as imposing such a limitation, which might imply a restricted construction of treaties to conform with s. 788(3).

In addition, the method by which Parliament gives effect to treaty obligations does not affect the way in which the courts resolve problems of interpretation that may arise where there is a discrepancy between the statutory wording and the wording of the treaty.[36] In *Garland v British Rail Engineering Ltd*,[37] Lord Diplock said:

'It is a principle of construction of UK statutes now too well established to call for citation of authority, that the words of a statute passed after the treaty has been signed and dealing with the subject matter of the international obligations of the UK, are to be construed, if they are reasonably capable of bearing such a meaning, as intended to carry out the obligation and not to be inconsistent with it.'

The conclusion of Lord Neuberger in *Boake Allen*[38] that the rule is only applicable to a legislative provision enacted to give effect to a specific treaty provision does not dispose of the issue. The purpose of s. 788 is plain. It acts as an umbrella which enables all treaties entered into by the UK with a view to relieving double taxation to be enacted into domestic law without the necessity of specific legislation. United Kingdom tax treaties have been

---

[35] *R. v Secretary of State for Foreign and Commonwealth Affairs, ex parte Rees-Mogg* [1994] QB 552 at 567; [1994] 1 All ER 457 at 467 per Lloyd LJ.

[36] *Salomon v Customs and Excise Commissioners* [1967] 2 QB 116; [1966] 3 All ER 871, CA. In that case, the treaty in question was not incorporated into or referred to in the statute. Notwithstanding this, Lord Denning MR said at 874: 'I think we are entitled to look at [the treaty] because it is an instrument which is binding in international law; we ought always to interpret our statutes so as to be in conformity with international law.' Russell LJ agreed with this where the statute is plainly intended to carry out the terms of the treaty. In *Cheney v Conn* (1964-1968) 44 TC 217; [1968] All ER 799, Ch.D., a claim that the charge to income tax was invalidated by provisions of a Geneva Convention prohibiting nuclear weapons on the basis that a substantial part of the tax was to pay for such weapons, was denied on the basis that the relevant part of the Convention was not enacted into domestic law and the taxing statute was clear and unambiguous in its terms.

[37] [1983] 2 AC 751 at 771; [1982] 2 WLR. 918 at 934 to 935, HL.

[38] See para. 10-200 above.

patterned on the OECD models for nearly five decades but each is unique. It avoids the necessity of examining changes in treaty practice or the outcome of negotiations in relation to particular treaties in order to determine whether they will or will not be enacted into domestic law. Since there are so many tax treaties, this approach obviates the need to introduce legislation relating to each individual treaty. Thus, although the implementation of tax treaties generally within specified limits is authorised by Parliament in advance, and the specific terms of the treaty become directly applicable through scheduling to an Order, the domestic legislation should be interpreted in a manner consistent with the treaty obligations.

The principle of construction enunciated by Lord Denning MR that 'we ought always to interpret our statutes so as to be in conformity with international law' is broader than merely reconciling different language in a statute with that in a particular treaty. As a party to the Vienna Convention on the Law of Treaties, regard must be had to the obligations that entails.[39] Article 26 of the Vienna Convention embodies the *pacta servanda sunt* principle, which requires treaties to be adhered to in good faith. Article 27 provides that a party may not invoke the provisions of its internal law as justification for its failure to perform a treaty. The only qualification to this is that a manifest violation of a provision of the internal law of a party regarding competence to conclude treaties may be invoked by that party in certain circumstances. The principle of construction embraces adherence to these obligations and not just the specific treaty obligation that is the subject of incorporation.[40] There is a presumption that Parliament intends to fulfil rather than break an international agreement.[41] Thus, where an Act is intended to give effect to a treaty, any doubt as to its meaning should, if possible, be resolved in favour of that which is consistent with the provisions of the treaty.[42]

It may be noted that while there appears no present appetite to amend s. 788 to ensure that the full effect of treaty obligations is beyond doubt despite recommendations that Parliament should reconsider s. 788.[43] A more fastidious approach has been found in enacting legislation in recent years to address cross-border collaboration between tax authorities.[44]

---

[39] See arts. 26 and 27 of the Vienna Convention.

[40] Vienna Convention on the Law of Treaties, art. 46.

[41] See *Salomon v Customs and Excise Commissioners*, above, n. 37, per Diplock LJ At 875.

[42] *Quazi v Quazi* [1980] AC 744 at 80S; [1979] 3 All ER 897 at 903, HL per Lord Diplock:

'Where Parliament passes an Act amending the domestic law of the United Kingdom in order to enable this country to ratify an international treaty and thereby assume towards other states that are parties to the treaty an obligation in international law to observe its terms, it is a legitimate aid to the construction of any provisions of the Act that are ambiguous or vague to have recourse to the terms of the treaty in order to see what was the obligation in international law that Parliament intended that this country should be enabled to assume.'

See also more recently *R. v Secretary of State for the Home Department, ex parte Brind* [1991] 1 AC 696.

[43] *UBS AG v R & C Commrs* (2005) Sp C 480 by Special Commissioners John FA Jones and Julian Ghosh at para. 41.

[44] This is addressed in chapter 20.

10-300   Retrospective effect

The implementing legislation authorises a degree of retrospectivity. Treaties may be given effect by virtue of s. 788 if they provide relief for tax:

- for periods before the passing of the Taxes Act 1988; or
- before the making of the treaty in question.

Provision may also be made in such circumstances as to income which is not subject to double taxation or chargeable gains which are not subject to double taxation.

It would appear that such retrospectivity is therefore subject to limitations. Whatever the authorisation given by s. 788(3) in relation to the ability of treaties to impose a charge not provided for under domestic law or to increase a charge imposed under domestic law, it is not clear that retrospective measures can only relieve or provide as to income or chargeable gains which is or are not subject to double taxation.

Such measures are typically contained in treaties where one is replaced by another, or in circumstances where the time delay between the negotiation of a treaty and its entry into force is lengthy as a result of protracted negotiations or delays in the ratification or exchange of instruments of ratification for domestic reasons in either contracting state.[45] Furthermore, an Order in Council which revokes an earlier Order may contain such transitional provisions as may be necessary or expedient as there is inevitably a delay between conclusion of a treaty and its final entry into force under domestic law. Current treaty practice is to provide for transitional measures in the terms of the treaty itself. Transitional measures implied unilaterally may well be in breach of a treaty obligation in certain circumstances.

10-350   Treaties made under old law

Section 789 of the Taxes Act 1988 also ensures continuity of enactment under domestic law of treaties made under the previous legislation relating to profits tax.[46] Thus, older treaties have effect in relation to corporation tax and income and gains chargeable to corporation tax in accordance with their terms where they are expressed to have effect in relation to profits tax and profits chargeable to profits tax. Accounting periods (the current term) are substituted for chargeable accounting periods.

Treaties made before 30 March 1971 which provide for exemption of income from surtax have effect as if they provided for that income to bear income tax at the basic rate or the lower rate, whichever is applicable, and are to be regarded for the purposes of computing total income, other than as that expression is now understood by the Taxes Act 1988, s. 835(5). Any reference in the Tax Acts to treaties under or by virtue of s. 788 include a reference to treaties having effect by virtue of s. 789.

---

[45] Article 28 of the Canada Treaty is a good example.

[46] Income Tax Act 1952 (ITA 1952), s. 347, or any earlier enactment corresponding to that section.

10-400   Effect of treaties

The precise effect of treaties in UK tax law and, in particular, whether treaties can impose or increase a tax liability beyond that provided as a matter of domestic law has been subject to some considerable debate.[47] Part of the controversy arises from the manner in which the implementing legislation has been drafted. Section 788(3) authorises that treaties shall 'have effect' insofar as they provide:

> '(b) for charging the income arising from sources, or chargeable gains accruing on the disposal of assets, in the United Kingdom to persons not resident in the United Kingdom;'

Arguably, this would authorise a treaty to impose a tax on the income or gains of a non-resident which was not taxable under domestic law. These authorising provisions are, however, subject to the provisions of Part XVIII generally. Section 788(1) refers to arrangements made 'with a view to affording relief from double taxation'. Thus, it would appear that the purpose of the treaty must be to relieve double taxation and that if s. 788(3)(b) creates a charge not existing under domestic law, then unless this was with a view to relieving double taxation, it would not be authorised. The HMRC approach to the issue is unequivocal. The HMRC *International Manual* (*INTM*) states that 'a double taxation agreement cannot impose a charge to tax where none exists at all in domestic law'.[48] The older *International Tax Handbook* simply notes[49] that where a treaty permits a liability to be imposed, this does not itself give rise to a charge if there is no general charge provided by domestic law.

Section 788(3) also authorises treaties to provide for conferring on non-UK residents the right to a tax credit under s. 231 in respect of qualifying distributions made to them by companies which are UK resident. The question as to whether treaties can impose a charge was argued in *Union Texas Petroleum Corporation v Critchley (HM Inspector of Taxes).*[50]

Article 10(2)(a)(i) of the 1975 US Treaty[51] provided that where a US corporation was in receipt of a dividend from a UK resident company, the recipient is entitled to a payment from the UK of a tax credit equal to one-half of the credit to which an individual resident in the UK would have been entitled had he or she received the dividend, subject to deductions withheld from such payment of an amount not exceeding 5 per cent of the amount or value of the dividend and of the amount of the tax credit paid to the US corporation. The US corporation argued that the payments to which it was entitled were amounts equal to one-half of the tax credit to which an individual resident in the UK would have been entitled had he or she received the dividends. It was argued that the reference to 'tax credits' in that subparagraph were not 'tax credits under section 86 of the FA 1972'. Accordingly, no deduction may be made from them, notwithstanding the concluding words of the treaty provision. The corporation was not assessable to UK income tax in respect of the dividends

---

[47] See Oliver, JDB, 'Double tax treaties in United Kingdom tax law', *BTR*, 388, (1970).

[48] At para. INTM152060.

[49] At para. 505.

[50] [1988] BTC 405; [1988] STC 691, Ch.D.; [1990] BTC 253; [1990] STC 305, CA.

[51] *Double Taxation Relief (Taxes on Income) (United States of America) Order* 1980 (SI 1980/568).

or the tax credit payment and the treaty itself imposed no liability to UK tax in respect of those amounts. It was also argued that the treaty itself did not impose a deduction requirement.

The Crown argued that a treaty has effect in English law and overrides anything to the contrary. Once the treaty extended the tax credit to a person, the credit is available for the purposes specified in s. 86 of the FA 1992. The US corporation is chargeable to income tax under Sch. F and the treaty had the effect of limiting that charge from the basic rate of tax to 5 per cent, which may be withheld from the payment in accordance with s. 86(4) of the 1972 Act. It was argued that s. 778(1)(d) could not apply because it did not incorporate any power to deduct taxes in circumstances such as existed under the US Treaty.

Harman J found the issue one of great difficulty to determine and noted in his judgement that his mind changed several times in the course of argument and of consideration. He upheld the Crown's argument on the incorporation of the treaty into UK law and held that the references to tax credits in art. 10 were references to tax credits provided by s. 86 of the Income and Corporation Taxes Act (ICTA) 1970. He accepted the Crown's submissions that the treaty should be read with a reasonable desire to understand its purpose, which was to fit the system of double tax relief into the system of tax credits on dividends introduced by the FA 1972. In this regard, it was plain that art. 10(2) as a whole was specifically intended to fit provisions for double taxation of dividends to the UK imputation system. The Crown had argued that s. 86(4) of ICTA 1970 provides for repayment of the tax credit which exceeds income tax chargeable on a taxpayer.

Although the treaty refers to a deduction from the payment due from the UK, interpreting the treaty as limiting that amount as provided in the treaty produces an economic result that was the same. The reasoning is therefore somewhat obscure, but the implication is that if the effect of the treaty is to achieve an economic result similar to that under domestic law, then the treaty presumably is capable of imposing a charge.

Although most treaties are implemented via s. 788 of the Taxes Act 1988, occasionally a legislative 'patch' is applied in order to deal with shortcomings. An example of this is Finance (No. 2) Act 1979, s. 16. This extended the benefit of the US Treaty to periods before the making of the Order in Council, notwithstanding that the treaty withdrew relief from tax for those periods. This is extremely rare and indeed in the *Union Texas* case,[52] the court appeared to accept the argument of the Crown that this provision did not have the effect of generally incorporating the treaty into UK law.

10-450   Putative treaties

Where a treaty is negotiated and executed, and its terms are carried out by one of the parties, but formal ratification has not taken place, the precise legal position is unclear. This unusual possibility arose in the context of the 1977 treaty with Ghana.[53] In the UK, the appropriate

---

[52] See above, n. 50.

[53] SI 1978/785.

Order in Council was made, and on 6 June 1978, the Inland Revenue announced that the treaty had entered into force.[54] The UK applied the treaty for some years, but in 1991, it emerged that the treaty had never been properly ratified in Ghana.[55] Article 27 of the 1977 treaty provided that the treaty was to come into force on the date when 'the last of all such things shall have been done in the United Kingdom and Ghana as are necessary to give the Convention the force of law in the United Kingdom and Ghana respectively'. The conditions precedent were never fulfilled and as a result, the treaty never entered into force and never had effect in either contracting state. Article 27 of the 1977 treaty provided for termination of the earlier 1947 treaty and since the entry into force was recognised to have potentially retrospective effect, permitted those provisions of the earlier treaty to continue to have effect if they were more beneficial until entry into force of the 1977 treaty. However, in effect the 1947 treaty was never terminated and was still in force in both countries.

The Inland Revenue ceased to apply the 1977 treaty once this was discovered and reapplied the 1947 treaty. By concession and in recognition of the 'wholly exceptional circumstances', the Inland Revenue offered the application of the most favourable terms of the two treaties during the period of mistake including permitting claims made out of time for a limited period.

The sensible approach adopted by the Inland Revenue obviated the need for detailed analysis of the strict legal position by taxpayers. Strictly, the 1947 treaty was in effect and taxpayers were entitled to rely on it. However, since taxpayers had been led to believe that the 1977 treaty was in effect, taxpayers had a legitimate expectation that they were entitled to rely on it, without having to look behind the steps taken at a diplomatic level between the contracting states.

10-500   State succession

As a matter of international law, state succession describes a variety of changes in the sovereignty over a particular treaty. Political changes in Central and Eastern Europe have in recent times impacted on the UK tax treaty network. In recent history, most cases have involved the dissolution of sovereign entities. Given the variety of possible changes that may occur, there are no general rules of international law to the effect that upon a succession of states, the benefit or burden of treaties of a predecessor state are transferred to the successor by reason of the succession. On the contrary, if a state is extinguished, its rights and obligations under treaties are generally extinguished also.

The dissolution of the Union of Soviet Socialist Republics was perhaps the most significant. The 1985 USSR Treaty was in effect brought to an end by the dissolution. The position was first clarified by the Inland Revenue in SP 3/92, issued on 1 May 1992. It indicated that the treaty was regarded as being in force between the UK and the Russian Federation. Other remaining former Soviet Republics were, by that time, recognised by the UK as independent sovereign states. In addition, those Republics committed themselves to continue to respect

---

[54] Inland Revenue press release, 6 June 1978.

[55] Inland Revenue press release, 31 January 1991.

all international obligations of the former Soviet Union. As a result, the provisions of the USSR Treaty continued to apply, with the exception of the Baltic States, Estonia, Lithuania and Latvia. The UK moved quickly to negotiate individual treaties with almost all of the successor states. A further update of the position was set out in SP4/01 in light of those negotiations. This indicated that, in some cases, states such as Armenia and Kyrgyzstan never regarded themselves bound by the USSR Treaty but the UK nonetheless applied the treaty to residents of those states until April 2002. The result has been that there have been no treaties in effect since that time.

Similar issues arose in relation to the dissolution of Czechoslovakia. Both successor states committed themselves to honour all international obligations of the former Federal Republic; the Czechoslovakia Treaty is treated as remaining in force between the UK and, respectively, the Czech Republic and the Slovak Republic.[56]

Likewise, a similar approach was taken in relation to the dissolution of Yugoslavia.[57] The Yugoslavia Convention is therefore treated as remaining in force between the UK and, respectively, Croatia and Slovenia. The status of these was updated in SP 3/04 and, most recently, in SP 3/07. The legal basis of the original statements appears to be a combination of recognition of the successor state by the UK and in effect a novation of the treaty by the successor state when it agrees to undertake the obligations. The later statements relating to the USSR Treaty reveal a practical and perhaps concessionary approach in the context of an obscure legal position.

Other changes in sovereignty have not so far raised problems in the tax treaty context. For example, the treaty with Namibia is an extension of the treaty with South Africa extended by Exchange of Notes on 8 August 1962 and amended by exchange of notes in 1967. Notwithstanding a finding by the International Court of Justice (ICJ)that South African occupation of Namibia (formerly South West Africa) was illegal, the agreement continued after the independence of Namibia in 1985.

The non-recognition of the homelands in South Africa similarly permitted treaty claims to be made by residents of those homelands pursuant to the South African Treaty. The reunification of the Federal Republic of Germany and the German Democratic Republic on 3 October 1990 brought about an automatic extension of the treaty with the Federal Republic to the territory of the former German Democratic Republic. The UK view was that treaties of the Federal Republic applied to the former territory of the German Democratic Republic. The German Ministry of Finance stated that it would apply those treaties from 1 January 1991.[58]

The return of Hong Kong to Chinese sovereignty has also produced unusual issues of state succession in the tax treaty context. Hong Kong maintains a tax system separate from China.

---

[56] SP 5/93.

[57] SP 6/93.

[58] The definition in art. 2(1)(b) of the treaty with the Federal Republic requires that 'the Federal Republic' when used in a geographical sense, means the territory in which the Basic Law for the Federal Republic of Germany is in force. Thus, the extension of the Constitution to eastern Germany extended the application of the treaty automatically.

The Chinese Treaty does not apply to Hong Kong. Unique to UK treaty practice, double tax measures relating to air transport are found in an air transportation agreement relating to Hong Kong and not in a separate tax treaty.[59]

10-550   Relationship between treaties and specific statutory provisions

As a matter of international law, every treaty in force is binding upon the parties to it and must be performed by them in good faith.[60] This is simply a codification of the longstanding principle *pacta sunt servanda*. In the context of tax treaties, implementation of this principle calls for changes in domestic law to give effect to treaty provisions. Generally, the introductory wording to s. 788(3), which requires treaties to take effect 'notwithstanding anything in any enactment', establishes the primacy of treaties over domestic law. The effect of such wording is to ensure that in all cases, treaties take precedence over domestic law. While this is relatively straightforward, in relation to legislation in force when the treaty comes into effect, the issue is problematic in the context of subsequent legislation because of the constitutional principle that no parliament can bind or restrict the legislative capacity of any future parliament.

10-600   Treaty override

The doctrine of parliamentary sovereignty clearly means that should it wish to do so, as a matter of domestic law, Parliament may legislate to override a treaty. To do so would be a clear breach of international law. The remedies for such a breach, however, lie not at the hands of individual taxpayers but in the hands of the other contracting state. The question of the fundamental relationship between domestic law and treaties has come before the courts on several occasions. In *Ostime (HM Inspector of Taxes) v Australian Mutual Provident*,[61] the simple point was made that the effect of the legislation is that, if and so far as there is any inconsistency between domestic law and the treaty, then the treaty having duly been given statutory effect must prevail over domestic law. The case was relatively straightforward on this point in the sense that the legislation in question predated the treaty.

In *IRC v Collco Dealings Ltd*,[62] the question was whether legislation enacted in 1955 overrode provisions of the treaty with Ireland dating back to 1926. The 1955 legislation was introduced to combat perceived abuse in relation to dividend stripping. The treaty between the UK and Ireland was not enacted by virtue of the mechanism now found in s. 788 of the Taxes Act 1988, but by way of specific legislation. It did not contain the wording making the treaty prevail 'notwithstanding any enactment'. It was argued that to apply the later legislation would create a breach of the treaty and would be inconsistent with the comity of

---

[59] See Chinese Treaty, art. 3(1)(a); Inland Revenue, *Tax Bulletin* (No. 151, October, 1996), p. 397, and Hong Kong Air Transport Treaty of 2 June 1998 (SI 1998/2566).

[60] Vienna Convention, art. 26.

[61] (1957) 38 TC 492.

[62] (1961) 39 TC 509.

nations and the established rules of international law. The potentially overriding domestic legislation had therefore to be construed so as to avoid this result. Viscount Simonds declined to accept the argument and said at 526:

> '[B]ut it is said in the first place that it [the taxpayer] is not entitled under an enactment but under an agreement which the appellant company, to add weight to the argument, prefer to call a treaty. But this contention cannot be accepted. The company has no rights under any agreement. Its rights arise from the act of Parliament which confirm the agreement and give it the force of law.'

He did not find the words in need of interpretation and adopted the view in *Maxwell on the Interpretation of Statutes*[63] which concludes: 'But if the Statute is unambiguous, its provisions must be followed, even if they are contrary to international law'.[64] His judgement on this was clearly influenced by the fact that the legislation in question was to counter perceived abuse. He continued:

> 'I am not sure upon which of these high sounding phrases, the appellant company chiefly relies. But I would answer that neither comity nor rule of international law can be invoked to prevent a sovereign state from taking what steps it thinks fit to protect its own revenue laws from gross abuse or to save its own citizens from unjust discrimination in favour of foreigners. To demand that the plain words of the statute should be disregarded in order to do that very thing is an extravagance to which this House will not, I hope, give here.'

Lord Morton of Henryton endorsed this view in somewhat less strident language, but he was nonetheless influenced by the anti-abuse nature of the provisions. He endorsed the views of Vaisey J in the High Court[65] that:

> 'The plain object of section 4(2) was to prevent what is colloquially called "dividend stripping", and if the decision of the Special Commissioners stands, residents in Ireland can do what their fellow taxpayers in this country are prohibited from doing. If that is the law, sobeit; but the consequence is not one which commands itself to me on general principles of justice or fairness.'

Lord Reed agreed with the conclusion but on somewhat different grounds. He noted that unless a limitation is implied, the later legislation enacted something inconsistent with the provisions of a treaty. He said:

> 'There is by no means so strong a presumption against Parliament having done that. Although the infringement of a treaty may cause loss to individuals, the only person properly entitled to complain of such infringement is the other party to the treaty. No doubt if that other party is aggrieved, the infringement is a breach of the comity of nations and there is a presumption that Parliament did not intend to act contrary to the comity of nations, but I do not think that there is necessarily a presumption that every infringement of a treaty is a breach of the comity of nations. After a treaty has been made, circumstances may alter and it may be reasonable to take unilateral action in the expectation that the other party to the treaty will not object. Indeed, the other party may have been consulted and have raised no objection.

> . . .

---

[63] Galpin, B, Maxwell, PB, and Wilson, R, *Maxwell on the Interpretation of Statutes*, 10th edn, Sweet & Maxwell, p. 143 and p. 149.

[64] In the High Court, this comment was also made with specific reference to 'any international treaty or arrangements', at 517.

[65] See at 517.

We do not know what happened in this case. But we do know that on a previous occasion, unilateral action was taken by section 52 of the Finance (No. 2) Act 1945 and this was followed by an alteration of the treaty in 1947 which altered the scope of the original tax exemption to correspond with the provisions of the 1945 Act.'

Lord Radcliffe recognised that statutory words apparently unlimited in scope may be given a restricted field of application if there is admissible ground for importing such a restriction and the consideration that if not construed in some limited sense, they would amount to a breach of international law, is well recognised as such a ground. However, he said that a supposed intention not to depart from the observance of the comity of nations is a much vaguer criterion by which to determine the range of a statute. When the departure consists in no more than a provision inconsistent with an inter-governmental agreement about taxation, which by its own terms is subordinated to the approval of the respective legislatures of the countries concerned and persists only so long as its terms are maintained in force as law by those legislatures, he argued that there is no useful aid at all to be obtained from this principle of interpretation. The arrangements between the UK and Ireland were unusual; modern tax treaty practice relies on s. 788 of the Taxes Act 1988 to give effect to treaty obligations rather than specific legislation.

The Privy Council, on an appeal from Ceylon, upheld Ceylonese legislation that was inconsistent with the Ceylon Treaty in *Woodend (KV Ceylon) Rubber Antiques Co. Limited v CIR.*[66] Although these cases are useful in considering general principles, they do not assist in interpreting s. 788(3), because they do not contain the words 'notwithstanding anything in any enactment'. Thus, as a matter of general principle, Parliament is presumed to intend to fulfil rather than break a treaty. Where, however, on an informed construction, there is no real doubt about the real meaning of an enactment, effect must be given to it even if it is not in accordance with a treaty or contrary to international law. The effect of the wording in s. 788(3), however, is that until Parliament exercises its power to override a treaty or treaties, it will not be presumed to do so and treaty provisions will prevail. In order successfully to override a treaty, clear express language to that effect must be used.

A most blatant and calculated instance of treaty override in the UK in the modern context is found in Taxes Act 1988, s. 812. This aims at withdrawing the right to obtain repayment of tax credits for companies which are present in or have associated companies in a unitary state. The language of the section is unambiguous. It provides that 'notwithstanding anything to the contrary in the arrangements', such companies are not entitled to repayment of tax credits which are provided for in a treaty. The section was enacted in order to retaliate against the introduction of unitary tax systems adopted by certain states in the US, most notably California. The legislation is not in force until an order to that effect has been made which requires approval by a resolution of the House of Commons. Although the Government indicated in 1993 that it would defer retaliatory action against the State of California following the passage of legislation by that state to modify its unitary tax law, no move has been made to bring these provisions into force. They remain on the statute, however. Such provisions are clear treaty override as defined by the OECD Committee on

---

[66] [1971] AC 321, PC.

Fiscal Affairs as 'the enactment of domestic legislation intended by the legislature to have effects in clear contradiction to international treaty obligations'.[67]

Similarly, legislation was enacted in relation to the treatment of UK resident members of partnerships controlled abroad in Finance (No. 2) Act 1987, s. 62. This arose out of *Padmore v IRC*.[68] The legislation here was clearly aimed at overriding the treaty. The statute sought to disapply treaties in relation to the income and capital gains of UK-resident partners. It requires that 'the [treaties] ... shall not affect any liability to tax in respect of the resident partners' share of any income or capital gains of the partnership'.[69]

Override by 'interpretation'

Another possible example of treaty override may be found in s. 808A of the Taxes Act 1988. The section provides for rules of interpretation of interest provisions where a special relationship is present. Although arguably declaratory of the rules of interpretation in some respects, the effect of s. 808A is to require certain older treaties, in which the effect of the special relationship provision on interest is merely to regulate the rate of interest without reference to the amount of debt, to impose by way of interpretation that the special relationship provision should take into account the amount of debt in all such treaties. It was explained by the Financial Secretary to the Treasury that 'we are now using this Bill to change the law to what we thought it was and to reflect the double taxation treaty'.[70] This is plainly not the case.

A similar device was adopted in relation to the formula for the repayment of tax credits on dividends. This arose out of the proceedings in *Union Texas Petroleum Co. v Critchley*.[71] In this case, the legislation does not purport to override the treaty. The Finance Act 1989, s. 115, simply says that 'the [treaty] shall be construed as providing'. These provisions were made retrospective other than in relation to judgements given before the announcement or in proceedings which had already commenced.

In the case of the legislation arising out of the *Padmore* and *Union Texas* cases, the Inland Revenue was (or believed it was about to be) on the losing side of cases before the courts. Since the Inland Revenue view of the interpretation of the treaty prevailed in Union Texas, the legislation did not in fact override the treaty. It may be described as attempted override. On the other hand, the suggestion that legislation overriding a judicial interpretation of a treaty where the Revenue has lost (as was apparently the case with the Taxes Act 1988, s. 808A) as a 'correction', is a facile excuse for a simple exercise of parliamentary supremacy.

---

[67] OECD Committee on Fiscal Affairs, Tax Treaty Override (1989).

[68] [1987] BTC 3; [1987] STC 36.

[69] This override has been perpetuated in the Taxes Act 1988, s. 112(4), (and ITTOIA 2005, s. 858, for income tax) despite the fact that the entity approach to taxing partnerships is no longer applied (Taxes Act 1988, s. 111, and for income tax, ITTOIA 2005, s. 848). It has been restated as 'always having had effect' in FA 2008, s. 58, and is retrospective to before FA 1987.

[70] House of Commons, 30 June 1992, at 452.

[71] [1988] BTC 405; [1988] STC 691.

No threat of losing a case appeared to have been at hand in the case of the introduction of the Taxes Act 1988, s. 808B, by FA 2000. This section imposes an interpretation of the 'special relationship' wording in treaties relating to royalties. The Inland Revenue stated in its document on double tax relief reform that in all cases, treaty benefits should be limited not only where the rate at which royalties are paid is excessive, but where in the absence of the special relationship, the arrangements under which the royalties are paid at all would not have been entered into. This in effect imposes a meaning on 'special relationship' not supported by all treaties. The extensive anti-avoidance rules incorporated in s. 808B can hardly be described as interpretation and are thus a clear treaty override.

The intention to override treaties could not be plainer in FA 2008, s. 59(1), which inserts ICTA 1988, s. 815AZA. This excludes UK residents from benefiting from provisions similar to art. 7 of the OECD Model in respect of profits of a trade, profession or business controlled or managed outside the UK or of an enterprise which is resident outside the UK.[72]

Until recently, the only case in which treaty override in relation to UK tax law has been challenged in the courts is *Collco Dealings Ltd* (and that in relation to the Republic of Ireland where there were specific and unusual legislative arrangements).[73] Plainly, such challenges must fail in relation to express and unambiguous override. This was the case in *Padmore (No. 2) v Commissioners of Inland Revenue*.[74] The taxpayer argued that Taxes Act 1988, s. 788(3), which appeared in Part XVII of the act, overrode s. 112(4), contained in Part IV of the act. Tax treaties, it was claimed, had effect 'notwithstanding anything in any enactment', but s. 788 itself was 'subject to the provisions of this Part'. Thus, an effective treaty override had to be contained in Part XVII.

The court held that the treaty had been overridden. An alternative construction would deprive Taxes Act 1988, s. 112, of all effect. Its purpose was to remove the exemption conferred on the taxpayer. The departure from the provisions of the treaty was plainly and deliberately made and thus there was no scope for any presumption. Parliament did not intend that ambiguous or unclear domestic law should have to be tested for compliance with treaty obligations.

Restraint in exercising parliamentary power in this way does indicate a compliant approach towards international law by the UK. Avoiding breaches of international law designed to demonstrate adherence to principles of international law will give other treaty parties confidence, which in turn will maintain the stability of the UK Treaty network.

There appears to have been no public indication of contracting states raising specific objections to these overrides. Notwithstanding, this, the consequence of a treaty override (or indeed the failure to implement a treaty in the first place) does not relive a contracting state of its obligations in international law. Tax levied pursuant to overriding domestic legislation will not be levied in accordance with the treaty. The other contracting state will not be

---

[72] The rationale for this override is on the basis of a rather tendentious view of art. 7. How treaties work is found in paras. 8 and 9 in the HMRC Explanatory Notes to s. 56 of FA 2008.

[73] See above, n. 62.

[74] [2001] BTC 36; [2001] STC 280, Ch.D.

required to give credit or otherwise relive double taxation that arises because of the override.[75] Mutual agreement procedure may be invoked by a dissatisfied taxpayer.[76] This possibility is recognised by HMRC, at least in relation to cross-border interest payments.[77]

10-650 Limiting access to treaties

Legislative devices have become more ingenious in seeking to narrow the potential application of treaties. A further category of relationship between treaties and domestic law reflects other attempts to limit availability of treaty benefits. In the capital gains area, several measures have appeared over the years in order to prevent access to treaty benefits through changes in residence. Such measures include Taxation of Chargeable Gains Act (TCGA) 1992, s. 83, which requires trustees becoming resident in a treaty country by virtue of tiebreaker provisions to be deemed to have disposed of assets which are treaty protected at the time that they become resident in the other contracting state. These rules cannot be regarded as treaty override, since the taxable events apply immediately before the taxpayer becomes resident in the other contracting state. Similarly, TCGA 1992, s. 84, prohibits rollover relief on replacement of business assets under s. 152 where new assets are acquired by trustees who are UK resident but are treated as non-resident for the purposes of a treaty and the assets in question are of a description 'specified' in the treaty. Again, these measures preclude a specific class of persons from qualifying for treaty benefits. Further provisions deal with capital gains and dual resident settlements. Section 88 requires gains of trusts to be attributed to beneficiaries if the trustees are UK resident but are treated as non-resident for treaty purposes and if the assets are of a kind that would qualify for treaty relief in the hands of a resident of the other contracting state. In *Boote v Banco do Brasil*,[78] the court upheld legislation designed to prevent branches of non-resident banks carrying forward or otherwise using losses resulting from income that was exempt by treaty notwithstanding a degree of retrospectivity.

10-700 Extension of treaty benefits

On the other hand, benefits are occasionally extended by domestic law beyond those given by treaty. Companies which are treated as resident in another contracting state by virtue of the application of a treaty are deemed to be non-resident for all purposes of the Taxes Act 1988 under FA 1994, s. 249, except the CFC rules.[79]

An exception is made in the case of the CFC charge by s. 747(1)(b) of the Taxes Act 1988 inserted by FA 2002, s. 90. It specifies that the general rule in s. 249 of the FA 1994, which deems a treaty non-resident to be non-resident for all corporation tax purposes to be disregarded for most CFC purposes (sub-clause (1)). It does not apply for the purpose of

---

[75] See chapter 14.

[76] See chapter 18.

[77] HMRC, *INTM*, para. INTM549060.

[78] [1997] BTC 140; [1997] STC 327, CA.

[79] FA 2002, s. 90 as amended by FA 2006, s. 78.

determining whether a company is a CFC, when testing whether the company is resident outside the UK. It does, however, apply in determining whether such a non-resident company is controlled by persons resident in the UK and whether profits of a CFC may be apportioned to a company resident in the UK pursuant to s. 747(4). Companies that cease to be UK resident, because they become resident in another country by virtue of the application of a tie-breaker contained in a treaty, are not liable to corporation tax (other than to the extent they are liable as non-residents) after they cease to be resident. They will henceforth, however, continue to be liable to the CFC charge. This is a rather surprising result. In *Bricom Holdings Limited v IRC* [1997] BTC 471 (CA), it was noted that the CFC charge is not corporation tax. It is a separate tax imposed as an anti-avoidance provision designed to protect the corporation tax. However, in the context of new s. 748(1B), the anti-avoidance provision will apply, notwithstanding that there is no principal charge to corporation tax which it is designed to protect. The effectiveness of this rule under EC law is questionable.[80]

---

[80] See chapter 3, para. 11-300.

The Legal Framework: European Law

Chapter 2

11-000   Introduction

The EC is established by treaty setting out its constituting provisions.[1] Community law within its area of competence is supreme and renders ineffective any UK legislative, administrative, or judicial act which is contrary to it. The British Parliament cannot override European law in the way other treaty obligations may.[2] Community law impacts on tax treaties in two respects. First, treaties are subject to the same tests on legality as are the domestic laws of member states. Second, certain areas of taxation traditionally occupied by treaties are now governed by European harmonisation measures.[3]

In one of the very earliest cases concerning tax (and a tax treaty),[4] the ECJ ruled that even in the absence of harmonisation of corporate tax, although a company's tax position depends on the national law applied to it, art. 43 (ex 52) of the EC Treaty unconditionally prohibits member states from laying down in their laws conditions for the pursuit of activities by persons exercising their right of establishment which differ from those laid down for their own nationals.

The ECJ has consistently reaffirmed this opinion that although as Community law stands, direct taxation is within the competence of the member states and, as such, does not fall within the purview of the Community, the taxation powers retained by the member states must nevertheless be exercised consistently with Community law.[5]

In the context of tax treaties the court has adopted the same rule, namely, in the absence of unifying or harmonising measures at Community level for the elimination of double

---

[1] Consolidated versions of the current treaty on EU and of the treaty establishing the EC, incorporating the amendments made by the Treaty of Athens, signed on 16 April 2003, are found in the Official Journal C 321E of 29 December 2006. Strictly, taxation is addressed by the treaty establishing the EC. The treaty establishing the EU addresses political integration. References in this book to articles are references to the treaty establishing the EC as contained in the Amsterdam Treaty. Articles were renumbered in the Amsterdam Treaty, which itself was in part a consolidating treaty. Cases before the renumbering have references to both old and new numbers. The term 'European law' is used to describe the laws of the Community and the Union in their entirety.

[2] This is now trite law. See, for example, European Communities Act 1972, s. 2; Case 14/64 *Costa v ENEL* [1964] ECR 585, ECJ; *R. v Secretary of State for Transport, ex parte Factortame Ltd* [1991] AC 603, HL.

[3] See below, chapter 13.

[4] *EC Commission v France* (Case C-270/83) [1986] ECR 273.

[5] See, for example, Case C-279/93, *Finanzamt Koln-Altstadt v Schumacker* [1995] BTC 251; [1995] STC 306; Case C-80/94, *Wielockx v Inspector der Directe Belastingen* [1995] BTC 415; [1995] STC 876; Case C-107/94, *Asscher v Staatssecretaris van Financien* [1996] BTC 563; [1996] STC 1025; Case C-307/97, *Compagnie de Saint-Gobain, Zweigniederlassung Deutschland v Finanzamt Aachen-Innenstadt* [2000] 854, ECJ; *Metallgesellschaft Ltd & Ors (Case C-397/98); Hoechst AG & Hoechst UK Ltd (Case C-410/98) v Commissioners of Inland Revenue & Attorney-General* [2001] BTC 99; [2001] ECR I-1727, para. 37; *Marks & Spencer plc v Halsey (HMIT)* (Case C-446/03) [2006] BTC 318 [2005] ECR I-10837, para. 29; and Case C-374/04 *Test Claimants in Class IV of the ACT Group Litigation v IR Commrs* [2008] BTC 305; [2006] ECR I-11673, para. 36.

taxation, the member states retain competence for determining the criteria for taxation on income and wealth with a view to eliminating double taxation by means of tax treaties among other instruments. Thus, member states remain at liberty to determine the connecting factors for the allocation of fiscal jurisdiction under such treaties. Nonetheless, such an allocation of fiscal jurisdiction does not permit member states to introduce discriminatory measures which are contrary to the Community rules.[6]

Fundamental freedoms

Direct tax measures are potentially capable of being tested under several articles of the EC Treaty:

(1) Article 12 (ex 6) prohibits any discrimination on grounds of nationality. This prohibition is framed on similar terms to the prohibition in art. 24(1) of the OECD Model Treaty.[7] The ECJ prefers to rely on the specific prohibitions in other parts of the EC Treaty.

(2) Article 18(1) (ex 8a) grants every citizen of the Union[8] the right to move and reside freely within the territory of the member states, subject to the limitations and conditions laid down in the EC Treaty and by the measures adopted to give it effect.

(3) Article 39 (ex 48) grants freedom of movement for workers. This entails the abolition of discrimination based on nationality as regards employment, remuneration and other conditions of work and employment. It includes the right, subject to accept offers of employment, to move freely within the EU and to stay in a member state during and after employment.

(4) Article 43 (ex 52) prohibits restrictions on the freedom of establishment of nationals of a member state in the territory of another member state, including restrictions on the setting up of agencies, branches or subsidiaries in any member state. Freedom of establishment includes the right to take up and pursue activities as self-employed persons and to set up and manage undertakings, in particular companies or firms.

(5) Article 48 (ex 58) extends the freedom of establishment rules to companies formed or managed in a member state.

(6) Article 49 (ex 59): prohibits restrictions on freedom of nationals of member states who are established in a member state to provide services within the EU.

(7) Article 56 (ex 73b) guarantees free movement of capital by prohibiting all restrictions on the movement of capital and payments between member states and between member states and third countries.

---

[6] *Bouanich v Skatteverket* (Case C-265/04) [2006] ECR I-923, paras. 50 and 51 (ECJ).

[7] See chapter 15, para. 24-150.

[8] Citizenship of the Union is established by art. 17 (ex 8) for every person holding the nationality of a member state. Citizenship of the Union complements and does not replace national citizenship.

Defences to restrictions

These fundamental freedoms are not unlimited. In addition to the limitations expressed in the freedoms themselves, defences to tax measures that would otherwise be in breech of the freedoms may be established on the basis of the following articles:

- *Article 46 (ex 56)*: public policy, public safety, public health; and
- *Article 58 (ex 73d)*: distinctions based on residence or place where capital is invested and to prevent infringement of national law, particularly taxation. This defence is restricted to art. 56 cases.

Since cases involving cross-border operations inevitably involve treaty issues, references to treaties appear in many cases concerning these freedoms that have come before the courts.

11-050   Personal scope

Article 12 (ex 6) of the EC Treaty prohibits discrimination on the grounds of nationality within the scope of application of the EC Treaty. The non-discrimination provisions are extended to companies or firms by art. 48 (ex 58) of the treaty. Thus, a company or firm formed in accordance with the law of a member state and having its registered office, central administration or principal place of business within the Community is to be treated in the same way as natural persons who are nationals of member states for these purposes. The definition is therefore not dissimilar from the definition of 'national' in art. 3 of the OECD Model read in conjunction with the definition of resident in art. 4(1) of the OECD Model.

The rules relating to discrimination based on nationality have also been extended to discrimination based on residence by the ECJ.[9] Citing *Sotgiu v Deutsche Bundespost*, the ECJ held in *Biehl*[10] that:

> 'The rules regarding equality of treatment forbid not only overt discrimination by reason of nationality but also all covert forms of discrimination which, by the application of other criteria of differentiation, lead to the same results.'

The ECJ recognised that a distinction based on residence, although applicable without distinction to nationals and non-nationals, should be viewed in the same way as a distinction based on nationality where the non-residents are in the main non-nationals. In *Schumacker*, Advocate General Leger noted[11] that 'the criterion of residence is the main pillar of international tax law. Chosen by almost every state in the world, it is given precedence over nationality'.

---

[9] The first occasion was in Case C-152/73 *Sotgiu v Deutsche Bundespost* [1974] ECR 153. This has been followed in a series of tax cases concerning individuals, such as: Case C-279/93, *Finanzamt Koln-Altstadt v Schumacker* [1995] BTC 251; [1995] STC 306; Case C-80/94, *Wielockx v Inspecteur der Directs Belastingen* [1995] BTC 415; [1995] STC 876, and Case C-107/94, *Asscher v Staatssecretaris van Financien* [1996] BTC 563; [1996] STC 1025; and in the case of companies, in Case C-1/93, *Halliburton Services BV v Staatssecretaris van Financien* [1994] BTC 8069; [1994] STC 655, and Case C-330/91, *R. v IRC, ex parte Commerzbank AG* [1993] BTC 299; [1993] STC 605.

[10] Case C-175/88, *Biehl v Administration des Contributions du Grand-Duche de Luxembourg* [1991] BTC 400; [1990] ECR 1-1779.

[11] See above, n. 6, para. 35 at 312.

While the extension of the principle to distinctions based on residence has been by the court's interpretation, the defence to restrictions on free movement of capital is explicitly on the basis of residence in tax matters was given limited approval in certain circumstances by amendments introduced in the Maastricht Treaty.[12]

Tax treaty benefits to non-residents

Member states may, in certain circumstances, be required to unilaterally give benefits to residents of other member states which they extend by treaty to their own residents. In *Compagnie de Saint-Gobain v Finanzamt Aachen Innenstadt*,[13] the ECJ considered *inter alia* the German Schachtelprivileg, a participation exemption granted by treaty with a non-EC-member country. Under it, companies holding a specified percentage of shares in other companies established in non-member countries are entitled to credit for underlying tax with respect do dividends paid against the corporation tax of the recipient. It also considered a similar exemption in respect of capital tax.

Under German group tax rules, subject to certain conditions, a permanent establishment of a foreign company may be included in the Organschaft. The German subsidiaries were treated as a single entity along with the permanent establishment for German tax purposes. Under these rules, the parent company (in this case the permanent establishment) is liable for tax on the group's aggregate results. The profits and losses of the other companies are included in the profits and losses of the principal company. Saint-Gobain, a French resident and incorporated company, operated through a permanent establishment in Germany. It held as part of the assets of the permanent establishment 10.2 per cent of a US corporation and effectively all of the shares of two German incorporated and resident subsidiaries. In this case, the permanent establishment was the principal company. The German companies had substantial holdings in companies established in Austria, Switzerland and Italy. Dividends were received from those companies and under the group profit transfer agreements were included in the income of the permanent establishment.

Under German law, the dividends were attributed to the permanent establishment in Germany and thus liable to German tax. As a general rule, Germany-resident companies are liable to unlimited (worldwide) liability to tax and permanent establishments to limited (German source) tax liability.

The German tax authorities refused to allow the benefit of treaties between Germany and the US and Switzerland respectively. In each case, dividends paid by US or Swiss companies were, subject to certain conditions, exempt from German tax on such dividends in the hands of German residents. These treaty exemptions were denied to the permanent establishment despite the fact that the dividends were included in the income of the permanent establishment.

The German tax authorities allowed credit (direct credit) in respect of tax withheld at source on dividends from the various countries. It, however, refused the underlying credit for

---

[12] Art. 73d (now 58) of the EC Treaty.

[13] Case C-307/97 [2000] STC 854, ECJ.

corporate tax paid by the foreign subsidiaries. Under German domestic law, the underlying credit was granted only to Germany-resident companies. There was no dispute that the concessions granted to domestic German groups resulted in a lighter tax burden.

The ECJ held all of the German provisions in question to be contrary to art. 43 (ex 52) and art. 48 (ex 58) of the EC Treaty because permanent establishments are less attractive than subsidiaries. This is because under German domestic law and bilateral treaties, the tax benefits are only granted to German subsidiaries. This restricts the freedom to choose the most appropriate legal form for the pursuit of activity in another member state.

The German Government sought to justify the discriminatory treatment on the basis that the situations of resident and non-resident companies are not generally comparable. This is particularly so because non-residents are only liable to limited tax liability whereas residents are subject to unlimited tax liability. The ECJ rejected this argument on the basis that the dividends were taxable in the hands of the permanent establishment, regardless of where the dividend paying companies were located; thus, the restriction to local source income was theoretical. In fact, the only difference was that the permanent establishment was not entitled to credit or exemption from tax on dividends from foreign shareholdings. The German Government argued that the measures were justified by the need to prevent a reduction in tax revenue, given the impossibility for the German authorities to compensate for the reduction in revenue if equal treatment were given by taxing dividends distributed by non-resident companies.

The ECJ rejected this argument, simply on the basis that it is not one of the grounds listed in art. 46 (ex 56) of the EC Treaty and cannot be regarded as a matter of overriding general interest which may be relied upon in order to justify unequal treatment.

It was further argued that the distinction was justified because there is no tax on the transfer of profits to the head office by a branch compared with the taxation of distributions by a subsidiary to a parent company. The ECJ did not accept that such advantages exist for permanent establishments, and even if they did, they could not justify a breach of the equal treatment required by art. 43 (ex 52).

Most favoured nation treatment

Do the fundamental freedoms of Community law oblige a member state to make available the benefits of a tax treaty negotiated with one member state to residents of another? The Commission has long held the view that the answer is no. In reply to a parliamentary question, the Commission indicated that Community law did not require a member state to grant automatically the withholding tax rate of its most favoured bilateral agreement to taxpayers of another member state which was not covered by that agreement.[14] On this basis, taxpayers of member states are limited to claiming the treaties concluded by the member state in which they are resident only. Thus, while they may be able to access treaties indirectly through the establishment of companies in other member states, they have no

---

[14] [1993] OJ C40/93.

entitlement to the application of more beneficial treaties concluded by the member states directly.

The issue was considered by the ECJ in *D. v Inspecteur van de Belastingdienst/ Particulieren/Ondernemingen Buitenland te Heerlen.*[15] The wealth of Mr D, a German resident, was comprised as 10 per cent of real property situated in the Netherlands, while the remainder was held in Germany. He was liable to Netherlands wealth tax, as a non-resident taxpayer, and as such did not qualify for personal allowances there. He argued that he was entitled those allowances under art. 25(3) of the Belgium–Netherlands Tax Treaty, which entitled a Belgian resident to the allowances in the Netherlands. He claimed that the difference, resulting from application of the Belgium–Netherlands Treaty, between his situation and that of a resident of Belgium in an equivalent situation amounts to discrimination prohibited by art. 56 of the EC Treaty (Free movement of capital). The court ruled that the proper comparison should be between the situation of a person resident in a state not party to such a treaty and that of a person covered by the treaty. The scope of a bilateral tax convention is limited to the persons referred to in it. In view of the court, the benefits in relation to the wealth tax could not be seen in isolation. The fact that the reciprocal rights and obligations in a bilateral treaty only apply to persons resident in one of the contracting states is an inherent consequence of bilateral double taxation conventions. Article 25(3) could not be regarded as a benefit separable from the remainder of the treaty, but it is an integral part and contributes to its overall balance. Thus, the court held that that Belgian resident and a non-Belgian resident are not in the same situation concerning wealth tax on real property situated in the Netherlands.

Exceptionally, a non-resident with a permanent establishment in a member state is regarded as being in a situation equivalent to that of a resident of that state. This access to treaty benefits is thus not unlimited. It applies where the national or resident of a member state exercises a fundamental freedom such as the right of establishment and in the context of that exercise is put in the same position as a resident or national of the contracting state in question.

A similar issue arose in *Test Claimants in Class IV of the ACT Group Litigation v Inland Revenue Commissioners.*[16] Certain treaties between the UK and other countries conferred, entitlement to payment of tax credits to qualifying non-resident individuals and companies resident in the other contracting states. For example, the UK–Netherlands Treaty granted a partial tax credit to a Netherlands-resident corporate shareholder on receiving dividends from a UK subsidiary, if that shareholder either alone or together with one or more associated companies controlled directly or indirectly 10 per cent or more of the voting power in the UK company subject to a limited rate of UK income tax.[17] Netherlands-resident 'portfolio' investors were entitled to a full tax credit in respect of the dividend. This treatment was more generous than in treaties with other member states. For example, the UK–France Treaty only conferred a tax credit if the dividend recipient held less than 10 per

---

[15] Case C-376/03 [2005] ECR I-5821.

[16] Case C-374/04 [2008] BTC 305

[17] Art. 10(3)(c).

cent of the voting power in the UK-resident company while others, such as the UK–Germany Treaty, conferred no such entitlement.

Applying its reasoning in the *D* case, the court concluded that arts. 43 EC and 56 EC do not prevent a member state (the source state). It also stated that the articles do not preclude agreeing by treaty with another member state for companies resident in the second state (the residence state) which receive dividends from a company resident in the source state to be entitled to a tax credit, without requiring the source state to extend the credit to companies resident in a third member state with which the source state has not concluded a treaty providing for such an entitlement.[18]

11-100   Treaties between member states

A distinction may be drawn between treaties concluded between member states and those concluded with third countries. Double taxation between member states is specifically addressed in art. 293 (ex 220) of the EC Treaty. It provides that:

> **'Article 293 (ex 220)**
>
> Member States shall, so far as is necessary, enter into negotiations with each other with a view to securing for the benefit of their nationals: ... the abolition of double taxation within the Community.'

Thus, member states are required to enter into negotiations with each other as necessary with a view to securing the abolition of double taxation within the Community for the benefit of their nationals. The scope and meaning of the article has been subject to much scholarly analysis[19] and debate but to limited consideration by the courts.

It has been argued that the expression 'so far as is necessary' limits the obligation to the extent that European measures have not already done so. Thus, to the extent that European law already occupies the field, member states individually would appear to have no obligation. It should be noted that the obligation is to enter into negotiations with a view to eliminating double taxation, rather than a legal duty to eliminate double taxation. The effect of this is therefore to preserve the right of member states to enter into treaties with each other. In addition, the subsidiarity principle introduced in the Maastricht Treaty[20] requires that the Community must act within the powers conferred upon it by the EC Treaty. However, areas which do not fall within its exclusive jurisdiction are only amenable to Community action if and so far as the objectives of the proposed action cannot be sufficiently achieved by member states.

The article itself does not prohibit double taxation. The application and scope of the article was considered by the ECJ in *Gilly v Directeur des Services Fiscaux du Bas-Rhin*.[21] The question put to the court was whether the objective of abolishing double taxation must be

---

[18] At paras. 92 and 93.

[19] See, for example, Gassner, W, Lang, M and Lechner, E (eds), *Tax Treaties and EC Law* (1996), Kluwer Law International.

[20] See art. 3b.

[21] Case C-336/96 [1998] BTC 335; [1998] STC 1014, ECJ.

regarded as having the status of a directly applicable rule under which double taxation may no longer take place, having regard for the time which member states have had to implement it. The taxpayers in that case argued that the article created legally binding rules directly applicable on which they could rely. Several member states appearing before the ECJ argued that the article does not have direct effect because it is not sufficiently clear and unconditional and does not confer on individuals a right to the abolition of all double taxation within the Community. The Commission argued that the article imposes on member states an obligation to enter into negotiations, if necessary. It does not oblige them to achieve a specific result. In the view of the Commission, the Franco–German Treaty did meet the objective of art. 293 (ex 220). The Advocate General regarded these provisions as not laying down an absolute obligation but as leaving member states with a wide discretion to decide whether to enter into negotiations. That discretion had been exercised by the contracting states when the treaty was signed in 1959 and when it was amended by successive protocols in 1969 and 1989. The taxpayer argued that the mere reduction of double taxation as opposed to its elimination did not meet the objective of art. 293 (ex 220).

The ECJ followed its earlier decision in *Ministere Public v Mutsch*[22] on another aspect of art. 293 (ex 220) that the article is not intended to lay down a legal rule directly applicable as such. It merely defined a number of matters on which the member states are to enter into negotiations with each other 'so far as is necessary'. The second indent of the article was held to indicate clearly that the abolition of double taxation within the Community is an objective of any such negotiations. Thus, although the abolition of double taxation within the Community is included among the objectives of the EC Treaty, it is clear from the wording of that provision that it cannot itself confer any rights on individuals which they might be able to rely on before their national courts.

Limits on the effect of treaties

In the absence of unifying or harmonising measures for the elimination of double taxation, member states are competent enough to determine the criteria for taxing income and eliminating double taxation. The means of achieving this includes bilateral treaties.[23] Although member states have retained their competence to enter into treaties with a view to eliminating double taxation, this competence must be exercised in a manner consistent with European law.

In *EC Commission v France*, the ECJ considered whether France was in breach of its obligations under the EC Treaty, in particular, art. 43 (ex 52), by not granting the benefit of shareholders' tax credits to branches and agencies in France of insurance companies established in other member states. The court ruled that by virtue of art. 43 (ex 52) freedom of establishment for nationals of one member state on the territory of another includes the right to take up and pursue activities and to set up and manage undertakings under the conditions laid down for its own nationals.

---

[22] Case 137/84 [1985] ECR 2681 at 2694-2695, para. 11.

[23] *Gilly* above, n. 21, at 1038, para. 24. The court referred particularly to treaties in accordance with the OECD Model.

The French Government argued that the difference in treatment arose by virtue of differences between the tax systems of member states and the existence of tax treaties. Different measures are necessary in each case, it argued, in order to take account of the differences between taxation systems which ought to be justified under art. 43 (ex 52). The tax rules in question were governed by double tax treaties between the relevant member states whose existence is expressly recognised in art. 293 (ex 220) of the treaty. Furthermore, the rules which were contested were necessary, in particular to prevent tax avoidance.

On the role of tax treaties, the ECJ held that rights conferred by art. 43 (ex 52) are unconditional, and a member state cannot make them subject to the contents of an agreement concluded with another member state. This clear statement has been reaffirmed in subsequent cases.[24] In particular art. 43 (ex 52) does not permit those rights to be made subject to a condition of reciprocity imposed for the purposes of obtaining corresponding advantages in other member states. Consequently, provisions in treaties between member states that do not comply with Community law are ineffective.

11-150   Treaties authorising discrimination

Where the treaty is not itself discriminatory but authorises discriminatory taxation by a contracting state, the treaty itself may escape attack. In *Finanzamt-Koln-Altstadt v Schumacker*[25] one of the questions put to the ECJ was whether it made any difference if the income in question was taxed in a member state in accordance with the treaty between the member states in question. The main point in issue was whether art. 39 (ex 48) of the EC Treaty allowed a Belgian resident who was otherwise in comparable circumstances with German residents to be denied equal tax treatment in Germany. In that case, there was no discussion of the treaty in question by the Advocate General or by the ECJ itself, other than pointing out that the unequal treatment in question – namely, denying a married Belgian resident the benefits of taxation by reference to the treatment of married residents and taxing him as a single person instead – was permitted in the state of employment in accordance with the applicable treaty. The underlying assumption seems to be that since art. 15(1) of the Belgian–German Treaty merely authorised the offending elements of German tax law. The provisions of the treaty were themselves not analysed or indeed strictly relevant and therefore discrimination lay in the German domestic law not in the treaty. Unlike the French authorities in *Commission v France*,[26] the German tax administration did not rely on the treaty to justify the discrimination in question.

11-200   Discriminatory treaties

Treaties may themselves give rise to discrimination. In *Saint-Gobain*, the German tax authorities included the shareholding in the American subsidiary in the domestic assets of

---

[24] For example, Case C-330/91: *R. v IRC, ex parte Commerzbank AG* [1993] BTC 299; [1993] STC 605, Advocate General's opinion.

[25] Case C-279/93 [1995] BTC 251; [1995] STC 306, ECJ.

[26] See above, n. 4.

the permanent establishment for the purpose of German capital tax. Germany did not allow an exemption for international groups, but did grant a concession, limited to domestic companies.

However, by virtue of art. 19 of the France–Germany Treaty, shareholdings of a German subsidiary in a foreign subsidiary of a French company not resident in Germany were excluded from German capital tax. As a result, the exemption from capital tax in relation to international groups also produced a tax burden on a permanent establishment of a foreign company which is different from that on a subsidiary of a foreign company. The German Government initially argued that the situation of a permanent establishment is different from a subsidiary, but it conceded the discrimination at the hearing. Thus, treaties may give rise to illegal discrimination if, as a result of their terms, taxpayers in like circumstance are not taxed equally.

A treaty which grants concessions to subsidiaries of a contracting state but fails to extend the same concessions to permanent establishments of a contracting state is a source of discrimination. In *Saint-Gobain*,[27] the result was not the ineffectiveness of the treaty, however, but the domestic law of the contracting state whose rules have been made discriminatory by application of the treaty. That the resident or national of another member state is treated more favourably in some respects does not cure or offset discriminatory inequality where it exists.

An unusual form of discrimination arising from non-discrimination provisions in double tax treaties arose in *XAB & YAB v Riksskatteverket*.[28] Swedish corporate income tax reliefs applied on the transfer of assets intra-group. They were applicable under Swedish law to companies in the same group – that is, where the parent owned at least 90 per cent of the subsidiary. The reliefs applied on condition that the companies were all established in Sweden or in a single other state with which Sweden has a treaty containing a non-discrimination clause. This was attacked as discriminatory against companies in groups established in more than one member state under arts. 43 (ex 52), 48 (ex 58), 56 (ex 73b) and 58 (ex 73d) of the EC Treaty.

In the case, 99.8 per cent of the shares of YAB were owned ultimately by XAB. About 58 per cent of those shares were owned directly by XAB. The balance were owned by other subsidiaries of XAB. A ruling was sought from the Swedish tax authorities on obtaining relief on intra-group transfers of assets in three circumstances:

- XAB owned all of the shares in YAB itself or through Swedish subsidiaries;
- 15 per cent of the shares in YAB were owned by ZBV, a Netherlands company wholly-owned by XAB; or
- ZBV and YGmbH, a Germany company wholly-owned by XAB, would each acquire 15 per cent of the shares in YAB.

Under Swedish domestic law, relief would be given in the first circumstance. Relief would also be given in the second circumstance on the basis it could be contrary to the non-

[27] See above, n. 13.

[28] Case C-200/98 [1999] ECR 1-8261.

discrimination clause of an applicable treaty – for example, that between Sweden and the Netherlands, for the relief to be denied. However, Swedish case law prohibited the cumulative application of two treaties, such as those between Sweden and Germany on the one hand, and Sweden and the Netherlands on the other. This was because the simultaneous application of two or more treaties was excluded on the basis that the provisions of each of those treaties applied only to undertakings of the contracting states and not to those of third states.

In upholding the claim of illegal discrimination, the ECJ noted that the freedom of establishment applies both to ensure that foreign nationals and companies are treated in the host member state in the same way as nationals of that state, as well as prohibiting the member state of origin from hindering the establishment in another member state.

These rules were held to be discriminatory.[29] Although each of the treaties in question was not discriminatory, when placed in context of the domestic law, the presence of a treaty containing the requisite provisions established discrimination when a third country was involved.

11-250   Treaty benefits neutralising discrimination

In *Bouanich v Skatteverket*[30] the court examined Swedish tax treatment of rules a payment in respect of a share repurchase. Where the repurchase was by a non-resident shareholder in connection with a reduction in share capital, it was taxed as a dividend without there being a right to deduct the cost of acquisition of those shares, whereas the same payment made to a resident shareholder is taxed as a capital gain with a right to deduct the cost of acquisition in calculating the gain. It ruled that this difference in treatment infringed art. 56 EC (Free movement of capital). The Swedish Government argued, however, that the position should be different where the tax system derives from a treaty (such as the France–Sweden Treaty) which fixes a lower maximum tax rate of dividends for non-resident shareholders than for resident shareholders (for whom it is treated as a capital gain). It further contended that interpretation of that treaty in the light of the OECD Commentary on the model only the nominal value of those shares is to be deducted from the share repurchase payment.

Thus, under the treaty, Ms Bouanich was permitted to deduct the nominal value of the shares from the taxable amount payable on the occasion of a repurchase of those shares with the balance taxed at the treaty rate of 15 per cent. By comparison, resident shareholders were taxed at the rate of 30 per cent on share repurchase payments after deduction of the cost of acquisition of the shares.

The court concluded that although member states remain at liberty to determine the connecting factors for the allocation of fiscal jurisdiction by treaty, this does not permit member states to introduce discriminatory measures. Article 56 EC (Free movement of

[29] The Swedish Government conceded that the rule in question was contrary to art. 43 (ex 52) and offered no justification, and the court ruled on this basis. It accordingly refused to consider the further grounds.

[30] Case C-265/04 [2006] ECR I-923 (ECJ).

capital) precludes such rules except where, on a case by case basis, non-resident shareholders are not treated less favourably than resident shareholders. This case-by-case calculation is a matter for member states.

Limitation on benefits

In the context of treaty shopping, questions arise as to whether Community law may invalidate anti-treaty shopping provisions contained in the national law of member states or treaties. The most important question is whether provisions inserted in treaties designed to limit the entitlement of residents of a contracting state which is an EU member state can be upheld. At the formative stage of the single market, the Commission appeared to be of the view that they should. The Ruding Committee report in its consideration of treaty aspects of European tax harmonisation gave particular attention to benefit limitation provisions. It noted that such provisions, though designed to minimise treaty shopping, can discriminate against enterprises of other member states. It also observed that despite this, member states continued to conclude treaties with such provisions. Similar views have been expressed by the Commission on several occasions. In the Commission's communication to the Council and to the European Parliament of 26 June 1992, reporting its conclusions on the Ruding Committee,[31] the Commission undertook to ensure that treaties which member states conclude between each other and with non-member countries are strictly in accordance with the principle of non-discrimination.

The Ruding Committee report expressed the view that art. 16 of the 1981 US Model Treaty (a form of which appears as art. 26 of the US–UK Treaty), a look-through provision, could be discriminatory under European principles. At the time, the Commission said that treaties concluded with non-member countries must be strictly in accordance with EC law and the Commission is to ensure that this position is observed.[32] In an information release at the time, the Commission said that treaties concluded with non-member countries must be strictly in accordance with EC law, and the Commission is to ensure that this position is observed.[33] Speaking at the time, the Taxation Commissioner, Mrs Scrivener, said that the Commission is studying treaties to consider if they disadvantaged companies in other member states. The protocol to the UK–Denmark Treaty signed on 16 October 1996 eliminating a look-through rule was no doubt a response to these concerns.

However, in *Test Claimants in Class IV of the ACT Group Litigation v Inland Revenue Commissioners*,[34] the court was asked to opine on the limitations on the benefit contained in the UK–Netherlands Treaty, which denied entitlement to the tax credit (that would otherwise exist) if the Netherlands-resident company was itself controlled by a company anywhere in the chain of ownership resident in a country whose treaty with the UK did not confer a tax credit on companies receiving UK-source dividends.[35]

---

[31] (SECTION 92)/118 Final.

[32] Commission Information Release dated 24 June 1992.

[33] Commission Information Release dated 24 June 1992.

[34] Case C-374/04 [2008] BTC 305. See above para. 11-050.

[35] Art. 10(3)(d)(i) of the UK–Netherlands Treaty at the time provided that:

Extending its reasoning in the *D* case,[36] the court concluded that arts. 43 EC and 56 EC do not prevent the operation of these provisions. Thus, the grant of a tax credit, the court ruled, cannot be regarded as a benefit separable from the remainder of the treaty, but it is an integral part of it and contributes to the overall balance of the treaty.[37] The reasoning on this issue is unconvincing. The circumstances in which these limitations on benefits apply are not analogous to the *D* case circumstances. These are not circumstances where a resident of a third country is seeking treaty benefits. The third country resident in these circumstances is merely seeking that the treaty between the source state and the residence state should not limit its benefits by reason of the investment by a third country resident in the residence state.

The court did not consider the analogous position of discriminatory treaties – illustrated by its decision in the 'Open Skies' decisions.[38] All these cases were essentially identical. By way of illustration, in the UK case[39] a declaration that concluding and applying an Air Services Treaty with the US which provided for the revocation, suspension or limitation of traffic rights in cases where air carriers designated by the UK are not owned by the UK or UK nationals was in breach of art. 52 of the EC Treaty (now 43 EC). The analysis in respect of the look-through rules in *ACT Class IV* ignores the disadvantage imposed by ownership of companies by residents of other member states.

Another similar concept (not discussed in ACT Class IV) was examined by the ECJ in *R. v Secretary of State for Transport, ex parte Factortame Ltd.*[40] The case involved 'quota hopping' a concept that might be regarded as analogous to treaty shopping. This involved the formation of companies in the UK by Spanish nationals. The directors and shareholders of the companies were mostly Spanish nationals. Fishing vessels which had previously been registered in Spain were re-registered as British vessels under the Merchant Shipping Act 1894. The purpose of this was to enable Spanish fishermen to access British fishing quotas.

According to the UK Government, these companies lacked any genuine link to the UK. As a result, new legislation was introduced in 1988 limiting eligibility for registration on a new register of British fishing vessels. Fishing vessels were only eligible to be re-registered if the vessel was British owned, managed and its operations were directed and controlled from within the UK. Similarly, any charterer or manager or operator of the vessel had to be a qualified person or company. Both legal and beneficial ownership in the vessel had to vest with a qualified person or companies.

'No tax credit shall be payable where the beneficial owner of the dividends is a company, other than a company whose shares are officially quoted on a Netherlands stock exchange ... unless the company shows that it is not controlled by a person or two or more associated or connected persons together, who or any of whom would not have been entitled to a tax credit if he had been the beneficial owner of the dividends.'

[36] See the *D* case, at para. 62.

[37] At para. 89.

[38] *EC Commission v UK, Denmark, Sweden, Finland, Belgium, Luxembourg, Austria and Germany*, Cases C-466/98, C-467/98, C-468/98, C-469/98, C-471/98, C-472/98, C-475/98 and C-476/98.

[39] Case C-466/98.

[40] [1991] 3 All ER 769.

A qualified company was one incorporated in the UK with its principal place of business there and with a minimum of 75 per cent legal and beneficial ownership by qualified persons. At least 75 per cent of the directors also had to be qualified persons.

A qualified person was a British citizen, resident and domiciled in the UK or a UK local authority. Administrative discretion was granted to dispense with nationality in the case of long-term residents who had lengthy involvement in the UK fishing industry. The ECJ held that it was contrary to Community law and art. 52 of the EC Treaty, in particular, to impose conditions requiring the legal and beneficial owners, charterers, managers and operators to be UK-resident and domiciled nationals. In the case of a company, the requirements that shareholders and directors be resident and domiciled was unjustifiable discrimination on grounds of nationality.

11-300 Avoidance and abuse of law

Early case law on tax avoidance as a justification for limiting fundamental rights under the EC Treaty suggested that the ECJ placed the establishment of the single market above the prevention of avoidance. In *EC Commission v France*[41] the ECJ considered whether France was in breach of its obligations under the EC Treaty – in particular, art. 43 (ex 52) – by not granting the benefit of shareholders' tax credits to branches and agencies in France of insurance companies established in other member states. The ECJ ruled that by virtue of art. 43 (ex 52) freedom of establishment for nationals of one member state on the territory of another includes the right to take up and pursue activities and to set up and manage undertakings under the conditions laid down for its own nationals.

The French Government argued that difference in treatment arose by virtue of differences between the tax systems of member states and the existence of tax treaties. Different measures are necessary in each case, it argued, in order to take account of the differences between taxation systems which ought to be justified under art. 43 (ex 52). The tax rules in question were governed by double taxation treaties between the relevant member states whose existence is expressly recognised in art. 293 (ex 220) of the EC Treaty. Furthermore, the rules which were contested were necessary in particular to prevent tax avoidance.

On the role of tax treaties, the ECJ held that rights conferred by art. 43 (ex 52) are unconditional and that a member state cannot make them subject to the contents of an agreement concluded with another member state. This clear statement has been reaffirmed in subsequent cases.[42] In particular, art. 43 (ex 52) does not permit those rights to be made subject to a condition of reciprocity imposed for the purposes of obtaining corresponding advantages in other member states. Consequently, provisions in treaties between member states that do not comply with Community law cannot stand. The court also rejected the risk of tax avoidance as justification in this context. It held that art. 43 (ex 52) does not permit any derogation from the fundamental principle of freedom of establishment on such a

---

[41] Case 270/83 [1986] ECR 273.

[42] For example, Case C-330/91: *R. v IRC, ex parte Commerzbank AG* [1993] BTC 299; [1993] STC 605, Advocate General's opinion.

ground. The court has not had occasion to consider the question of abuse and treaties since that decision. The jurisprudence in this area has, however, advanced considerably.

Tax base erosion

The related notion of erosion of the tax base as a justification for limiting fundamental rights under the EC Treaty was also rejected by the ECJ in *ICI v Colmer*.[43] This was put beyond doubt in *Metallgesellschaft Ltd & Ors (Case C-397/98); Hoechst AG & Hoechst UK Ltd (Case C-410/98) v Commissioners of Inland Revenue & Attorney-General*, when it was said:[44]

> 'It is settled case law that diminution of tax revenue cannot be regarded as a matter of overriding general interest which may be relied upon in order to justify a measure which is, in principle, contrary to a fundamental freedom.'

Meaning of tax avoidance

An early indication of the attitude of the court in this area was in *Imperial Chemical Industries plc (ICI) v Colmer (HM Inspector of Taxes)*.[45] There, group relief at the time was subject to the requirement that the holding company's business consist wholly or mainly in the holding of shares in UK companies. The ECJ ruled that this requirement amounted to a restriction on the freedom of establishment for companies and therefore infringed art. 43 (ex 52). The UK tax avoidance defence was swiftly dismissed as follows:

> 'As regards the justification based on the risk of tax avoidance, suffice it to note that the legislation at issue in the main proceedings does not have the specific purpose of preventing wholly artificial arrangements, set up to circumvent UK tax legislation, from attracting tax benefits, but applies generally to all situations in which the majority of a group's subsidiaries are established, for whatever reason, outside the UK. However, the establishment of a company outside the UK does not, of itself, necessarily entail tax avoidance, since that company will in any event be subject to the tax legislation of the state of establishment.[46]'

The court has followed this approach in subsequent decisions in this area. This brief statement set out the court's formulation on the meaning of 'tax avoidance', namely, 'wholly artificial arrangements, set up to circumvent UK tax legislation' which it has adhered to consistently.[47] Second, member state legislation (and by extension tax treaty provisions) can be justified on this basis only if its specific purpose is to do so. General tax rules that apply to all cases meeting the description in the rule cannot be so justified. Third, certain transactions do not constitute tax avoidance within this meaning. In *ICI v Colmer*, establishment of a subsidiary in another member state itself does not of itself constitute avoidance. Similarly, in *Hughes de Lasteyrie du Saillant v Ministère de l'Économie, des*

---

[43] Case C-264/96 [1998] BTC 304; [1998] STC 874.

[44] [2001] BTC 99, at para. 59; [2001] STC 452, at para. 59.

[45] Case C-264/96 [1998] BTC 304

[46] At para. 26.

[47] See, for example, below, *Cadbury Schweppes*, para. 55, and Thin Cap, para. 74.

Finances et de l'Industrie[48] a transfer of residence from one member state to another to establish a business did not itself imply tax avoidance.

This formulation was refined considerably in *Cadbury Schweppes plc & Anor v Inland Revenue Commissioners*.[49] Again it ruled, this time in the context of the UK Controlled Foreign Companies legislation that the mere fact that a resident company establishes a subsidiary, in another member state cannot set up a general presumption of tax evasion (avoidance) and justify a measure which compromises the exercise of a fundamental freedom guaranteed by the treaty.[50] Here the rule was expressed:

> 'It follows that, in order for a restriction on the freedom of establishment to be justified on the ground of prevention of abusive practices, the specific objective of such a restriction must be to prevent conduct involving the creation of *wholly artificial arrangements which do not reflect economic reality, with a view to escaping the tax normally due on the profits generated by activities carried out on national territory.*[51]'

The artificiality the court appeared to contemplate was in the exercise of the fundamental freedom (in that case the right of establishment in art. 43). This is to be identified by reference to objective circumstances showing that, despite formal observance of the conditions laid down by Community law, the objective pursued by freedom of establishment has not been achieved. That objective is to allow a nationals to set up in another member state to carry on activities there, and thus assist economic and social interpenetration within the Community in the sphere of activities as self-employed persons.[52] Freedom of establishment is intended to allow a Community national to participate, on a stable and continuing basis, in the economic life of a member state other than his or her state of origin and to profit therefrom.[53] That involves an actual establishment intended to carry on genuine economic and is ascertainable by third parties with regard, in particular, to the extent to which the establishment physically exists in terms of premises, staff and equipment.[54]

In order to find that there is such an artificial arrangement, there must also be a subjective element consisting in the intention to obtain a tax advantage. This must go beyond any advantage of low taxation resulting from establishment in a particular member state[55] and intend to escape the tax normally due on the profits generated by activities carried out on national territory of the home member state.

---

[48] Case C-9/02 [2006] BTC 105.

[49] Case C-196/04 [2008] BTC 52.

[50] At para. 50.

[51] At para. 55. Emphasis added.

[52] See Case 2/74. *Reyners v Belgium* [1974] ECR 631, para. 21.

[53] *Cadbury*, para. 54.

[54] *Cadbury*, paras. 66 and 67.

[55] *Cadbury*, para. 49.

Proportionality

This high threshold was echoed in *Test Claimants in the Thin Cap Group Litigation v Inland Revenue Commissioners.*[56] There it was argued that the then UK thin-capitalisation rules complied with the arm's-length principle in art. 9 of the OECD Model. Plus, most UK treaties contain a provision permitting the respective competent authorities to agree a compensating adjustment, whereby any increase in taxable profits in the state of the borrowing company is matched by a corresponding reduction in taxable profits in the state in which the lending company is established. The court ruled that the thin-capitalisation rules were not based on a mere allocation of taxing powers between the UK and its treaty partners, which would be the case if they were aimed at relieving double taxation but a unilateral measure to prevent profits being untaxed.[57] The provisions thus constituted a restriction on the right of establishment. However, such thin-capitalisation rules have a legitimate purpose in preventing the reduction of profits made by a subsidiary funded by way of loans, rather than equity capital – thereby allowing that subsidiary to transfer profits to a parent company in the form of deductible interest rather than non-deductible dividends. Such a measure must be a proportionate response, which is only satisfied if the legislation provides:

> 'For a consideration of objective and verifiable elements which make it possible to identify the existence of a purely artificial arrangement, entered into for tax reasons alone, and allows taxpayers to produce, if appropriate and without being subject to undue administrative constraints, evidence as to the commercial justification for the transaction in question and, secondly, where it is established that such an arrangement exists, such legislation treats that interest as a distribution only in so far as it exceeds what would have been agreed upon at arm's length.[58]'

These standards are equally applicable to anti-avoidance measures in tax treaties as much as they apply to domestic provisions. The extent to which the measures included meet this standard in UK treaties[59] remains largely untested.

Procedural requirements

Normal compliance obligations involved in claiming treaty benefits will not give rise to an infringement of community rights. In *FKP Scorpio Konzertproduktionen GmbH v Fiananzamt Hamburg-Eimsbuttel,*[60] German compliance obligations required a certificate confirming exemption under a treaty to be produced by the person claiming treaty benefit as a precondition to the non-deduction of tax source made to a non-resident service provider. The income in question was exempt from German tax under the Netherlands–Germany Treaty. The court rejected the argument that these administrative steps constituted a restriction on the freedom to provide services and art. 49 (ex 59). Although the requirements constituted an obstacle to the freedom to provide services, by making it more difficult for a

---

[56] Case C-524/04 [2008] BTC 348.

[57] *Thin-Cap*, paras. 50 to 52.

[58] *Thin-Cap*, para. 92.

[59] See chapter 16.

[60] Case C-290/04.

non-resident, the obstacle was justified in order to ensure proper functioning of the procedure for taxation at source.[61]

11-350   Treaty effect on defences to restrictions

In the same way as treaties may engage the fundamental freedoms, they may also impact on the defences available to member states to what are otherwise *prima facie* breaches of Community law.

Waiver of cohesion

The initial justification for discriminatory taxation accepted by the ECJ is where the discrimination is necessary to maintain the cohesion of the tax system. In *Wielockx v Inspecteur der Directe Belastingen*[62] the question of the effect of art. 18[63] of the OECD Model on discrimination was considered. The ECJ held that a non-resident taxpayer who received almost all of his or her income in the state where he or she worked as a physiotherapist and had a fixed base under art. 14(1) of the Belgium–Netherlands Treaty[64] but was not entitled to set up a pension reserve qualifying for deductions under the same tax conditions as a resident self-employed taxpayer, suffered discrimination. The Netherlands Government argued that the discrimination was justified on the basis that it was necessary to maintain the cohesion of the tax system.[65] The court, however, concluded that although a state may base the cohesion of its tax system on the principle of a correlation between the deductibility of contributions and taxation of pensions, it may also reject that principle. The court referred to art. 18 of the OECD Model, which reads as follows:

'Subject to the provisions of paragraph 2 of Article 19 [concerning *inter alia* civil servants' pensions], pensions and other similar remuneration paid to a resident of a contracting state in consideration of past employment shall be taxable only in that state.'

The Belgium–Netherlands Treaty had identical terms to art. 18 of the OECD Model. Advocate General Leger also referred in his opinion[66] to art. 22 of the Belgium–Netherlands Treaty[67] and noted that income of a resident of one contracting state not otherwise dealt with in the treaty was taxable only in the state of residence. The effect of treaties which are an integral part of national tax law and override domestic tax rules is that the cohesion applies at another level. Thus, he argued, domestic cohesion is waived and cohesion is established at a treaty level. In that case, he concluded, the result was that pension contributions are deductible in the country of payment even if the right to receive the pension is in the hands of a non-resident. Consequently, there is no requirement of a rigorous correlation between deductibility of contributions and taxation of pensions in order to secure cohesion of the

---

[61] At paras. 58 and 59.

[62] Case C-80/94 [1995] BTC 415; [1995] STC 876, ECJ.

[63] 'Pensions and similar payments'.

[64] 'Independent personal services'.

[65] Case C-204/90, *Bachman v Belgium* [1994] STC 855, ECJ.

[66] At para. 53, at 884.

[67] 'Other income'.

domestic tax system. Thus, where cohesion of the domestic tax rules is waived by treaty, it may not be relied upon as a justification for discrimination. The same conclusion was reached in *Danner*.[68]

Cross-border coherence of tax systems

The court subsequently rejected the notion that coherence may be established cross-border by the operation of the arm's-length principle under art. 9 of the OECD Model in *Lankhorst-Hohorst GmbH v Finanzamt Steinfurt*.[69] Lankhorst-Hohorst GmbH ('Lankhorst-Hohorst'), a German incorporated and resident company, was wholly owned by a Netherlands-resident parent company. The ultimate Dutch parent company loaned money at interest to Lankhorst-Hohorst, repayable over ten years in annual installments. The loan was intended as a substitute for capital and was accompanied by a letter of support under which the lender would waive repayment if third party creditors made claims against Lankhorst-Hohorst.

The German tax authorities treated the interest paid to the Dutch parent company as a distribution of profits and taxed it as such under German thin-capitalisation rules because as a result of Lankhorst-Hohorst's excessive indebtedness and its inability to provide security, it could not in fact have obtained a similar loan from any third party.

Member state governments argued that since the rules on thin capitalisation are intended to prevent the arbitrary transfer of the tax liability from one country to another and to ensure that the tax is charged in the place where the profit is actually made, there could be no finding of discrimination between the tax arrangements applicable to cross-border operations and those applicable to domestic operations.

The Commission supported this view but referred to the risk of double taxation where the German company is subject to German corporation tax on the deemed distribution whilst the foreign shareholder still reports interest it has received in its earnings in the Netherlands. The Commission argued that a member state which classifies interest as a covert distribution of profits must also ensure that there is liaison on the matter with the state in which the parent company is registered, so that a corresponding adjustment can be made. In the absence of any such adjustment, the risk of double taxation cannot be ruled out. art. 9(2) of the OECD Model[70] resolves this, as it is consistent with the principle of proportionality, and ensures the correct sharing of the right to tax, on the one hand, and the tax revenue of the member states involved, on the other.

The court rejected the application of the need to ensure the coherence of the applicable tax systems by reference to the arm's length principle. It ruled that there must be a direct link between deduction, on the one hand, and taxation of the sums received, on the other. In the case of *Bachman*,[71] this link was preserved since both were in respect of the same taxpayer. In *Lankhorst-Hohorst* the court found no such direct link where the subsidiary of a non-

---

[68] Case C-136/00, *Rolf Dieter Danner*, para. 41.

[69] Case C-324/00 [2003] BTC 254.

[70] See chapter 8, para. 17-700.

[71] See above.

resident parent company suffers less favourable tax treatment and no tax advantage to offset such treatment can be identified.[72]

11-400   Specific treaty provisions

The following section explores specific treaty provisions and how they relate to the framework of European law.

Permanent establishment

In *Futura Participations SA and another v Administrations des Contributions*,[73] the question arose as to whether the deduction of losses could be made conditional on maintaining accounting records within a member state. The Luxembourg Government relied in part on the Luxembourg–France Treaty to justify requiring branch accounts to be kept there. It argued that under art. 4(2) of the treaty, income may only be charged to tax which arises from economic activity conducted within the territory through the permanent establishment. It also argued that art. 4(4) provides that the competent authorities of both contracting states shall, where necessary, agree to lay down apportionment rules if there are no proper accounts showing clearly and precisely the profits attributable to the establishments in their respective territory. From this, the Luxembourg authorities argued that actual profits of the permanent establishment must be taxed and that the apportionment rules only apply where there are no proper accounts showing clearly and precisely the profits referable to the particular establishment. Article 21(2) of the Luxembourg–France Treaty provided that where a taxpayer resident in France has a permanent establishment in Luxembourg, the provisions relating to loss carry-forwards are to be applicable on the same conditions as they are to taxpayers resident in Luxembourg. This meant that the accounts had to be kept in Luxembourg. It was argued that there was no discrimination, because Luxembourg companies were required to keep accounts at their head office which was also in Luxembourg.

In supporting the Luxembourg Government, the UK referred to the OECD Model and Commentary.[74] According to these authorities, it was argued that although contracting states are not obliged to require taxpayers to keep separate accounts, the commentary suggests that this is the most accurate and reliable method of establishing losses. Since the signatory member states have a margin of discretion in deciding the most appropriate way for establishing losses, a state cannot be prevented from choosing the best and most accurate method. According to this argument, effective fiscal control is only possible if losses are ascertained on the basis of proper accounts.

The Advocate General acknowledged[75] that the Model Convention does not expressly require separate accounts. However, in his opinion, the commentary merely points out that

---

[72] At para. 42.

[73] Case C-250/95 [1997] STC 1301, ECJ.

[74] At para. 42, at 1309.

[75] At para. 47, at 1310.

precise figures relating to profits and losses could be obtained only on the basis of proper accounts and that this method is therefore to be used in normal cases. This does not mean that accounts must be kept at the branch. He also pointed out that the OECD Model cannot apply conclusively to Community law with respect to the question raised in this case.

The UK further argued[76] that with reference to the commentary it is quite normal for well-run businesses to produce separate branch accounts. This, the Advocate General reasoned, did not mean that the separate accounts had to be kept at the branch. The Advocate General noted that the permanent establishment rule contained in art. 4 and the provisions relating to elimination of double taxation in art. 24(2)(2), which maintain the principle of territoriality do not contravene Community law, even in relation to the carrying-forward of losses. The relevant provision here was, rather, art. 21(2), which provides that where a French resident has a permanent establishment in Luxembourg, provisions dealing with losses there are subject to the same conditions as are applicable to Luxembourg residents. This simply refers to the tax law of member states which requires taxpayers to keep proper accounts. Extension of this condition to branches of a non-resident company is, however, incompatible with Community law in the view of Advocate General Lenz. The court agreed[77] that the territoriality principle did not itself entail any prohibited discrimination. In finding the rule discriminatory, the ECJ did not address specifically the argument raised by the UK about the interpretation of the treaty.

Employment income

The terms of a treaty itself were sought to be impugned in *Gilly v Directeur des Services Fiscaux du Bas-Rhin*.[78] The case is significant in several respects. It is most important because it considered the impact of European law on important aspects of tax treaties. Mr and Mrs Gilly were resident in France near the German border. Mr Gilly, a French national, taught in a French state school. Mrs Gilly, a dual French-German national, taught in a state school in Germany, in the frontier area.

Under French domestic law, income tax was payable on the aggregate income of the spouses regardless of where received. The French progressive rates were applied and the spouses could not opt to be taxed separately. In calculating allowances and deductions for family commitments, account is taken of taxable income in France. In their particular case, because income from French sources was less than one-half of the total income (Mr Gilly's share of the income being 45 per cent), they were assessed as having to pay more income tax than if they were taxed separately.

In Germany, Mrs Gilly was not entitled to the preferential scale for married couples, known as splitting. She was automatically deemed to be single because her husband was not a German resident. In her case, application of splitting would have resulted in reducing her tax liability in Germany. Thus, despite being deemed to be a single taxpayer without children,

---

[76] At para. 48, at 1310.

[77] At para. 22, at 1317.

[78] See above, n. 21.

she was in fact married and had two dependent children. A credit was given in France for tax paid abroad, which reduces the double taxation slightly but does not eliminate it.

In its submission, the European Commission argued that the application of French law to the couple's total income and of German law to Mrs Gilly's income from Germany constitutes, by reason of the way in which her marital status is taken into account, an obstacle which is incompatible with the principles governing the freedom of movement of workers. The taxpayers argued that provisions of the Franco–German Treaty were discriminatory and illegal under European law.

Articles 13, 14 and 16 of the Franco–German Treaty contained a variety of rules which determined whether employment income was taxable in the country of residence or the country of source. Article 13(1) of the treaty set out the principle as regards taxation of income from employment. It did not accord with the OECD Model in that it gave exclusive jurisdiction to tax to the place of performance. It read:

> 'Subject to the provisions of the following paragraphs, income from dependent work shall be taxable only in the Contracting State in which the personal activity in respect of which it is received is carried out. In particular, salaries, wages, pay, gratuities or other emoluments shall be deemed to constitute income from dependent work, together with all similar benefits paid or awarded by persons other than those referred to in Article 14.'

Article 13(5)(a) contained an exception to the general rule that income is to be taxed where the work is carried out, applicable to frontier workers. They were to be taxed in their state of residence. The article provided that:

> 'By way of exception to paragraphs 1, 3 and 4, income from dependent work earned by persons who work in the frontier area of one Contracting State and who have their permanent home in the other Contracting State, to which they normally return each day, shall be taxable only in that other State.'

The UK does not presently have provisions relating specifically to frontier workers in its treaties and the issue is not addressed in the OECD Model. Article 14(1) of the Franco–German Treaty established a further special rule in respect of remuneration and pensions from the public sector. They were, in principle, taxable in the paying state. The article specifies that:

> 'Salaries, wages and similar remuneration, and retirement pensions, paid by one of the Contracting States, by a Land or by a legal person of that state or Land governed by public law to natural persons resident in the other state in consideration for present or past administrative or military services shall be taxable only in the first State. However, that provision shall not be applicable where the remuneration is paid to persons having the nationality of the other State without being at the same time nationals of the first State; in such cases, the remuneration shall be taxable only in the State in which such persons are resident.'

This accords in part with art. 19(1)(a) of the OECD Model. It differs materially from the OECD Model in that it distinguishes between nationals of one contracting state and dual nationals.

Article 16 of the Franco–German Treaty laid down a special rule applicable to teachers who are temporarily resident in the contracting state other than the one in which they are normally resident. Under these rules, taxation jurisdiction remained with the state of their normal residence. Thus, the article required that:

'Teachers resident in one of the Contracting States who, in the course of a period of temporary residence not exceeding two years, receive remuneration in respect of teaching in a university, college, school or other teaching establishment in the other state shall be taxable in respect of that remuneration only in the first State.'

The OECD Model does not contain the specific provision for cross-border teachers although many treaties, including UK treaties, contain such provisions. The commentary does not discourage such provisions. The cumulative effect of these treaty clauses is to vary the tax consequences for employed individuals depending upon whether they:

- are teachers or not;
- are frontier workers;
- are in the public or private sector;
- have the nationality of the state applying them;
- are dual nationals; or
- are short-term visiting teachers.

The question for the ECJ was whether art. 39 (ex 48) of the EC Treaty, which guarantees free movement of workers, precludes the application of these treaty provisions. The court noted[79] that whilst abolition of double taxation within the Community is one of the objectives of the EC Treaty, no unifying or harmonising measure for the elimination of double taxation has been adopted at the Community level – and nor have the member states concluded any multilateral convention to that effect.[80] In the absence of such measures, member states are competent to determine the criteria for taxation of income and wealth with a view to eliminate double taxation. In particular, it was not regarded as unreasonable for member states to base their treaties on the OECD Model Convention.

There are a number of possibilities with special rules for frontier workers, state employees and teachers who are temporarily resident in a contracting state. Thus, different connecting factors allocate taxing jurisdictions in different circumstances. Nationality is one of the factors in relation to state employees. The ECJ did not regard the use of nationality as the criterion for allocating fiscal jurisdiction as discriminatory. This was because in the absence of unifying or harmonising measures adopted in the Community context, the contracting states are competent to define the criteria for allocating their powers of taxation as between themselves with the view to eliminating double taxation. The rule relating to public sector employees was based on the OECD Model. The court accepted the commentary on that article that the principle is justified by 'the rules of international courtesy and mutual respect between sovereign states' and 'is contained in so many of the existing conventions between OECD members that it can be said to be already internationally accepted'.[81] The ECJ thus appears to be recognising a new defence specifically in the context of treaties: if a treaty is based on a provision of the OECD Model and if the OECD Model reflects internationally

---

[79] At para. 23, at 1038.

[80] Except the convention of 23 July 1990 on the elimination of double taxation in connection with the adjustment of profits of associated enterprises, [1990] OJ L225/10.

[81] At para. 32, at 1039.

accepted practice, then its legitimacy may be supported. This observation was not strictly necessary for the decision based on the competence of the contracting states. The court noted that the second part of art. 14(1) of the Franco–German Treaty abandoned the paying state principle, where nationals of the other contracting state are involved. The court noted that throughout the OECD provisions on state employees, nationality is, however, a relevant criterion. In any event, even if the whole art. were ineffective, Mrs Gilly would still have been taxable in Germany under other provisions. The court also found that the taxpayers had not established that they had been disadvantaged by the choice of the paying state as the state competent to tax income earned in the public sector. The disadvantages lay in the domestic rules of the two contracting states respectively and, in particular, in relation to their graduated rates of tax.

The ECJ also rejected the argument that art. 6 (ex 7) of the EC Treaty (the general prohibition on discrimination on grounds of nationality) prohibited nationality as the criterion for allocating taxing jurisdiction. In accordance with longstanding law, the general prohibition of discrimination on grounds of nationality only applies independently to situations governed by Community law in which the treaty lays down no specific prohibition of discrimination. In this case, the issue was governed by art. 39 (ex 48).

In the view of the Advocate General, the criteria in the EC Treaty which have the purpose only of determining the power to tax certain income are neutral with regard to freedom of movement for workers because in the two states concerned, they do not in tax matters treat workers of other member states less favourably than or differently from their own nationals who are in the same situation. He was further of the view that it cannot be discriminatory to provide that remuneration of an employed person is taxable in the state where he works or in the state where he resides, or by the state paying the remuneration. It is necessary in the final analysis to refer to the criterion of the recipient's nationality in order to decide which of the two states is to tax it. In his view, the consequences of the application of the treaty distributive provisions could not be regarded as capable of deterring a worker from exercising his or her freedom of movement between the two member states in question. The allocation of taxing jurisdiction in these circumstances was not regarded as constituting prohibited discrimination.

Article 39 (ex 48) of the EC Treaty did not preclude the application of provisions such as those in arts. 13(5)(a), 14(1) and 16 of the Franco–German Treaty, under which the tax regime applicable to frontier workers differs depending on whether they work in the private sector or the public sector (and where they work in the public sector). It also depends on whether, when working in the public sector, they have only the nationality of the state of the authority employing them and whether the regime applicable to teachers differs depending on whether their residence in the state in which they are teaching is for a short period or not.

Elimination of double taxation: foreign tax credit

The *Gilly* case also considered whether the treaty rules for eliminating double taxation contained in the Franco–German Treaty were compatible with art. 39 (ex 48) of the EC Treaty. Article 20(2)(a)(cc) of the Franco–German Treaty, as amended by the protocol signed on 28 September 1989, read as follows:

'2. Double taxation of persons resident in France shall be avoided in the following manner:

(a)   Profits and other positive income arising in the Federal Republic and taxable there under the provisions of this Treaty shall also be taxable in France where they accrue to a person resident in France. The German tax shall not be deductible for calculation of the taxable income in France. However, the recipient shall be entitled to a tax credit to be set against the French tax charged on the taxable amount which includes that income. That tax credit shall be equal . . .

(b)   for all other income, to the amount of the French tax on the relevant income. This provision shall apply in particular to the income referred to in Articles ... 13(1) and (2) and 14.'

These rules are based on art. 23B of the OECD Model in accordance with the 'ordinary credit method'. A similar approach is adopted in UK treaties.

The tax credit mechanism adopted by the Franco–German Treaty was not incompatible with European law. The ECJ recognised the distinction between the full credit method and the ordinary credit in that double taxation could be fully avoided only by a credit equal to the amount of tax charged in Germany. The court stressed that it is not the object of a treaty to ensure that tax in one state is no higher than that which the taxpayer would be subject to in the other. The object is simply to prevent the same income from being taxed in each of two states. The court accepted the arguments of several member states that if the state of residence were required to accord a tax credit greater than the fraction of its national tax corresponding to the income from abroad, it would have to reduce its tax in respect of the remaining income. This would entail a loss of revenue for it and would thus encroach on its sovereignty in matters of direct taxation. That the tax in the source country exceeded the tax in the residence country on the income from the source country, in conjunction with the distributive provisions of the treaty authorising taxation in the source state, therefore permitting excess foreign tax, is likewise not contrary to art. 39 (ex 48).

11-450   Treaties with third countries

The position in relation to treaties between a member state and a non-EU country is more complex. Article 307 (ex 234) of the EC Treaty provides that rights and obligations arising from agreements between member states and third countries concluded before entry into force of the EC Treaty are not affected by the provisions of that treaty. In the context of the UK, art. 5 of the 1972 Act of Accession[82] provides that art. 307 (ex 234) of the EC Treaty is to apply to new members (including the UK) to agreements or conventions concluded before accession. It therefore has no application to UK treaties concluded from accession on 1 January 1973. In *EC Commission v Italy*,[83] the ECJ held that art. 307 (ex 234) is limited to guaranteeing rights of third countries arising out of pre-existing agreements. There are currently only 26 such treaties with countries which are not presently EU members. The vast majority of these are with Commonwealth countries following the old colonial style.

---

[82] [1972] OJ Spec, ed., 27 March, p. 14.

[83] Case 10/61 [1962] ECR 1.

In *R. v Secretary of State for Transport, ex parte Factortame Ltd*,[84] Advocate General Mischo noted that as long as the rights of non-member countries are not involved, a member state cannot rely on the provisions of a pre-existing treaty with third states in relation to intra-Community matters.[85]

Thus, a discriminatory provision imposed by the third country in a treaty subject to art. 307 (ex 234) may not be liable to attack. However, art. 307 (ex 234) does require member states to take all appropriate steps to remedy the inconsistency with Community law. This imposes a higher obligation than the duty of member states to 'so far as necessary, enter into negotiations . . . with a view to the abolition of double taxation' imposed in respect of intra-Community treaties. The UK has been subject to these rules for some 23 years; if there are incompatibilities with Community law in those old treaties, it is unlikely that the UK has discharged its obligation to take all appropriate steps as this would of necessity involve seeking renegotiation of the treaty in question.

Treaties entered into since accession will not benefit from the protection of art. 307 (ex 234). Therefore, even if the limitation provisions are solely for the benefit of a non-EU member state, they fall to be tested in the same way as treaties between member states.

In the UK 'Open Skies Case',[86] a bilateral treaty, was concluded between the UK and the US in 1946. Another agreement replaced it with effect from 23 July 1977, the date upon which it was signed and entered into force.

The UK argued that the protection afforded by art. 234 extends to the rights and obligations arising from such treaties; accordingly, the question of whether a pre-accession agreement has been amended or even replaced since the accession of the member state concerned to the Community is of only secondary importance. Furthermore, the UK contended that the right granted by the later agreement was originally conferred by the first treaty and had not changed in substance. Even though their wording was not in all respects the same, reflecting the different structure of the two treaties, they were, in substance, identical.

The ECJ observed that art. 234 is of general scope and applies to any international treaty, irrespective of subject matter, which is capable of affecting application of the EC Treaty.[87] The purpose of art. 234(1) is to make it clear, in accordance with the principles of international law,[88] that application of the EC Treaty does not affect the duty of the member state concerned to respect the rights of non-member countries under a prior agreement and to perform its obligations thereunder. In ruling that the transitional relief did not apply, the court found that the rights and obligations of the US and the UK flowed not from an agreement before but from an agreement after the accession of the UK to the European

---

[84] Case C-221/89 [1991] 3 All ER 769.

[85] See Case 286/86, *Ministere Public v Deserbais* [1988] ECR 4907 at 4926.

[86] *EC Commission v UK*, Case C-466/98.

[87] At para. 23.

[88] Art. 30(4)(b) of the Vienna Convention on the Law of Treaties.

Communities.[89] The preamble to the second treaty recited that it was concluded 'for the purpose of replacing' the first, in particular, in order to take into account the development of traffic rights between the contracting parties. It thus gave rise to new rights and obligations between those parties. It was not possible to attach the rights and obligations which flowed from the second treaty to the first.[90]

Non-EU nationals or residents will not be in a position to claim the benefits of Community law other than in relation to art. 56 (free movement of capital).[91] In *R. v IRC, ex parte Commerzbank AG*,[92] the UK argued that the refusal to make the repayment supplement to a non-resident under the Taxes Act 1988, s. 825, as it then stood, was justified in part by the existence of the US Treaty. The UK argued, *inter alia*, that the treaty removed the possibility of discrimination against non-resident companies since they were exempt from the tax which only resident companies would pay. It was therefore by virtue of the application of the treaty that there is no discrimination with respect to the conditions concerning the recovery of overpaid tax.

However, in upholding the taxpayers' case that it had been discriminated against, the ECJ did not deal with the US–UK Treaty issues. The decision did, however, establish clearly that discrimination on the basis of fiscal residence within a national territory falls to be treated in the same manner as overt discrimination by reason of nationality.

The facts of the case are unusual because a national and resident of a member state (Germany) was able to claim the benefit of the US–UK Treaty. In most treaty claims involving third countries, the person claiming treaty benefits from a member state will be a non-EU national who will not be likely to have standing to enjoy the protection of Community law.

The first case to reach the ECJ on tax treaties with non-member states was *Saint-Gobain*.[93] It was argued by the German Government that treaties with non-member countries were not within the sphere of Community competence. This, it argued, is a matter for member states that are at liberty to conclude bilateral treaties with non-member countries. On the basis that bilateral treaties are based on the principle of reciprocity, the balance inherent in such treaties would be disturbed if the benefit of their provisions were extended to companies established in member states which were not parties to them. The court, however, said that it was settled that taxing powers must be exercised consistently with Community law. The balance and reciprocity of treaties concluded with non-member states in question would not be jeopardised by a unilateral extension of the category of recipients in Germany of the tax advantages provided for by those treaties. It would not in any way affect the rights of non-member countries which are parties to the treaties and would not impose any new

---

[89] At para. 26.

[90] At para. 26.

[91] Case C-446/04, *Test Claimants in the FII Group Litigation*, [2008] BTC 222, paras. 179–181; Case C-157/05, *Holböck* [2007] ECR I-4051, paras. 33 and 34; Case C-112/05, *Commission v Germany* [2007] ECR I-8995, para. 18; and *Skatteverket v A.*, Case C-101/05.

[92] [1991] BTC 161.

[93] See above, n. 13.

obligations on them. The court noted, in any event, that German domestic law had been amended in this respect, extending the credits and exemptions to permanent establishments of non-resident companies. It was argued by the Swedish Government that in extreme situations, extending the scope of bilateral treaties could lead to no tax being produced at all. This was rejected in the particular case since it had not been argued that there was a risk of non-taxation in any country.

Community law could be invoked in relation to a treaty with a third country where a company resident in a member state acquires or establishes a company resident in another member state. If the second company's entitlement to benefits under a treaty with a third country is denied, the second company would appear to have standing to impugn the treaty provision.[94] The claim would be against the country of residence rather than that of the third country which denied the treaty benefit.

A further possibility might exist where an EU national resident in a treaty country outside the EU is denied benefits. Unless a right under the EC Treaty is exercised, the equal treatment guaranteed by the EC Treaty may not be invoked.[95]

Fiscal supervision and third countries

The ECJ has consistently held that Directive 77/799[96] may be relied on by a member state in order to obtain from the competent authorities of another member state all the information enabling it to ascertain the correct amount of tax.[97] As a result, lack of information by a member state in the intra-Community context has not been held to inhibit the effectiveness of tax administration so as to justify a restriction on fundamental freedoms.

This is not always the case in dealings with third countries; for example, see the decision in *Skatteverket v A*.[98] Under Swedish law, where distributions from a foreign company which is established in a state within the EEA or in a state with which Sweden has concluded a tax treaty, including provision on exchange of information, the distributions are exempt from corporate income tax. The Sweden–Switzerland Treaty contained no exchange-of-information provision but did include a MAP to, among other things, resolve any difficulties or doubts arising as to the interpretation or application of the treaty. At the time of conclusion, it was clear that the Swiss delegation considered the only information that could be exchanged was that needed to ensure proper application of the treaty and that would prevent improper application of it. It was also apparent that Sweden took formal note of that declaration and did not seek to include any express provision on the exchange of information. The court ruled that a restriction on the free movement of capital is justified where compliance with requirements for a tax advantage can be verified only by obtaining information from the competent authorities of a third country. Thus, it is, in principle, legitimate for a member state to refuse to grant that advantage if it proves impossible to

---

[94] Case C-1/93, *Halliburton Services BV v Staatssecretaris van Financien* [1994] BTC 8069; [1994] STC 655.

[95] Case C-221/89, *R. v Secretary of State for Transport, ex parte Factortame Ltd* [1991] All ER 769, at para. 19.

[96] See chapter 20, para. 29-200.

[97] See *Rolf Dieter Danner*, Case C-136/00 at para. 47 and cases cited in it.

[98] Case C-101/05.

obtain such information from that country – in particular, because that country is not under any treaty obligation to provide information.[99]

11-500   Treaties and compensation for breach of EC law

In March 2001 the ECJ ruled that affording groups of companies the right to make a group income election where they were resident in the UK but denying them that right where the parent companies were not resident in the UK infringed the freedom of establishment in art. 43 (ex 52).[100] The court also held that affected companies were entitled to an effective legal remedy of reimbursement or reparation of the financial loss which they have sustained and from which the Revenue and the Government benefited as a result of the advance payment of tax by the UK subsidiaries. Compensation was thus payable for loss of the use of the money paid as ACT between the date of payment and the date when the ACT was used by being set off against the subsidiary company's mainstream corporation tax liabilities. The appropriate compensation was determined by reference to compound interest.[101]

In the case of UK subsidiaries whose parent companies were resident in member states where the relevant treaty permitted the payment of tax credits, the question of whether this compensation was to be reduced by amount of those tax credits arose. The House of Lords[102] held unanimously that it was to be so reduced, overturning the unanimous decision of the Court of Appeal,[103] which had upheld the ruling of the High Court.[104] While each of the five law lords gave different reasons, the essential difference between their views and those of the courts related to whether the compensation ought to be determined by reference to the loss suffered by the UK subsidiaries (as the persons who had suffered improper imposition of *ACT*) or by the group comprising the UK subsidiaries and parent companies resident in other member states. The tax credits were paid to the parent companies. Lords Hope and Scott referred, in particular, to the decision of the ECJ in *Metallgesellschaft v IRC*,[105] where the remedy was said to be that of both the parent company and the subsidiary.

---

[99] At para. 63.

[100] *Metallgesellschaft Ltd & Ors (Case C-397/98); Hoechst AG & Hoechst UK Ltd (Case C-410/98) v Commissioners of Inland Revenue & Attorney-General* [2001] BTC 99.

[101] *Sempra Metals Ltd (formerly Metallgesellschaft Ltd) v IRC & Anor* [2007] BTC 509; [2007] UKHL 34.

[102] *Pirelli Cable Holding NV & Ors v IRC* [2006] UKHL 4.

[103] [2004] BTC 50; [2003] EWCA Civ 1849.

[104] [2003] BTC 218; [2003] EWHC 32 (Ch).

[105] Case C-410/98 [2001] BTC 99.

Interpretation of Tax Treaties

Chapter 3

12-000   Introduction

The interpretation of tax treaties is a subject that has received considerable attention over the years. The starting point of most of the analysis has been whether treaties are essentially contractual in nature or a form of legislative enactment. Therefore, should they be subject to the ordinary rules of statutory interpretation or should they be interpreted by rules of international law applicable to the interpretation of international agreements? Are they to be construed in the same way as any other fiscal legislation or are there specific rules?

The difficulty in coming to any conclusion is that treaties are, in effect, both. They are agreements between sovereign states, but under UK constitutional rules, in order to give effect to them under domestic law, they also acquire the status of legislative instruments. This duality of status has led some to conclude that treaties must be interpreted at both levels and that different rules might apply at each level. Tax treaties are interpreted by domestic courts and not supranational tribunals (with the exception of the ECJ which has thus far refrained from interpretation).

How do the rules of treaty interpretation differ from rules for interpretation of domestic statutes? In *Steele v EVC International NV (formerly European Vinyls Corp (Holdings) BV)*,[1] Morritt LJ commented[2] that it is debatable whether the principles expressed by Mummery J differ from those now applied in the construction of domestic legislation. Since the *EVC* case involved the construction of domestic law provisions incorporated by reference into the treaty, the comments of Morritt LJ do not illuminate the issue further.

Some writers have been quick to spot inconsistencies in the approach of the courts. The reality is that there is a specific body of law relating to the interpretation of treaties which does overlap to a greater or lesser extent with the rules applicable to the interpretation of tax statutes. Where they overlap, few difficulties arise – where they do not, a distinct body of rules applies.

The courts have traditionally articulated the view that treaties are agreements and are required to be interpreted in accordance with particular rules. For example, in *Belgium Government v Postlethwaite*,[3] Lord Bridge of Horwich said that:[4]

---

[1] [1996] BTC 425; [1996] STC 785, CA.

[2] At 797g.

[3] [1987] 2 All ER 985, HL.

[4] At 991.

'A treaty is a "contract between two sovereign states and has to be construed as such a contract. It would be a mistake to think that it had been construed as though it were a domestic statute" [*R v Governor of Ashford Remand Centre, ex parte Beese* [1973] 3 All ER 250 at 254 per Lord Widgery CJ] . . . It must be remembered that the reciprocal rights and obligations which the high contracting parties confer and accept are intended to serve . . . [a certain purpose]. To apply to . . . treaties, the strict cannons appropriate to the construction of domestic legislation would often tend to defeat rather than serve this purpose.'

Similarly, in the tax treaty context, Harman J said in *Union Texas Petroleum Corp. v Critchley (Inspector of Taxes)*:[5]

'I consider that I should bear in mind that this double tax agreement is an agreement. It is not a taxing statute, although it is an agreement about how taxes should be imposed. On that basis, in my judgement, this agreement should be construed as *ut res magis valet quam pereat*, as should all agreements. The fact that the parties are "high contracting parties", to use an old description, does not change the way in which the Courts should approach the construction of any agreement.'

Notwithstanding these comments, Harman J, only one paragraph later, relied on comments of Lord Dunedin in *Whitney v IRC*,[6] a case that involved construing domestic legislation, for the proposition that 'a statute is designed to be workable, and the interpretation thereof by a court should be to secure that object'.

How helpful these statements are and what their precise import may be is far from clear. The courts have for some time adopted a liberal approach in interpreting international treaties. In *Re Arton (No. 2)*,[7] Lord Russell CJ said:

'In my judgement, these treaties ought to receive a liberal interpretation . . . which means no more than they should receive their true construction according to their language, object and intent.'

Subsequently, in construing the Carriage of Goods by Sea Act 1924, which adopted the Hague Rules, in *Stag Line Limited v Foscolo, Mango and Co.*,[8] Lord MacMillan said:

'It is important to remember that the Act of 1924 was the outcome of an international conference and that the rules in the Schedule have an international currency. As these rules must come under the consideration of foreign courts, it is desirable in the interest of uniformity that their interpretation should not be rigidly controlled by domestic precedents of antecedent date, but rather that the language of the rules should be construed on broad principles of general acceptance.'

This approach was adopted by Lord Atkin, who said:[9]

'For the purpose of uniformity, it is, therefore, important that the Courts should apply themselves to the consideration only of the words used without any predilection for the former (English) law, always preserving the right to say that words used in the English language which

---

[5] [1988] BTC 405; [1988] STC 691, at 707, Ch.D.

[6] (1924-26) 10 TC 88.

[7] [1896] 1 QB 509, at 517.

[8] [1932] AC 328, HL.

[9] At 343.

have already in the particular context received judicial interpretation, may be presumed to be used in the sense already judicially imputed to them.'

This approach has been followed in a number of cases involving non-tax treaties.[10] In *James Buchanan and Co. v Babco Ltd,*[11] Viscount Dilhorne said:

'In construing the terms of a convention, it is proper and indeed right, in my opinion, to have regard to the fact that conventions are apt to be more loosely worded than acts of Parliament. To construe a convention as strictly as an act may indeed lead to a wrong interpretation being given to it.'

12-050   Vienna Convention on the Law of Treaties

Whatever the past approaches to treaty interpretations, they have become less significant since the conclusion of the Vienna Convention on the Law of Treaties. In *Fothergill v Monarch Airlines Limited,*[12] Lord Diplock said:

'In exercising its interpretative function . . . in the case of Acts of Parliament giving effect to international conventions concluded after the coming into force of the Vienna Convention on the law of treaties, I think an English court might well be under a constitutional obligation to [have recourse to "travaux preparatoires"]. By ratifying that Convention, Her Majesty's Government has undertaken an international obligation on behalf of the UK to interpret future treaties in this manner and since under our constitution, the function of interpreting the written law is an exercise of judicial power and rests with the Courts of Justice, that obligation assumed by the UK falls to be performed by those Courts.'

Article 4 of the Vienna Convention provides that it applies only to treaties concluded by states after its entry into force with regard to such states. It entered into force in accordance with art. 84 on 27 January 1980 (the 30th day following the date of deposit of the 35th Instrument of Ratification or Accession).

The UK has only some 30 treaties still in force that were concluded prior to that date, and not all countries who are parties to more recent treaties are parties to the Vienna Convention. Most of the important cases, in which the rules of interpretation of tax treaties have been considered in detail, involve treaties which were concluded prior to that date. Strictly speaking, on its terms, the Vienna Convention only applies to treaties that are concluded with contracting states who are parties to the Vienna Convention. Is the application of the Vienna Convention consequently restricted to post-1980 treaties with Vienna Convention contracting states? Lord Diplock, in the *Fothergill* case, noted that what is said in arts. 31 and 32 of the Vienna Convention does no more than codify already existing public international law.[13] On this basis, it would appear that in the UK courts, there ought to be little distinction on the basis that the Convention is merely a codification of existing customary international law. Lord Fraser of Tullybelton had reservations, however, on the

---

[10] *Riverstone Meat Co. Pty. Ltd v Lancashire Shipping Co. Ltd* [1961] AC 807, HL; *Fothergill v Monarch Airlines Ltd* [1981] AC 251, HL.

[11] [1973] 3 All ER 1048, HL.

[12] See above, n. 10.

[13] At 282.

extent of the authoritative value of the Vienna Convention. On the other hand, has the codification of customary law, at least among the parties to the Vienna Convention, arrested the development of customary international law which changes to meet developments?[14] Different rules of interpretation may apply as a result depending upon the contracting state in question.

12-100 *Commerzbank* principles

The most comprehensive recent statement of the courts' approach was set out in *IRC v Commerzbank AG*[15] by Mummery J. The treaty in question was not governed by the Vienna Convention. Nonetheless, the principles articulated drew on both traditional sources and the Vienna Convention as follows:

'(1) It is necessary to look first for a clear meaning of the words used in the relevant article of the Convention, bearing in mind that "consideration of the purpose of an enactment is always a legitimate part of the process of interpretation": per Lord Wilberforce [in *Fothergill*] at p. 272 and Lord Scarman at p. 294. A strictly literal approach to interpretation is not appropriate in construing legislation which gives effect to or incorporates an international treaty: per Lord Fraser at p. 285 and Lord Scarman at p. 290. A literal interpretation may be obviously inconsistent with the purposes of the particular article or of the treaty as a whole. If the provisions of a particular article are ambiguous, it may be possible to resolve that ambiguity by giving a purposive construction to the convention looking at it as a whole by reference to its language as set out in the relevant UK legislative instrument: per Lord Diplock at p. 279.

(2) The process of interpretation should take account of the fact that: "The language of an international convention has not been chosen by an English parliamentary draftsman. It is neither couched in the conventional English legislative idiom nor designed to be construed exclusively by English judges. It is addressed to a much wider and more varied judicial audience than is an Act of Parliament which deals with purely domestic law. It should be interpreted, as Lord Wilberforce put it in *James Buchanan & Co. Ltd. v Babco Forwarding & Shipping (UK) Ltd.* [1978] AC 141, 152, 'unconstrained by technical rules of English law, or by English legal precedent, but on broad principles of general acceptation'": per Lord Diplock [in *Fothergill*] at pp. 81–282 and Lord Scarman at p. 293.

(3) Among those principles is the general principle of international law, now embodied in art. 31(1) of the Vienna Convention on the Law of Treaties, that "a treaty should be interpreted in good faith and in accordance with the ordinary meaning to be given to the terms of the treaty in their context and in the light of its object and purpose". A similar principle is expressed in slightly different terms in MacNair on the "Law of Treaties" (1961) at p. 365, where it is stated that the task of applying or construing or interpreting a treaty is "the duty of giving effect to the expressed intention of the parties, that is, their intention as expressed in the words used by them in the light of the surrounding circumstances". It is also stated at p. 366 of that work that references to the primary necessity of giving effect to "the plain terms" of a treaty or construing words according to their "general and ordinary meaning" or their "natural signification" are to be a starting point or prima facie guide and, "cannot be allowed to obstruct the essential quest in the

---

[14] *Trendtex Trading Corp Ltd v Central Bank of Nigeria* [1977] 1 QB 529, CA, in which Lord Denning discusses the developing nature of customary international law and concludes that courts give effect to these changes without legislation.

[15] [1990] BTC 172; [1990] STC 285 ChD at 297–298.

application of treaties, namely the search for the real intention of the contracting parties in using the language employed by them."

(4) If the adoption of this approach to the article leaves the meaning of the relevant provision unclear or ambiguous or leads to a result which is manifestly absurd or unreasonable recourse may be had to "supplementary means of interpretation" including "travaux preparatoires": per Lord Diplock [in *Fothergill*] at p. 282 referring to art. 32 of the Vienna Convention, which came into force after the conclusion of this double taxation Convention, but codified an already existing principle of public international law. See also Lord Fraser at p. 287 and Lord Scarman at p. 294.

(5) Subsequent commentaries on a convention or treaty have persuasive value only, depending on the cogency of their reasoning. Similarly, decisions of foreign courts on the interpretation of a convention or treaty text depend for their authority on the reputation and status of the Court in question: per Lord Diplock [in *Fothergill*] at pp. 283–284 and per Lord Scarman at p. 295.

(6) Aids to the interpretation of a treaty such as "travaux preparatoires", international case law and the writings of jurists are not a substitute for study of the terms of the convention. Their use is discretionary, not mandatory, depending, for example, on the relevance of such material and the weight to be attached to it: per Lord Scarman at p. 294.'

The *Commerzbank* principles have become the received view of the UK courts' approach. In *UBS AG v Revenue and Customs Commissioners*, Etherington J noted that 'there is no dispute between the parties that the correct approach of the Court to the interpretation of the Treaty is that described by Mummery J in *IR Commrs v Commerzbank AG*'.[16] In *Memec plc v IRC*,[17] Robert Walker J commended the whole of the above passage for careful study. He summarised the *Commerzbank* principles as follows:

'(1) the approach should be purposive;

(2) it should be international, not exclusively English;

(3) it should have regard to art. 31(1) of the Vienna Convention;

(4) recourse may be had to supplementary means of interpretation such as "travaux preparatoires";

(5) subsequent commentaries and decisions of foreign courts have persuasive value only;

(6) recourse to "travaux preparatoires", international case law and the writings of jurists is discretionary, not mandatory.

The Court of Appeal has recognised the official commentaries on successive versions of the OECD Model Convention as supplementary means of interpretation: see *Sunlife Assurance Co of Canada v Pearson (HMIT)* (1986) 59 TC 250 at pp. 330–331; [1986] BTC 282 at p. 296.'

In the Court of Appeal, Peter Gibson LJ noted agreement between the taxpayer and the Inland Revenue on the correctness of the approach articulated by Mummery J in *IRC v*

---

[16] [2006] BTC 232 [2006] EWHC 117 (Ch) para. 27. In addition to UBS, it has also been cited by Special Commissioners in *Sportsman v IR Commrs*. (1998) Sp C 174; *Jiminez v The Inland Revenue Commissioners* (2004) Sp C 419 (meaning of art. 37(3) of the Vienna Convention on Diplomatic Relations); *Stevens, Garnham & Payne v The Inland Revenue Commissioners* (2004) Sp C 411 (meaning of art. 5(3) of the UK–Switzerland Social Security Convention) and *Trevor Smallwood Trust v R & C Commrs* (2008) Sp C 669.

[17] [1996] BTC 590; [1996] STC 1336, p. 1349.

Commerzbank. Lord Justice Gibson noted the comment of Mummery J that 'interpretation should take account of the fact that a convention is not designed to be construed exclusively by English judges but is addressed to a wider judicial audience'. He added that 'in the case of a double taxation agreement, the judicial audience is, in addition to the judges found in the constituent parts of the UK, only the judges to be found in the Courts of the other contracting party. It is not to be assumed that the convention is addressed to a wider international audience than that'.[18]

While this may be true in one technical sense, because almost all UK tax treaties are bilateral, it is not true in the context of treaties generally. All treaties are based on successive model treaties which have been developed at a multilateral level. The use of more or less standard provisions throughout the global treaty network is increasing. Reference is made in countries around the world to treaty interpretation by foreign courts. It would certainly not be true in relation to the EC Arbitration Convention and even considering the UK treaty network alone, identical provisions are found in many instances in bilateral treaties between the UK and other contracting states. Both the *Commerzbank* case (concerning the 1945 US Treaty) and the *Memec* case (concerning the German Treaty) were in respect of treaties that were not governed by the Vienna Convention. Any failure to explore the detailed application of the Vienna Convention to these cases is therefore to be expected.

12-150   General rule of interpretation

Given the lack of systematic judicial analysis based specifically on the principles of the Vienna Convention, the convention is used in this work principally as an outline to examine the way in which UK courts have addressed the issues expressed in it. The general principles are set out in art. 31 as follows:

'(1)   A treaty shall be interpreted in good faith in accordance with the ordinary meaning to be given to terms of the treaty in their context and in the light of its object and purpose.

(2)   The context for the purpose of the interpretation of a treaty shall comprise, in addition to the text, including its preamble and annexes:

(a)   any agreement relating to the treaty which was made between all the parties in connexion with the conclusion of the treaty;

(b)   any instrument which was made by one or more parties in connection with the conclusion of the treaty and accepted by the other parties as an instrument related to the treaty.

(3)   There shall be taken into account, together with the context:

(a)   any subsequent agreement between the parties regarding the interpretation of the treaty or the application of its provisions;

(b)   any subsequent practice in the application of the treaty which establishes the agreement of the parties regarding its interpretation;

(c)   any relevant rules of international law applicable in the relations between the parties.

(4)   A special meaning shall be given to a term if it is established that the parties so intended.'

---

[18] [1998] BTC 251; [1998] STC 754, CA at p. 776.

The ordinary meaning of terms

As is the case with statutory interpretation, the ordinary meaning of words is the first limb of the principle. The courts have principally relied on the ordinary meaning of words, rather than any alleged purpose of a treaty article. In *IRC v Commerzbank*,[19] Article XV of the old (1945) US Tax Treaty provided:

'Dividends and interest paid by a [US corporation] shall be exempt from tax by [the UK] except where the recipient is a citizen, resident or corporation of the [UK]. This exemption shall not apply if the corporation paying such dividend or interest is a resident of the [UK].'

The Inland Revenue argued that the treaty did not confer benefits on anyone other than residents or citizens of the US. The treaty was lacking by more modern comparison, because it had no general reference to its personal scope. It was held that the natural and ordinary meaning of the words of art. XV was clear. Interest paid by US corporations was exempt from UK tax, except where the recipient was a UK citizen resident or corporation.

Similarly, in *Strathalmond v IRC*,[20] the same wording was considered in relation to dividends. The court decided that it exempted from UK tax, US dividends and interest paid to a US citizen resident in the UK who was not within the definition of 'resident of the United Kingdom'. This was because US citizens were excluded from that definition.

In *Padmore v IRC*,[21] the wording of the treaty was central to the conclusion that a Jersey-resident partnership with no permanent establishment in the UK is not subject to tax here. In the High Court, Peter Gibson J rejected an argument from the Crown that the general scheme of the Jersey Treaty was relevant in determining the meaning of the 'profits of a Jersey enterprise' under para. 3(2) of the treaty. He said:

'The proper starting point is the language of para. 3(2). That to my mind is unequivocal in its meaning. All the industrial or commercial profits of a Jersey enterprise are not to be subject to United Kingdom tax, and that on its face plainly means those profits whether earned in Jersey or in the United Kingdom or elsewhere.'

He rejected the idea that any wider considerations would compel a different conclusion. Again, in the Court of Appeal, Fox LJ said that:

'Article 3(2) is expressed in language of very considerable width. It relieves from United Kingdom taxation all the profits of a Jersey enterprise (subject to an exemption which is not relevant). That enterprise in the present case is a partnership. The partnership is not an entity distinct from the partners. The profits belong to them. As a matter of construction of this wide language, I see no words which exclude the individual partner's share of the profits from the exemption. The exemption is in general terms and I see no reason why the greater does not include the less.'

---

[19] See above, n. 15.

[20] (1972) 48 TC 537.

[21] [1989] BTC 221; [1989] STC 493, CA.

Despite noting the anomaly between the treatment of partnerships, sole traders and shareholders resident in the UK, he said:[22] 'I do not think these are sufficient to displace what seems to me the natural meaning of Article 3(2)'.

In *Sun Life Assurance Company of Canada v Pearson*,[23] the intention of the drafters of the treaty was central. Vinelott J said:

'The problem is to identify those provisions of the law of the United Kingdom which the framers of the treaty intended to describe in Article 6(7). Once it is accepted that section 430 (as amended by the 1956 and 1965 Acts) was a provision, and indeed the only provision which the framers of the treaty had in mind, the question whether or not it was accurately described as relating to the liability of an overseas life assurance company to tax in respect of income from investment of its life assurance fund becomes a barren one.'

The second question was whether legislative amendments were provisions 'relating to . . . liability to tax' within art. 6(7) of the Canadian Treaty, and if they were, whether the changes were or were not minor modifications not affecting the general character of the provisions in force on 6 December 1995, which the treaty preserved. The Crown sought to argue that the domestic law provisions in question relating to the right of recovery of income tax deducted at source from a UK investment income were not provisions relating to the liability to tax of an overseas insurance company within art. 6(7). The court regarded that view as resting on too narrow a construction of the words 'relating to the liability to tax'. In the light of art. 6(2), Vinelott J concluded that those words referred clearly to the overall liability of a Canadian enterprise carrying on business through a permanent establishment in the UK to UK tax, including the tax on income from investments in the UK made for the purpose of the business carried on by that permanent establishment.

Similarly, the Court of Appeal in that case[24] rejected the argument that 'profits' in art. 7 of the 1980 Canadian Treaty had a different meaning from 'commercial and industrial profits' found in the earlier Canadian Treaty and in the Australian Treaty. It focused on the ordinary meaning of the words set in the context of the treaty as a whole and supported by the OECD Model Commentary, an analysis of the changes in comparison with the previous treaty and similar provisions in the Australian Treaty. This approach seems to suggest that more complex tools of interpretation are required for the most difficult questions, rather than that the ordinary meaning of words is inappropriate as the primary tool of interpretation.

A further case which considered art. XV of the old 1945 US Treaty and relied on other methods of interpretation was *IRC v Exxon Corp.*[25] That case involved a dividend paid by a US corporation resident in the UK to its parent company, a US corporation resident for tax purposes in the US. The question was whether the expression 'a resident of the other contracting party' in the second sentence of art. XV should be interpreted in accordance with the residence definitions set out in art. 2(1)(g) 'resident of the United Kingdom' and (1)(h) 'resident of the United States' or whether it should be treated as a 'term not otherwise

---

[22] At 379.

[23] [1984] BTC 223; [1984] STC 461.

[24] [1986] BTC 282; [1986] STC 335.

[25] [1982] BTC 182; [1982] STC 356, Ch.D.

defined' for the purposes of art. 2(3) of the treaty. The argument for the taxpayer that the plain meaning of the words was to be adopted, said Goulding J, was 'to simply accept the consequence that the second sentence of the Article has either probably or certainly failed to achieve whatever purpose its framers intended'. The Crown argued that the broad policy behind the second sentence was clear, namely to deny exemption for dividends or interest paid to a US company by a subsidiary trading and managed in the UK and merely incorporated in the US. The learned judge agreed that the intended purpose of the second sentence of art. XV could be discerned and that the plain meaning of the words used meant that the expression 'resident of the other contracting party' does not import residence definitions. He said:

> 'In coming to this conclusion, I bear in mind that the words of the Convention are not those of a regular Parliamentary draftsmen, but a text agreed upon by negotiation between two contracting governments. Although I am thus constrained to do violence to the language of the Convention, I see no reason to inflict a deeper wound than necessary. In other words, I prefer to depart from the plain meaning of the language only in the second sentence of Article 15 and I accept the consequence (strange though it is) that similar words mean different things in the two sentences.'

The plain meaning of words was applied in *Steele v EVC International NV*[26] in interpreting art. 10 of the Netherlands Treaty in relation to entitlement to repayment of the dividend tax credit. The repayment of the credit was denied where the company paying the dividend is controlled by a person or two or more associated or connected persons who would not have been entitled to the credit directly. The question of association or control was applicable if 'under the laws of the United Kingdom relating to the taxes covered by this Convention, he or they could be treated as having control of it for any purpose' (art. 10(3)(d)(ii)). It was argued by the taxpayer that the mischief at which the article was aimed was treaty shopping and that this purpose is sufficiently achieved if the rules relating to connection only apply to persons who are genuinely connected, that is otherwise than through the mere coincidence of their exercising joint control of the company in question. Such an argument would require the exclusion of the Taxes Act 1988, s. 839(7), which connects together persons acting together to secure or exercise control of a company.

Lightman J in the High Court dismissed this argument on the basis that the words in the treaty 'for any purpose' clearly embrace connection under s. 839(7). He said: 'Whether this is just may be a matter on which strong opinions may be held, but that is not enough to prevent the language used being given its full effect'.[27]

On appeal, after summarising the *Commerzbank* principles of interpretation, Morritt LJ Said:[28] 'The use of the word "could" in conjunction with "any purpose" seems to me to exclude any requirement that there is some substantive issue ... other than the availability of the tax credit for the purpose of which the connection arises or is relevant'. The wording was to the effect that the persons in question could be treated as connected for any purpose, not for all purposes. He did not think that these conclusions arose from an unduly literal

---

[26] [1996] BTC 425; [1996] STC 785, CA.

[27] [1995] BTC 32; [1995] STC 31, at 51b, Ch.D.

[28] [1996] BTC 425 at 437; [1996] STC 785 at 797, CA.

construction of the Convention. Although accepting the provision as an anti-avoidance measure designed to prevent the artificial creation of entitlement to tax credits, he said that it was fanciful to suppose that the draftspeople of the Convention intended to restrict the application of those provisions in cases in which they already applied or to limit those which did apply. Thus, the purposive construction which contended that the clause referred to a restricted definition of control was rejected.

In *Trevor Smallwood Trust v R & C Commrs*, Drs AN Brice and JF Avery Jones held that the in relation to art. 13(4) of the Mauritius Treaty, the 'plain words "taxable only" in the Treaty Residence state mean what they say.' There would thus be no scope for any basis of taxation in the non-treaty residence state.[29] The ordinary meaning of words has prevailed before the Special Commissioners in other recent decisions.[30]

Context

Article 31 of the Vienna Convention requires the ordinary meaning of terms to be given in their context. Context is explained, but not exhaustively defined in art. 31(2). The context for the purpose of interpretation of a treaty comprises primarily the text including its preamble and annexes.

It has become quite common, particularly in treaties with non-OECD countries, to have exchanges of notes signed concurrently with the conclusion of treaties. These are typically written in order to modify, explain or clarify particular issues in a treaty. As already noted, such exchange of notes either constitute treaties themselves as a matter of international law, or form part of the formal treaty by reference and are included in the statutory instruments bringing the formal treaty into effect. The real implication of the introductory wording of art. 31(2) is that the context of a treaty is all of its constituent parts, rather than individual elements.

In accordance with the 1963 and the 1977 OECD Models, UK treaties invariably have the following title: 'Agreement between the Government of the United Kingdom of Great Britain and Northern Ireland and the Government of [the Sultanate of Oman] for the avoidance of double taxation and the prevention of fiscal evasion with respect to taxes on income and capital gains.'

A typical preamble reads:

> 'The Government of the United Kingdom of Great Britain and Northern Ireland and the Government of the Sultanate of Oman desiring to conclude an agreement for the avoidance of double taxation and the prevention of fiscal evasion with respect to taxes on income and gains, have agreed as follows:'

---

[29] (2008) Sp C 669, para. 103.

[30] *UBS AG v Revenue and Customs Commissioners* (2005) Sp C 480; *Stevens, Garnham & Payne v The Inland Revenue Commissioners* (2004) Sp C 411.

This formulation is of longstanding use and shows up in every tax treaty. In *Imperial Chemical Industries Limited v Caro*,[31] it was observed by Lord Evershed MR[32] that 'it is proper to notice the avowed object' of the treaty as stated in its heading. In that case, it was regarded as important to demonstrate that the treaty was intended to cover not only income tax, but other taxes such as the national defence contribution subsequently known as profits tax. Donovan LJ also said:[33]

'Does the direction in Article XII of the Agreement on its true construction allow credit to be given more than once? I think that question can be answered either way without doing violence to the express language of the agreement; and one must seek to answer, I think, from the general tenor of that document and its subject matter. The subject matter includes among other things profits tax and since it is levied upon the actual income of a period and not the conventional basis of the income of some other period, there could never be any question of allowing credit for Australian tax twice against profits tax.'

In *Avery Jones (Rowley's Administrator) v CIR*,[34] a claim was made on behalf of a deceased estate for exemption from UK income tax under art. XV of the old US Treaty. Dividends and interest paid by a corporation of one contracting state were exempt from tax by the other 'except where the recipient is a citizen resident or corporation of that other contracting party'. Although she was UK resident for domestic purposes, as a US citizen she was not resident in the UK within art. 11 of the treaty as a result of the Strathalmond decision.[35] The taxpayer argued that the expression 'citizen' in art. XV referred only to a citizen of the US and not to a British subject, as the expression was not reciprocal so far as it concerned citizens, because the term 'citizen' of the UK was unrecognised in UK law. This view was upheld by the High Court. The Special Commissioner rejected the idea that no meaning should be given to the phrase. Notwithstanding difficulties as a matter of construction, it seemed to the court untenable to adopt such a view. It therefore accepted the arguments put forward by the Crown. In the court's view, it did less violence to the language of the agreement to hold that the deceased as a British subject and citizen of the UK and colonies was a citizen of the UK, than to hold that she was not. The court noted that if any sensible meaning is to be attributed to the term, it must include the taxpayer or else 'the Court would have to decide that the provision was completely meaningless, a course which is never taken on the construction of any document, let alone a solemnly negotiated international treaty, save where there can be no other possible course available'. The court observed that art. XV was not the only place in which reference to citizenship occurs. It also occurred in art. 20A(1) and occurs there in a context which could not only be restricted to US citizens. Similarly, protection given to teachers under art. XVIII applied on the basis of citizenship. The court rejected the idea that the draftspeople of the treaty intended art. XV to apply equally on the basis of reciprocity, as well as the notion that the citizenship concept only applied in relation to US citizens.

---

[31] (1958-1961) 39 TC 374.

[32] At 379.

[33] At 390.

[34] (1973-1978) 51 TC 443; [1976] STC 290.

[35] See above, n. 20.

Another case in which 'paid' was held to mean just that and not to mean 'payable' was *Union Texas Petroleum Corp v Critchley.*[36] Again, this conclusion was reached on the basis of the context in which it was used. The issue was whether a deduction from the amount of the dividend and associated tax credit was to be calculated before or after the deduction itself. In a related provision, reference was made to the dividend and tax credit 'paid' without reduction for the deduction. The inference from this was that it was after deduction in all other cases, including the provision being interpreted. As a result, words were in effect ignored in order to prevent the provision having no effect. Context in this sense was the dividend article of the US Treaty and not the treaty as a whole. Since the article was substituted by protocol, conceivably the 'treaty' in this context was the protocol rather than the treaty as a whole amended by the protocol. This distinction was not made by the court, however.

In the Court of Appeal, the question was whether the absence of a definition of dividends in art. 18 (the tax credit) signifies that it is to be construed in that article as having the same meaning as in art. 6(4), or as having a meaning indicated by art. 2(3), which allows UK domestic law to determine its meaning. The overall context of the term 'dividends' was taken into account noting that the draftsperson of the treaty was careful to say whether a term defined only in a distributive article is to have the same meaning in another but not every article. In some articles of the treaty, arts 3(5) and 23(3)(b), references to dividends are construed as having the art. 4(4) meaning, but that was because both related to tax withheld on a dividend and so implicitly cross-referred to art. 4.

In *IRC v Vas,*[37] the court considered the context of provisions relating to exemption for teachers, including the position of art. 21[38] and its relationship with other articles in the Hungarian Treaty, to consider the effect of the exemption not applying. Vinelott J urged that caution should be exercised in searching for purpose from the context of a treaty, because treaties represent negotiated compromise for which policy reasons may not be discernable from the terms of the treaty other than where the OECD Model is followed.

In *Memec plc v IRC,*[39] Peter Gibson LJ analysed the whole scheme of the German Treaty and the relationship between the definition, the distributive articles and the rules for elimination of double taxation in considering whether a distribution from a German silent partnership which was treated as a dividend in art. VI(4) for withholding tax purposes was also a dividend for the purposes of qualification for underlying credit paid under art. XVIII, the tax credit provision.[40]

Article 31(2) of the Vienna Convention includes, in the context of a treaty, any agreement relating to it which was made between the parties in connection with the conclusion of the treaty, and any instrument made by a party in connection with the conclusion of the treaty

---

[36] See above, n. 5.

[37] [1990] BTC 52; [1990] STC 137, Ch.D.

[38] 'Visiting teachers'.

[39] [1998] BTC 251; [1998] STC 754, CA

[40] For an example that demonstrates the context in relation to a social security treaty, see *Stevens, Garnham & Payne v The Inland Revenue Commissioners* (2004) Sp C 411, para. 44.

and accepted by the other parties as an instrument relating to the treaty. The extent of this is therefore precisely prescribed. First, both in relation to agreements and instruments, they must be made in connection with the conclusion of the treaty. Any agreement must be between the parties to the treaty and in relation to an instrument made by less than all parties to the treaty, it must be accepted by the others as an instrument related to the treaty.

In UK treaty practice, there are almost no examples of agreements relating to individual treaties other than notes exchanged. It has occasionally been suggested that the commentary to the OECD Model may be viewed as such an agreement. In *IRC v Commerzbank AG*,[41] it was said that subsequent commentaries on a treaty have persuasive value only. The Crown, in that case, sought support from a joint statement issued by the United States Internal Revenue Service and the Board of Inland Revenue in 1977.[42] The statement was made pursuant to art. 20A of the old (1945) US Treaty, which authorises competent authorities to agree on the interpretation of provisions. Mummery J regarded this statement as having no authority in English courts. It expresses the official view of the revenue authorities of the two countries. That view, he said, may be right or wrong.[43] Although art. 20A authorises the competent authorities to communicate with each other directly to implement the provisions of the Convention and to 'assure its consistent interpretation and application', it does not confer any binding or authoritative effect on the views or statements of the competent authorities in the English courts. The treaty in question, however, was not one governed by the Vienna Convention. This may be an instance where the rules might differ between a treaty where the Vienna Convention applies and where it does not. Articles 31(3)(a) and 31(3)(b) of the Vienna Convention require that such mutual agreement, although not binding, must be taken into account when interpreting the treaty. There is no indication as to customary international law on this point. Two competent authority agreements between HMRC and the United States Internal Revenue Service have been made under the 2001 US Treaty.[44] The status of these agreements derives from the authority given under art. 26(3) of that treaty to make such agreements.

In *Sun Life Assurance Company of Canada v Pearson*,[45] when the use of the commentary was first considered, it was noted that the articles in question were drawn in identical terms to the provisions of the 1977 OECD Model Treaty and that both the UK and Canada were member countries – therefore, the point was not decided. In commenting on the allocation of income, the judge noted that any doubts he had about the position would be dispelled by the commentary. This was despite the fact that the 1977 commentary was not a commentary on the 1967 Canadian Treaty, which had a different origin. He noted, however, that 'the views of the experts who sat on the Fiscal Committee on the Regulation of Double Taxation are entitled to very great weight'. Indeed, the commentary is referred to for support in relation to several aspects of the decision. The court also referred to the background of the 1967 treaty,

---

[41] [1990] BTC 172; [1990] STC 285, Ch.D.

[42] Published in [1977] *BTR*, 494.

[43] [1990] BTC 172; [1990] STC 285 at 302c.

[44] The competent authority agreements comprise one regarding the qualification of certain UK pension or other retirement arrangements of 1 May 2005, and a United Kingdom/United States Dual Consolidated Loss competent authority agreement signed on 6 October 2006.

[45] [1984] BTC 223; [1984] STC 461, Ch.D.

both in relation to the domestic law context and the OECD recommendation of 30 July 1963 adopting the 1963 Draft Convention. The Court of Appeal[46] did not reiterate the point that the commentary related to the 1977 model, but simply noted that it is common ground that the court is entitled to consider the commentary on the authority of *Fothergill v Monarch Airlines Ltd*.[47] In summarising the *Commerzbank* principles of interpretation in *Memec*, the judge referred to the commentary as a supplementary means of interpretation.

Article 31 (3) of the Vienna Convention seems to distinguish between those agreements and instruments which form part of the context under art. 31(2), and those which are to be taken into account together with the context. This does seem to suggest that even if it is correct that their consideration is mandatory, it ought to have a value which is lower than those agreements and instruments which form part of the context.

Object and purpose

Article 31 of the Vienna Convention requires a treaty to be interpreted in the light of its object and purpose. In *Commerzbank*, for example, it was said that 'a literal interpretation may be obviously inconsistent with the purposes of the particular article or of the treaty as a whole'.[48] The earliest recognition of the object of the treaty was found in *Ostime v Australian Mutual Provident Society*.[49] Upjohn J said:[50]

> 'My approach to the relief order (which enacts the Australian Treaty) is that its whole object is to relieve from double taxation, and that therefore one is looking to those profits or surpluses which by the law of Australia or the UK, as the case may be, are made the subject of taxation.'

Full recognition of the object and purpose interpretation, and of Article 31(1), is found in *IRC v Commerzbank*.[51] In that case, the court also referred[52] to the customary international rule as expressed by McNair in *The Law of Treaties*,[53] where it was stated that the task of construing or interpreting a treaty is 'the duty of giving effect to the expressed intention of the parties'. In this respect, McNair said that the plain terms of a treaty or construing words according to their general and ordinary meaning or their natural signification are to be a starting point or a prima facie guide and 'cannot be allowed to obstruct the essential quest in the application of treaties, namely the search for the real intention of the contracting parties using the language employed by them'.

Mummery J said:[54] 'I can find no sufficient indication of the purposes of the Convention or in its surrounding circumstances, or in the provisions in articles other than Article 15 to

---

[46] [1986] BTC 282; [1986] STC 335, CA.

[47] See above, n. 10 at 280.

[48] See above, n. 15, per Mummery J at 297j.

[49] (1956-1960) 38 TC 492.

[50] At 505.

[51] 51 See above, n. 37.

[52] 52 At 301.

[53] McNair, AD, *The Law of Treaties* (1961), Oxford: Clarendon Press.

[54] At 304d.

qualify the clear words'. The House of Lords, in *Ostime v Australian Mutual Provident Society*,[55] did not rely on this approach in coming to the same conclusion. In *ICI v Caro*,[56] it was argued that the manifest intention of the two governments was to prevent double taxation. In that case, the Court of Appeal recognised that its conclusions on the meaning of the treaty gave rise to double taxation, but said that the only safe guide is to give effect to the plain meaning of the words.

A similar approach may be seen in relation to the *EVC* case. In that case, the court refused to accept that the purpose of the limitation of benefits was to prevent tax avoidance and that its application should therefore be restricted to circumstances which did entail such avoidance. Again, it preferred to rely on the plain meaning of words. In *Memec plc v IRC*,[57] the Chancery Division held that a purposive approach should be adopted so as to construe the treaty in as symmetrical a way as possible, unless the language is clearly against such a construction. Although the principle was not rejected by the Court of Appeal, it concluded that the symmetry which the judge sought required treating a special definition as a general definition and this did not do justice to the 'coherent and careful drafting of the convention amid the protocol'. The symmetry contended for was not intended by the drafters of the treaty.

The Special Commissioners decision in *A Sportsman v IRC*[58] may be viewed as a purposive interpretation using the preamble as a statement of purpose in this regard. In that case, reference was made to the preamble in the French Treaty and the fact that it indicates a dual purpose of avoiding double taxation and preventing fiscal evasion with respect to taxes on income. It was noted that the statutory instrument bringing the treaty into effect itself was designed to afford relief from double taxation. The issue arose as to whether credit should be given for tax payable under the treaty, as well as tax actually paid. The Special Commissioners ruled that the taxpayer had confused literal and ordinary meaning. They said:[59]

> 'Double taxation conventions are not to create or allocate taxing rights, but to prevent double taxation. Taxing rights already exist. By entering into a double taxation convention, each government relinquishes all or part of its taxing rights according to domestic law in certain circumstances; one country gives up its claim in recognition of the fact that the other is going to take it. However, if there is no actual taxation by one country, there is nothing in the object and purpose of the convention to prevent taxation by the other.'

The Special Commissioners noted that the second stated object of the treaty is prevention of fiscal evasion. They ruled that if art. 24(a) (foreign tax credit) were to be construed in the manner in which the taxpayer contended, that object could be defeated. Sovereign states do not, as a matter of principle, enforce one another's revenue laws. To give credit in country A for tax payable but not paid in country B would encourage evasion of tax in country B by a taxpayer incurring a tax liability there and then returning to country A without meeting that

[55] See above, n. 48.

[56] See above, n. 31.

[57] See above, n. 39.

[58] (1998) Sp C 174.

[59] At 295.

liability. Since the taxpayer's interpretation makes evasion easy, thereby defeating a stated purpose of the treaty, that tends to suggest that the interpretation should be rejected. While this line of reasoning is clearly flawed, it illustrates an attempt at a purposive approach to treaty interpretation.[60]

Lord Nicholls of Birkenhead said in *Pirelli Cable Holdings & Ors v Revenue and Customs Commissioners* that art. 10(3)(c) of the Netherlands Treaty, 'like all documents, must be interpreted purposively. So, in answering these questions it is important to have in mind how they come to arise at all'.[61] Thus, the article could not be construed as allowing a tax credit to a resident of the Netherlands in the absence of advance corporation tax as this would be contrary to the stated purpose of the article, namely to provide a tax credit to a resident of the Netherlands in the same circumstances as to a UK resident.

12-200   Supplementary means of interpretation

Article 32 of the Vienna Convention provides for supplementary means of interpretation. It reads:

> 'Recourse may be had to supplementary means of interpretation including the preparatory work of the treaty and the circumstances of its conclusion, in order to confirm the meaning resulting from the application of Article 31, or to determine the meaning when the interpretation according to Article 31:
>
> (a)   leaves the meaning ambiguous or obscure; or
> (b)   leads to a result which is manifestly absurd or unreasonable.'

No explanation is provided as to what constitutes supplementary means other than to say that it includes the preparatory work of the treaty and the circumstances of its conclusion. Supplementary means are clearly viewed as an aid to interpretation conducted in accordance with art. 31 of the Vienna Convention. The purpose of this recourse is to either to confirm the meaning resulting from the application of art. 31 or determine the meaning when art. 31 interpretation leads to ambiguous or obscure meaning or leads to a result which is manifestly absurd or unreasonable.

These rules are regarded as codifying customary international law. *Fothergill* preceded the decision in *Pepper v Hart*,[62] and the House of Lords was therefore keen to distinguish *Hansard*, which at that time could not be resorted to for the purpose of ascertaining what ambiguities or obscure provisions mean, from 'travaux preparatoires'. The distinction was explained by Lord Diplock in *Fothergill* thus:[63]

> 'It is however otherwise with that growing body of written law in force in the United Kingdom which, although it owes its enforceability within the United Kingdom to its embodiment in or authorisation by an Act of Parliament, nevertheless owes its origin and its actual wording to

---

[60] For an example of the consideration of the use of the preamble in relation to a social security treaty, see *Stevens, Garnham & Payne v The Inland Revenue Commissioners* (2004) Sp C 411 para. 42.

[61] *Pirelli Cable Holdings & Ors v Revenue and Customs Commissioners* [2006] BTC 181; [2006] UKHL 4, para. 13.

[62] [1992] BTC 591; [1992] STC 898, HL.

[63] See above, n. 10, at 281.

some prior law-preparing process in which Parliament has not participated, such as the negotiation and preparation of a multilateral international convention ... which Her Majesty's Government wants to ratify on behalf of the United Kingdom but can only do when the provisions of the convention have been incorporated into our domestic law.

Accordingly, in exercising its interpretive function of ascertaining what the delegates to an international conference agreed upon by their majority vote in favour of the text of an international convention, where that text itself is ambiguous or obscure, an English Court should have regard to any material which those delegates themselves had thought would be available to clear up any possible ambiguities or obscurities.'

The conditions for the use of 'travaux preparatoires' were set out by Lord Wilberforce in *Gatoil International Inc. v Arkwright-Boston Manufacturers Mutual Insurance Company:*[64]

'First that the material is public and accessible; secondly, that it clearly and undisputedly points to a definite legislative intention.' In relation to preparatory works, the Special Commissioner said in *Commerzbank,*[65] following Lord Scarman in *Fothergill,* that 'preparatory work are only aids in the interpretation of the relevant words of the treaty. If they appear to disclose an intention which cannot even with the best will in the world be read into the words of the treaty, then they are obviously not aids at all.'

In the UK, the confidential nature of tax treaty negotiations means that in most cases, detailed preparatory work in the form of notes of meetings, exchanges of correspondence and the like are unavailable.

OECD Model Commentary

The most important publicly available document is the commentary to the OECD Model. The OECD Model forms the basis of the UK negotiating position. HMRC takes the view that 'Where the text of a provision of a double taxation agreement follows the wording of the OECD Model or has substantially similar wording then the guidance in the commentary on the OECD Model may be used as an aid to interpretation of that double taxation agreement.'.[66] The commentary itself advocates its own use.[67]

Commentary to the OECD Model is now routinely referred to by the courts but its exact status as an interpretative tool is yet to be fully explored and the courts have not refined the tests as to when it is required to be used, when it may be used, and its position in the hierarchy of interpretive rules. The commentary to the OECD Model is an important aid to interpretation in *Sun Life Assurance Company of Canada v Pearson,*[68] when the use of the commentary was first considered by a UK court, it was noted that the articles in question were drawn in identical terms to the provisions of the 1977 OECD Model Treaty, and that both the UK and Canada were member countries. In commenting on the allocation of income, the judge noted that any doubts he had about the position would be dispelled by the

---

[64] [1985] AC 225 at 263.

[65] At 294h.

[66] HMRC, *INTM*, para. INTM152070

[67] Introduction, para. 28-30

[68] [1984] BTC 223; [1984] STC 461, Ch.D.

commentary. This was despite the fact that the 1977 commentary was not a commentary on the 1967 Canadian Treaty, which had a different origin. He noted, however, that 'the views of the experts who sat on the Fiscal Committee on the Regulation of Double Taxation are entitled to very great weight'. Indeed, the commentary is referred to for support in relation to several aspects of the decision. The court also referred to the background of the 1967 treaty, both in relation to the domestic law context and the OECD recommendation of 30 July 1963 adopting the 1963 Draft Convention. The Court of Appeal[69] did not reiterate the point that the commentary related to the 1977 model, but simply noted that it is common ground that the court is entitled to consider the commentary on the authority of *Fothergill v Monarch Airlines Ltd.*[70]

In summarising the *Commerzbank* principles of interpretation in *Memec*, the judge referred to the commentary as a supplementary means of interpretation.

The effect of amendments to the commentary is likely to become of increasing importance. Publication of the 1963 OECD Draft Treaty was accompanied by a commentary which remained unchanged until the 1977 OECD Model with its commentary despite important work in the subject by the OECD in the interim. Again that remained until updated in 1992 and for the first time, it was published in looseleaf rather than book form. The adoption of looseleaf format was perhaps a harbinger of acceleration in the rate of change – the Model Treaty and commentary are now updated every three years. Other changes affect the utility of the commentary. The manner in which the OECD undertakes examination of treaty issues has become more transparent and it is now normal for discussion drafts to be published for public consultation and for submissions by non-governmental interested parties also to be published (curiously, while the source of public comment is made known, the contributions at governmental level and from participating countries remains secret). In one sense, the commentary has become an ongoing work in progress. The OECD itself has expanded from a small group of highly industrialised countries to include a broader range of members with a wider spectrum of perspectives on tax treaties. This has made consensus harder to maintain and the number of Observations and Reservations entered by member countries increases with each update. The commentary to the 2008 model reveals a further source of significant increase in the volume of Observations and Reservations. Under the Outreach Programme the OECD encourages non-member countries to participate and has started to collect comments from them on the commentary.[71]

Thus far, little attention has been paid to distinctions between treaties made after the various Model Conventions and their Commentaries have been published. The first decision to grapple with the dynamic nature of the commentary is *Trevor Smallwood Trusts v R & C Commrs.*[72] In struggling with the meaning of 'place of effective management' in Article 4(3) of the Mauritius Treaty, the Special Commissioners reviewed the commentary through its development in particular, from the 1977 version, the 2000 amendments as well as the 2001

---

[69] [1986] BTC 282; [1986] STC 335, CA.

[70] See above, n. 10 at 280.

[71] Therefore, this may be of some persuasive value in the context of treaties with states that participate in this process.

[72] (2008) Sp C 669.

discussion draft, which included changes proposed (at the time of the case but now adopted in the 2008 model). That treaty is based on the 1977 OECD Model. The Special Commissioners said 'Our view is that the negotiators on both sides could be expected to have the Commentary in front of them'.[73] This view usefully places the commentary in the category of preparatory work within art. 32 of the Vienna Convention, and as such as a supplementary means of interpretation. However they continue (obiter):

'The negotiators on both sides] can be expected to have intended that the meaning in the Commentary should be applied in interpreting the Treaty when it contains the identical wording.'

This conclusion is not consistent with the use of supplementary material in art. 32, which makes the use of such material permissive to address ambiguous or obscure language or when the ordinary methods of interpretation in art. 31 lead to manifestly absurd or unreasonable results. The exaggerated role of the commentary is compounded by the Special Commissioners expanding the observation thus:

'If the Commentary contains a clear explanation of the meaning the term it seems clear that the parties to the Treaty intended that such explanation should be more important than the ordinary meaning to be given to the terms of that phrase. This is either on the basis that the existence of the model and Commentaries demonstrate that the parties intended it as a special meaning within article 31(4) of the Vienna Convention, or that the Vienna Convention does not purport to be a comprehensive statement of the method of treaty interpretation.'

Such a conclusion would elevate commentary existing at the time of negotiations to part of treaty and, in effect, substitute the wording of the treaty with that of the commentary. The decision does, however, return to the real question of existing commentary as preparatory work in relation to a treaty between the UK and a non-OECD country in noting that the negotiators may be expected to have the commentary in front of them:

'This is as much true of the United Kingdom which is a member of the OECD as it is of Mauritius, which is not. The difference is that the United Kingdom had the opportunity of stating that it disagreed with any part of the commentary by making an Observation, while Mauritius did not, although the commentary does now contain Observations by a number of non-OECD member countries, but not including Mauritius.'

This remark raises complex issues in compressed language. Interpretation of treaty involves uncovering the intention of the contracting parties and not of a party to the treaty. Therefore, if at the time the commentary was adopted there was no opportunity for a non-OECD member country to comment, it is inappropriate to assume that common intention of contracting states was to adopt that version of the commentary or at all, particularly in the face of the ordinary meaning of terms. Where an observation is entered, it is clear that the other contracting state does not hold the view contained in the commentary. In such a case it is stretching the notion of agreement to conclude that the common intention of the contracting states is to adopt the meaning or approach adopted in the commentary.

The decision in *Smallwood* also usefully considers the role of developments to the commentary subsequent to the conclusion of the treaty. The question is approached thus:

---

[73] Para. 98.

'99. The relevance of Commentaries adopted later than the Treaty is more problematic because the parties cannot have intended the new commentary to apply at the time of making the Treaty. However, to ignore them means that one would be shutting one's eyes to advances in international tax thinking, such as how to apply the treaty to payments for software that had not been considered when the Treaty was made. The safer option is to read the later commentary and then decide in the light of its content what weight should be given to it.'

This careful approach may be contrasted with the treatment by the Court of Appeal in *Indofood International Finance Ltd v JP Morgan Chase Bank NA*,[74] where it uncritically applied the commentary as amended in 2003 to the meaning of 'beneficial ownership' in treaties between Indonesia and Mauritius made in 1996 (neither OECD members) and made even earlier between Indonesia and the Netherlands.

There is no suggestion in the case that, under the Vienna Convention principles, versions of the commentary made after the conclusion of a treaty is an 'agreement' made by the parties relating to a treaty between OECD members. If that were to be the case, it would be required to be included in the context of a treaty. Likewise, the courts do not appear to view the commentary as a subsequent agreement or practice required to be taken into account under art. 31(3). They are thus supplementary and courts are permitted but not bound to consider them.

The Special Commissioners in *Smallwood* also examined proposed amendments to the commentary as part of a recommendation to Working Party 1, which has responsibility for the OECD Model but considered 'that this should be treated with considerably more caution because it has not been adopted by the OECD'.[75]

Despite enormous effort in developing the commentary, the courts have not always found it helpful in resolving questions of construction. In *Smallwood*, for example, the close examination of the commentary as described above merely led to the conclusion that 'the matter is not free of controversy within the OECD'.[76] Similarly, in *UBS*, the lack of assistance from the commentary compelled the conclusion that the ordinary meaning of terms was the appropriate approach.[77]

Other multilateral statements, such as the *United Nations Model Double Taxation Convention between Developed and Developing Countries*, and the *United Nations Manual for the Negotiation of Bilateral Tax Treaties between Developed and Developing Countries*, may be helpful in some cases. The same might be said of those treaty partners that have their own model treaties, subject to the difficulty that unilateral statements of one of the contracting states will not normally be regarded as qualifying under this heading of the Vienna Convention.

---

[74] [2006] BTC 8003 [2006] EWCA Civ 158.

[75] Para. 128.

[76] Para. 126.

[77] *UBS AG v HMRC* (2005) Sp C 480, para. 11

There are no cases involving the commentary to the United Nations Model Convention.[78] This commentary has not been updated, and, as a result, some of the more difficult temporal issues will not arise. In the context of non-OECD treaties, it is also arguable that given the influence of the OECD Model, that commentary may also be useful in the context of treaties with non-OECD member states.

Other treaties

Recourse has been made in several cases to parallel treaties. For example, in *Sun Life Assurance Company of Canada v Pearson*,[79] the taxpayer placed reliance on the decision of the court in *Ostime v Australian Mutual Provident Society*,[80] which considered identical provisions in art. 3 of the Australian Treaty as supporting the interpretation of the same provisions in the Canadian Treaty. In *Padmore v IRC*,[81] the Court compared the Swiss Treaty with the Jersey Treaty in order to conclude that additional wording appearing in the Swiss Treaty would have to have been included in the Jersey Treaty in order to reach the interpretation contended for by the Crown. Similarly, the fact that partnerships were referred to specifically in the US Treaty but not in the Jersey Treaty was argued to mean that the Jersey Treaty did not deal with partnerships. The court noted that the provisions of other treaties are not of assistance in construing a particular treaty. Other countries may have negotiated different bargains. In *IRC v Vas*,[82] the difference between the US and Hungarian treaties dealing with visiting teachers was addressed by reference to the law in Hungary and a comparison between the expression in the earlier US Treaty and the Hungarian Treaty in order to consider the provision in question.

Treaties between third countries may also be referred to on occasion. The Court of Appeal, however, in *Memec*[83] has questioned how much assistance can be obtained from treaties where the UK is not a party to them. In that case, Morritt LJ noted differences in the wording between the German–Swiss Treaty and the UK–Germany Treaty in the context of determining the meaning of the term 'dividends' under the UK–Germany Treaty. In placing reliance on such treaties, it is not only necessary to find similarly worded provisions in a similar context within the treaty, but also to identify a similar approach to the interpretation of treaties adopted by the courts responsible for construing the treaty in question.

Writings of jurists

The writings of jurists have had a somewhat uneven reception by the courts in the context of interpreting tax treaties. On the hand, writers such as Brownlie and McNair have been readily accepted by the courts in expressing principles of customary-international law relating to interpretation of treaties. Commentary by jurists on specific provisions have been

---

[78] It was referred to but not quoted in *Indofood International Finance Ltd v JP Morgan Chase Bank NA* [2005] BTC 8023 [2005] EWHC 2103 (Ch), para. 26.

[79] See above, n. 45.

[80] See above, n. 49.

[81] See above, n. 21.

[82] See above, n. 37.

[83] See above, n. 39.

more equivocal. In *Commerzbank*,[84] Mummery J said that reliance on commentaries was persuasive only and depended on the cogency of reasoning. In that case, the Inland Revenue relied heavily on the opinions of eminent jurists on international law, Sir Ian Brownlie and McNair, particularly in the absence of any preparatory work. The Special Commissioner relied on statements in Brownlie and McNair that the burden of proof was on the Crown to rebut the presumption that the words of art. XV of the US Treaty should bear their plain and ordinary meaning.

In *Memec*,[85] this view was echoed by Robert Walker J. The Crown sought to introduce extracts of *Klaus Vogel on Double Taxation Conventions*. Initially, the taxpayer objected to the extracts on the grounds that they constituted 'surmise and guesswork'. Ultimately in reply, the objection was modified and the taxpayer's counsel drew the Special Commissioners' attention to an extract not quoted by the Crown in support of their own case. The Special Commissioners admitted the relevant extracts but 'found them to be of little assistance and much of Herr Vogel's commentary is verging on the incomprehensible'.[86] The position changed somewhat in the High Court, where Dr. Vogel was referred to as 'an eminent German expert'.[87] This time, the Inland Revenue argued 'that his view is tentative and reliance on it is not mandatory and depends on its cogency'.

The views were ultimately expressed to be of some help, but not by themselves to be determinative. In the Court of Appeal, it was said that 'the views of an acknowledged expert in this field, as Professor Vogel undoubtedly is, deserve respect'.[88]

In *Trustees of Wensleydale's Settlement v IRC*,[89] Dr. Vogel's work was again referred to on the meaning of 'place of effective management' in the Irish Treaty. Although no views were expressed about the comment in the book, the Special Commissioners clearly placed reliance on it.[90]

Foreign judgements

The courts have taken a critical approach to foreign cases, although in *Fothergill v Monarch Airlines Limited*,[91] Lord Scarman said 'the decisions of a Superior Court or the opinion of a Court of Cassation will carry great weight'. Thus, although the desirability of a common approach was fostered by the Vienna Convention, and indeed observations in the introduction to the commentary read that 'harmonisation of these conventions in accordance with uniform principles, definitions, rules and methods, and agreement on common

---

[84] See above, n. 15.

[85] See above, n. 17.

[86] At 1343a.

[87] At 1356j.

[88] [1998] BTC 251 at 261; [1998] STC 754 at 768b, CA. See also the dissenting view of Sir Christopher Staughton at 770j.

[89] (1996) Sp C 73; [1966] STC SCD 241.

[90] See *Indofood International Finance Ltd v JP Morgan Chase Bank NA* [2005] BTC 8023 [2005] EWHC 2103 (Ch); [2006] BTC 8003 [2006] EWCA Civ 158 citing with approval Philip Baker's commentary on the OECD Model Convention; *Caglar & Ors v Billingham (HMIT)* (1996) Sp C 70 citing various authors on public international law

[91] See above, n. 10.

interpretation, became increasingly desirable', the courts have proceeded cautiously. In *Commerzbank*,[92] the Crown relied on the decision of the United States Court of Claims in *Great West Life Assurance Company v United States*.[93] That case was on the effect of art. 12 of the treaty between the US and Canada. It granted exemption in terms similar to art. XV of the United Kingdom – United States Treaty. Mummery J noted:[94]

> 'That decision is of some interest as illustrating the basis on which the United States taxes foreign corporations trading in the United States, but it is of no real assistance in these cases because it is clear from the report that different principles were applied by the Court to the interpretation of that Convention than an English Court would have applied in accordance with the decision of the House of Lords in *Fothergill v Monarch Airlines Limited*.'

In particular, he referred to US case law to the effect that the meaning given a treaty by an appropriate government and governmental agency is of great weight. The US court, he said, was greatly influenced in its decision by the fact that the Departments of State and Treasury had interpreted art. 12 of the United States – Canada Treaty as not conferring the exemption claimed and had negotiated other treaties on that basis. No such principle is applied by the English courts to the provision of a treaty; he therefore did not find that decision of much assistance in the present case.

In *Memec*,[95] where the meaning of the term 'dividends' was under examination in the German Treaty, reference was made to a decision of the German Bundesfinanzhof in construing the treaty between Germany and Switzerland. In the Court of Appeal, Morritt LJ noted that the German decision was on a differently worded article in a different context in a different treaty, and questioned how much assistance can be obtained from other treaties, particularly when the UK is not a party to them. A similar approach was adopted in *Padmore v IRC*.[96] Although foreign decisions were not accepted in *Commerzbank* and *Memec*, the courts have nonetheless looked at them with great care.[97] In *Memec*, the court noted that it was not apparent in the German–Swiss Treaty whether the applicability of art. 10(6) was in issue, but in art. 28 of that treaty it appeared to have been concerned to preserve the rights to apply withholding tax on dividends in the country of source and therefore a wide meaning of 'dividends' was natural in that context. The court thus distinguished the treaty without having to comment on the approach of the German court.[98]

In *QRS 1 Aps and others v Frandsen*,[99] the court was called on to consider whether the enforcement of a judgement obtained by a liquidator on behalf of a foreign tax administration was a 'Revenue matter' within the meaning of art. 1 of the Brussels Convention on Jurisdiction and the Enforcement of Judgements in Civil and Commercial

---

[92] See above, n. 15.

[93] A.F.T.R. 2nd 82-1316.

[94] At 302f.

[95] See above, n. 39.

[96] See above, n. 21.

[97] See above (the discussion regarding *Commerzbank*).

[98] See also the dissenting opinion of Sir Christopher Staughton.

[99] [1999] BTC 8023; [1999] STC 616.

Matters. In this regard, the court referred to a report of Professor Peter Schlosser on the 1978 Accession Convention by which the UK acceded to the Brussels Convention and to *Dicey and Morris on the Conflict of Laws*.[100] French decisions and writers on the subject were also considered. The court formulated the problem thus:[101]

> 'There is no definition of "Revenue matters" in the Convention and no decision of the Court of Justice of the European Communities bearing on the point. What then, one must ask, would the original member states themselves regard as Revenue matters for this purpose? Do they subscribe to the legal principle enshrined in Dicey's r3 and in particular that part of the rule barring the indirect enforcement of foreign revenue laws.'

Simon Brown LJ noted[102] that 'there is no reason to doubt that the rule in France is just as fundamental and far reaching as in England and that it is rightly described in both jurisdictions as a rule international application. I should add that we were shown no contrary jurisprudence from any other member state'.

12-250   Statutory rules of interpretation

As a rule, unless domestic law meanings are required to be applied to treaty provisions, the interpretation rules contained in domestic tax law are inapplicable. An important exception was enacted in 1992 in relation to the meaning of 'special relationship' for the purpose of treaty provisions relating to interest. Section 808A of the Taxes Act 1988 applies where a treaty makes provision for interest and contains the special relationship wording. That wording is defined in s. 808A(2)(b) as, where owing to a special relationship, the amount of interest paid exceeds the amount which would have been paid in the absence of the relationship, the treaty provisions only apply to the last mentioned amount.

Special relationship

A series of specific interpretation rules are imposed. These require that the special relationship provision be construed as requiring account to be taken of all factors including:

- whether the loan would have been made at all in the absence of the relationship;
- the amount which the loan would have been in the absence of the relationship; and
- the rate of interest and other terms which would have been agreed in the absence of the relationship.[103]

It further requires the provision to be construed as requiring the taxpayer to demonstrate that there is no special relationship or where there is one, to show what the amount of interest would have been in the absence of such a relationship.[104] Where a company makes a loan to

---

[100] Collins, L, *et al.* (eds.), *Dicey and Morris on the Conflict of Laws*, 12th edn (1993), vol. 1, p. 97.

[101] Simon Brown LJ at 628j.

[102] At 629f.

[103] Taxes Act 1988, s. 808A(2).

[104] *Ibid*, s. 808A(3).

another with which it has a special relationship, and the making of loans generally is not part of the lender's business, that fact is to be disregarded.[105]

The factors listed do not apply where the special relationship provision in the treaty expressly requires regard to be had to the debt on which the interest is paid in determining the excess interest and accordingly expressly limits the factors to be taken into account.[106]

The reason for the statutory interpretation provision is somewhat obscure. It arises out of the Special Commissioners' decision apparently in 1992, the details of which have not been published. One might surmise that the Commissioners concluded that the OECD Model wording permitted only an adjustment based on the rate of interest charged and not on the amount of debt overall. Since the decision was never appealed, it was presumably acquiesced to by the Revenue, which sought the inclusion of the section in legislation. The interpretation rule itself is also in need of some interpretation. In particular, subsection (5), which excludes the application of the rule. It appears to disapply the provision where the treaty itself requires regard to be had to the debt on which the interest is paid. This notion is extended by the wording 'and accordingly expressly limits the factors to be taken into account'. It is unclear whether the presence of a provision requiring regard to be had to the debt on which the interest is paid is itself to be construed as an express limit or whether particular wording expressing a limitation must be found in the treaty. A reservation by the UK and changes in the OECD Model Treaty now reflect this position in any event.

A similar provision was enacted in relation to royalties in the FA 2000. Article 12(4) of the OECD Model contains a provision denying the relief from source state tax to the extent that, by reason of a special relationship between the payer and the beneficial owner of the royalties, or between both of them and some other person, the amount of the royalties, having regard to the use, right or information for which they are paid, exceeds the amount which would have been agreed upon by the payer and the beneficial owner in the absence of such relationship. It has been UK Treaty negotiating policy, to omit from that clause the words 'having regard to the use, right or information for which they are paid'. In most cases those words are replaced by the phrase 'for whatever reason', but sometimes no alternative wording is included. In either event, the Inland Revenue stated in its document on double tax relief reform that its view of the intention of this provision is that it should apply where not only the rate at which royalties are paid is excessive but also, in the absence of the special relationship, the arrangements under which the royalties are paid at all would not have been entered into.[107]

12-300   Other references to domestic law

The most important general rule of interpretation applies to terms used in a treaty but not defined in it. Article 3(2) requires that:

[105] *Ibid*, s. 808A(4).

[106] *Ibid*, s. 808A(5).

[107] The Inland Revenue, 'Double taxation relief for companies', a discussion paper (1998).

'As regard the application of the Convention by a contracting state, any term not defined therein shall, unless the context otherwise requires, have the meaning which it has under the law of that state concerning the taxes to which the Convention applies.'

This clause is found in all UK treaties. Although reference has been made to this article in a large number of cases, there are still several outstanding issues which have not been addressed by the courts. In *Ostime v Australian Mutual Provident Society*,[108] the court was called on to address whether the Australian Treaty prevented the attribution of investment income to the UK branch of a non-resident non-mutual insurance company. It was argued that the treaty did not deal with purely notional or conventional profits and that 'industrial or commercial profits' defined in art. 2(1)(i) of the treaty must be given its natural and ordinary meaning. Article 2(3) (art. 3(2) of the OECD Model) had no application. On that basis, the Crown argued that industrial or commercial profits could not include purely notional or fictitious profits, but could only refer to real or actual profit. Since there are none as a matter of domestic law, the treaty has no application. The court proceeded on the basis that the domestic law of the source state (that is, the UK) was the relevant law. In *Imperial Chemical Industries Ltd v Caro*,[109] the income in question was from Australian sources. However, in construing the operation of the tax credit granted under art. 12 of that treaty in the context of the preceding-year basis of assessment, it was provided that the reference to income referred to income as determined for UK purposes (that is, the residence country). The case is perhaps an unusual one given the former preceding year basis, which resulted in a total mismatch. In addition, the court was moved by the general purpose of the treaty in avoiding double taxation and was therefore inclined not to permit the same credit to be granted twice. It seems unlikely that it will establish any principle beyond the specifics of the now abolished preceding year basis in the context of deciding which contracting state laws should apply. In the House of Lords, in *Pirelli Cable Holdings & Ors v Revenue and Customs Commissioners*, Lord Scott of Foscote, when interpreting art. 10(3)(c) of the Netherlands and Italian treaties, under which a Netherlands, or Italian, resident company could claim 'one half of the tax credit to which an individual resident in the United Kingdom would have been entitled had he received those dividends', noted that there is no definition anywhere in those treaties of the expression 'tax credit'. In each case he applied art. 3(2) of each treaty to adopt the expression 'tax credit' as defined in s. 832(1) of the Taxes Act 1988.[110]

There are also numerous instances where a treaty makes specific reference to domestic law. For example, see the Netherlands Treaty (1980), art. 10. Similar references may be found to the law of the other contracting states. This commonly applies in relation to tax-sparing provisions which are described by reference to the legislation in the other contracting state. Similarly, entities established in other contracting states are frequently described by reference to the domestic law of the other contracting state. The limitation of benefits provisions of art. 10(3)(d)(i) of the Netherlands Treaty (1980) referred to companies whose shares are officially quoted on a Netherlands stock exchange and which comply in certain

---

[108] See above, n. 48.

[109] See above, n. 31.

[110] [2006] BTC 181; [2006] UKHL 4, paras. 64 and 65.

respects with Council Directive 79/279/EEC.[111] In such a case, interpretation in accordance with Community law is required. These provisions illustrate a 'special meaning within art. 31(4) of the Vienna Convention'.

12-350   Treaties in more than one language

Although many UK treaties are concluded in English only, a large number are concluded in at least two languages. Where this is the case, the practice is to agree on the authoritative value of each text. Typical language in this regard is found, for example, in the execution provisions of the Canadian Treaty, which reads: 'Done in duplicate at London in the English and French languages, both texts being equally authoritative'.

The interpretation of treaties authenticated in two or more languages is addressed in the Vienna Convention. Article 33 reads as follows:

'(1)   When a treaty has been authenticated in two or more languages, the text is equally authoritative in each language, unless the treaty provides or the parties agree that, in case of divergence, a particular text shall prevail.

(2)   A version of the treaty in a language other than one of those in which the text was authenticated shall be considered an authentic text only if the treaty so provides or the parties so agree.

(3)   The terms of the treaty are presumed to have the same meaning in each authentic text.

(4)   Except where a particular text prevails in accordance with paragraph 1, when a comparison of the authentic texts discloses a difference of meaning which the application of Articles 31 and 32 does not remove, the meaning which best reconciles the texts, having regard to the object and purpose of the treaty, shall be adopted.'

The courts in the UK have not had to consider language versions of tax treaties other than in English. The opportunity to do so has arisen on occasion in relation to other non-tax treaties and, in this context, Lord Wilberforce said in *Fothergill v Monarch Airlines Ltd*:[112]

'My Lords, some of the problems which arise when the Courts of this country are faced with texts of treaties or conventions in different languages were discussed in *James Buchanan & Co. Ltd. v. Babco Forwarding & Shipping (United Kingdom) Ltd.*, [1978] AC 141. It is obvious that the present represents a special and indeed unique case.

Here it is not only permissible to look at a foreign language text, but obligatory. What is made part of English law is the text set out in Schedule 1, i.e. in both Part I and Part II, so both English and French texts must be looked at. Furthermore, it cannot be judged whether there is an inconsistency between two texts unless one looks at both. So, in the present case the process of interpretation seems to involve:

(1)   Interpretation of the English text, according to the principles upon which international conventions are to be interpreted (see *Buchanan's* case and *Stag Line Ltd. v. Foscolo, Mango & Co. Ltd.* [1932] AC 328, 350).

---

[111] Dated 5 March 1979.

[112] See above, n. 10, at 272.

(2)   Interpretation of the French text according to the same principles but with additional linguistic problems.

(3)   Comparison of these meanings.

Moreover, if the process of interpretation leaves the matter in doubt, the question may have to be faced whether 'travaux preparatoires' may be looked at in order to resolve the difficulty'

This approach does not differ from the Vienna Convention Guidelines. In *Memec*, the court rejected an 'over-subtle point' based on the wording of the French version of the 1963 Draft Model Tax Convention on the meaning of 'dividend' for underlying credit purposes.[113] However, the French version of the 1977 OECD Model was relied upon by the Special Commissioners in *Trevor Smallwood Trusts v R & C Commrs* (2008) Sp C 669 to interpret the expression 'effective management' in art. 4(3) of the Mauritius Treaty and by the Court of Appeal in *UBS AG v Revenue and Customs Commissioners*.[114]

12-400   Human rights and the European Convention on Human Rights

Although the UK was among the first signatories to the European Convention on Human Rights (ECHR) in 1951, it was only in 1998, as a result of the Human Rights Act 1998, that the key elements of the convention were enacted into the law of the UK. Section 3 of the Human Rights Act 1998 creates a general requirement that all legislation, whether past or future, must be read and given effect in a way which is compatible with the legislation. It does this by providing that all legislation, primary and secondary, whenever enacted, must be read and given effect in a way which is compatible with convention rights. It will no longer be necessary for there to be ambiguity in order to have resort to the convention. This legislation creates a new hierarchy in the context of tax treaties. Thus, although s. 788 of the Taxes Act 1988 generally makes domestic law subject to tax treaties, s. 3 of the Human Rights Act 1998 now makes even this provision subject to the application of the convention. As a result, all tax treaties and their implementation must comply with the Human Rights Act and the convention. This is likely to have an increasing impact, particularly in relation to issues such as exchange of information and the non-discrimination provision of tax treaties.

---

[113] See above, n. 39, at 767. See, however, the dissenting opinion of Sir Christopher Staughton at 770-771.

[114] [2007] BTC 285 [2007] EWCA Civ 119, para. 23.

Scope of Tax Treaties: Taxes Covered and Territorial Scope

Chapter 4

13-000 Taxes covered

All treaties specify the taxes that are within their scope. The UK does not follow the OECD Model entirely in this respect. Typically, paras. 1 and 2 of art. 2 of the OECD Model specify the relevant taxes in general terms. A number of treaties, particularly those with Eastern European countries, do, however, adopt the OECD Model in describing the taxes covered in general terms. The Lithuanian Treaty provides an example:

> '2(1) This Convention shall apply to taxes on income and on capital gains imposed on behalf of a Contracting State or of its political subdivisions or local authorities, irrespective of the manner in which they are levied.
>
> 2(2) There shall be regarded as taxes on income and on capital gains all taxes imposed on total income or on elements of income including taxes on gains from the alienation of movable or immovable property.'

Identification of the UK taxes is important, firstly, in relation to determining the application of a treaty to residents of other contracting states. It also will specify the UK taxes against which foreign tax payable under the treaty may be credited. Treaties with countries where there are Federal constitutions may or may not extend the taxes to state or provincial taxes. The Canadian Treaty is limited to Federal tax (art. 2(1)(a)), as is the case with the US (art. 2(3)(a) (2001 treaty)). On the other hand, the Russian Treaty applies to taxes imposed 'on behalf of a contracting state or of its political subdivisions or local authorities' (art. 2(1)).

The most common UK approach is to describe the particular taxes covered by the treaty in question. This is reflected, for example, in the Bulgarian Treaty, art. 2(1) which reads:

> 'The taxes which are the subject of this Convention are:
>
> (a) in the UK:
>
>   (i) the income tax;
>   (ii) the corporation tax; and
>   (iii) the capital gains tax; (hereinafter referred to as "United Kingdom tax");'

Income tax or comprehensive treaties will typically cover all direct taxes. Thus, National Insurance contributions and similar charges are always excluded from these treaties, even though they are levied in parallel with income tax. The vintage of the treaty reflects the taxes levied at the time. Given the age of the treaty network, the taxes described in many treaties are often no longer in effect. For example, the German Treaty, art. 1(1)(b), covers the 'income tax (including surtax), the corporation tax and the capital gains tax'. Surtax was abolished from the year 1973–74 and was followed by the income tax system with graduated rates. Other early treaties make no reference to capital gains tax or corporation tax. See, for example, Belize, art. 1(1)(a), which refers to 'income tax (including surtax) and profits tax'.

Changes in the tax system are, however, catered for. This is covered by wording, of which art. 2(4) of the Korean Treaty is typical (see below):

> '2(4) The Convention shall apply also to any identical or substantially similar taxes which are imposed after the date of signature of this Convention in addition to, or in place of the existing taxes. The competent authorities of the Contracting States shall notify each other of any substantial changes which have been made in their respective taxation laws.'

The abolition of surtax and profits tax does not give rise to any uncertainty about whether the income tax in its present form is within those older treaties. Likewise, corporation tax is substantially similar. The same is true, it is suggested, where the capital gains tax is not referred to in a treaty.

There is, however, little guidance on these expressions. In *Ashanti Goldfields Corporation Limited v Merrifield* (1934) 19 TC 52, an income tax was imposed on holders of mining concessions in the Gold Coast Colony (now Ghana). The taxpayer, a UK-resident company, was expressly exempt from that tax. Evidence was presented that the reason for the exemption was because the company was paying a royalty based on its gross receipts from mining and oil extraction prior to the introduction of the tax. The Gold Coast Colony tax was itself creditable, and it was argued that the royalty on gross receipts corresponds to a 5 per cent tax on net profits and is a payment of the relevant tax, which corresponds with UK income tax. This argument failed.

The proper criteria for deciding whether a foreign tax corresponds to income and corporation tax were examined in *Yates v GCA International Limited*.[1] For the purposes of double tax relief, foreign tax must 'correspond to UK income tax' or corporation tax. Both parties agreed that this meant it should be in character or function or to be similar to. The Revenue accepted that the Venezuelan tax was charged on income but contended that it did not correspond to income tax or corporation tax in the UK. The Revenue formed this conclusion on the basis that the Venezuelan tax is a tax levied on 90 per cent of gross receipts and is not a tax on turnover. Scott J, however, looked at the Venezuelan Tax Code as a whole, which permitted the deduction of expenses generally. In this particular case, net income was deemed to be 90 per cent of gross receipts. Although this was unrealistic in the circumstances, it was not appropriate to pick out certain elements of the Venezuelan rules since as a whole they serve the same function as income tax and corporation tax do in the UK.

In *Bricom Holdings Limited v IRC* [1997] BTC 471; [1997] STC 1179 (CA), it was held that the CFC's charge under Taxes Act 1988, s. 747, was not corporation tax but a separate charge. It was argued that it is, however, 'substantially similar' to corporation tax. The difference between the CFC charge and corporation tax is principally that the tax is charged

---

[1] [1991] BTC 107; [1991] STC 157 (ChD).

only on UK-resident companies having interests in CFCs. It is not charged on the profits of the UK company itself, but on profits calculated basically, as for corporation tax, except that capital gains are not included. Certain assumptions must be made, such as that the company is not a close company and that it is not part of the group of the controlled foreign company apportioned to it and the only reliefs are as set out in Schedule 26. At para. 25, the Special Commissioners considered the tax base to be the most important factor in determining similarities, suggesting that a tax computed on the same base as corporation tax but charged on a specific class of company with some variations appropriate to that class, might well be substantially similar to corporation tax. The Special Commissioners considered that there were differences in not only the class of company charged but also the computation of profits – the person taxed on those profits and the reliefs available to be set off against it. The matter, they said, is one of degree, but they were inclined to the view that the differences from corporation tax are not so great as to prevent the CFC charge from being substantially similar to corporation tax. United Kingdom domestic law differs from treaties in this respect. Section 788 authorises treaties to make provisions for relief in relation to income tax and corporation tax. Authority for treaties to affect taxes 'of a similar character' only applies to the taxes imposed by the other contracting state.[2] Since the taxpayer's claim failed in the Court of Appeal on other grounds, this issue was not considered further.

Other taxes which feature or have featured in treaties include development land tax and petroleum revenue tax. Development land tax was abolished for events after 18 March 1985 by FA 1985, s. 93. At the time, the Revenue Statement of Practice SP4/84 expressed the view that development land tax was not covered by treaties entered into before it was enacted. It was specifically included in a number of treaties concluded in the 1960s, 1970s and 1980s up to the time of its repeal. Petroleum revenue tax is accepted as a tax similar to income tax, capital gains tax and corporation tax. Where a foreign tax is specifically identified in a treaty, then credit must be given. In relation to those treaties that follow the OECD Model in describing the taxes generally, it will be necessary to identify the taxes that are within the scope of the treaty. In most cases, these are helpfully identified in the HMRC *Double Tax Relief Manual*, although the absence of reference to specific taxes may mean that it is possible to argue that certain taxes not considered by the HMRC are within the scope of the treaty. The obligation on member states to exchange information on significant developments does not raise important issues for taxpayers.

13-050 Territorial scope

All UK treaties specify their territorial scope. Definitions of the expression 'United Kingdom' may vary from treaty to treaty. An early form is found in the Seychelles Treaty. Article 2(1)(a) reads:

> '2(1) In this Arrangement, unless the context otherwise requires–
>
> (a) The term 'United Kingdom' means Great Britain and Northern Ireland, excluding the Channel Islands and the Isle of Man.'

---

[2] S. 788(1)(c).

This closely matches the definition in the Interpretation Act 1978, Sch. 1, where the UK is defined to mean 'Great Britain and Northern Ireland'. Other early treaties, such as Israel, art. 2(1)(a), are in similar terms without the exclusion for the Channel Islands and Isle of Man.

However, virtually all treaties since the 1960s carry a more extended definition to include the UK areas of the Continental Shelf.[3] Even in those treaties, where there is no exclusion of the Channel Islands and the Isle of Man, these are not part of the UK. The UK is a party to the Convention on the Territorial Sea and the Contiguous Zone (Geneva, 29 April 1958; TS (3) 1965; CMND. 2511). Pursuant to this Convention, the sovereignty of a state extends beyond its land territory and its internal waters to a belt of sea adjacent to its coast referred to as the territorial sea (see art. 1(1)). The breadth of the area which constitutes territorial waters is not generally settled in international law and the precise scope may be dependent upon specific treaties for the purposes of those treaties and particular domestic statutes. In general, the UK adheres to a three-mile limit. In *Clark v Oceanic Contractors Inc.* ([1982] BTC 417; [1983] STC 35 (HL)), it was accepted that employees' duties performed in the UK sector of the North Sea were outside the UK. Although accepting that all UK statute is in principle territorial, it did not assist in determining what the precise boundary of that territory is.

It may be noted that the treaty provisions defining the territory of the other contracting state are not mirrored with the UK definitions. Each contracting state's territory is normally defined in accordance with its own constitutional norms. Thus, for example, landlocked countries such as Austria and the Czech Republic do not include any jurisdiction beyond territorial seas (Austria, art. 3(1)(b), and Czechoslovakia, art. 3(1)(b)). Some unusual variations are found in the Channel Islands. For example, in the case of Guernsey, it is defined as 'any island in which the Income Tax (Guernsey) Law 1950 is in force'.[4] In the case of Jersey, although 'United Kingdom' is defined, 'Jersey' is not.[5]

Under customary international law, the sovereignty of a state extends to the airspace above its territorial lands and sea. There appears to be no general upper limit of airspace. There are several treaties dealing with outer space. Pursuant to the Treaty on Principles Governing Activities of States in the Exploration and Use of Outer Space, Including the Moon and Other Celestial Bodies, outer space is free for exploration and use by all states.[6] There is no clearly defined lower limit. This is clearly material to activities carried on in space, particularly at lower levels, for example, whether a low level geostationary satellite constitutes a permanent establishment.

Inland waterways form part of the territorial waters of the UK. This includes rivers, lakes and sea areas which lie on the land ward side of the low waterline along the coast.[7] The

---

[3] See chapter 12, para. 21-150.

[4] Art. 2(1)(b).

[5] See *BTR* (1990), 302 to 312.

[6] 27 January 1967; TS 10 (1968); CMND. 3519.

[7] Territorial Waters Order in Council 1964, arts. 2–5.

operation of boats in these areas is nonetheless treated as the equivalent to international transport activity in treaties patterned on the OECD Model 8(2). United Kingdom treaty policy is, however, to exclude such activity from the benefit of art. 8.

Access to Treaty Benefits: Fiscal Domicile, Personality and Nationality

Chapter 5

14-000   Who is entitled to the benefits of a tax treaty?

The starting point of any analysis is art. 1 of the OECD Model Convention. This specifies that the 'Convention shall apply to persons who are residents of one or both of the contracting states'. The commentary to the OECD Model notes that, in principle, residents of a state should be entitled to treaty benefits.

This approach of the OECD is reflected in more recent UK treaties. The vast majority of treaties that the UK has entered into adopt the OECD Model, art. 1. There are, however, some 25 older treaties which do not include an article describing the scope of application of the treaty. Most of the treaties that do not have an article equivalent to art. 1 of the OECD Model are with Commonwealth countries. Other countries that do not have a general scope article include the treaties with Israel, the Isle of Man, Jersey and Guernsey. The extent to which some treaties limit their benefits to certain kinds of residents only is considered in chapter 16.[1]

14-050   Personality

In most cases, it will be necessary to be both a 'person' and a resident of one or both contracting states. The term 'person' is defined in treaties following the OECD Model to include 'an individual, a company and any other body of persons'. Thus, any entity endowed with legal personality will be a person for treaty purposes. These expressions may be contrasted with the domestic definitions contained in the Taxes Act 1988, s. 832(1):

> '"Body of persons" means any body politic, corporate or collegiate, and any company, fraternity, fellowship and society of persons whether corporate or not corporate ...
> "Company" is defined to mean ... any body corporate or unincorporated association, but does not include a partnership. '

The application of similar provisions was considered by the court in *Padmore v IRC*.[2] The Jersey Treaty contained a definition similar but not identical to the OECD Model. Although 'person' is deemed to include any 'body of persons, corporate or not corporate', no definition of 'body of persons' appears in the treaty. Article 2(3) of the treaty, however,

---

[1] The US Treaty follows the OECD Model broadly. However, it prefaces the general scope of art. 1 with: 'except as specifically provided'.

[2] *Padmore v IRC* [1989] BTC 221; [1987] BTC 3; [1987] STC 36, Ch.D.

provides that in the application of the treaty by the UK or Jersey, any term not otherwise defined must have the meaning which it has under the laws of the UK or Jersey, or as the case may be, relating to the taxes which are the subject of the Treaty, unless the context requires otherwise. Again, this is the OECD approach.

Partnerships do not have legal personality under Jersey or English law. Despite this, at that time, for UK income tax purposes, a partnership was assessed to trading profits on the partnership and was assessed separately from any other tax chargeable to the partners. Jersey income tax was similarly assessed. Residence for tax purposes was ascribed to partnerships by reference to management and control under both UK and Jersey law. The Court of Appeal decided that the definition of person was comprehensive and that a partnership is, as a matter of ordinary language, a body of persons. The Court refused to apply the domestic meaning.

Following the *Padmore* decision, the UK sought to include provisions in its treaties designed to protect its right to tax UK-resident partners on their share of income and gains of a foreign partnership, where the partnership qualifies for exemption from UK tax. An example is found in the Uzbekistan Treaty, and it reads:

> '24(1) Where, under any provision of this Convention, a partnership, joint venture or other entity is entitled, as a resident of Uzbekistan, to exemption from tax in the United Kingdom on any income or capital gains, that provision shall not be construed as restricting the right of the United Kingdom to tax any member of the partnership, joint venture or other entity who is a resident of the United Kingdom on his share of such income or capital gains; but any such income or gains shall be treated for the purposes of Article 22 of this Convention as income or gains from sources in Uzbekistan.'

The main effect of this provision is to compel transparency from the perspective of UK taxation with respect to UK participants in partnerships, joint ventures or other entities. Since such entities may not be treated as transparent in the other contracting state and subject to local taxation, the income or gains of UK participants is treated as foreign source income for the purpose of applying credit for foreign tax paid. The precise scope of application of the rule may give rise to difficulties. This is only partly addressed by reference to the definitions in, for example, art. 3 of the Uzbekistan Treaty, which treats a partnership or joint venture under Uzbekistan law as a taxable unit (art. 3(2)). The term 'company' means any body corporate or any entity which is treated as a body corporate for tax purposes. As a result, entities not treated as a body corporate for tax purposes under Uzbekistan law (but which might be 'taxable units') will be subject to transparent treatment in the UK with respect to UK-resident participants.

United Kingdom legal systems also contain anomalies in this respect.[3] A limited liability partnership formed under the Limited Liability Partnerships Act 2000 is a body corporate with legal personality separate from that of its members. Fiscal transparency is given, not by treating the LLP as transparent, but by generally treating its activities for tax purposes as not

---

[3] And similar legislation for Scotland and Northern Ireland.

carried on by it but by its members.[4] Thus, while the LLP itself may be a 'person' within art. 1, it will not be a resident of a contracting state from a UK tax perspective.

Foreign entity characterisation

In *Padmore*, the characterisation of the entity was the same for both UK and foreign purposes. The characterisation of a foreign entity as a company is to be determined (in England) for domestic purposes under the rules of English conflict of laws by reference to the general law of the country of incorporation in the case of a corporate entity. English law will recognise the existence of a corporation duly created in a foreign country as a matter of common law.[5] Whether the entity in question is a corporation will depend on the law of the country where it is formed.

The only statutory recognition of this rule applies if a question arises whether a body which purports to have or, as the case may be, appears to have lost corporate status under the laws of a territory which is not a recognised state should or should not be regarded as having legal personality as a body corporate under the law of any part of the UK. Under the Foreign Corporations Act 1991, if it appears that the laws of that country are at that time applied by a settled court system in that territory, the question and other material questions relating to the body must be determined and account must be taken of those laws as if the territory were a recognised state.

There are few cases either in tax or general law on this. An entity which according to its proper law possesses certain aspects of separate personality may not necessarily be regarded as a corporation. In *Von Hellfeld v Rechnitzer & Mayer Freres & Co.*,[6] it was held that a French partnership could not be sued in its own name in the absence of evidence that by French law, the partnership was a different legal entity from its partners. In *Dreyfus v IRC*,[7] the court referred to French law in determining whether a Societe en nom collectif (SNC) constituted a company or not. UK-resident members in the SNC successfully proved that under French law, an SNC was a legal person. Consequently, the members were not liable to UK super tax on the entity's profits as they arose. In that case, the question was whether the entity was a partnership or a company. HMRC now views the SNC as transparent; see also *Ryall v du Bois Co. Ltd*,[8] where a German GmbH was treated on analogy to an English private company.

As a result of these rules, the possibility arises for entities to be treated as corporations for UK tax purposes even though in the country of their formation, they may be deemed to be fiscally transparent by the local tax law.

Administrative practice has adopted somewhat different terminology in dealing with entity classification. HMRC describes entities as fiscally 'transparent' or 'opaque'. In the case of a

---

[4] See ITTOIA 2005, s. 863.

[5] *Lazzards Bros & Co. v Midland Bank Ltd* [1933] AC 289, HL.

[6] [1914] 1 Ch. 748, CA.

[7] [1956] AC 39.

[8] (1933) 18 TC 431.

'transparent' entity, the member is regarded as being entitled to a share in the underlying income of the entity as it arises. A member in an 'opaque' entity is taxed only on the distributions made by the entity.[9] HMRC has published a list of entities that it has examined and regard as being transparent or opaque.[10] It does not regard the expressions 'transparent' and 'opaque' as being interchangeable with 'partnership' or 'body corporate'. Thus, although a partnership is fiscally transparent for the purpose of UK tax on income, a fiscally transparent entity is not necessarily a partnership. The *Stamp Duty Manual* also contains a list of entities which have been considered as bodies corporate for the purpose of stamp duty.

The criteria that HMRC applies in deciding whether a UK resident has an interest in a foreign business entity which results in UK tax on the resident's share of profits of the entity as they arise or whether they are taxed on distribution only is determined according to matters such as:

(a) legal existence separate from that of its members;
(b) the existence of share capital or something else which serves the same function as share capital;
(c) whether the business is carried on by the entity itself or jointly by its members;
(d) whether members are entitled to share in its profits as they arise or amount of profits to which they are entitled depend on a decision of the entity or its members after the period in which the profits have arisen to make a distribution of its profits;
(e) is the entity or are the members responsible for debts incurred as a result of carrying on the business;
(f) do the assets used for carrying on the business belong beneficially to the entity or the members.

Treaty classification

The precise manner in which an entity is classified for treaty purposes will depend upon the particular treaty in question. Article 3(1)(b) of the OECD Model defines a company as any body corporate or other entity which is treated as a body corporate for tax purposes. Although the first part of the definition is similar to the UK domestic law definition, it requires the status of a body corporate to be determined by reference to tax rules rather than the general law. Apart from the statutory provisions, UK tax law determines corporate status by reference to the general law. This definition itself does not explain which contracting states tax purposes are relevant in this respect. The country of residence will apply its law in deciding whether a 'person' is a resident of that contracting state. Where a foreign entity is treated as a corporation for UK purposes and qualifies for treaty benefits, the significance of this classification varies from treaty to treaty. Thereafter, it refers to the contracting state for the purposes of the tax of the contracting state where the convention is to apply. In other words, where UK tax is in question, UK classification is relevant. This would, as described above, point to the domestic general law of the other contracting state. Most UK treaties, and indeed the OECD Model, do not generally distinguish between benefits available to

---

[9] *Tax Bulletin* (No. 83, June 2006).

[10] *Ibid.*

companies as opposed to other taxpayers. Classification as a company will principally determine entitlement to treaty benefits as a person resident in a member state.

Treaty benefits and transparent entities

The 2001 US Treaty addresses fiscal transparency directly. Article 1(8) specifies that an item of income derived through a person that is fiscally transparent under the laws of either contracting state is regarded as derived by a resident of a contracting state to the extent that the item is treated for the purpose of the tax law of that contracting state as the income of the resident. This corresponds in general to the administrative practice adopted by HMRC, which takes the view that for UK tax purposes, limited liability companies (LLCs) formed under the laws of various states of the US should be regarded as taxable entities and not as fiscally transparent. They do not in principle recognise LLCs as qualifying for treaty benefits, but accept treaty claims from LLCs to the extent that the income in question is subject to US tax in the hands of those members of the LLC who are residents of the US.[11] The logical extension of this treatment is to permit benefits under the treaty for a member of a US LLC resident in a third country, and not to deny it by virtue of participation in the LLC.

Subsequent treaties have addressed this issue in more detail. For example, residence state classification is treated as determinative by art. 4(5)(a) of the Japanese Treaty, which requires the source state to accord treaty benefits to residents of the other state who are the members of a transparent entity established in the same state as the members, without regard to the way in which it would be treated in the source state. Similarly, where the state of residence of an entity and its members treats the entity as the taxpayer, then the source state must grant treaty benefits on that basis regardless of the source state classification of the entity.[12] On the other hand, where the entity is established in the source state and the entity is treated as non-transparent in the other state, treaty benefits are not available in respect of its income.[13]

Fiscal transparency

The fact that an entity does not qualify as a 'person' will not automatically produce fiscal transparency. In *Memec plc v Inland Revenue Commissioners*,[14] a UK company (Plc) was the silent partner in a silent partnership under German law with a German resident and incorporated company (GmbH). It made a capital contribution to GmbH and obtained in return a contractual right to payment of 87.84 per cent of the annual profits of the partnership. Under German law, GmbH remained the owner of the business assets and of the income from those assets. Plc, as the silent partner, had no proprietary interest in the assets. GmbH ran the business. A silent partnership has no separate legal personality under German law.

---

[11] DT 19853A.

[12] UK–Japan Treaty, art. 4(5)(b).

[13] See UK–Japan Treaty, art. 4(5)(c), and 2008 UK–France Treaty, which elaborates on these concepts further.

[14] [1998] BTC 251; [1998] STC 754, CA.

The dispute involved whether the income should be identified as dividends from a trading subsidiary of the silent partnership, divisible and distributable after expenses as prescribed by the partnership agreement or should be identified as Plc's contractual right under the partnership agreement to payment of the prescribed share of partnership profit.

After considering the categorisation of entities under both foreign and English law, Robert Walker J[15] concluded that the arrangement embodied in the silent partnership was not transparent. Transparency, he said, is normally associated with a situation where the ultimate recipient of the underlying income in question has a beneficial interest in it from the start. If the income is not transmuted at some intermediate stage, for example, by the need for trustees to exercise a discretion or by its being packaged so as to reach the ultimate recipient in the form of a fixed annuity or other form which is different from the underlying income, then the entity is transparent. This view was shared by the Court of Appeal.

In this case, the UK company did not receive or become entitled to dividends paid by the trading subsidiary. It was only entitled to an amount determined by reference to the dividends rather than the dividends themselves. Consequently, it could not qualify directly for treaty relief by way of credit for underlying tax paid by the trading subsidiary.

14-100   Residence

The following section discusses the issues surrounding residence.

Are treaty benefits for residents of contracting states only?

As a matter of UK law, the absence of wording defining the scope of application of the treaty means that residents of third countries may be entitled to the benefit of treaties that their country of residence is not a party to. This point was clearly made by the High Court in *Inland Revenue Commissioners v Commerzbank AG and Inland Revenue Commissioners v Banco do Brasil SA.*[16] The 1945 US Treaty at that time contained no general scope provision. Article XV specified that:

> 'Dividends and interest paid by a corporation of one contracting party shall be exempt from tax by the other contracting party except where the recipient is a citizen, resident or corporation of that other contracting party. This exemption shall not apply if the corporation paying such dividend or interest is a resident of the other contracting party.'

The crucial issue in the case was whether the two banks incorporated in Germany and Brazil respectively were entitled to claim the benefit of an exemption from UK tax on interest paid to their UK branches by US corporations under the US Treaty. The Inland Revenue argued vigorously that treaty benefits ought not to be conferred on persons who were not residents or citizens of the US. Before the Special Commissioners, the Inland Revenue solicitor argued that benefits should not be so conferred unless they were explicitly included. It was argued that in bilateral treaties there is a presumption against an intention to benefit third

---

[15] In the Chancery Division [1996] BTC 590; [1996] STC 1136.

[16] [1990] BTC 172; [1990] STC 285, Ch.D.

parties. This was rejected by the Special Commissioners, and similarly by the High Court. In the *Banco do Brasil* case,[17] the Commissioner noted that the State of Brazil was not involved and that all private persons, including those connected with the state entering into the agreement, are in this context third parties. In the *Commerzbank* decision, the Special Commissioner was of the view that the question of third party rights was only concerned with the acquisition of rights by third party states. He preferred the view of McNair's *Law of Treaties*[18] to the effect that, provided that the necessary implementation by municipal law has been carried out, there is nothing to prevent the nationals of single 'third states' in the absence of any express or implied provision to the contrary from claiming the rights or becoming subject to the obligations created by a treaty.

It was also argued before the Commissioners that almost all of the articles of the treaty were concerned with citizens, residents and corporations of contracting parties. The Commissioners found that this particular article was not. It was also argued by the Inland Revenue before the Commissioners that there was a general principle of treaties that the branches of non-resident corporations should be taxed in the country in which they were situated. No support for this was found other than a reference to the OECD Model Convention and the Commissioner noted that unusual provisions do find their way into treaties.

In the case of Brazil, there was no treaty. The Special Commissioner merely noted that this would mean that the Brazilian authorities could not participate in competent authority proceedings. The Inland Revenue tried to argue that in the context of *Commerzbank*, the German–US Treaty operated to exempt from US taxation the amounts of interest paid to the branch which were the subject of the appeal. The Special Commissioner regarded it as incongruous if the effect of an article of the UK–US Treaty were to depend on the existence of otherwise of a treaty between one or other of those countries or one or more third countries.

On appeal to the High Court, Mummery J was firmly of the view that the natural and ordinary meaning of the words of art. XV was clear. Interest paid by US corporations was exempt from UK tax except where the recipient was a UK citizen, resident or corporation. This was so despite the fact that the claim for treaty benefits was made by a Brazilian and German resident respectively.

The submission by the Crown was that the treaty read as a whole dealt almost exclusively with the right to tax or waive the right to tax citizens or residents of and corporations of a contracting party. In the absence of express words to that effect, this ought to mean that the article in question should have been interpreted as not waiving the right to tax a corporation of a non-contracting party. Mummery J noted, however, that the Crown did accept, by the time the case reached the High Court, that there was no legal reason why a treaty cannot deal with rights and obligations of persons other than citizens, residents and corporations of the contracting parties. The court observed that at the time, the treaty did not contain wording equivalent to art. 1 of the OECD Model Convention.

---

[17] At 293.

[18] McNair, AD, *The Law of Treaties* (1961), Oxford: Clarendon Press.

Mummery J concluded that this construction did not give rise to any manifestly absurd or unreasonable consequences. There was no sufficient indication in the purpose of the treaty or in its surrounding circumstances or in the provisions other than the article in question to qualify the clear words. There were articles in the treaty which did not exclude persons from non-contracting parties from tax exemptions conferred by the treaty. There are also articles which expressly identify those who come within the benefit of the provisions and confine the scope of the provisions to those who are citizens or residents of one of the contracting parties. There was no such express restriction in art. XV. The exemption was therefore defined by reference to the character of the source of income and not to any characteristic of the recipient of the income from that source.

The decision has been criticised, particularly on the basis that McNair's statement does not support the proposition claimed by the court.[19] Nonetheless, the decision was not appealed and treaties should be read against the background of this decision.

Most of the treaties that do not contain a personal scope article are with Commonwealth countries and are very old. In each of these treaties, the scope of application generally emerges from the text of individual provisions and there do not appear to be any major lacunae of the kind which gave rise to the *Commerzbank* case.

Non-discrimination

The UK has not included the final sentence of art. 24(1) of the OECD Model into any treaties. That sentence states specifically that nationals of a contracting state may not be discriminated against even if they are not resident in either of the contracting states in question. The wording is the only express recognition of the extension of treaty benefits to residents of third countries in the model.

14-150   Who is a resident for treaty purposes?

The concept of 'resident of a contracting state' fulfils a crucial role in determining the treaty's personal scope of application. In the majority of treaties which contain a personal scope article, qualification as a resident of a contracting state is the *sine qua non* of a claim to treaty benefits. The approach to residence as adopted in UK treaties has an impact on the ability of persons in third countries to benefit from treaties, in addition to resolving dual residence problems.

OECD definition

The vast majority of treaties follow the OECD models. A number follow the 1963 OECD Draft Convention, which states that a 'resident of a contracting State' means any person who under the law of that state is liable to tax therein by reason of his domicile, residence, place of management or any other criterion of a similar nature. The 1977 model added the wording to exclude from this term any person who is liable to tax in that state in respect only

---

[19] [1990] *BTR* 388 at 391. See also Vogel, K, *Klaus Vogel on Double Taxation Conventions*, 2nd edn (1994), p. 5.

of income from sources in that state or capital situated therein. The current version, as it appears in the Iceland Treaty, reads:

'Article 4: Fiscal domicile

4(1) In this convention, the term "resident of a Contracting State" means any person who, under the laws of that State, is liable to tax therein by reason of his domicile, residence, place of management or any other criterion of a similar nature. But this term does not include any person who is liable to tax in that State in respect only of income or capital gains from sources in that State.'

The commentary notes that this is intended to apply to various forms of personal attachment to a state which form the basis of comprehensive taxation, that is, a worldwide basis. The second sentence of the definition, added in 1977, was intended to exclude a person subject only to taxation limited to income from sources within that state. The commentary on this second sentence was amended in 1992 to take into account the Conduit Company Report. The commentary now expresses the view that according to its wording and spirit, this sentence would exclude from the definition of a resident of a contracting state, foreign held companies exempted from tax on their foreign income by privileges tailored to attract conduit companies.

The commentary does, however, recognise that this has inherent difficulties and limitations. It must therefore be interpreted restrictively because otherwise it might exclude from the scope of treaties all residents of countries adopting a territorial principle in their taxation a result, which, the commentary says, is clearly not intended.

In the context of treaty shopping, this amended text in the commentary seems a clumsy and ineffective method of attempting to restrict treaty benefits. It is far from clear that the wording of the article has the effect contended for in the revised commentary. Indeed, the natural wording might instead suggest that all taxpayers on a source basis only would be excluded from treaty benefits rather than those specifically foreign-owned companies designed to attract conduit operations. It seems unlikely that such an approach would be upheld by the courts simply on the strength of the commentary, particularly in the light of other anti-avoidance provisions available and, specifically, look-through and excluded entity rules. It is submitted that such specific provisions are the only realistic method of countering the issue raised in this paragraph of the commentary. The negotiating position of the UK, revealed in treaties signed since the OECD Commentary was amended, would suggest that the Revenue places little faith in this interpretation to prevent conduit operations.

Colonial definition

The older treaties, following the colonial pattern, adopt an entirely different approach to the question of residence. They generally state that a UK resident is any person resident in the UK for UK tax purposes and not resident in the other contracting state for the purpose of that state's tax and vice versa. In the case of companies, they are normally regarded as resident in the UK for treaty purposes if their business is managed and controlled in the UK and resident in the other contracting state if the business is managed and controlled in that contracting state. For example, the treaty with Grenada reads:

'2(g) The terms "resident of the UK" and "resident of Grenada" mean respectively any person who is resident in the UK for the purposes of United Kingdom tax and not resident in Grenada for the purposes of Grenada tax and any person who is resident in Grenada for the purposes of Grenada tax and not resident in the UK for the purposes of UK tax; and a company shall be regarded as resident in the UK if its business is managed and controlled in the UK and as resident in Grenada if its business is managed and controlled in Grenada.'

The HMRC view is that the management and control test for companies does not prevent the operation of the first test, which refers to the domestic law of the contracting states.[20] It is on this basis, for example, that HMRC argues that exempt companies in the Channel Islands cannot claim treaty benefits. This conclusion is far from clear and may not be consistent with the specific exclusions of tax-favoured entities from entitlement to treaty benefits or HMRC's approach, as shown by the Crown's arguments in *Forth Investments Ltd v IRC*.[21]

The practical application of this form of residence clause came before the courts in the *Forth Investments* case. This involved a company incorporated in Barbados under the International Business Companies (Exemption from Income Tax) Act 1965. Essentially, that act allows Barbados companies that are foreign owned and do not carry on business in Barbados to pay tax at a reduced rate of $2\frac{1}{2}$ per cent. Unlike the current version, the 1949 Barbados Treaty did not exclude international business companies from claiming treaty benefits.

In the *Forth Investments* case, evidence indicated that the shares in the company were issued to a Bahamas company. It emerged that the structure formed part of a complicated arrangement to avoid UK tax and ultimately a UK-resident individual accepted liability under s. 478 of ICTA 1970.[22] Although the arrangement did not form part of the subject matter of the case it likely induced a degree of scepticism about the facts presented.

The Inland Revenue refused to allow the claim on the basis that it was not satisfied that the company was resident in Barbados. The company had submitted a treaty claim form duly completed together with a certificate of authentication from the Barbados Deputy Commissioner of Inland Revenue. Only some of the additional information in support of the claim had been submitted, including the names and addresses of directors, a list of directors meetings and copies of some but not all minutes of those meetings. The case ultimately turned on the admissibility of evidence that the business of the company was managed and controlled in Barbados and the certificate by the taxation authorities of Barbados that the company was a resident of Barbados. The court also rejected an argument that the company must be viewed as resident in Barbados if it was accepted that the company was subject to tax in Barbados because it would only be subject to tax if it was resident and that this had been accepted by the Inland Revenue. This argument was regarded by Brightman J as circular, and residence was not found to have been admitted by the Revenue.

The case was decided on the basis of evidentiary issues only. It is, however, implicit in the decision that the court considered that it was entitled to consider the treaty definition of residence quite separately from how it was treated for the tax laws of the other contracting

---

[20] HMRC, *International Tax Handbook*, para. 520.

[21] (1971-1977) 50 TC 617; [1976] STC 399, Ch.D.

[22] Now ITA 2007, s. 721.

state. The company was treated as a resident of Barbados by the Barbados tax administration. This was not determinative or even influential and evidence of the tax treatment in Barbados was dismissed as hearsay. There was no suggestion that this meant that the first test of residence in the treaty was satisfied. The exclusion of the evidence was on procedural grounds and not too much should be read into the decision. Despite this, the treaty definition of management and control only was applied to determine the residence of the company for treaty purposes.[23]

Thus, unlike the OECD test, which refers simply to the domestic definition of the contracting states, the colonial style treaty adopts its own definition of corporate residence. While most Commonwealth countries adopt a form of management and control test of company residence, presumably a UK court would interpret the concept in accordance with UK law; there may be a divergence of approach between the UK and a foreign country, resulting in a company being resident for treaty purposes although not necessarily for the purposes of the other contracting state's domestic law. These treaties refer to 'management and control' rather than to 'central management and control'.

Deemed residents

It has become the practice, at least in treaties with major industrial nations to expand the definition of residence beyond that in art. 1 of the OECD Model. Residence is defined in art. 4(1) of the 2001 US Treaty in a manner that is more consistent with the OECD Model but includes a reference to citizenship. Several uncertainties in interpreting the OECD wording are also addressed. These include specific inclusion of pension schemes and other employee benefit schemes that are exempt from tax, as well as religious, charitable, scientific and other institutions that may similarly be exempt from tax under domestic law.[24] A similar approach is found in the 2006 Japan Treaty,[25] and the 2008 France Treaty contains the following:

'4(4) The term "resident of a contracting State" shall include where that Contracting State is France any partnership, group of persons or any other similar entity:

(a)   which has its place of effective management in France;

(b)   which is subject to tax in France; and

(c)   all of whose shareholders, associates or members are, pursuant to the tax laws of France, personally liable to tax therein in respect of their share of the profits of that partnership, group of persons or other similar entity.'

14-200   Dual residence: the tie-breaker

A person who is resident in both contracting states falls within the person scope of treaties. Where this happens, modern treaties seek to resolve the question in favour of one of the contracting states for the purpose of applying the treaty under art. 4(2) of the OECD Model,

---

[23] See *Trevor Smallwood Trusts v R & C Commrs* (2008) Sp C 669, para. 68, where a certificate of residence from the tax authorities in Mauritius was uncontested and the only evidence of Mauritian residence.

[24] Art. 4(3).

[25] Art. 4(1).

in the case of individuals, and art. 4(3), in other cases. Once the residence is resolved in favour of one of the contracting states, the treaty is read as if the person is a resident of that state only. Dual residence can arise in two contexts. First, concurrent continuous residence will occur when both states regard the person as resident within their territory during the same period under their respective domestic laws. This will arise from conflicting criteria in the UK and the other contracting state. Thus, an individual may live in France but by regularly visiting the UK for around three months a year (but exceeding 90 days in a tax year), the individual will be treated (at least according to HMRC Practice)[26] as resident in the UK. This will be the case despite also being resident in France for French tax purposes.

The second case of dual residence is where a person is consecutively resident in the two states by moving from one to the other part way through the tax year, and as a result being resident in both states but at different times. This second case is of particular importance in UK treaty practice because there is no differentiation of tax treatment during such periods of residence and non-residence in a single tax year under domestic law for income tax or capital gains tax purposes.[27] In such cases it will be necessary to test the residence of the taxpayer at the time the relevant item of income or gain arises such as when a dividend is paid for the purpose of applying the dividend article (OECD Model, art.10) or when an asset is disposed of for the purpose of applying the capital gains article (OECD Model, art. 13).

These circumstances occurred in *Trevor Smallwood Trust v R & C Commrs*,[28] where the trust in question was resident in Mauritius under Mauritian domestic law from 19 December 2000 to 2 March 2001 ('the Mauritius Period') and resident in the UK under UK domestic law from 2 March 2001 to 5 April 2001 ('the UK Period'). Both the Revenue and the taxpayer agreed that is it possible to apply the treaty to residence for part of the year but disagreed on the consequences.[29] The taxpayer argued that residence for treaty purposes at the moment of alienation only is relevant, or in the alternative (with which the Revenue agreed) the whole of the Mauritius Period. Both parties agreed that the consequence is that, during the Mauritius Period, the trustee is a resident only of Mauritius for the purpose of the treaty. Both parties also agreed that, if there is dual residence, it is to be dealt with by applying the tie-breaker and that this should apply separately to each period.[30] The Special Commissioners preferred to rely on their own third hypothesis that 'liability to tax is equated to treaty residence in Article 4(1)'. In other words, chargeability to tax under TCGA 1992, s. 2, means residence for treaty purposes even though s. 2 only requires residence for part of the year, and the disposal need not take place in that part. If that were the case the non-resident is UK resident throughout the tax year, and thus the tie-breaker is always engaged. This third approach is neither supported by the wording of TCGA 1992, s. 2, nor art. 4(1) and is plainly contrary to the purpose of the treaty as a whole and art. 4 in particular. In coming to this conclusion, the Special Commissioners claimed support (wrongly) from

---

[26] IR 20, para. 3.2.

[27] TCGA 1992. s. 2(1).

[28] (2008) Sp C 669.

[29] See chapter 11, para. 20-000.

[30] The language of TCGA 1992, s. 83A, is drafted on this assumption. See chapter 11, para. 20-150.

para. 10 of the commentary to art. 4 of the OECD model added in 2000 (after the Mauritius Treaty was made):

'The facts to which the special rules [i.e. the tie-breaker in article 4(2) applicable to individuals] will apply are those existing during the period when the residence of the taxpayer affects tax liability, which may be less than an entire taxable period. For example, in one calendar year an individual is a resident of State A under that State's tax laws from 1 January to 31 March, then moves to State B. Because the individual resides in State B for more than 183 days, the individual is treated by the tax laws of State B as a State B resident for the entire year. Applying the special rules to the period 1 January to 31 March, the individual was a resident of State A. Therefore, both State A and State B should treat the individual as a State A resident for that period, and as a State B resident from 1 April to 31 December.'

The paragraph quoted supports the contrary conclusion, namely that split year treatment is the appropriate result in cases of consecutive residence where the taxpayer is resident in both states throughout the tax year under both domestic laws.

Resolving dual residence: individuals

Domestic law on individual residence lends itself to dual residence problems. First, residence for part of a tax year means residence for the whole tax year. There are no statutory rules which apportion tax years of arrival and departure as a matter of law between periods of residence and non-residence. Second, the UK applies two separate tests of residence in this context, namely *residence simpliciter* and ordinary residence. Third, the question of residence is essentially one of fact and a matter of degree. In particular, the circumstances of a taxpayer's visits to the UK may be of such a nature or may be either prolonged or repeated, so as to cause the taxpayer to become resident even though on average he or she spent only something over a quarter of the tax year in the UK.[31] Moreover, such visits may also make a taxpayer ordinarily resident.[32]

This means that regular visitors to the UK, for a significant minority of their time, will become resident. Other anomalies may arise in relation to dual residence resulting from the unusual UK tax year ending on 5 April. Conversely, total absence throughout a tax year is not necessarily conclusive of non-residence.[33] Under the Taxes Act 1988, s. 334, where a Commonwealth citizen or citizen of the Irish Republic whose ordinary residence has been in the UK, leaves the UK for a purpose only of occasional residence abroad, then such an individual will be regarded during that period of absence as actually residing in the UK. This applies where 'a person who is not for a time actually residing in the UK, but who has constructively his residence there because his ordinary place of abode and his home is there, although he is absent for a time from it, however long continued that absence may be'.[34]

---

[31] *Lysaght v IRC* [1928] AC 234.

[32] *Levene v IRC* [1928] AC 217.

[33] See *Reed v Clark* [1985] BTC 224; [1985] STC 325, Ch.D.

[34] *Lloyd v Sulley* (1884) 2 TC 37, at 42.

Resolution of dual residence in UK treaties is far from uniform. In the case of dual resident individuals, this is addressed in treaties patterned on the OECD Model. A typical example is found in art. 3(2) of the French Treaty, which reads as follows:

'Where by reason of the provisions of paragraph (1) an individual is a resident of both Contracting States, then this case shall be determined in accordance with the following rules:

(a)   He shall be deemed to be a resident of the Contracting State in which he has a permanent home available to him. If he has a permanent home available to him in both Contracting States, he shall be deemed to be a resident of the Contracting State with which his personal and economic relations are closest (centre of vital interests).

(b)   If the Contracting State in which he has his centre of vital interests cannot be determined, or if he has not a permanent home available to him in either Contracting State, he shall be deemed to be a resident of the Contracting State in which he has an habitual abode.

(c)   If he has an habitual abode in both Contracting States or in neither of them, he shall be deemed to be a resident of the Contracting State of which he is a national.

(d)   If he is a national of both Contracting States or of neither of them, the competent authorities of the Contracting States shall settle the question by mutual agreement.'

There have been no cases on the detailed application of the tie-breaker. *Squirrell v R & C Commrs*[35] is the only UK decision that refers to art. 4(2) but is unsatisfactory in that the taxpayer was unrepresented and made only confused written submissions. Nonetheless, the Special Commissioner's helpful comments do shed light on important aspects of the operation of the tie-breaker. The taxpayer was a UK national married to a US citizen. He lived and worked in the UK until 17 October 2000, when he left to live in the US with his wife. He was resident and ordinarily resident in the UK until 17 October 2000 and not resident and not ordinarily resident from the following day. He worked for British Airways plc until 31 March 2000. On 1 April 2000, he received a termination payment, which was in lieu of notice of £92,957.89, from which UK income tax at 23 per cent was deducted under PAYE. He claimed exemption from UK tax under the (1975) US Treaty on the basis that the income was taxed in the US jointly with that of his wife, who was taxable there throughout the year as a citizen. However, no claim was made in either country to determine his residence status under art. 4(2) for the purposes of the treaty and without it the treaty could not be applied. However, the result was the same from the UK point of view as it would have been taxable in the UK under art. 15 (Employment income) because of either residence or performing duties in the UK when it was earned. The Special Commissioner noted that taxpayer applied for treaty relief in the wrong country.

Dual residence: companies

Although treaties patterned on the OECD Model contain tie-breaker provisions, a number of early treaties do not. Those following the colonial pattern (see Grenada above) define residence both positively and negatively. A resident of a contracting state is a resident of one contracting state who is not also resident in the other contracting state. The effect of these treaties is that dual residents are excluded from treaty benefits. The 1975 US Treaty contained a tie-breaker in relation to individuals and trusts (arts. 4(2) and (3)). There were no provisions for resolving dual residence of companies. Dual resident companies were specifically addressed in art. 1(2). They were not entitled to claim any relief or exemption

---

[35]   (2005) Sp C 493.

from tax under the treaty with limited specified exceptions. Similar definitions of residence were found in the 1946 US Treaty, with the additional criteria of citizenship. This gave rise to considerable difficulties of application.[36] The 2001 US Treaty provides no tie-breaker for a person other than an individual who is a resident of both contracting states. Where dual residence of persons other than individuals occurs, art. 4(5) of that treaty requires the competent authorities of the contracting states to endeavour to determine by mutual agreement the mode of application of the treaty to those persons. If they do not, such persons are not entitled to claim any treaty benefit except those provided by para. 4 of art. 24(4), art. 25 (Non-discrimination) and art. 26 (Mutual Agreement Procedure).

The impact of treaty residence on domestic law

Where a company is treated as resident in the UK for domestic tax purposes but is treated as resident outside the UK and not resident in the UK for the purposes of any treaty, then it is treated as not resident in the UK for all domestic tax purposes.[37] This is except in relation to the case of the controlled foreign company charge by s. 747(1)(b) of the Taxes Act 1988, inserted by FA 2002, s. 90. In such a case, the company is therefore non-resident for all other purposes. This treatment is automatic and no claim for relief under the relevant treaty is required.[38] A company resident in the UK as a result of its place of incorporation or place of central management and control will clearly be a resident of the UK under this definition. If the central management and control is also in another jurisdiction, the company will still be a UK resident, at least for the purposes of art. 4(1) of the OECD Model.

Central management and control

From 15 March 1988, a company which is incorporated in the UK is regarded as resident there.[39] Certain limited exceptions apply to some UK incorporated companies which were prior to that date resident outside the UK.[40] Companies incorporated outside the UK continue to be subject to the case law test, which applied to all companies prior to 15 March 1988. This test was enunciated at the beginning of the twentieth century in *De Beers Consolidated Mines v Howe*,[41] in which Lord Loreburn said:

> 'A company resides, for the purposes of income tax, where its real business is carried on . . . I regard that as the true rule; and the real business is carried on where the central management and control actually abides.'

Successive cases have consistently applied the central management and control test. The question of where central management and control actually abides is one of fact. It is distinguished from the place where the company's trade or business is conducted. Under UK

---

[36] See *Strathalmond v IRC* (1972) 48 TC 537, *Avery Jones v IRC* (1973-1978) 51 TC 443; [1976] STC 290 and *IRC v Exxon Corporation* [1982] BTC 182; [1982] STC 356.

[37] FA 1994, s. 249(1).

[38] *Ibid.*, s. 249(3).

[39] FA 1988, s. 66.

[40] *Ibid.*, Sch. 7.

[41] (1906) 5 TC 198.

domestic law, a company may be resident in two jurisdictions.[42] Thus, central management and control can be divided on a geographical basis, so that a company can have a dual residence.

Management and control

Treaties following the colonial pattern refer to 'management and control', rather than 'central management and control'. It may be argued that the two are distinct notions – with 'central management and control' under domestic law referring to the highest level of decision-making authority and 'management and control' referring to a lower level of management of the company's business. The attraction of such an approach is that it may assist in resolving some dual residence conflicts. If the two expressions are synonymous, then only a more limited category of conflicts over residence are addressed.

Place of effective management

The tie-breaker in the case of dual corporate residence under the OECD Model is found in art. 4(3) of the Italian Treaty, and it reads as follows:

'4(3) Where by reason of the provisions of paragraph (1) of this Article a person other than an individual is a resident of both Contracting States, then it shall be deemed to be a resident of the Contracting State in which its place of effective management is situated.'

There is little authority on the application of the tie-breaker in UK law. As a matter of administrative practice, the Inland Revenue changed its view as between the 1997 and 1992 Model Conventions. At one time, its view was that the UK concept of 'central management and control' meant the same thing as 'place of effective management'; there was a note to this effect in the commentary on the 1977 OECD Model Double Taxation Convention. HMRC now no longer believes that necessarily to be so, and the note did not appear in the 1992 edition of the OECD Model. The place of effective management, it says, is generally understood to be the place where the head office is – not the head office in the sense of the registered office but the central directing source, the place where one would expect to find, for example, the finance director, the sales director and, if there is one, the managing director. The company records would normally be found there together with the senior administrative staff.[43]

The Revenue is of the view that its revised idea of effective management is nearer to other EU member states' management tests than is central management and control. Nevertheless, the Revenue believes it is not that easy to divorce effective management from central management and control, and, in the vast majority of cases, they will be located in the same place.

Current administrative practice is contained in Statement of Practice SP1/90, para. 22, which reads as follows:

---

[42] *Swedish Central Railway Co. Ltd v Thompson* (1925) 9 TC 342.

[43] HMRC, *International Tax Manual*, para. INT348.

'The Commentary in paragraph 3 of Article 4 of the OECD Model records the United Kingdom view that, in agreements (such as those with some Commonwealth countries) which treat a company as resident in a state in which "its business is managed and controlled", this expression means "the effective management of the enterprise". More detailed consideration of the question in the light of the approach of Continental legal systems and of Community law to the question of company residence has led the Revenue to revise this view. It is now considered that effective management may, in some cases, be found at a place different from the place of central management and control. This could happen, for example, where a company is run by executives based abroad, but the final directing power rests with non-executive directors who meet in the United Kingdom. In such circumstances the company's place of effective management might well be abroad but, depending on the precise powers of the non-executive directors, it might be centrally managed and controlled (and therefore resident) in the United Kingdom.'

HMRC now says that 'effective management will normally be located in the same country as central management and control but may be located at the company's true centre of operations, where central management and control is exercised elsewhere'.[44]

The first judicial decision to address the tie-breaker is *Trustees of Wensleydale's Settlement v IRC*.[45] The case turned on whether the trustees of a settlement were deemed to be resident in the Republic of Ireland by virtue of the tie-breaker in the UK–Irish Treaty. In that case, reference was made to *Klaus Vogel on Double Taxation Conventions* in which it was said that the 'place of management' in German Treaty practice is very similar to the 'place of effective management', since the former depends on factual conditions. This followed German case law, which established that the place of management is the centre of top level management, that is, where the management's important policies are actually made.

In the *Wensleydale* case, both the taxpayer and the Inland Revenue agreed that the 'centre of top level management' was a good description of the place of effective management. Cases dealing with 'central management and control' were referred to in this respect. On the facts, the Special Commissioner found that the Irish-resident trustees acted as such in name rather than in reality. Although the trustee signed all the documents placed before her, the Special Commissioner believed that she would have fallen in with whatever the settlor requested. The distinction in this case was thus between management that was effective as opposed to management that was apparent or ineffective. The case offers little assistance in addressing the distinction between 'central management and control' and effective management, particularly as both the taxpayer and the Inland Revenue offered as authority cases which deal with the domestic law concept of central management and control.

Wood v Holden[46] concerned a Netherlands incorporated company that had a Dutch trust company as its sole director. It was ultimately owned by non-UK resident trustees for the benefit of Mr and Mrs Wood. The company only undertook the purchase and sale of shares as part of an arrangement to avoid capital gains tax devised and implemented by a UK-based firm of accountants. Revenue claimed that the company was UK resident. Before the Special

---

[44] HMRC, *INTM*, para. INTM120070.

[45] (1996) Sp C 73; [1996] STC SCD 241.

[46] (2004) Sp C 422; [2005] BTC 253 [2005] EWHC 547 (Ch); [2006] BTC 208 [2006] EWCA Civ 26.

Commissioners,[47] the case for the Revenue was that the Dutch trust company did not in fact take the decisions but did what it was told to do by Mr R or by the UK-based firm of chartered accountants acting on his behalf. Special Commissioners Wallace and Brice agreed, holding that the mere physical acts of signing resolutions or documents by the directors are insufficient for actual management. What is needed, they said, is an effective decision as to whether or not the resolution should be passed and the documents signed or executed. The taxpayer argued that in relation to art. 4(3) of the UK–Netherlands Treaty, 'actual management' was synonymous with 'effective management'. The Special Commissioners, however, accepted the the Revenue contention that in the context of the case there is no difference between central management and control and the place of effective management. The context was that only two decisions the company were made: a purchase and sale of certain shares. The place of effective management, they concluded, 'must be the place where effective management decisions are taken'. They found no indication that any effective management decisions were taken in the Netherlands.[48] This finding followed from their understanding of central management and control.

Their decision was reversed by both the High Court and the Court of Appeal in relation to central management and control on the basis that influencing company policy by persons who are not authorised to make decisions as part of the constitutional organs of the company is not an exercise of central management and control, at least in cases where the functions of those organs have not been 'usurped'. Although the case was decided on domestic law grounds, Park J, in the High Court, commented on the place of effective management and formulated the test thus:

> 'Article 4(3) requires there to be identified a "place" of effective management, and it has to be a place situated in one of the two States [and] when it comes to applying the detailed wording of article 4(3) what was the "place ... situated" in the UK which was Eulalia's "place of effective management"?[49]'

The Court of Appeal did not address the point.

Indofood International Finance Ltd v JP Morgan Chase Bank NA[50] involved the Indonesia–Netherlands Tax Treaty in a commercial dispute governed by English law in which the issue was whether 'reasonable measures' could have taken when the Indonesia–Mauritius Tax Treaty terminated, thereby increasing the rate of withholding tax. The company was entitled to redeem the notes in the case of a tax increase unless such measures could be taken. The note holders argued that interposing a Dutch company between the issuer and the parent company was such a measure. Chancellor Sir Andrew Morritt expressed the following views:

> 'As counsel for the issuer pointed out the test, as elaborated by the OECD Commentary, refers to the place where "key" decisions are taken. The provisions of the trust deed and, more particularly, of the note conditions show clearly that they must be taken by the parent

---

[47] At that stage under its anonymised name, *R v Holden* (2004) Sp C 422.

[48] At para. 146.

[49] At para. 77.

[50] [2006] BTC 8003; [2006] EWCA Civ 158.

guarantor. Whilst I do not doubt that the board of directors of Newco would be permitted to determine what to do with the handling charges and equity capital and would be responsible for complying with the requirements of Dutch law, those are hardly the "key" decisions. Let it be assumed that the issuer and Newco are otherwise resident in Holland and the question arose whether to interpose Newco it is, in my view, plain beyond doubt that such a decision and the terms of any interposition would not be left to the issuer or Newco but would be decided by the board of the parent guarantor. In particular it would not be left to the board of the issuer or of Newco to decide whether to assign or to accept the benefit of the loan agreement between the parent guarantor and the issuer and if so on what terms. Questions in relation to any subsequent migration, substitution or interposition of another company between the parent guarantor and Newco or between Newco and the issuer would be decided by the board of the parent guarantor. In my view it is plain that the place of effective management of the issuer is Indonesia and that the place of effective management of Newco, if interposed between the parent guarantor and the issuer, would be Indonesia too.[51]'

The other two judges in the Court of Appeal declined to decide the case on this point but Chadwick LJ would not have found the Newco resident in Indonesia. He observed:

'It is unnecessary to decide whether the Indonesian court would hold, also, that Newco was not resident in the Netherlands on the ground that its "effective management" (in the context of article 4(4) of the Dutch DTA) was situated in Indonesia. On that point my provisional conclusion differs from that reached by the Chancellor; but I do not think that any useful purpose would be served by a detailed analysis. I prefer not to decide the point in the present case. I should add, however, that had I reached the conclusion that on the balance of probabilities the Indonesian Tax Court would hold that Newco was resident in the Netherlands, I would have had no doubt that the point was so finely balanced that it would not be reasonable to expect a commercial organisation to enter into arrangements which would lead, inevitably, to the need to test that point in litigation.[52]'

The case is unsatisfactory in several respects, including that there was no indication of Newco being treated as resident in Indonesia under its domestic law, so the tie-breaker would not have been engaged and that the English court was asked what an Indonesian court would have decided in relation to a hypothetical Dutch company. In *Trevor Smallwood Trusts v R & C Commrs*,[53] having decided that the trusts were dual resident, the Special Commissioners, Drs Avery Jones and Brice, then turned to the meaning of place of effective management in art. 4(3) of the UK–Mauritius Treaty. The facts are similar to *Wood v Holden* in that they concern an arrangement whereby a UK-resident individual sought to avoid capital gains tax on the sale of shares, this time owned by a trust whose residence was under scrutiny. The taxpayer and the Revenue clashed over whether, or to what extent, place of effective management (POEM) differed from central management and control (CMC). This, the Special Commissioners considered, misses the point:

'The two concepts serve entirely different purposes. CMC determines whether a company is resident in the UK or not; POEM is a tie-breaker the purpose of which is to resolve cases of dual residence by determining in which of two states it is to be found. CMC is essentially a one-country test; the purpose is not to decide where residence is situated, but whether or not it

---

[51] At para. 57.

[52] At para. 75.

[53] (2008) Sp C 669.

is situated in the UK. POEM, on the other hand, must be concerned with what happens in both states since its purpose is to resolve residence under domestic law in both states, caused for whatever reason, which could include incorporation in one state and management in the other, or different meanings of management applied in each state, or different interpretations of the same meaning of management applied in each state, or divided management.'

On the meaning of 'effective', they said:

'Effective is used elsewhere in the OECD Model and the Treaty in "effectively connected" in articles 10, 11 and 12 which is an odd use of English. We believe "effective" should be understood in the sense of the French *effective* (*siège de direction effective*) which connotes real, French being the other official version of the model, though not of the Treaty. ... Accordingly, having regard to the ordinary meaning of the words in their context and in the light of their object and purpose we approach the issue of POEM as considering in which state the real management of the trustee qua trustee is found.'

They adopted, based on the expression in *Trustees of Wensleydale's Settlement v IRC*,[54] 'realistic, positive management' as the place of effective management. Despite such incisive analysis, the Special Commissioners fell into the same trap as Special Commissioners Wallace and Brice in *Wood v Holden* by confusing the influence of the UK-based accountants who promoted the scheme and their client with the trustees who as a matter of trust law manage the trust.

OECD discussion paper

In February 2001, the OECD published a paper, 'The impact of the communications revolution on the application of "place of effective management" as a tie-breaker rule'. The paper notes that there is no definition of 'place of effective management', and extremely limited guidance is given on its meaning in the commentary. The paper comments on the central management and control concept, as adopted in English-speaking countries, as well as the 'place of management' concept adopted by some Continental countries. The paper does not draw a clear distinction between the notions of central management and control, place of management and place of effective management, although it recognises that the analysis is based on the experience of a limited number of countries.

The underlying concern, however, is that, as a result of the communications and technological revolution, the way in which people run their businesses is changing fundamentally. As a result of sophisticated telecommunication technology and fast efficient transportation, it is no longer necessary for a person or group of persons to be physically located or meet in any one place to run a business. This increased mobility and functional decentralisation may have a significant impact on the incidence of dual-resident companies and the application of the place of effective management tie-breaker rules. The Revenue position on this is understood to be that where directors use modern communication technologies, such as video-conferencing, telephone or email chat facilities, to conduct board meetings, if part of the decision-making takes place in the UK, the company is UK resident. In the Revenue's view, if one director is present in the UK when this takes place, this is sufficient. This, it says, can then be addressed by application of the tie-breaker in the context of dual residence involving treaty countries.

---

[54] At para. 6.

The OECD paper was considered in *Trevor Smallwood Trusts v R & C Commrs*,[55] and the amendments to the OECD Commentary to art. 4, para. 24.4, included in the 2008 version. The Special Commissioners deduced from it that the subject was not free of controversy within the OECD. The points that emerge from both *Smallwood* and the OECD paper are that, first, that the purpose of the place of effective management test is to resolve dual residence cases and must be construed accordingly. (There can thus only be one place of effective management.) Second, in a world where residence is commonly determined by reference to either incorporation or some form of management test, it is management that prevails over incorporation.[56] Third, it is not the same as central management and control, although both may be present in the same state. Fourth, it is necessary to weigh up what happens in both states. The factors will not be the same in every case. 'Some sort of management', such as operating a bank account in the name of the trustees, carries less weight than realistic, positive management.[57] Fifth, points from other cases are that a 'place' where effective management is conducted is a good indicator, particularly where there is none in the other state. Sixth, the notion of 'management' in the case a legal person is of necessity by reference to that exercised through its own constitutional organs fulfilling their functions according to its governing law (such as the board of directors) unless the functions of those constitutional organs are 'usurped'. The term 'usurped' is used to indicate circumstances where management and control is exercised independently of, or without regard to, those constitutional organs; and, by extension, a distinction must be made between proposing, advising and influencing the decisions which the constitutional organs in and the taking of those decisions.

Triangular cases

Can a person otherwise resident in a third country locate the management and control of his or her business in a treaty country following the colonial pattern in order to benefit from a particular UK Treaty adopting this formulation? In considering this question, it should be borne in mind, in particular, that under UK domestic law,[58] a company may be resident in two places at the same time. It is therefore not inconceivable that a company may be entitled to treaty benefits under this model, even though it also resident in a third country. In the *Commerzbank* case, it was pointed out that treaties between two non-UK companies would have no bearing on the application of a treaty between the UK and a contracting state. Consequently, the application of tie-breaker provisions in a treaty between two other countries would not have a bearing on the application of the UK Treaty. The only possible exception might be in relation to a foreign provision analogous to the FA 1994, s. 249.

Dual residence: trusts

A trust is not an individual, so dual residence is addressed by art. 4(3). Trusts have some similarities with companies in this context. A company is a legal person. A trust is not a

---

[55] At paras. 125 to 127.

[56] It is no doubt for this reason that treaties with the US have not included such a test. The US domestic test is incorporation only, so all dual residence cases would automatically default to the UK, which adopts a management-based test.

[57] See *Trustees of Wensleydale's Settlement v IRC*, para. 6.

[58] *Swedish Central Railway Co. Ltd v Thompson* [1925] AC 495, HL. See HMRC, *International Tax Handbook*, para. 338.

person but a relationship, and it is treated as a notional person for UK tax purposes. Thus, the trustees of a settlement are collectively to be treated as a single 'deemed person' for the purposes of the Income Tax Acts, unless the context requires otherwise.[59] Under English law concepts, while a company is, by its constitution, normally managed by its directors, a trust is managed by its trustees. The domestic rules for determining the residence of trusts may easily give rise to questions of dual residence. Unlike the residence of a company, the residence of a trust is by reference to the residence of its trustees, not where it is managed and controlled. For income tax and capital gains tax purposes, the position is straight forward where all the trustees are either resident or non-resident. The trust residence follows their residence. However, where there is more than one trustee, the trustees will be treated as UK resident if one is UK resident (regardless of the number of non-resident trustees) and the settlor is or was resident, ordinarily resident or domiciled in the UK at the time of settlement of the trust.[60] By contrast, if the settlor was not resident, ordinarily resident or domiciled, then the trust is non-resident despite the presence of any number of UK-resident trustees, as long as there is a single non-resident trustee. A similar rule applies to the residence of deceased estates.[61] Thus, trustees may be UK resident even where a majority are outside the UK and the administration of the trusts takes place outside the UK.

In *Trustees of Wensleydale's Settlement v IRC*,[62] one trustee was an English solicitor UK resident and the other was the wife of an Irish solicitor resident in Ireland. Special Commissioner David Shirley found that the place of effective management was not in Ireland, where management appeared limited to operating a bank account compared with the place actual decisions were taken. In *Trevor Smallwood Trust v R & C Commrs*,[63] there were no mixed residence trustees. The trustee was only in Mauritius during the Mauritian period and only in the UK during the UK period. The resolution of such consecutive residence cases ought to be simple. There can be no effective (or any other) management in a contracting state during a period in which there is no trustee present in that state to exercise it. The treaty position in relation to capital gains during a year of partial treaty-non residence was overridden in FA 2005, which is now TCGA 1992, s. 83A.[64]

Dual residence: partnership

A partnership is not treated as an entity separate and distinct from its partners, and tax liability is determined by reference to the partners.[65] As a result, the question of dual residence of a partnership does not arise. The only context in which the residence of a partnership can arise is in relation to the treaty override for UK-resident partners of foreign resident firms.[66] The effect of these provisions is to make UK-resident partners liable to

---

[59] ITA 2007, s. 474(1).

[60] ITA 2007, s. 476; TCGA 1992, s. 69A.

[61] ITA 2007, s. 834.

[62] (1996) Sp C 73.

[63] (2008) Sp C 669.

[64] See chapter 11, para. 20-150.

[65] ICTA 1988, s. 111(1).

[66] ITTOIA 2005, s. 858(1)(a)(i).

income tax on their share of partnership profits despite the presence of a treaty. The central management and control test will apply.[67]

Administrative resolution of dual residence

Several treaties do not adopt the place of effective management as a mechanism to resolve dual residence. This appears to an increasing tendency in UK treaty practice. Of the treaties and protocols negotiated since 2001, this has been the case in relation to treaties with Canada, Chile, Japan, Lithuania, Macedonia, Moldova and the Netherlands, and the US. A current example is the UK–Lithuania Treaty, which reads:

> '4(3) Where by reason of the provisions of paragraph (1) of this Article a person other than an individual is a resident of both Contracting States, the competent authorities of the Contracting States shall endeavour to settle the question by mutual agreement. In the absence of such agreement, for the purposes of the convention, the person shall not be entitled to claim any relief or exemption from tax provided by this convention.'

HMRC says of such provisions:

> 'Exceptionally, a tie-breaker may not contain an objective test which can be applied unilaterally by HM Revenue & Customs. For example, the tie-breaker in the treaty with Canada and in the 2003 treaty with the USA depends on agreement between the Competent Authorities of the two states. In such a case, the FA94/S249 rule can apply only when a claim for relief under the treaty which requires the determination of residence has been made and residence has been formally awarded to the other country.[68]'

As a matter of principle, this approach to resolving dual residence is unsatisfactory in several respects. First, taxpayers are unable to self-assess their basic status. Second, there is in most cases no obligation on the contracting states to reach agreement. Third, there are no criteria specified to provide guidelines for any possible agreement.[69] Fourth, unless and until mutual agreement is reached, the dual-resident taxpayer is largely excluded from treaty benefits. It is an invitation to arbitrary and intransigent behaviour, compounded by the secrecy of the process, which even if on the part of one contracting state can have profound consequences and no remedy for the taxpayer.

14-250   Nationality

Broadly speaking, nationality is not material to tax liability in the UK. Notwithstanding this, nationality is material to a number of aspects of tax treaties. It represents the residual test for determining the residence of an individual for treaty purposes before the matter is to be addressed by the competent authorities.[70] It may also determine liability to tax in respect of

---

[67] See generally *Padmore v IRC* [1987] BTC 3; [1987] STC 36, Ch.D.

[68] HMRC, *INTM*, para. INTM120070.

[69] An exception is found in art. 4(3) of the UK–Canada Treaty, which requires 'place of effective management, the place where it is incorporated or otherwise constituted and any other relevant factors' to be taken into account. The generality of this list effectively adds nothing.

[70] See chapter 5, para. 14-150.

government service under art. 19.[71] It is also relevant in respect of certain prohibitions against discrimination pursuant to art. 24, including the giving of jurisdiction to the country of nationality under mutual agreement procedure. It may also be relevant to the taxation of social security pensions.[72]

The form of definition commonly used from 1981 is reflected in the Mauritian Treaty of 11 February 1981. Article 3(1)(c) reads:

'(a) the term "national" means:

(i) in relation to the UK, any citizen of the UK and Colonies, or any British subject not possessing that citizenship or the citizenship of any other Commonwealth country or territory, provided that in either case he has the right of abode in the UK; and any legal person, partnership, association or other entity deriving its status as such from the law in force in the UK;'

Nationality has been a troublesome concept in UK treaties, largely as a result of the complexities of British nationality arising from its colonial past. Early treaties with colonies or former colonies typically contain no reference to nationality. Other early treaties contain references to nationality, but no definition.[73] Other early treaties, such as Cyprus, define a UK national as 'any citizen of the UK and colonies who derives his status as such from his connection with the UK' (art. 3(1(j)(ii)). In *Avery Jones v IRC*,[74] it was held that the citizenship 'of the UK and colonies' was the only concept of citizenship in UK law. As a result, the reference to a UK citizen in a treaty meant a reference to such citizenship. Therefore, there are presently two categories of individuals who qualify as nationals under most treaties:

- British citizens; and
- Commonwealth citizens who have the right of abode in the UK.

Nationality may also be bestowed on other persons and relationships for treaty purposes. This status is generally only relevant in respect of non-discrimination. Thus, a partnership, association or other entity deriving its status as such from the law in force in the UK is a UK national for treaty purposes. This would include companies and other bodies corporate, and would appear to include trustees. This extension of nationality beyond individuals has disappeared in the recently negotiated 2008 France Treaty.[75] Under domestic law, there is no reference to UK nationals. The current expression 'Commonwealth citizen' has in effect the same meaning. It has limited significance. Section 278(2) of ICTA 1988 extends personal allowances and reliefs to non-residents who are *inter alia* Commonwealth citizens.

---

[71] See chapter 10, paras. 19-600 and 19-750.

[72] See chapter 10, para. 19-650.

[73] See Israel and Germany. See, in particular, Germany, where a number of treaty provisions are governed in part by nationality.

[74] (1976) 51 TC 443.

[75] Art. 3(1)(c).

Permanent Establishment

Chapter 6

15-000   Cornerstone of cross-border business taxation

Permanent establishment forms the cornerstone of treaty rules relating to the taxation of cross-border business. In all treaties, it constitutes the minimum threshold that must be met before business profit may be taxed in a host country. Modern treaties specify that the profits of an enterprise of a contracting state may be taxable only in that state unless the enterprise carries on business in the other contracting state through a permanent establishment situated therein. This key principle is normally contained in art. 7(1). That article deals with the allocation of profits to such a permanent establishment should it exist under the rules in art. 5. Several articles make specific and narrow exceptions to these rules. Where investment income in the form of interest, dividends, royalties or items not specifically referred to in the treaty ('other income') is attributable to a permanent establishment, then the usual limitations on taxing those items of income are disapplied.[1] Likewise, authority to tax capital gains in the host state is in part by reference to the existence of a permanent establishment.[2] Employment income in respect of duties performed in a host country by a short stay employee is also made dependent upon the existence of a permanent establishment in that state.[3] Discriminatory tax measures against permanent establishments are prohibited.[4]

15-050   Meaning of permanent establishment

There are two notions of permanent establishment embodied in art. 5 of the OECD Model:

(1)   *physical permanent establishment:* this is a fixed place of business through which the business of the enterprise is wholly or partly carried on; and

(2)   *agency permanent establishment:* this applies to dependent agents exercising their authority to contract.

Certain limited functions are excluded from constituting a permanent establishment by way of exception to these two basic concepts. The common thread to these exclusions is their preparatory or auxiliary nature. The definition of permanent establishment in art. 5 of the Model Convention has remained remarkably constant. It has not been amended since the

---

[1] Arts. 10(4), 11(5),12(3) and 21(2).

[2] Art. 13(2).

[3] Art. 15(2)(c).

[4] Art. 24(3).

1977 Model Convention. Indeed, the differences between the 1963 Draft Convention and the 1977 model are relatively minor. In addition, the UK has concluded a limited number of treaties that give effect to a newer third basis for the existence of a permanent establishment broadly in line with UN Model Treaty, art. 5(3)(b), so that the mere provision of services in the source state will constitute a permanent establishment. Despite the consistency of language in the model treaties, the outcome of negotiation has produced widely differing permanent establishment articles in the UK Treaty network. While these basic fixed place of business and agency concepts are common to all treaties, the precise definition of each varies enormously from treaty to treaty. Treaties patterned on the models draw a distinction between physical and agency permanent establishments, but a number of early treaties do not make this distinction very clear. Thus, in the Isle of Man Treaty, the core definition reads as follows:

> '**Article 2(1)(k)** The term "permanent establishment" when used with respect to an enterprise of one of the territories, means a branch, management or other fixed place of business, but does not include an agency unless the agent has, and habitually exercise, a general authority to negotiate and conclude contracts on behalf of such enterprise.'

This approach may be contrasted with the standard language found in treaties patterned on the various models from 1963 onwards. An early example is Namibia, where each is separately identified, so that the term 'permanent establishment' means:

> '(k)(i) a fixed place of business in which the business of the enterprise is wholly or partly carried on;
>
> a person acting in one of the territories on behalf of an enterprise of the other territory – other than an agent of an independent status to whom sub-paragraph (vi) applies – shall be deemed to be a permanent establishment in the first-mentioned territory if he has, and habitually exercises in that territory, an authority to conclude contracts in the name of the enterprise.'

Each aspect will be further examined in this chapter. In FA 2003 the permanent establishment concept was included in domestic law.[5] The domestic definition is primarily relevant to corporation tax and draws heavily on the model, art. 5, but is not coextensive with it.

15-100   Interpretation of permanent establishment

There are no reported cases in the UK on the meaning of permanent establishment. Consequently, ordinary principles of treaty interpretation must be applied. Administrative practice and the extent to which domestic law coincides with treaty provisions are of particular importance.

The UK has a tradition of active participation in the OECD Committee on Fiscal Affairs and, in particular, its working parties responsible for both the Model Tax Convention and the commentary. In general, the HMRC does not adopt an independent interpretation of

[5] FA 2003, s. 148.

permanent establishment but relies heavily on the OECD Commentary.[6] For some time, a single observation on the commentary was entered by the UK in relation to dependent agents contracting in their own name.

The UK has a single observation to the commentary on art. 5 (para. 45.5) and a single reservation (para. 52).

15-150   Physical permanent establishments

A current expression of the meaning of physical permanent establishment is found in art. 5(1) of the Lithuanian Treaty:

> '5(1) For the purposes of this Convention, the term "permanent establishment" means a fixed place of business through which the business of an enterprise is wholly or partly carried on.'

This wording is coextensive with domestic legislation for corporation tax purposes.[7] The relevance is, however, different. In the context of corporation tax under domestic law, permanent establishment is important where a trade is carried out in the UK by a non-resident company. The expression 'business', used in both art. 5(1) of most treaties and the FA 2003, s. 148, is broader than 'trade'. In *American Leaf Blending Co. SDN BHD v Director General of Inland Revenue* [1978] STC 561 (PC), Lord Diplock said that 'in the case of a company incorporated for the purpose of making profits for its shareholders, any gainful use to which it puts any of its assets *prima facie* amounts to the carrying on of a business'. The concept of business is wider than that of 'trade'. The carrying on of business usually calls for some activity on the part of whoever carries it on, although depending on the nature of the business, the activity may be intermitted with long intervals of quiescence in between. The court accepted that every isolated act of a company of a kind authorised by its Memorandum necessarily constitutes the carrying on of a business. More recently, in *Jowett v O'Neill and Brennan Construction Limited*,[8] the outer limits of this rule were indicated. Thus, although normally where a company laid out assets and earned an income return, it would be carrying on a business that is not an inevitable legal conclusion, there may be exceptional cases. In that case, merely holding an interest-bearing bank account was not regarded as carrying on a business.[9] In the context of non-resident companies, the activities must constitute a key element of the trade to attract corporation tax liability under domestic law,[10] but the wider meaning may be relevant in relation to the existence of a foreign permanent establishment for the purpose of crediting any foreign tax.[11]

---

[6] HMRC's commitment to the commentary in this respect is not unambiguous: 'A lot of our interpretation of treaty PE is based on the commentary to Article 5 of the Model Treaty'. (HMRC, *International Tax Manual*, para. INTM264050).

'Usually all member states will fully support the interpretation included in the commentary. Where this is not the case, a member state will record either an "observation" or a "reservation" at the end of the commentary paragraphs for a particular treaty article'. (HMRC, *International Tax Manual*, para. INTM266030).

[7] FA 2003, s. 148(1)(a).

[8] [1998] BTC 133; [1998] STC 482 (ChD).

[9] See also *Revenue and Customs Commissioners v Salaried Persons Postal Loans Limited* [2006] EWHC 736(Ch).

[10] ICTA 1988, s. 11(1).

[11] See HMRC, *International Tax Handbook*, para. ITH 849.

15-200   Administrative practice

The HMRC understanding of the concept of permanent establishment is set out in *INTM*, para. INTM266030, which says:

'The general definition of a permanent establishment contains three requirements, namely:

(a)   there must be a place of business, normally premises, although it can, in certain circumstances be machinery or equipment;

(b)   the place of business must be fixed, that is, have a certain degree of permanence; and

(c)   the business must be carried on through this fixed place of business, normally by the personnel of the enterprise.'

This is essentially a paraphrase of para. 2 of the OECD Commentary on art. 5. Much of the discussion in the *International Manual* on this subject proceeds in a similar vein.[12] Where the HMRC guidance is to recognise a permanent establishment in narrower circumstances either for domestic law or treaty purposes, then, as a practical matter, the narrower view will apply. Automated equipment and certain aspects of electronic commerce are in point.[13]

15-250   Permanent establishments in e-commerce

Changes to the commentary on the Model Tax Convention adopted by the Committee on Fiscal Affairs on 22 December 2000 in the context of e-commerce may also give an indication of how these issues might be viewed in the context of permanent establishments constituted by automated equipment in related technology. Modern examples include: fixed automated telecommunications equipment, such as backhaul ducts and cables; POP, transmission and switching equipment; backbone local loop; ducts and cables; leased lines; indefeasible rights of use; and capacity deals.

The commentary to art. 5(1) now, rather confusingly, indicates that human intervention is not a requirement for the existence of a permanent establishment in the case of the operation of computer equipment or certain other automatic functions,[14] although personnel or agents are normally required to some extent where the business is carried on 'mainly through automatic equipment'.[15] Usually personnel conduct the business of the enterprise and although the commentary is still accurate in the context of e-commerce, it was not intended to rule out that a business may be carried on at least partly without personnel.

Specifically, in the context of e-commerce, the changes to the commentary make it clear that in many cases, the issue of whether computer equipment at a given location constitutes a permanent establishment will depend on whether the functions performed through that equipment exceed the preparatory or auxiliary threshold. An e-tailer, essentially a content

---

[12] HMRC, *INTM*, paras. INTM266050 to INTM266080.

[13] HMRC, *INTM*, paras. INTM266090 and INTM266100.

[14] Para. 42.6

[15] Para. 10.

provider,[16] is an example of a trading function that might be fully carried out automatically through a website on a server that the OECD regards a capable of constituting a permanent establishment.

The UK has refused to participate in this consensus. Its view was first expressed in the Inland Revenue press release of 11 April 2000 to the effect that:

> 'In the UK, we take the view that a website of itself is not a permanent establishment. And we take the view that a server is insufficient itself to constitute a permanent establishment of a business that is conducting e-commerce through a website on the server. We take that view regardless of whether the server is owned, rented or otherwise at the disposal of the business.[17]'

The UK observation to the commentary on art. 5 expresses the matter more narrowly, saying that a server used by an e-tailer of itself, or together with websites, cannot constitute a permanent establishment. The result of these statements is that the presence of a server will simply be one of the factors, among others, to take into account in determining whether or not a permanent establishment exists. By implication, it is difficult to see the UK recognising a permanent establishment that has no human participation. In this regard, recourse may be had to the more traditional view in relation to the maintenance and operation of fixed automatic equipment explained in paras. 8 and 10 of the OECD commentary on art. 5. Thus, for example, the operation of equipment by a non-resident company for its own account in the UK may constitute a permanent establishment even if the activities of local personnel are restricted to setting up, operating, controlling and maintaining such equipment.

The above analysis may simply reflect a traditional view of whether a non-resident is trading in the UK through a branch or agency updated to deal with trade via automated equipment where there is no other presence.[18] It is also difficult to see how fully enabled trading websites on servers differ from other automated equipment.

15-300 The illustrative list

Most treaties contain a list of deemed physical permanent establishments. The Estonian Treaty reflects the model in this respect:

> '5(2) The term 'permanent establishment' includes especially:
>
> (a) a place of management;
> (b) a branch;
> (c) an office;
> (d) a factory;
> (e) a workshop;

---

[16] Para. 42.9 of the commentary on art. 5 defines an e-tailer as an enterprise that carries on the business of selling products through the internet.

[17] Now in *INTM*, para. INTM266100.

[18] See para 15-450 regarding agency permanent establishments below.

(f)   a mine, an oil or gas well, a quarry or any other place of extraction of natural resources;'

It will immediately be observed that the domestic illustrative list in the FA 2003, s. 148(2), includes these items.

Negotiation practice varies widely as to whether other facilities are deemed to constitute a fixed place of business. A number of very early treaties, such as Antigua and Barbuda art. 2(1)(k), contain no illustrative list. In the natural resource sector, UK domestic law (FA 2003, s. 148(2)(f)) deems an installation or structure for the exploration of natural resources to be a permanent establishment. Most treaties only regard a place of exploitation as constituting a fixed place of business. Exceptions to the majority in this respect include the Australian Treaty (art. 5(2)(f)) and the Chilean Treaty (art. 5(2)(f)). Surprisingly (since a place of exploration t is included in the US Model Double Tax Treaty), this is not the case in the 2001 US Treaty.

Other more unusual deemed permanent establishments include 'a store or other sales outlet' (Guyana art. 5(2)(c)) and 'a warehouse in relation to a person providing storage facilities for others' (Bangladesh art. 5(2)(f)), or 'an assembly workshop or agricultural establishment' (Bolivia art. 5(2)(d)), 'premises used as a sales outlet for receiving or soliciting orders' (India art. 5(2)(f)). These provisions are normally included at the request of the other contracting state.

At least as far at those items in the model, it is clear that, these are *prima facie* permanent establishments only and that to be a treaty permanent establishment, any of these types of places would also need to have the general attributes of a fixed place of business within art. 5(1).

15-350   Branch

Permanent establishment is defined in most treaties to include in art. 5(2)(b) *inter alia* 'a branch'. As a matter of domestic law, in order to be liable to tax on its trading income, a non-resident has long been required to carry on a trade within the UK through a 'branch or agency'. A branch or agency is defined, rather unhelpfully, as 'any factorship, agency, receivership, branch or management'.[19]

There is limited judicial commentary on the concept. In *Greenwood v FL Smidth & Co*,[20] Atkin LJ commented in the context of the place of business which the partnership in *Sulley v Attorney-General* had in England: 'It is immaterial whether this organisation is an "agency or a branch"'.[21] In *IRC v Brackett*,[22] the Special Commissioners took the view that the Jersey company in question was 'effectively trading only in the UK through Mr Brackett' and that it would be perverse to hold that the company was not within the charge to tax 'because of

---

[19] ICTA 1988, s. 834(1); FA 2003, s. 126(1).

[20] (1922) 8 TC 193, HL.

[21] (1860) 2 TC 149.

[22] [1986] BTC 415; [1986] STC 521, Ch.D.

some semantic difficulty in fitting its arrangements within the wording of the definition of a branch or agency'. The High Court did not consider this question. It was dealt with as a composite expression in *Sun Life Assurance Co. of Canada v Pearson.*[23]

The notion of a branch is one which also gives rise to difficulties under other areas of domestic law. For example, in relation to company law, foreign companies are obliged to register where a branch is established in the UK. The English statute simply says that a branch means anything which is a branch for the purpose of the EU Eleventh Company Law Directive.[24] The directive itself contains no definition of branch.

There is likewise very little administrative guidance on the meaning of 'branch'. The Revenue states in the *International Tax Manual*[25] that it has been advised that the presence of a principal (in the case of a sole trader or partnership) or of employees on a more or less regular basis is likely to be an essential ingredient of a branch (although employees may also be agents). What is perhaps important in the context of the application of treaties is that if this is indeed correct, then as a matter of domestic law, non-resident companies might be trading in the UK, but would not do so through a branch or agency where there is no human intervention.

While this view may pre-date recent discussions in relation to e-commerce, there is no suggestion that it has been viewed as inapplicable to other forms of activity where the trade is carried on mainly through automatic equipment. On this basis, it seems that even though in the treaty context a permanent establishment might be constituted by such automatic equipment, as a matter of domestic law, there may be no branch or agency in the UK and therefore a non-resident company would not be within the charge to UK corporation tax in any event and the question of treaty protection would not arise. A rather crude view is found in the HMRC *International Tax Manual*:[26]

> 'Most people recognise a branch of a foreign business when they see one and the impression given to the public is helpful in deciding whether or not a branch exists. For example there are many branches of foreign banks that trade on the High Streets of many towns and cities in the UK.'

A traditional bank branch may be illustrative on the basis that the business of the bank was done there but this is no more than a fixed place of business. It emphasises the need for an analysis of the functions actually performed in all cases.

15-400   Building site and construction or installation projects

Although some early treaties contain no provision relating to construction sites, building or assembly projects (for example, Jersey and Seychelles), many treaties address this issue. Under domestic law, a building site or construction or installation project is simply included

---

[23] [1986] BTC 282; [1986] STC 335, CA, by Fox LJ at 350.

[24] 89/666; [1989] OJ L395/36.

[25] At para. 842.

[26] HMRC, *INTM*, para. INTM264090.

on the illustrative list of deemed fixed places of business (FA 2003, s. 148(2)(h)). This is at variance with the model and not found in most treaties. The common approach is adopted by art. 5(3) of the Russian Treaty, which reads:

'5(3) A building site or construction or installation project constitutes a permanent establishment only if it lasts more than twelve months.'

A number of treaties, particularly those with developing countries, adopt a six-month, rather than a 12-month rule (see, for example, the Omani Treaty, art. 5(3)). A slightly different formulation is found in the Papua New Guinea Treaty, which refers to a site or project lasting more than 183 days in any 365-day period (art. 5(3)).

The scope of such articles also varies widely. Many treaties follow the UN Model and include supervisory services connected building site or construction or installation project.[27] The Nigerian Treaty additionally includes in art. 5(2)(i):

'Installation or the provision of supervisory activities in connection therewith incidental to the sale of machinery or equipment where the charges payable for such activities exceed 10 per cent of the free on board sale price of the machinery or equipment.'

The somewhat surprising identification of building and installation activity separately in art. 5(3) is explained by HMRC, in *International Tax Manual*, para. INTM266130. as follows:

'The OECD member states have made this type of activity the subject of a specific rule because of the frequency with which it caused difficulties of interpretation. And, for clarity in the Model Treaty, 12 months duration has been taken to be a sufficient indication that the activity is a fixed place of business permanent establishment.'

The better view is that it is an extension of the illustrative list but that a specific duration of such sites or projects is made explicit. This was clearly understood by the drafter of the domestic permanent establishment definition in the FA 2003, s. 148(2)(h), by placing building sites or construction or installation projects within the illustrative list. No duration is specified in the domestic definition so the general principle applies to its interpretation.

15-450   Agency permanent establishments

A permanent establishment may exist despite the absence of a fixed place of business as a result of contractual relationships that give rise to a dependent agency. Such permanent establishments are addressed in art. 5(5) and (6) of the model. The Swedish Treaty is an example, the relevant part of which reads as follows:

'5(5) Notwithstanding the provisions of paragraphs (1) and (2) of this Article, where a person … is acting on behalf of an enterprise and has, and habitually exercises, in a Contracting State an authority to conclude contracts in the name of the enterprise, that enterprise shall be deemed to have a permanent establishment in that State in respect of any activities which that person undertakes for the enterprise.'

---

[27] See Kazakhstan Treaty, art. 5(3)(a).

These provisions track loosely the UK domestic machinery for assessing non-residents trading in the UK, which are now contained in the opaquely drafted FA 1995, ss. 126 and 127, and which, for practical purposes, only applies to persons other than companies. Under that legislation, any person who is a 'branch or agency' of a non-resident trading in the UK is jointly liable with the non-resident for the tax and compliance obligations relating to the trade.[28] For this purpose, 'branch or agency' means any factorship, agency, receivership, branch or management.[29]

The Revenue view at the time these provisions were introduced was that the domestic law was in line with the principles contained in the model. The main difference, they said, is that there is no requirement in the absence of a treaty for the non-resident to have a fixed presence in the UK before earned income may be taxed.[30] Thus, on this basis, the important elements of treaties from a UK income tax perspective are in relation to physical permanent establishments.

Mention should also be made of one of the earliest cases dealing with trading in the UK, *Erichsen v Last*.[31] In that case, a Danish company had marine cables at three points in the UK. Telegraph messages from the UK to foreign destinations passed first over the lines of the Post Office and then through the marine cables of the taxpayer onwards to their foreign destinations. The company was found to be trading in the UK. In the Court of Appeal, two out of the three judges agreed that it was simply the fact that contracts were made in the UK that gave rise to the trading. The fact that the lines were in the UK made no difference. Cotton LJ considered that it did not matter whether they used their own lines or those of others. Brett LJ went further to say that it is immaterial whether any part of the cable is in the UK. By contrast, Lord Jessell, the Master of the Rolls, in dissenting, was of the view that either receiving payment for messages sent from abroad or transmitting messages from stations in the UK abroad could constitute trading. He offered the analogy of a railway company with a station at Dover and Calais. A foreign company established at Calais carrying passengers from Dover to Calais would be trading in Dover, as regards the passengers carried from Dover to Calais. However, physical establishment as a requirement for trading in the UK was rejected by the majority.

15-500   Corporation tax

The position for companies changed in 2003 as the domestic definition of agency permanent establishment differs markedly from the treaty meaning. The relevant parts of FA 2003 read:

'148(1) For the purposes of the Tax Acts a company has a permanent establishment in a territory if, and only if– . . .

(b) an agent acting on behalf of the company has and habitually exercises there authority to do business on behalf of the company.'

---

[28] FA 1995, s. 126(1).

[29] FA 1995, s. 126(8). See discussion on the meaning of 'branch' at para. 15-350 above.

[30] Inland Revenue, *Tax Bulletin* (August 1995), p. 238.

[31] (1881) 1 TC 351, 4 TC 422.

The scope and nature of the authority in the invariable treaty language refers to persons having and habitually exercising 'an authority to conclude contracts' in the name of the enterprise. The UK domestic legislation simply refers to an agent's 'authority to do business on behalf of the company'.

The distinction between trade and business in UK domestic law has already been noted.[32] As has already been noted, in the context on non-residents liability to UK income, capital gains or corporation tax, it is only authority in either case that related to trading in the UK that is relevant, but wider authority may be relevant in other contracting states in connection with the ability of UK residents to credit foreign tax against their UK liability.

HMRC clearly recognises the contractual nature of the agent's authority in domestic law and the authority of persons to conclude contracts as the basis for agency permanent establishment. Although it interprets the domestic definition widely,[33] it considers its meaning by reference to the law of contract and agency both in relation to the domestic definition[34] and the treaty definition.[35] In the treaty context, HMRC suggests that actions carried out for and binding the principal constitute authority to conclude contracts. The example it gives is of a contract arranged by an agent in the UK to deliver goods owned by a foreign principal to a customer. This, HMRC says, would be treated for UK tax purposes as though the foreign principal had contracted in the UK for the delivery.[36] If the foreign principal is providing delivery services, the actions of the UK agent may be concluding contracts on its behalf in the example, but arranging delivery for goods sold by a foreign principal would not (unless the contract on behalf of the principal is made by delivery). Such actions may constitute part of 'business' carried on under the domestic definition.

Habitual exercise of the authority is required in both domestic law and treaty agency to give rise to a permanent establishment. When considering the early provisions relating to 'regular agents' under domestic law in *Nielsen, Andersen & Company v Collins (H.M. Inspector of Taxes)*,[37] Scrutton LJ said:[38]

> 'The contrast intended to be drawn is between casual employment, temporary employment, for a transaction or few transactions, and regular appointment of a permanent agent who is there as representing the foreigner.'

In *Willson v Hooker*,[39] 'regular agency' was likewise distinguished from 'casual or occasional agency'. In that case, only a single trading transaction was entered into. However, the appellant was the person through whom all the relevant steps comprised in the transaction were carried out and thus not a casual agent.

---

[32] See para. 15-150 above.

[33] HMRC, *INTM*, para. INTM264070.

[34] HMRC, *INTM*, para. INTM264100.

[35] HMRC, *INTM*, para. INTM266160.

[36] HMRC, *INTM*, para. INTM266160.

[37] 13 TC 91.

[38] At p. 122.

[39] [1995] BTC 461; [1995] STC 1142, Ch.D.

English contract law does not distinguish between agents who contract in the names of their principals and those who contract in their own names as undisclosed agents for their principals. Treaties following the OECD pattern refer to agents who have authority 'to conclude contracts in the name of the enterprise'. The commentary to the model was amended in 1994 to adopt the approach previously taken by the UK in an observation[40] to the effect that a person is an agent whether contracting in his or her own name or that of the enterprise.[41] Outcomes may differ where foreign contract law is involved.[42]

15-550   Independent agents

The existence of an independent agent will not give rise to a permanent establishment. Article 5(5)[43] only applies to an agent 'other than an agent of an independent status to whom paragraph (6) of this Article applies'. The Swedish Treaty continues:

> '5(6) An enterprise shall not be deemed to have a permanent establishment in a Contracting State merely because it carries on business in that State through a broker, general commission agent or any other agent of an independent status, provided that such persons are acting in the ordinary course of their business.'

This exclusion is not limited to agency permanent establishments in art. 5(5). An independent agent cannot fulfil the functionality necessary to carry on business at a fixed place to constitute a physical permanent establishment within art. 5(1) either as a result of the wide language of art. 5(6).

United Kingdom domestic law has long contained similar exclusions in relation to the machinery for assessing non-residents trading in the UK. The current domestic legislation which applies for income tax purposes – that is, FA 1995, s. 127(1) – identifies the following categories:

> '(a)   an agent of the non-resident who does not act in relation to the transactions in the course of carrying on a regular agency for the non-resident;
>
> (b)   brokers who:
>
> (1)   carry on the business of a broker;
>
> (2)   carry out the transaction on behalf of the non-resident in the ordinary course of that business;
>
> (3)   where the remuneration received by the broker in respect of the transaction is not less than the rate than that which would have been customary for that class of business;
>
> (c)   investment managers subject to the provisions of section 127(3); and
>
> (d)   Lloyds members' agents or managing agents of a syndicate where the non-resident is a member of Lloyds.'

---

[40] Formerly at para. 45 of the commentary to art. 5.

[41] Commentary to art. 5, para. 32.1.

[42] For example, HMRC, *INTM*, para. INTM46540.

[43] See the Swedish Treaty referred to above.

An early predecessor of FA 1995, ss. 126 and 127 legislation (section 373(1) of Income Tax Act 1952), was considered by the courts in *Fleming v London Produce Company*.[44] In that legislation, the reference to a 'broker' included a general commission agent. The court determined that, first, a general commission agent must have 'broker-like qualities'. Second, the exemption only applied to non-residents who merely employed brokers in the ordinary way, even if they regularly employ the same one. A general commission agent is one who holds himself out as being ready to work for clients generally and who does not in substance confine his activities to one principal or an insignificant number of principals.

The expression 'independent agent' is used in FA 1995 only in Sch. 23, and is there only to distinguish between the liability of independent agents and others. An independent agent is not liable to civil penalties or surcharge in respect of certain acts which he or she did not participate in or consent to, and is entitled to indemnities from his or her non-resident principal.[45] In this context, an independent agent means, in relation to the non-resident, any person 'who is the non-resident's UK representative in respect of any agency from the non-resident in which he was acting on the non-resident's behalf in an independent capacity'. For this purpose, a person:

> 'Shall not be regarded as acting in an independent capacity on behalf of the non-resident unless, having regard to its legal, financial and commercial characteristics, the relationship between them is a relationship between persons carrying on independent businesses that deal with each other at arm's length.'

Sections 126 and 127 of FA 1995 were repealed for corporation tax purposes by the introduction of the permanent establishment test for non-resident companies trading in the UK in 2003. The Finance Act 2003 draws a clear distinction between the machinery and charging provisions. Section 148(3) is categorical in that 'a company is not regarded as having a permanent establishment in a territory by reason of the fact that it carries on business there through an agent of independent status acting in the ordinary course of his business'. Schedule 26 supplements s. 148(3) with respect to excluding independent agents as regards transactions carried out through a broker, investment manager or Lloyd's agent[46] by prescribing the circumstances in which each is regarded as an agent of independent status acting in the ordinary course of his business. For these purposes, a person is regarded as acting in an independent capacity on behalf of a company only if the relationship between them, having regard to its legal, financial and commercial characteristics, is a relationship between persons carrying on independent businesses that deal with each other at arm's length.[47] Schedule 26 does not contain define 'broker' and investment managers or Lloyd's agents are merely examples of others agents who may be of independent status acting in the ordinary course of their business. They are thus safe harbours under domestic law and not aids to the construction of treaty independent agent provisions.

This wording is carried over to FA 2003, para. 7(2), Sch. 23. In FA 2003, Sch. 26, the language is now of general application in relation to whether brokers, investment managers

---

[44] (1968) 44 TC 582.

[45] FA 1995, Sch. 23, paras. 5 and 6.

[46] S. 152(1)(a).

[47] Sch. 26, para. 7(2).

and Lloyds agents are independent or not. The Revenue has long taken the view that independent agent in Sch. 23 is intended to have the same meaning as in the model 'except that it is not limited to agents ejusdem generis with broker or general commission agents'.[48] The OECD Commentary does not require dealings at arm's length and thus the domestic statutory formulation of independence is more restrictive than the treaty expression.[49]

However, the broad nature of the language does not provide clear guidance and consequently detailed examination of the facts and circumstances will be required on a case by case basis.

Treaties patterned on the UN Model may contain their own threshold for independence as shown by the Jordanian Treaty:

'5(6) … when the activities of such an [independent] agent are devoted wholly or almost wholly on behalf of that enterprise or its associated enterprises, and the transactions are not made under arm's length conditions, he will not be considered an agent of an independent status within the meaning of this paragraph.'

HMRC appears to consider that where English contract law is concerned, an agent is not an independent agent if he or she has the characteristics of a dependent agent and habitually exercises that authority, whether doing so in his or her own name or that of the enterprise.

Paragraph 852 of the *International Tax Handbook* suggests that the making of contracts in the name of the principal would be regarded by civil law countries as a characteristic of a dependent agent, whereas contracts made in the agent's own name would be characteristic of independent status. It continues:

'In our law, if contracts are made on behalf of and with the authority of the principal, the relationship of the agent to the principal is not affected by whether the contract is made in the name of the principal or the agent's own name. So agents, who in all other respects would be dependent agents according to the model, could in our law make contracts in their own name. We would not wish such agents to be regarded as agents of independent status under a treaty and therefore resist the literal meaning of "in the name of" and argue that the word should be interpreted as "on behalf of" which is an acceptable translation of the words "au nom de" which appears in the French version of the Model Convention.'

This approach has been included in the OECD Commentary since 1994.[50]

15-600   Services and permanent establishments

It will be apparent that business profits arising from the provision of services by an enterprise of one state in another state, will only be taxable in the other state if the business is carried, on at least in part, through a fixed place of business. The conclusion of contracts to provide services does not itself give rise to profits, but the performance of the service

---

[48] HMRC, *International Tax Handbook*, para. 963.

[49] OECD Commentary to art. 5, paras. 36 to 39.

[50] At para. 32.

does. Consequently, an agency permanent establishment will not be sufficient to give taxing jurisdiction. The UN Model Treaty between developed and developing countries has long advocated broader taxing jurisdiction for source countries including the recognition of a permanent establishment where services are performed in the source country over a period of time. The UN Model approach is exemplified by art. 5(3) of the UK–Botswana Treaty, which provides that:

'5(3) The term "permanent establishment" likewise encompasses:

. . .

(b) the furnishing of services, including consultancy services, by an enterprise through employees or other personnel engaged by the enterprise for such purpose, but only where activities of that nature continue (for the same or connected project) within the Contracting State for a period or periods aggregating more than 183 days in any twelve-month period commencing or ending in the fiscal year concerned.'

The UK appears willing to agree to provisions of this kind and they appear in a variety of forms in treaties including those with Chile, India, South Africa and in the Taiwan arrangement. These provisions may apply to different kinds of services. For example, 'professional services and other activities of an independent character'[51] or services including managerial services, other than those taxable as royalties and fees for technical services are covered.[52] Likewise, the duration for the performance of the services varies, so that in the Indian Treaty, activities must continue for periods aggregating more than 90 days within any 12month period, or services are performed within that State for an associated enterprise for periods aggregating more than 30 days within any 12-month period,[53] while in the Kazakhstan Treaty consultancy services must be provided for more than 12 months.[54] These provisions are inserted at the instance of the UK's treaty partners. Nonetheless, they apply equally to services provided by residents of those states in the UK and may give rise to an income or corporation tax liability permitted by those treaties.

15-650 Deemed activity and permanent establishments

A number of treaties, particularly those that follow the UN Model, identify particular activities that will, if undertaken, constitute a permanent establishment without meeting the fixed place of business or, in some cases, agency requirements. Examples include toll manufacturing, that is, manufactures or processes in that State for the enterprise goods or merchandise belonging to the enterprise,[55] maintaining substantial equipment for rental or other purposes within that other state for a period of more than 12 months.[56]

---

[51] Chile, art. 5(3)(b), South Africa, art. 5(3)(b).

[52] India, art. 5(2)(k).

[53] India, art. 5(2)(k)(i) and (ii).

[54] Kazakhstan, art. (5(3)(c)).

[55] UK–Jordan Treaty, art. 5(5)(b).

[56] UK–Australia Treaty, art. 5(3) (b) (excluding equipment let under a hire-purchase agreement).

The UN Model also makes special permanent establishment rules for insurance business, which is found, for example, in the UK–Indonesia Treaty (below):

'5(6) An insurance enterprise of a Contracting State shall, except with regard to re-insurance, be deemed to have a permanent establishment in the other Contracting State if it collects premiums in the territory of that other State or insures risks situated there through an employee or through a representative established there who is not an agent of an independent status.'

Difficulties with insurance business are recognised by the OECD, but it does not regard it as appropriate to include model provisions.[57] Some of these difficulties are reflected in the high proportion of cases involving treaties and insurance companies in the UK courts examined throughout this book.

15-700   Preparatory or auxiliary activities

Where a permanent establishment exists as a result of either the fixed-place-of-business rule or the agency rule, it will nonetheless not be treated as being a permanent establishment if, in relation to the business of the company as a whole, the activities carried on are only of a preparatory or auxiliary character. This applies both in relation to physical and agency permanent establishments. The extent of 'preparatory or auxiliary' activities is illustrated by art. 5(4) of the UK–Turkey Treaty thus:

'5(4) Notwithstanding the preceding provisions of this Article, the term "permanent establishment" shall be deemed not to include:

(a)   the use of facilities solely for the purpose of storage, display or delivery of goods or merchandise belonging to the enterprise;

(b)   the maintenance of a stock of goods or merchandise belonging to the enterprise solely for the purpose of storage, display or delivery;

(c)   the maintenance of a stock of goods or merchandise belonging to the enterprise solely for the purpose of processing by another enterprise;

(d)   the maintenance of a fixed place of business solely for the purpose of purchasing goods or merchandise, or of collecting information, for the enterprise;

(e)   the maintenance of a fixed place of business solely for the purpose of carrying on, for the enterprise, any other activity of a preparatory or auxiliary character;

(f)   the maintenance of a fixed place of business solely for any combination of activities mentioned in subparagraphs (a) to (e) of this paragraph, provided that the overall activity of the fixed place of business resulting from this combination is of a preparatory or auxiliary character.'

The domestic law[58] is to similar effect, although, perhaps, the drafting is more modern. The functions enumerated in subparagraphs (a) to (d) above all relate to trade in goods only with the exception of collection of information. Services are thus addressed only by the general rule that functions of a preparatory or auxiliary character only negate the existence of a permanent establishment.

---

[57] Commentary to art. 5, para. 38.

[58] FA 2003, s. 148(4).

In *Birmingham & District Cattle By-Products Co Ltd v IRC* (1919) 12 TC 92, the first three months of the company's activities consisted of installing machinery, obtaining premises, engaging staff and arranging for the supply of by-products all of which were found to be preparatory to trade rather than trading. Nearly 100 years later, Special Commissioner Charles Hellier said in *Mansell v R & C Commissioners*:

> 'It seems to me that a trade commences when the taxpayer, having a specific idea in mind of his intended profit making activities, and having set up his business, begins operational activities – and by operational activities I mean dealings with third parties immediately and directly related to the supplies to be made which it is hoped will give rise to the expected profits, and which involve the trader putting money at risk: the acquisition of the goods to sell or to turn into items to be sold, the provision of services, or the entering into a contract to provide goods or services: the kind of activities which contribute to the gross (rather than the net) profit of the enterprise.[59]'

In relation to the negotiation of contracts, he said:

> 'It does not seem to me that carrying on negotiations to enter into the contracts which, when formed, will constitute operational activity is sufficient. At that stage no operational risk has been undertaken: no obligation has been assumed which directly relates to the supplies to be made. Not until those negotiations culminate in such obligations or assets, and give rise to a real possibility of loss or gain has an operational activity taken place. Until then, those negotiations may be part of setting up the trade but they do not to my mind betoken its commencement.[60]'

Although these cases deal with temporal issues, they do indicate a dividing line between operational activities and those that are preparatory in the sense of merely facilitating the operational activities. However, HMRC guidance and the OECD Commentary view 'preparatory or auxiliary' as a single composite expression rather than two separate concepts. The HMRC view is:

> 'In deciding whether or not a fixed place of business of a non-resident enterprise is used for activities of a preparatory or auxiliary nature, consider the following factors:
>
> (a) Are the services it performs so remote from the actual realisation of profits by the enterprise that it would be difficult to allocate any part of the profit to the fixed place of business? If they are, then the fixed place of business will not be a permanent establishment. The benchmark to gauge the activities against are those of the trade as a whole entity...
>
> (b) Does the activity of the fixed place of business form an essential and significant part of the enterprise as a whole? A fixed place of business whose general purpose is identical to the general purpose of the enterprise is not used for activities of a preparatory or auxiliary nature.
>
> Note that the exclusion of activities of a preparatory or auxiliary nature from the definition of a permanent establishment only applies if these activities are solely for the non-resident enterprise. If the activities are performed not only for the enterprise but also for other

---

[59] (2006) Sp C 551, para. 93.

[60] *Ibid.*, para. 94.

[61] HMRC, *INTM*, para. INTM266120. See also OECD Commentary to art. 5, paras. 21–30.

enterprises, including other companies in the same group, then the fixed place of business will not be within the scope of the exclusion.[61]'

This view emphasises the distinction between core and non-core elements of the business, so that non-core, supporting functions are recognised as preparatory or auxiliary.

These exclusions are not universally recognised, however. In the UK–India Treaty, for example, a person, other than an independent agent, acting for or on behalf of an enterprise, is deemed to be a permanent establishment if he or she habitually maintains a stock of goods or merchandise from which he or she regularly delivers goods or merchandise for or on behalf of the enterprise.[62]

15-750   Parent companies and subsidiaries as permanent establishments

Modern treaties such as that with Cyprus specify that:

'5(7) The fact that a company which is a resident of one of the Contracting States controls or is controlled by a company which is a resident of the other Contracting State, or which carries on business in that other Contracting State (whether through a permanent establishment or otherwise), shall not of itself constitute either company a permanent establishment of the other.'

This curious provision is not found in the domestic definition of permanent establishment in the FA 2003, s. 148. The statement does, however, emphasise, along with art. 9 (Associated enterprises), that tax is imposed on each legal person separately rather than on the group, and that the actual course of interaction between the parent and subsidiary must be examined.

---

[62] Art. 5(4)(b), incorporating art. 5(4)(b) of the UN Model.

Distributive Provisions of Income Tax Treaties

Chapter 7

16-000   Allocation of taxing jurisdiction

The distributive provisions of income tax treaties constitute the heart of the treaty system. These rules allocate taxing jurisdiction between the contracting states and determine the source of income and agreed maximum levels of taxation in source states. Any remaining double taxation after the application of these rules falls to be addressed by the double tax relief article (OECD Model, art. 23), which in the UK generally allows credit for foreign tax paid against related UK tax liability. In the context of non-UK residents, the distributive articles determine the limits of the UK tax base. Collectively, the distributive provisions cover the whole of the UK tax system. As with domestic law, treaties have evolved significantly since the oldest of them was first negotiated. Furthermore, given the fact that each treaty is individually negotiated with its own trade-offs, taking into account the interests of both contracting states, there is a wide variation in the detail. There is, as a result, no substitute for examining the precise wording of each treaty in considering its application.

Treaties patterned on the OECD Model allocate taxing jurisdiction in relation to any particular item of income or gain according to one of three approaches. First, exclusive taxation by the country of residence may be authorised. This is the starting point of the OECD Model which allows the country of residence broad authority to tax. Where exclusive jurisdiction is granted to the country of residence, then the other contracting state may not tax the item.[1]   Second, taxing jurisdiction may be allocated concurrently to the country of residence and to the country of source of the income or situs of the asset. The majority of distributive provisions specify when this may be the case. Within this category, treaties may impose a maximum amount of tax. This is most commonly the case in relation to dividends, interest and royalties.[2] Where double taxation arises by reason of concurrent taxing jurisdiction, relief may be claimed pursuant to art. 23.[3] Third, exclusive taxing jurisdiction may be granted to the country of source. In this last category, exclusive taxing jurisdiction emerges frequently from the exemption granted in the residence country under art. 23B of the OECD Model, rather than in the distributive provisions themselves. The scheme of distributive provisions of the UN Model Treaty is similar to the OECD Model but seeks to widen the range of circumstances in which source countries are entitled to exercise taxing

---

[1] *Trevor Smallwood Trust v R & C Commrs* (2008) Sp C 669 at para. 103.

[2] See chapter 9, paras. 18-100, 18-150 and 18-200.

[3] See chapter 14.

jurisdiction. The UN Model is styled to apply 'between developed and developing countries', and it is implicit that the residence countries are assumed to be developed, capital exporting countries with developing countries being implicitly the source jurisdictions. The extent to which this continues to reflect trade and investment patterns may be open to question. It is, however, noticeable that a shift in emphasis among the OECD members as reflected in the 2008 commentary to the OECD Model hints at adopting a similar stance to that found in the UN Model, such as recognition of service permanent establishments.[4]

The distributive provisions of treaties allocate the right to tax. They do not require a state to exercise that right. For example, many UK treaties authorise a positive rate of tax on dividends but, generally, as a matter of domestic law, this right is not exercised. There may, as a result, be circumstances where the item is not liable to tax in either jurisdiction. For example, a disposal of shares by a UK-resident company of shares in a Mauritian company qualifying for the substantial shareholding exemption within TCGA 1992, Sch. 7AC, may not be subject to tax in the UK and precluded from Mauritian tax by art. 13 of the UK–Mauritius Treaty. Although the principal purpose of treaties as commonly set out in their title is the avoidance of double taxation,[5] there is no overarching principal that denies treaty benefits where such taxing jurisdiction is not exercised by the other contracting state. To the extent that contracting states wish to limit the availability of benefits in such circumstances, specific limitations to that effect are normally included.[6]

16-050 Classification of sources

The broad classification of sources of income for treaty purposes parallels the schedular system of UK taxation to a large extent.[7] Table 7.1 is a general guide to assist classification under treaty and domestic law in relation to the main UK sources and the common application of treaty provisions to them. It will be noted that within certain broad categories, various sectors are identified for special treatment. This is most notable in relation to business profits where shipping and air transportation, as well as artists and sportspeople, have their own rules.[8] Similarly, in the employment area, general rules are provided for dependent personal services with specific treatment applicable to directors' fees, artists and sportspeople, pensions and government services.[9]

Delimiting the boundaries between the categories does give rise to difficulties under both domestic law and treaties independently. It should be emphasised that these broad classifications will form a general guide only and that treaty classification and domestic law

---

[4] Commentary to OECD Model, art. 5, paras. 42.11ff. See chapter 6, para. 15-600.

[5] In *Imperial Chemical Industries Limited v Caro* (1960) 39 TC 374 by Lord Evershed MR at 379.

[6] See chapter 16.

[7] The schedular system largely survives only for corporation tax purposes. This overall approach to the drafting of tax treaties reflects the long-standing influence of the UK on thinking about double taxation relief in the OECD.

[8] See chapter 8.

[9] See chapter 10.

classification will not necessarily coincide in all cases. For example, in *Memec plc v IRC*,[10] the treaty meaning of 'dividend' under the German Treaty was not the same as the domestic meaning of the expression for the purpose of credit in relation to underlying tax under the Taxes Act 1988, s. 799. Changes in classification also occur both in domestic law and treaties, such as the abolition of the charge under Sch. C by the FA 1996 in domestic law and the abandonment of art. 14 for independent personal services under the latest OECD Model (29 April 2000), with those activities being subsumed in the notion of business profits under arts. 5 and 7. A further source of complexity in dealing with treaties arises from potential mismatches in classification between the UK and the other contracting state. This may arise because of different legal analysis of the underlying issues, differing approach to the determination of the source of income for tax purposes or interpretation of the treaty.

Table 7.1: General guide to classification under treaty and domestic law

Treaty article	Domestic source – corporation tax	Domestic source – other taxpayers
Art. 6 – income from immovable property	Sch. A	ITTOIA 2005 – property income
Art. 7 – business profits	Sch. D, case I	ITTOIA 2005 – trading income
Art. 8 – transport	Sch. D, case I	Trading income
Art. 10	Sch. F	Dividends from UK-resident companies; dividends from non-UK-resident companies
Art. 11 – interest	Sch. D, case III	ITTOIA 2005 – interest
Art. 12 – royalties	Sch. D, case III	ITTOIA 2005 – receipts from intellectual property
Art. 13 – capital gains	Chargeable gains	Chargeable gains
Art. 14 – independent personal services		ITTOIA 2005 – trading income
Art. 15 – dependent personal services		ITEPA 2003 – employment income
Art. 16 – directors' fees		ITEPA 2003 – employment income
Art. 17 – artistes and sportsmen		ITEPA 2003 – employment income; ITTOIA 2005 – trading income
Art. 18 – pensions		ITEPA 2003 , Pt. 9 – pension income
Art. 19 – government service		ITEPA 2004 – employment income
Art. 20 – students		Various
Art. 21 – other income		Various

---

[10] [1998] BTC 251; [1998] STC 754, CA.

Business Profits

Chapter 8

17-000   Business profits

The permanent establishment article, in conjunction with the business profits article, forms the core of the treaty regime regulating the taxation of cross-border business activities. Article 7(1) of the OECD Model sets out the general rule. It is reflected in art. 7(1) of the Italy Treaty, which reads as follows:

> 'The profits of an enterprise of a Contracting State shall be taxable only in that State unless the enterprise carries on business in the other Contracting State through a permanent establishment situated therein. If the enterprise carries on or has carried on business as aforesaid, the profits of the enterprise may be taxed in the other State but only so much of them as is attributable to that permanent establishment.'

Thus, the right to tax profits is, in the first instance, granted exclusively to the state of residence of an enterprise. The most important exception to the general rule is where the enterprise carries on business through a permanent establishment in the other contracting state.

Article 7(1) refers to profits of an enterprise that carries on business through a permanent establishment. The starting point is that 'profits' means all profits. The scope of the article is then restricted by art. 7(7), which specifies that where profits include items of income which are dealt with separately in other articles, then those articles are not affected by the business profits article. It is thus a general provision which may be excluded by more specific rules. Special rules may apply for the two specific types of business or income. These normally include, in treaties following the current OECD Model, income from immovable property, profits from the operation of ships all aircraft in international traffic, business activities of entertainers and sportsmen and as well as dividends, interest and royalties. Earlier OECD style treaties further distinguish independent personal services from business profits, as is the case with treaties adopting the UN Model. A number of treaties with developing countries also draw a distinction between the provision of certain services provided through a permanent establishment and others where there is no permanent establishment. Article 7(7) is absent, however, from a number of UK treaties.

The effect of this article is that such profits can only be taxed in the state of residence of the enterprise. Any domestic law of the other contracting state seeking to tax these profits would be prevented from doing so.[1] This has been overridden, however, by the FA 2008, s. 59, from 12 March 2008 by the insertion of s. 815AZA into ICTA 1988, so that article does not

---

[1] In *Trevor Smallwood Trust v R & C Commrs* (2008) Sp C 669, para. 103 on the equivalent rule for capital gains. See chapter 11, para. 20-000.

prevent income of a person resident in the UK being chargeable to income tax or corporation tax. Thus, where business profits, for example, are attributed to a UK resident under ITA 2007, Pt. 13, Ch. 2 (Transfer of Assets Abroad), no treaty protection will be available in the UK to such a resident.[2]

17-050   Enterprise

An 'enterprise of a contracting state' is normally defined in art. 3(1)(d) to mean an 'enterprise carried on by a resident of a contracting state' and has been present in treaties at least since the 1963 OECD Draft. Several definitions were added to art. 3 of the OECD Model in 2000. 'Enterprise' now 'applies to the carrying on of any business'.[3] The term 'business' includes 'the performance of professional services and of other activities of an independent character'.[4] The newer definitions are not found in treaties concluded in the 20th century and comprise the majority of UK treaties. The expression 'enterprise' is not a term of art used generally in UK domestic tax law. In treaty language, which is more common in civil law jurisdictions and in this context, 'enterprise' is likely the same or similar to 'business'.[5] This would appear to be supported by the new definitions, although the commentary indicates that these should be understood by reference to domestic law.[6] The use of 'enterprise' may not be identical in all parts of a treaty. In *Boake Allen Ltd & Ors (including NEC Semi-Conductors Ltd) v Revenue and Customs Commissioners*,[7] the reference to 'enterprise' in art. 25(5) (non-discrimination on the basis of ownership) and in similar treaties was taken, without discussion, to refer to the companies that were the subject of the alleged discrimination and not the business they undertook. A similar approach was taken in *Sun Life Assurance Co. of Canada v Pearson* by Fox LJ, who said, 'SLAC is a "Canadian enterprise" for the purposes of the treaty'[8] in relation to the attribution of profits to a UK permanent establishment. The definitions now in art. 3, which refer to activities rather than to persons, appear more suited to art. 7 questions.

A fair rewrite of the treaty language might be that 'business profits of a resident of one contracting state are taxable exclusively in that state in the absence of a permanent establishment in the other contracting state'. Thus, business profits may only be liable to tax in the other contracting state if the resident carries on business there through a permanent establishment. In such circumstances, tax in the contracting state is limited to the amount of profits attributable to the permanent establishment. However this is expressed, the breadth of the principle is made clear by the policy explained in the OECD Commentary: unless a

---

[2] See chapter 1, para. 10-600 on the treatment of UK-resident partners.

[3] OECD Model, art. 3(1)(c).

[4] OECD Model, art. 3(1)(h).

[5] See the discussion in chapter 6, para. 15-150, on the meaning of business.

[6] Commentary to art. 3, paras. 4 and 10.2.

[7] [2007] BTC 414; [2007] UKHL 25.

[8] 59 TC 250 at p. 323.

permanent establishment exists, the enterprise is insufficiently engaged in the economy of the state to justify taxing its profits.[9]

While articulating this principle is relatively straightforward, determining the profits attributable to a permanent establishment is one of the more difficult issues in the application of tax treaties. The principles to be applied in attributing profits are set out in the remaining paragraphs of art. 7.

17-100   Which profits are 'business' profits?

The notion of 'business' has a wide meaning in UK domestic tax law but does not generally express taxing jurisdiction (other than in the context of property business,[10] which is addressed under art. 6 (income from immovable property)). 'Profits' in art. 7(1) covers all profits of an enterprise in principle, and since it applies to all profits other than those dealt with specifically in other articles, addresses all residual profits. In *Sun Life Assurance Co. of Canada v Pearson*,[11] the Court of Appeal discussed the meaning of profit in art. 7 at length, concluding that in art. 7(4) of the 1980 Canadian Treaty, it referred to investment income of a non-resident life insurance company and not to its 'income less expenses'. Its meaning must therefore be understood in the context of particular circumstances.

Treaties following the colonial pattern and some other early treaties refer to 'commercial and industrial profits' in the context of permanent establishment provisions. This term may not be coextensive with 'profits' in art. 7 of the OECD Model, as noted by Vinelott J in the High Court in the *Sun Life* case.[12] The scope of the expression varies from treaty to treaty, where different sources of income are included or excluded.

The most important and common application of art. 7 is in respect of trade profits. In domestic law, a non-UK resident is chargeable to income tax:

- on profits of a trade carried on wholly in the UK; or
- in the case of a trade carried on partly in the UK and partly elsewhere, on the part of profits of the trade carried on in the UK.[13]

The charge to corporation tax under Sch. D, Case I, on non-resident companies, tracks the language of art. 7(1) more closely:

> "11(1) A company not resident in the United Kingdom is within the charge to corporation tax if, and only if, it carries on a trade in the United Kingdom through a permanent establishment in the United Kingdom.

---

[9] OECD Commentary to art. 7, para. 9.

[10] Sch. A, Taxes Act 1988, s. 15, for corporation tax and ITTOIA, Pt. 3 for income tax.

[11] See above, n. 5.

[12] 59 TC 250, p. 310. See also *Ostime v Australian Mutual Provident Society* 38 TC 492.

[13] ITTOIA 2005, s. 6(2).

If it does so, it is chargeable to corporation tax, subject to any exceptions provided for by the Corporation Tax Acts, on all profits, wherever arising, that are attributable to its permanent establishment in the UK.[14]'

17-150   Attribution of profits to a branch

Allocation of profit to a permanent establishment is a controversial and awkward issue both in domestic and treaty practice. There have generally been two conceptual approaches to the attribution of profits. At one end of the scale is the 'relevant business activity approach', which treats the profits of the permanent establishment as those profits arising from the business activity in that permanent establishment. The tax is thus in respect of profits arising from transactions undertaken with third parties at or by that permanent establishment. At the other end of the scale is the 'functionally separate enterprise' approach, which emphasises the words 'and dealing wholly independently with the enterprise of which it is a permanent establishment'. This requires the recognition of 'dealings' between the permanent establishment and other parts of the enterprise, which are to be taken into account in determining the profits of the permanent establishment.

United Kingdom practice in the past, which originated in, and continues with respect to, the domestic income tax treatment, appears to have followed the former approach. The UK administrative application of the separate entity hypothesis was that it is only a tool for allocating such profits as exist with an enterprise and does not permit transactions between the permanent establishment and other parts of the enterprise to be hypothesised.[15] The permanent establish legislation introduced in FA 2003 represents something of a midpoint in the sense that statutory authority for domestic law purposes is given to a separate enterprise approach for companies liable to corporation tax in certain respects but not in all.

The OECD Commentary to art. 7 until 2008 largely endorsed the relevant business activity approach. The 2008 version adopts an extreme version of the functionally separate enterprise approach now styled the 'Authorised OECD Approach'. This followed a study that has run for over ten years and has yet to be completed. The 263-page final version of the 'Report on the attribution of profits to permanent establishments' was approved by the OECD Council on 17 July 2008 and includes a preface and four parts. Part I sets out general considerations for attributing profits to permanent establishments. The additional parts address the financial sector, where doing business in permanent establishment form is especially common, that is, banking (part II), global trading in financial instruments (part III) and insurance (part IV). Intended as an exercise in interpretation of art. 7, the project overreached that objective and its conclusions cannot be accommodated within the existing art. 7. Consequently, the OECD Committee on Fiscal Affairs strategy was, first, to include in the 2008 revised commentary on art. 7 that part of the report that it considers does not

---

[14] ICTA 1988, s. 11.

[15] Inland Revenue, *Banking Manual*, app. 9A. This manual has since been withdrawn but contained the essence of the 'Nolan Opinion' on the attribution of profits to branches of foreign banks operating in the UK. Lord Nolan (when practising at the Bar) provided a reasoned legal opinion on the attribution of profits of permanent establishments that formed the basis of agreement between the foreign banks and the Inland Revenue.

conflict with art. 7 and, second, to release a discussion draft of a new art. 7 to give effect to those parts that need a new legal framework. This was released on 7 July 2008.

The UK approach to treaties follows the OECD Model and is illustrated by Article 8(2) of the Thai Treaty which reads:

> 'Where an enterprise of a Contracting State carries on business in the other Contracting State through a permanent establishment situated therein, there shall in each Contracting State be attributed to that permanent establishment the profits which it might be expected to make if it were a distinct and separate enterprise engaged in the same or similar activities under the same or similar conditions and dealing wholly independently with the enterprise of which it is a permanent establishment.'

The article makes it clear that the attribution is to be undertaken in each state – the state where the permanent establishment is located – for the purpose of determining liability there and the residence state for the purpose of granting relief from double taxation. Although it is widely suggested that the separate enterprise theory permits part of an enterprise to make a profit 'dealing' with other parts of the enterprise, this proposition fails on two grounds. First, there is the legal impossibility of a person self-transacting. The theory confuses 'separate enterprise' with 'separate legal entity'. Second, it requires reading art. 7(2) in isolation rather than in the context of the article as a whole. The profits that are to be attributed to a permanent establishment are the 'profits of the enterprise' in art. 7(1). There can never be a profit in the permanent establishment if the person engaged in the enterprise makes a loss as a whole. Furthermore, in authorising the attribution of the profits of the enterprise as a whole, the direction to each state to make the attribution implies that the head office accounts should determine profits to be attributed in the event of a conflict with the state where the permanent establishment is located.

17-200   Domestic attribution – income tax

The legal basis for attributing profits to a UK branch of a non-resident for income tax under domestic law is obscure. Historically, assessment was on a branch or agency through which the trade was carried on. The same was true for non-resident companies whose chargeable profits were any trading income arising directly or indirectly through or from the branch or agency, and any income from property or rights used by or held for the branch or agency.[16]

There is little direct authority as to the method of determining income which arises 'directly or indirectly' through or from the branch or agency. In an early case, *Pommery and Greno v Aptthorpe*,[17] on the question of whether non-residents were trading in the UK, Denman J said:[18]

> 'It may be that there may be some difficulty in some respects as to the manner of calculating the amount of expenditure to be put against profits, whether it would be a proper course to look at the goods sent over to England and then to consider what profits they make, putting a fair

---

[16] Taxes Act 1988, s. 11(2), prior to amendment by FA 2003.

[17] (1886) 2 TC 182.

[18] At 189.

valuation on them as they arrive, and as the money is transmitted, or whether it would be necessary in such a case to look more minutely at the profits and losses upon the whole trade carried on partly in France and partly in England. . . . That is a matter of quantum, a matter for the consideration of persons skilled in dealing with such matters as assessing profits of trade.'

This passage has been cited by the Revenue as an early description of the arm's length principle. The problems of allocation in a non-treaty context are well illustrated in *Yates v GCA International Ltd*.[19] In that case, an English company entered into a contract with a Venezuelan company to provide certain services. The remuneration was divided between work performed in the UK and work performed in Venezuela. Under the Venezuelan Tax Code, income was regarded as arising from a Venezuelan source *inter alia* if the originating cause of the income was within Venezuela or for services rendered to Venezuelan residents or technical services utilised in the country; however, for the purpose of determining the extent to which credit was available in the UK under what is now the Taxes Act 1988, s. 790(4), it was provided that the income in question must arise in the territory imposing the tax. Scott J (as he then was) concluded that English law concepts as to identification of the place where income arises had to be applicable in determining to what extent the contractual remuneration was 'income arising in' Venezuela. He held that apportionment of the source of profits was possible and that the Special Commissioners made the obvious apportionment, namely based on the contract itself, which he did not disturb.

In the *Sun Life* case, the court considered whether, in the context of the Canadian Treaty, insurance policies were made at or through a branch or agency in the UK in the following circumstances. A Canadian insurer divided its business into divisions. The British division comprised not only territories within the UK but also the Republic of Ireland, Malta, Guernsey, Jersey and the Isle of Man. The Court of Appeal concluded that the branch or agency was constituted by the whole of the operation within the UK and that the offices outside the UK, such as in the Republic of Ireland, had no authority to conclude any insurance business. They were merely administrative channels whereby proposals reached London, where they were effectively dealt with and where the policies were issued.

Little changed until the enactment of FA 1995, which introduced both substantive and procedural changes to the taxation of non-residents. The question of determining profits of non-residents was debated in Parliament as a result of perceived inadequacies of the proposed legislation.[20] In the course of the debate in the Standing Committee on the Finance Bill, the Government reaffirmed that 'the arm's length principle applies generally to the measure of profits brought into charge on a non-resident'. The Government was unwilling to see amendments to the legislation, but thereafter the Revenue issued a statement in *Tax Bulletin*,[21] with the agreement of the major tax professional bodies, to the effect that the arm's length principle as set out in the OECD Model Treaty and OECD publications applies to the measure of profits chargeable on a non-resident in respect of trading in the UK as a matter of law, irrespective of whether a treaty applies. In law, a branch is not a separate legal person from the company to which it belongs but part of it. The Finance Act 1995, s. 126(4),

---

[19] [1991] BTC 107; [1991] STC 157, Ch.D.

[20] *Hansard*, HC Standing Committee D, 2 March 1995, p. 547.

[21] August 1995, p. 234.

states that for the purpose of that section (determining the liability of UK representatives of a non-resident (that is the branch or agency)), the representative is to be treated as if he or she were a separate and distinct person from the non-resident. This may give some statutory support for the separate enterprise hypothesis as a matter of domestic law.

The statutory transfer pricing provisions in the Taxes Act 1988, Sch. 28AA, do not themselves apply to the attribution of profits between a UK branch and other parts of a non-resident's business. However, it should be borne in mind that if a non-resident is within the UK tax charge, transactions between it and other companies where there is common management, control or capital as determined under the Taxes Act 1988, Sch. 28AA, para. 4, will be within the UK transfer pricing rules. Thus, the determination of the transfer prices will be at two levels: first, between the person and the other parts of the group, and, secondly, between the head office and the UK permanent establishment. Both levels are relevant to UK tax.

General arm's length principles are, however, imported into the treaty rules contained in art. 7(2) of the OECD Model, which require the profits attributed to a permanent establishment to be those which the establishment would have made if instead of dealing with its head office, it had been dealing with an entirely separate enterprise under conditions and at prices prevailing in the ordinary market. The application of the separate entity hypothesis has been examined by the courts in relation to treaties with Australia, Canada and the Netherlands. Two of these cases dealt with the attribution of profits of overseas life assurance companies to permanent establishments in the UK. The domestic legislation which provided for profit on a notional basis was itself designed to overcome difficulties of allocation. In *Ostime v Australian Mutual Provident Society*,[22] Lord Radcliffe identified the problems of art. 7(2) thus:[23]

'It is not left wholly to the will of the United Kingdom taxing authorities to decide the basis on which that attribution of commercial profits is to be made. Article [7(2)] provides by its terms for a basis which in effect requires the hypothesis that the branch is an independent enterprise dealing as an independent entity at arm's length with the head office. The profits which emerge from a calculation based on this hypothesis are to be deemed to be income derived from sources in the United Kingdom.

I do not think that it is open to us to decide what would be the consequences of taxing the respondent's commercial profits according to this new formula. It is by no means easy to see what other hypotheses are required or excluded by the central hypothesis. In his view, the formula of allocating notional profits could not be applied to the hypothetical independent enterprise "without violating the very hypothesis ... designed to lay down the basis of taxability."'

In the same case, Lord Denning described the test in his dissenting judgement as:

'The Agreement goes on to say how this amount is to be ascertained. It is by means of a given hypothesis. You are to treat the establishment here as if it were completely independent of the Australian head office and were dealing at arm's length with it, and you are to estimate the

---

[22] (1958) 38 TC 492, HL.

[23] At 517.

profits which such an independent enterprise might be expected to derive on its own, and then tax it on the amount so ascertained.'

The importance of the way in which branch activity is actually conducted is highlighted in *General Reinsurance Company Ltd v Tomlinson*.[24] A Dutch reinsurance company operated a branch in the UK. It maintained a portfolio of investment built up from the profits of its reinsurance business in London, made up of UK investments and certain dollar investments held in New York. Decision-making about the portfolio took place in the Netherlands. Investment income in this context was regarded as profits obtained in the carrying-on of the company's business. This applied to profit on US investments, even though they were specifically earmarked for possible US claims. Since the US business was done by the company in London, the investment income was part of its profit as a matter of domestic law. In that case, it was considered that if the permanent establishment was to be treated as an independent enterprise, it must be considered to be necessary for it to have a portfolio of investments in order to carry on its business. Although the court recognised that there were difficulties in deciding what the appropriate size of the portfolio was, in that case, the court determined that because the London portfolio was built up from past profits of the business of the branch, there was nothing to suggest that the London portfolio was either too large or too small for the amount of the business carried on by the London branch.

17-250　Domestic attribution – corporation tax

The introduction of the permanent establishment concept into domestic law in 2003 brought with it art. 7(2) attribution rules for corporation tax purposes:

'11AA(2) There shall be attributed to the permanent establishment the profits it would have made if it were a distinct and separate enterprise, engaged in the same or similar activities under the same or similar conditions, dealing wholly independently with the non-resident company.[25]'

The Taxes Act 1988, s. 11AA,[26] specifically sets out rules for the determination of profits attributable to a permanent establishment. Section 11AA(2) adopts broadly the wording of art. 7(1) of the OECD Model Treaty. Thus, there is to be attributed to the permanent establishments the profits it would have made if it were a distinct and separate enterprise engaged in the same or similar activities under the same or similar conditions dealing wholly independently with the non-resident company. The exact scope and extent, to which the permanent establishment is to be treated as a distinct and separate enterprise, and what the effect of this is, are themselves somewhat controversial in treaty terms. The legislation does not address this fully. However, certain assumptions are to be built into the attribution by s. 11AA(3). First, it must be assumed that the permanent establishment has the same credit rating as the non-resident company. Second, it must also be assumed that the permanent establishment has equity capital of an amount not less than it would have had operating as a distinct and separate entity. Third, its loan capital may not exceed the amount it would have

---

[24] (1970) 48 TC 81.

[25] Taxes Act 1988.

[26] Inserted by FA 2003, s. 149.

had if it had that amount of equity capital. No definition of 'equity capital' or 'loan capital' is given.

The new legislation specifies that no deductions may be made in respect of costs in excess of those that would have been incurred on these assumptions. No definition of 'costs' in this context is provided.

Schedule A1 to ICTA 1988 supplements the provisions in s. 11AA in determining the profits attributable to the permanent establishment.[27] The schedule builds on the separate enterprise principle contained in s. 11AA(2). It specifies that in accordance with the separate enterprise principle, transactions between the permanent establishment and any other part of the non-resident company are treated as taking place on such terms as would have been agreed between parties dealing at arm's length. Again, no explanation is given as to what constitutes a 'transaction'. This absence is particularly important since, in principle, there can be no transactions within a legal entity. This general principle is made subject to certain exceptions. First, the general provision as to allowable deductions applies whether or not the expenses are incurred by or reimbursed by the permanent establishment. The amount of expenses is the actual cost to the non-resident company.[28] Second, no deduction is allowed in respect of royalties paid or similar payments made by the permanent establishment to any other part of the non-resident company in respect of the use of intangible assets held by the company. This does not, however, prevent a deduction in respect of any contribution by the permanent establishment to the costs of creation of an intangible asset.[29]

Deductions in respect of payments of interest or other financing costs by the permanent establishment to other parts of the non-resident company are generally prohibited. It is only in relation to such costs payable in respect of borrowing by the permanent establishment in the ordinary course of a financial business carried on by the permanent establishment that the prohibitions do not apply. In this context, financial business means banking, deposit taking, money lending, debt factoring, or business similar to any of those, as well as dealing in commodity or financial futures.[30] Special rules apply to non-resident companies engaged in financial business which deal with the attribution of financial assets and profit-rising in order to address the manner in which loans are treated as made by the non-resident company to the permanent establishment, as well as separate rules where the permanent establishment is acting as an agent or intermediary.[31] An anti-avoidance provision has been introduced to deal with transfer of assets not carried out for valid commercial reasons, which include the obtaining of a tax advantage.[32] Where goods or services are provided by the non-resident company to the permanent establishment, then the separate enterprise principle applies if the goods or services are of a kind that the company supplies in the ordinary course of its business to third parties dealing with it at arm's length. If not, then the provision of goods or

---

[27] S. 11(6).

[28] Sch A1, para. 3.

[29] Sch. A1, para. 4.

[30] Sch. A1, para. 5.

[31] Paras. 9 and 10.

[32] Para. 8.

services is dealt with as an expense incurred by the non-resident company for the purposes of the permanent establishment.[33]

Deductions are to be allowed for expenses incurred for the purposes of the permanent establishment including executive and general administrative expenses so incurred, whether in the UK or elsewhere.[34] This is consistent with the approach in the OECD Model, art. 7(3). Deductibility only applies to expenses of a kind that would give rise to deduction if incurred by a company resident in the UK.

The branch capital requirements are intended to assimilate permanent establishments to subsidiaries. As a result, a thin capitalisation approach is intended by HMRC in relation to financing of the branch. This approach imputes the same or similar activities under the same or similar conditions to the branch as a separate entity. The effect is to limit the amount of debt in respect of which interest may be deducted by the branch.

17-300 Financial institutions

Since the main targets of the legislation are foreign banks operating through branches in the UK, it is perhaps surprising that only a small part of the legislation is devoted to such institutions. Part 3 of Sch. A1 sets out rules for financial institutions. They are identified by reference to banks as defined in ICTA 1988, s. 840A. However, similar principles may also apply to non-resident companies that are not banks (para. 7). This complex drafting, read in conjunction with para. 5 makes it clear that the rules apply to non-resident companies with permanent establishments in the UK engaged in financial business. This means banking, deposit taking, money lending or debt factoring, as well as similar businesses. It also includes dealing in commodity or financial futures.

17-350 Authorised OECD approach

The approach now adopted by the OECD in its 2008 report, labelled 'The working hypothesis' during the earlier phases of the study, requires the following steps in order for the OECD to apply its version of the functionally separate enterprise approach:

(1) The permanent establishment must be hypothesised as a distinct and separate enterprise. This requires a functional and factual analysis of the permanent establishment in order to determine the functions of the hypothesised distinct and separate enterprise and the economically relevant characteristics relating to the performance of those functions.

(2) The profits of the hypothesised distinct and separate enterprise must be determined based on a comparability analysis. Since there are no transactions between a branch and a head office within a single entity, this requires an analogy to dealings. The

---

[33] Para. 6.

[34] S. 11AA(4).

working hypothesis refers to the dealings between the permanent establishment and the enterprise of which it is a part. Dealings relate to events which ought to be recognised for the purpose of attributing profits, since there are no contractual terms. Accounting records, together with any contemporaneous internal documentation, are to be used in order to hypothesise the 'terms of the dealing'.

(3)   The OECD transfer pricing guidelines are to be applied by analogy to such dealings.

The precise application of this approach is controversial, and despite its authoritative sounding title, it is not universally accepted. Within the OECD, around half of the member countries have entered observations or reservations in connection with the 2008 revised commentary to art. 7, and some 24 non-member countries have already registered positions on it. Its status as far as UK law is concerned remains as an aid to interpretation.[35] At the time of the introduction of FA 2003, the Revenue indicated that the new legislation does not imply an incorporation of the draft OECD working hypothesis. As a result, apart from the rules relating to the attribution of capital, there are no changes, it says, in the rules for allocating profits to branches.

In the exchange of notes of 24 July 2001, with respect to the US 001), explicit endorsement is given to the OECD Transfer Pricing Guidelines as the mechanism by analogy for determining the profits attributable to a permanent establishment. However, the exact effect of this statement is unclear.

17-400   Deduction of expenditure

Deduction of expenditure of a permanent establishment is given express recognition in art. 7(3) of the OECD Model. For example, that article in the UK–Macedonia Treaty reads:

'7(3) In determining the profits of a permanent establishment, there shall be allowed as deductions expenses which are incurred for the purposes of the permanent establishment, including executive and general administrative expenses so incurred, whether in the State in which the permanent establishment is situated or elsewhere.'

This clarifies the method of allocating expenses prescribed by art. 7(2). It specifies that in determining the profits of a permanent establishment, deduction of expenses must be allowed where they are incurred for the permanent establishment. This includes executive and general administrative expenses incurred where they are in the state in which the permanent establishment is situated or otherwise. As a result, the place where the expenditure is incurred is irrelevant and a deduction must be allowed for the overhead costs related to the permanent establishment.

Treaties adopting the approach of the UN Model make it clear that intra-enterprise dealings cannot be recognised. One version is found in the UK–Mexico Treaty, which modifies art. 7(3) thus:

'7(4) . . . However, no such deduction shall be allowed in respect of amounts, if any, paid (otherwise than by way of reimbursement of actual expenses) by the permanent establishment

---

[35] See chapter 3, para. 12-200.

to the head office of the enterprise or any of its other offices, by way of royalties, fees or other similar payments in return for the use of patents or other rights, or by way of a commission, for specific services performed or for management, or, except in the case of a bank, by way of interest on money lent to the permanent establishment.'

It is clear that the authorised OECD approach cannot properly apply in the case of treaties adopting similar language. There is an assumption that charges of this kind are only made to permanent establishments by head offices and not the other way around. No such limit is placed on payments by head offices to permanent establishments.

17-450   Customary methods of allocation

Article 7(4) authorises the application of customary methods of attributing profits to permanent establishments. Its terms are reflected in art. 7(4) of the Romanian Treaty which reads as follows:

'Insofar as it has been customary in a Contracting State to determine the profits to be attributed to a permanent establishment on the basis of an apportionment of the total profits of the enterprise to its various parts, nothing in paragraph (2) of this Article shall preclude that Contracting State from determining the profits to be taxed by such an apportionment as may be customary; the method of apportionment adopted shall, however, be such that the result shall be in accordance with the principles embodied in this Article.'

The significance and application of these provisions has been highlighted in cases involving determining the UK profits of overseas life assurance companies. Under domestic law, overseas life insurance companies have been taxed on a conventional basis; the conventional profits for this purpose are arrived at by reference to the proportion of investment income corresponding to the proportion of business done in the UK and the whole of the business. In *Ostime v Australian Mutual Provident Society*,[36] the court considered the 1947 Australian Treaty. 'Industrial or commercial profits' was narrowly defined in the treaty and specifically excluded income in the form of dividend, interest, rents, royalties, management charges or remuneration for personal services. The provisions attributing profits to a permanent establishment in art. III(2) did not contain wording preserving conventional methods of attributing income. The treaty, as a result, overrode the application of the domestic rule.

In the *Sun Life* case, the treaty provision relating to customary methods was considered by the Court of Appeal.[37] It concluded that there was no doubt as to the customary nature of the domestic statute law of attribution based on a fraction of worldwide income which had been in place since 1915. The court noted that article 7(4) of the OECD Model does not require a close correspondence of the method permitted by that article and the separate enterprise principle in art. 7(2). Consequently, it held that art. 7(4) authorises some computation based on apportionment of total profits. Insofar as a conventional method is to give effect to the separate enterprise principle, it must to some degree be crude in its operation. The limits of art. 7(4) are imprecise and the court was not prepared to say that the domestic law was not in accordance with the principles of art. 7. Although apportioning total profits by reference to a

---

[36] See above, n. 22.

[37] See above, n. 11.

formula is not an attribution of profits on a separate enterprise basis, the customary nature of the UK rules meant that the domestic law gave reasonable effect to the principles of art. 7.

17-500   Independent personal services

Under domestic law, income tax is charged on the profits of any profession or vocation under ITTOIA 2005, s. 5. This is distinguished in certain respects from the income of a trade, but the territorial scope of the charge is identical.[38] For many years, UK treaties, particularly those patterned on the OECD 1963 draft and 1977 model, have distinguished between business profits in art. 7 and 'professional services and other activities of an independent character' referred to in art. 14.

One such treaty is the UK–Belgium Treaty, which provides that:

'14(1) Income derived by a resident of a Contracting State in respect of professional services or other activities of an independent character shall be taxable only in that State unless he has a fixed base regularly available to him in the other Contracting State for the purpose of performing his activities. If he has such a fixed base, the income may be taxed in the other State but only so much of it as is attributable to that fixed base.'

A fixed base in this context is somewhat similar in concept to a fixed place of business in art. 5(1), although the expression is not elaborated on to the same extent. There is no equivalent to agency permanent establishment in art. 14, emphasising that it is the performance of services, rather than the contracting to provide services, that gives rise to profit. The fixed base must be regularly available to the person providing the services for the purpose of providing his or her services. In other words, authority to tax is personal rather than a reference to an enterprise. The absence of any equivalent to art. 7(2) means that only a relevant business (professional) activity basis of attribution is permitted. It is not always clear which activities fall within business profits as opposed to independent personal services. Article 14 of the UK–Belgium Treaty continues:

'14(2) The term "professional services" includes, especially, independent scientific, literary, artistic, educational or teaching activities as well as the independent activities of physicians, lawyers, engineers, architects, dentists and accountants.'

There are similar problems of defining the boundaries under domestic law. A profession generally involves an occupation requiring purely intellectual skill or manual skill controlled by the intellectual skill of the operator, such as painting.[39] It is about fact and degree. The essential question is the degree of intellectual skill involved.[40] The Revenue practice is generally to deal with independent personal services by analogy to business profits.[41] The Revenue guidance notes that although the article is mainly concerned with individuals who carry on a profession, it can also be relevant to an individual who carries on a trade. This addresses the lack of common boundary between 'trade' and 'profession or vocation' under

---

[38] ITTOIA, s. 6(3).

[39] *IRC v Maxse* (1919) 12 TC 41.

[40] *Currie v IRC* (1921) 12 TC 245.

[41] Inland Revenue, *Double Taxation Manual*, para. 1740.

ITTOIA, Pt. 2, on the one hand, and, on the other hand, the treaty concepts of 'business profits' in art. 7 and 'independent personal services' in art. 14. It also addresses distinctions between trade and professions in old cases that seem improbable in the modern context. Thus, a photographer is a trader[42] while a jockey carries on a vocation.[43]

Article 14 was deleted from the OECD Model on 29 April 2000 on the basis of an OECD report entitled 'Issues related to article 14 of the OECD Model Tax Convention'.[44] The deletion was based on the fact that there were no intended differences between the concepts of permanent establishment as used in art. 7 and fixed base as used in art. 14, and between how profits were computed and tax was calculated according to whether art. 7 or 14 was applied. The United Kingdom – United States 001) was the first UK treaty to adopt this approach. Article 14 does not appear, and the term 'business' is defined to include the performance of professional services and other activities of an independent character, as recommended by the OECD. This was carried out to prevent a restrictive interpretation of 'business' which might exclude such activities. However, this change in the US Treaty alters the basis on which cross-border professional partnerships are taxable, moving them to an enterprise basis.[45]

17-550   Technical service fees

Several treaties with developing countries make an important exception to the permanent establishment principle in the context of fees for technical services. An example is found in the Gambian Treaty. Article 14 reads in part:

'(1)   Fees for technical services arising in one of the territories and paid to a resident of the other territory may be taxed in that other territory.

(2)   Notwithstanding the provisions of Article 7, such fees may also be taxed in the territory in which they arise and according to the law of that territory; but where such fees are paid to a resident of the other territory who is subject to tax there in respect thereof the tax so charged in the territory in which the fees arise shall not exceed 15 per cent of the gross amount of the fees arising there.'

Thus, where technical services are provided, they may be taxed in the country of source, despite the absence of a permanent establishment. These articles are included at the instance of the other contracting states and are commonly aimed at protecting withholding taxes on gross fees paid to non-residents for consulting services. The rate of tax is usually linked to the rate set with respect to royalties. The article gives primary taxing rights over the fees to the country in which the fees arise, this being deemed to be the country of which the payer is a resident.[46]

---

[42] *Cecil v IRC* (1919) 36 TLR 164.

[43] *Wing v O'Connell* [1927] IR 84.

[44] Adopted by the Committee on Fiscal Affairs on 27 January 2000.

[45] US Treaty, art. 3(1)(d).

[46] HMRC, *INTM*, para. INTM153140.

These articles cause significant problems in determining the boundary between cases that concern technical services compared with independent personal services or business profits, as well as distinctions between technical service fees and royalties. Early versions of these articles contained fairly simple definitions. For example, art. 14(3) of the Gambian Treaty reads:

> 'The term "fees for technical services" as used in this Article means payments of any kind to any person, other than to an employee of the person making the payments, in consideration for any services of a technical or consultancy nature.'

This definition does not assist greatly in identifying the boundaries between, for example, professional services which are 'technical' on the one side, and payments for 'know-how', which may fall within the royalty article. Later versions, such as art, 13 of the Indian Treaty (1993), contain lengthy descriptions of technical services with amounts deemed to be included and excluded. Technical service provisions may not apply where there is a permanent establishment, thus encouraging permanent establishments in the context of technical services, so as to avoid taxes on a gross basis. From a UK perspective, this will be important in the context of technical service contracts performed abroad, where tax on a gross basis may lead to effective taxation at rates in excess of UK rates. In some treaties, such as Gambia, a recipient of such fees can elect to have tax charged on a net basis. In addition, such treaties typically deem the source of payments to be the country in which the payer is resident. This will permit a UK resident to obtain credit for the tax paid, notwithstanding that the work is done in the UK.

17-600   Shipping and air transport

The allocation of taxing jurisdiction in respect of shipping and air transport is found in several kinds of treaties. It is always contained in comprehensive income tax treaties. It is also frequently found in treaties covering only shipping and air transportation, such as treaties with Algeria, Brazil, Cameroon, Ethiopia, Iran, Jordan, Lebanon, Saudi Arabia and Zaire. In the case of Hong Kong, relief from double taxation in relation to shipping and air transportation is included in a broader commercial treaty addressing those industries generally.

The UK–Mauritius Treaty is typical of UK treaties following the OECD Model, as shown here:

> '8(1) Profits from the operation of ships or aircraft in international traffic shall be taxable only in the Contracting State in which the place of effective management of the enterprise is situated.

> 8(2) If the place of effective management of a shipping enterprise is aboard a ship then it shall be deemed to be situated in the Contracting State in which the home harbour of the ship is situated, or, if there is no such home harbour, in the Contracting State of which the operator of the ship is a resident.

> 8(3) The provisions of paragraph (1) of this Article shall also apply to profits from the participation in a pool, a joint business or an international operating agency.'

The OECD Model also restricts taxation to the management state in respect of boats engaged in inland waterways transport, but this provision is normally excluded from UK treaties in line with a reservation in art. 8 of the OECD Model.[47] Until 2005, the UK reserved the right to include in the article profits from leasing of ships or aircraft on a bareboat basis and from the leasing of containers.[48] A number of treaties diverge from the OECD Model, by applying different connecting factors giving rise to the right to tax profits from these sources, such as the port of registry,[49] residence,[50] or management and control plus head office[51] – although the general thrust of it is to permit taxation in one state only in respect of international traffic. A UK-resident company that is within the Tonnage Tax regime in FA 2000, Sch. 22, and therefore exempt from corporation tax on its 'relevant shipping profits', may nonetheless qualify for such benefits.

17-650 Artists and sportspeople

Entertainers and athletes constitute a further category of business identified for special treatment. Some treaties, following the old colonial pattern, simply exclude entertainers from the personal services articles (for example, Belize and Germany). Others (for example, Gambia) contain no specific provision, leaving entertainers within the general rule for personal services. The common thread in treaty provisions aimed at artists and sportspeople is that they authorise taxation of the income of such individuals in the contracting state where their professional activities are exercised, despite the absence of a permanent establishment or fixed base. Thus, art. 17(1) of the Danish Treaty reads:

> 'Notwithstanding the provisions of Articles 14 and 15, income derived by a resident of a Contracting State as an entertainer, such as a theatre, motion picture, radio or television artiste, or a musician, or as an athlete, from his personal activities as such exercised in the other Contracting State, may be taxed in that other State.'

A number of treaties make exceptions for certain kinds of performances. For example, state-sponsored visits, non-profit organisations and official cultural exchanges are excluded in art. 17 of the Austrian Treaty. Others, such as art. 19(1) of the Hungarian Treaty, contain a *de minimis* provision for gross receipts not exceeding £8,000. In some cases, the exclusion for state-sponsored visits and non-profit organisations only applies to those organisations. Others, such as the Canadian Treaty, art. 16, also exclude their employees.

In 1974, the Committee on Fiscal Affairs added wording to the 1963 OECD Draft Convention to deal with amounts accruing to persons other than the entertainer or athlete. An example of this is found in art. 18(2) of the New Zealand Treaty (as shown below):

> 'Where income in respect of personal activities exercised by an entertainer or an athlete in his capacity as such accrues not to the entertainer or athlete himself but to another person, that

---

[47] Commentary on art. 8, para. 32.

[48] OECD Commentary on art. 8, para. 34.

[49] UK–Greece, art. 5.

[50] UK–Malta, art. 8(1).

[51] UK–Brazil, art. 3.

income may, not withstanding the provisions of Articles 8, 15 and 16, be taxed in the Contracting State in which the activities of the entertainer or athlete are exercised.'

These rules do not apply under art. 16(2) of the US Treaty if the recipient of the payment establishes that neither the entertainer nor sportsperson nor persons related thereto participate directly or indirectly in the profits of that other person in any manner. In *Agassi v Robinson (HM Inspector of Taxes)* [2006] BTC 372; [2006] UKHL 23, the taxpayer was a famous US-resident professional tennis player who played in the UK for a limited number of days each year. He had set up a company incorporated and resident in the US which he controlled and through which he entered into endorsement contracts with two manufacturers of sports clothing and equipment, neither of which was resident or had a tax presence in the UK. His company received payments in the US from the manufacturers. The House of Lords held (Lord Walker of Gestingthorpe dissenting) that the payments were in respect of 'relevant activity' in the UK within what is now ITTOIA 2005, s. 13, and therefore liable to income tax on those payments. When the matter was heard before the Special Commissioners,[52] it was common ground that the treaty with the US did not prevent any of the charges to tax.

Some treaties also include activities providing the services of public entertainers as constituting a permanent establishment (for example, the Jamaican Treaty, art. 4(4)(a)). The manner in which performers and sportsmen are taxed under domestic law varies considerably according to their circumstances. Commonly, such individuals may be employees subject to tax under ITEPA 2003 or exercising a trade or profession under ITTOIA 2007, Pt. 2. Entertainers may also receive royalties typically in respect of copyright or similar rights. Where the source of income is employment or copyright royalties, withholding will apply under PAYE,[53] or in the case of copyright royalties.[54] While there is no general withholding mechanism in respect of income taxed under ITTOIA, Pt. 2, a withholding mechanism in respect of foreign entertainers applies pursuant to ITA 2007, ss. 966 to 970, and the Income Tax (Entertainers and Sportsmen) Regulations 1987 (SI 1987/530).

17-700   Associated enterprises

All income tax treaties contain provisions equivalent to art. 9 of the OECD Model authorising the application of domestic transfer pricing rules. The Canadian Treaty, patterned on the OECD Model, reads as follows:

'9(1) Where:

(a)   an enterprise of one of the Contracting States participates directly or indirectly in the management, control or capital of an enterprise of the other Contracting State; or

(b)   the same persons participate directly or indirectly in the management, control or capital of an enterprise of one of the Contracting States and of an enterprise of the other Contracting State;

---

[52] Sub nom *Set & Ors v Robinson (HMIT)* (2003) Sp C 373, an anonymised decision at that stage.

[53] ITEPA 2003, Pt. 11, and related regulations.

[54] ITA 2007, s. 906.

and in either case conditions are made or imposed between the two enterprises, in their commercial or financial relations, which differ from those which would be made between independent enterprises, then any profits which would but for those conditions have accrued to one of the enterprises, but by reason of those conditions have not so accrued, may be included in the profits of that enterprise and taxed accordingly.'

In the UK, the insertion of Sch. 28AA to the Taxes Act 1988, replacing s. 770, had the stated objective of enacting art. 9 of the OECD Model into domestic law. This is given statutory effect by para. 2, which despite its infelicitous drafting requires the domestic law to be construed so as to conform with art. 9 and the 'Transfer pricing guidelines for multinational enterprises' (the 'Transfer Pricing Guidelines').[55] Accordingly, HMRC states that 'the scope of Schedule 28AA can be no wider than the scope of Article 9, as informed by the OECD Transfer Pricing Guidelines.'[56]

There are two hurdles to be overcome before an adjustment to the profits of an enterprise may be adjusted. First, there must be the required participation in management control or capital within art.9(1) (a) or (b). These expressions are not defined in the article but Sch. 28AA, para. 4, specifies when a person participates directly or indirectly in the management, control or capital of another person for the purposes of the domestic rule. Indirect participation under the domestic law includes participation which is deemed to exist by virtue of broad attribution rules.[57] These take the domestic expressions outside the scope of those found in the treaty language.

The second hurdle to overcome is that the conditions between the two enterprises in their commercial and financial relations must be other than on arm's length terms. The commentary on art. 9 of the OECD Model[58] and the 'Transfer Pricing Guidelines'[59] make it clear that this refers to the totality of terms of the transactions entered into by the two enterprises. The domestic rule recognises the transactional basis explicitly.[60]

HMRC confirms that the term 'provision' is broadly analogous to the phrase 'conditions made or imposed' in art. 9, and embraces all the terms and conditions attaching to a transaction or series of transactions. Although, HMRC says, the term provision is arguably wider than the phrase 'conditions made or imposed', it must never be interpreted as such.[61]

Where the two requirements are met, then the profits of the enterprise whose profits are less than they would be but for the actual transaction, may be adjusted upwards to reflect what they would have been if the transaction was at arm's length. This upward-only adjustment is made to the tax computation only. It does not require the transaction to be at arm's length or deem it to be so for tax or indeed any other purposes.

---

[55] Approved by the Council of the OECD on 27 June 1995.

[56] HMRC, *INTM*, para. INTM432040.

[57] Sch. 28AA, para. 4(3).

[58] Para. 1.

[59] Approved by the Council of the OECD on 27 June 1995, Ch. 1.

[60] Sch. 28AA, paras. 1(1) and 1(2).

[61] HMRC, INTM, para. INTM432040.

Any such upward-adjustment of profits carries with it the risk of double taxation, because the same profits will be included in the tax computations of the two enterprises. Article 9(2) of the UK–Japan Treaty broadly follows the OECD Model in providing a mechanism to address such double taxation:

> '9(2) Where a Contracting State includes, in accordance with the provisions of paragraph 1 of this Article, in the profits of an enterprise of that Contracting State – and taxes accordingly – profits on which an enterprise of the other Contracting State has been charged to tax in that other Contracting State and the competent authority of that other Contracting State agrees that the profits so included are profits which would have accrued to the enterprise of the first-mentioned Contracting State if the conditions made between the two enterprises had been those which would have been made between independent enterprises, then that other Contracting State shall make an appropriate adjustment to the amount of the tax charged therein on those profits. In determining such adjustment, due regard shall be had to the other provisions of this Convention.'

Article 9(2) confers entitlement to corresponding adjustments in a contracting state where there is an increase in tax liability in the other contracting state as a result of a transfer pricing adjustment. Such adjustments are not automatic, and the mutual agreement procedure under art. 25 is invariably invoked. Many older UK treaties do not contain art. 9(2) (see, for example, the Kenyan Treaty), but the modern trend appears to be to include it. In those treaties that do not, the mutual agreement procedure is the only basis for the making of corresponding adjustments. Schedule 28AA permits adjustments by claim in relation to UK transactions but not cross-border transactions.[62] The mutual agreement procedure must therefore be invoked.[63]

---

[62] Paras. 6 to 6C.

[63] See chapter 18.

Income from Property

Chapter 9

18-000   Introduction

This chapter examines income from property, sometimes described as investment income. It covers income from immovable property, (OECD Model, art. 6), dividends (OECD Model, art. 10), Interest (OECD Model, art. 11) and royalties (OECD Model, art. 12). The common characteristic is that the amount under consideration is an economic rent derived from the ownership of an asset. In each case the income may by received in the course of a business or as a personal investment. Where the amount is part of a business, the interaction between these articles and those discussed in chapter 8 requires careful consideration. The treatment of dividends interest and royalties within the EU is now also subject to the application of Community law.[1]

18-050   Income from immovable property

Article 6 of the OECD Model Treaty provides that income from immovable property may be taxed in the state in which the property is situated. Immovable property is given the meaning under the law of the contracting state in which the property is situated. The OECD Model was amended in 1977 to specify that income from immovable property includes income from agriculture or forestry. It also defined immovable property to include property accessory to immovable property, livestock and equipment used in agriculture and forestry, rights to which provisions of general law respecting landed property apply, usufruct of immovable property and rights to variable or fixed amounts as consideration for the working of or the right to work, mineral deposits, sources and other natural resources. Ships, boats and aircraft are not to be regarded as immovable property under this definition. Under domestic law, several of these activities are treated as trading. These include farming and market gardening[2] and the commercial occupation of land in the UK,[3] although the commercial occupation of woodlands in the UK is not a trade.[4] Certain other activities are not treated as trading but their profits are calculated as if they were. These include:[5]

- mines and quarries (including gravel pits, sand pits and brickfields);
- ironworks, gasworks, salt springs or works, alum mines or works, waterworks and streams of water;

---

[1] See chapter 13.

[2] ITTOIA 2005, s. 9.

[3] ITTOIA 2005, s. 10.

[4] ITTOIA 2005, s. 11.

[5] ITTOIA 2005, s. 11.

- canals, inland navigation, docks and drains or levels;
- rights of fishing;
- rights of markets and fairs, tolls, bridges and ferries; and
- railways and other kinds of way.

Most of these businesses will likely, but not necessarily, need to be conducted through a fixed place, emphasising the need for careful classification in accordance with the particular treaty. Some treaties make explicit the overlap between this article and the more general business profits provisions, such as the UK–Argentina Treaty, which provides:

> '6(4) The provisions of paragraph (1) and (3) of this Article shall also apply to the income from immovable property of an enterprise and to income from immovable property used for the performance of independent personal services.'

The situation of property is normally to be determined under the general conflict of law rules. Most importantly, land is situated in the country where it lies. However, in relation to choses in action, they are normally situated in the country where they are properly recoverable or can be enforced. Chattels are situated in the country where they are located at any given time. The classification of property between movables and immovables is adopted in civil law systems. However, in English law, the important distinction is between realty and personalty. Income from land is perhaps the easiest source of income from immovable property to identify in this context. Income from land is dealt with under ITTOIA 2005, Pt. 4, and distinguishes between a person's UK property business, which consists of generating income from land in the UK,[6] and a person's overseas property business, which consists of the same activity from land outside the UK.[7] A similar classification applies for companies subject to corporation tax under Sch. A in the case of UK-situated land[8] and Case V, Sch. D, in the case of foreign-situated land.[9]

In this regard, both freehold and leasehold interests in land in England are regarded as immovable. A mortgagee's interest in land in England, including his or her right to payment of the debt, is regarded as an interest in an immovable. However, in the treaty context, mortgage interest is normally dealt with under art. 11 (interest) on the basis that the more general provisions relating to immovable property are overridden by the specific reference in art. 11(3), so that 'interest' includes income from 'debt claims of every kind whether or not secured by a mortgage'. In the 2001 UK–US Treaty, the expression 'real property', rather than 'immovable property', is used in art. 6. Modern treaties with other common law jurisdictions adopt the same approach,[10] but older ones use the OECD language.[11] Treaties following the colonial model do not contain an immovable income article. Since such treaties are often not comprehensive, they do not generally limit the UK right to tax income from land.

---

[6] ITTOIA 2005, s. 264.

[7] ITTOIA 2005, s. 265.

[8] ICTA 1988, s. 15.

[9] ICTA 1988, s. 70A.

[10] UK–Australia, art. 6(2).

[11] UK–New Zealand, art. 7(2).

Article 6(3) normally provides that the rights of the contracting state where the immovable is situated apply to 'income derived from the direct use, letting or use in any other form of immovable property'. This wording is not apt to cover deemed income arising in relation to the anti-avoidance provisions of ITA 2007, Pt, 14, Ch. 3.[12]

Timeshares

Spain is a popular location for second homes owned by UK individuals. In order to address uncertainty as to the imposition of Spanish tax against UK holders of timeshares, art. 6(3) of the Spanish Treaty was amended by protocol,[13] so that income from the use or letting of timeshare rights in respect of immovable property situated in a contracting state (which are owned by a resident of the other contracting state and which are for a period or periods which in the aggregate do not exceed four weeks in any calendar year) are excluded. In the computation of the period or periods, all timeshare rights owned by a resident of a contracting state in respect of immovable property situated in the other contracting state are to be taken into account.

Article 6 does not prejudge the manner in which the income is to be taxed, thereby permitting the deduction of tax from income of a person whose usual place of abode is outside the UK ('the non-resident'), and which is or may become chargeable under Sch. A, or as the profits of a UK property business.[14]

Real estate investment trusts

The expression real estate investment trust (REIT) originated in the US but has now entered into common usage. Its generic form is described by the OECD as:

> 'A widely held company, trust or contractual or fiduciary arrangement that derives its income primarily from long-term investment in immovable property (real estate), distributes most of that income annually and does not pay income tax on income related to immovable property that is so distributed. The fact that the REIT vehicle does not pay tax on that income is the result of tax rules that provide for a single-level of taxation in the hands of the investors in the REIT.[15]'

In the UK, a REIT is a company or group to which FA 2006, Pt. 4, applies.[16] Only UK-resident companies that carry on a Sch. A or overseas property rental business may qualify.[17] Qualifying REITS are exempt from corporation tax on their property rental business profits.[18] Distributions by a REIT to its shareholders are treated as profits of a UK property

---

[12] Taxes Act 1988, s. 776, on the disposal of interests in land in the case of companies.

[13] SI 1995/765.

[14] ITA 2007, s. 971, and SI 1995/2902.

[15] OECD Commentary on art. 10, para. 67.1.

[16] FA 2006, s. 103(3).

[17] FA 2006, ss. 104 and 106(3).

[18] FA 2005, s. 119(1).

business for income tax payers and Sch. A profits for corporation tax payers.[19] These distributions are paid under deduction of tax at the basic rate.[20] Although the distribution is treated as UK property income, it does not fall into non-resident landlord income subject to income tax that may be deducted net of expenses.[21] Distributions are not regarded by HMRC as income from immovable property within art. 6 but as dividends within art. 10.

18-100   Dividends

Dividends and other distributions from the UK-resident companies are generally not liable to income tax in the hands of non-residents as a matter of domestic law. The legislative route to this simple treatment is convoluted: dividends and other distributions from the UK companies are within the charge to income tax under ITTOIA, Pt. 4, Ch. 3 or Ch. 5. There is no provision for the deduction of tax at source on such amounts; dividends and other distributions from UK companies are 'disregarded income'.[22] The liability to tax of a non-resident in relation to 'disregarded income' is restricted to the amounts deducted at source.[23]

An exception to this rule is made in relation to distributions by REITs.[24] Such distributions bear tax deducted at source at the basic rate.[25] The imputation system, introduced in 1973, was largely abolished in 1999 but continues to provide for a tax credit for qualifying dividends paid to UK-resident individuals and certain non-residents.[26] However, tax credit only applies insofar as the distribution is brought into charge to income tax. It is not repayable.

Dividend articles

Certain elements of UK treaties reflect art. 10 of the OECD Model. The text of these dividend articles varies widely, however, in UK treaties. The UK has undergone numerous changes in its domestic law relating to taxation since the oldest of the current existing treaties were negotiated some 60 years ago. At one end of the spectrum are those treaties that do not contain dividend articles at all, such as those with Guernsey, Jersey and the Isle of Man. A second group of treaties simply provides for exemption from tax on dividends paid by a company resident in one contracting state to a shareholder resident in the other, or limiting the rate of tax to be deducted to rates specified in the treaty. The third category of treaties provides for repayment of tax credits and followed the introduction of the imputation system of corporation tax into the UK in 1973. The treaty entitlement to repayment of tax credits was only been extended to selected treaty partners. Current UK policy is to withdraw

---

[19] FA 2006, s. 121(1).

[20] ITA 2007, s. 973, and SI 2006/2867, reg. 3.

[21] FA 2006, s. 121(2)(c).

[22] ITA 2007, s. 813(1)(a) with s. 825(1)(a).

[23] ITA 2007, s. 811(3).

[24] ITA 2007, s. 973, and SI 2006/2867, reg 3.

[25] 20 per cent in 2008–09, FA 2008, s. 1(2)(a).

[26] ITTOIA 2005, s. 397.

this benefit where it has previously been provided. Repayment of tax credits is only contemplated in a handful of treaties, such as Belgium, Italy, Luxembourg and Sweden. In any event, the net amount payable to the shareholder under such treaties after the permitted withholding is less than the tax credit repayment, so no claims for relief are processed.[27] A fourth class of dividend article has emerged at the other end of the spectrum, with the introduction of REITs specifying the tax treatment applicable to distributions by them to treaty resident shareholders including under the UK – Saudi Arabia, UK–France and UK–Netherlands treaties.

Tax deducted at source

Since the UK does not presently impose a tax on dividends paid by UK-resident companies to non-residents under its domestic law, the effect of treaty provisions on outward bound dividends is narrow. HMRC takes the view that distributions paid by UK-resident REITs fall within the dividend articles of treaties and not the articles dealing with income from immovable property. In line with art. 10 of the OECD Model, the manner in which such tax may be reduced is reflected in the UK–Malaysia Treaty as follows:

'10(1) Dividends paid by a company which is a resident of a Contracting State to a resident of the other Contracting State may be taxed in that other State.

(2) However, such dividends may also be taxed in the Contracting State of which the company paying the dividends is a resident and according to the laws of that State, but if the recipient is the beneficial owner of the dividends and subject to tax in respect of the dividends in the other Contracting State, the tax so charged shall not exceed:

(a)   5 per cent of the gross amount of the dividends if the beneficial owner is a company which controls, directly or indirectly, at least 10 per cent of the voting power in the company paying the dividends;

(b)   10 per cent of the gross amount of the dividends in all other cases.'

Companies controlling at least 10 per cent of the voting power in the UK-resident company qualify for a preferential maximum rate of tax in the overwhelming majority of treaties. This preferential rate may in practice not be available in respect of distributions by REITs as a result of measures in the REIT legislation designed to discourage REITs from having shareholders who qualify for the preferential rate. A REIT that makes a distribution to a person with more than the permitted maximum shareholding is subject to tax on a notional amount treated as income received by the REIT.[28] A person who controls (directly or indirectly 10 per cent or more of the voting rights in a company exceeds the maximum permitted shareholding).[29] REITs are required take reasonable steps to prevent the possibility of such a distribution being made.[30] As a result, REITs will normally have mechanisms to prevent any company from routinely qualifying for the reduced rate for substantial voting participation.

---

[27] Inland Revenue, *Tax Bulletin* (February 1999), p. 626.

[28] SI 2006/2864, reg. 10(1).

[29] FA 2006, s. 114(1)(c).

[30] SI 2006/2864, reg. 10(1)(b).

The treatment of distributions by REITs is not uniform, even in the few treaties that address the issue. The UK – Saudi Arabia Treaty refers to a 'property investment vehicle'.[31] This is defined in a protocol to the treaty to mean 'a widely held investment vehicle that distributes most of its income – from immovable property within the meaning of article 6 (income from immovable property) – on which it is exempt from tax'.[32] Such dividends qualify for a 15 per cent maximum tax rate in the source state, compared with 5 per cent in all other cases. By contrast, certain distributions are precluded from benefiting from reduced rates of tax in the 2008 UK–France Treaty. The exclusion applies to:

> 'Dividends paid out of income or gains derived from immovable property within the meaning of art. 6 (Income from immovable property) by an investment vehicle:
>
> a   which distributes most of this income annually; and
> b   whose income or gains from such immovable property are exempted from tax;
>
> where the beneficial owner of those dividends holds, directly or indirectly, 10 per cent or more of the capital of the vehicle paying the dividends.[33]'

While the OECD Model only seeks to distinguish between the recipients of dividends generally and corporate shareholders with a substantial participation (typically 10 per cent or more) in the voting control of the dividend-paying company, UK treaties increasingly address other classes of shareholder. The UK – United States Treaty eliminates taxation of dividends for qualifying residents with 80 per cent or more of the voting power of the company paying the dividends for a 12-month period ending on the date the dividend is declared.[34] Other companies may also qualify if they are listed on a recognised stock exchange or controlled by such companies,[35] as well as certain closely held companies or if the relevant competent authority agrees.[36] The UK–Japan Treaty provides the same treatment in respect of shares representing at least 50 per cent of the voting power of the company paying the dividends for the period of six months.[37] In each case the availability of this relief is ring-fenced by detailed and lengthy limitation of benefits provisions.

Pension funds or pension schemes also frequently qualify for the elimination of tax in the source state in modern treaties.[38] The 2008 UK–France Treaty limits the rate of French tax on dividends paid by French companies to UK pension funds to 15 per cent, but it is silent on dividends by UK companies to French pension funds.[39] Religious, charitable, scientific,

---

[31] Art. 10(2)(a).

[32] Protocol, art. 5(a).

[33] Art. 11(5).

[34] Art. 10(3)(a)(i).

[35] Art. 10(3)(a)(ii).

[36] Art. 10(3)(a)(ii).

[37] Art. 10(3)(a).

[38] UK–US, art. 10(3)(b); UK–Japan, art. 10(3)(b); 2008 UK–Netherlands, art. 10(2)(b)(ii).

[39] Art. 11(1)(d).

cultural, or educational organisations exempt from tax under the domestic law of their home states qualify for exemption under the UK–Netherlands Treaty.[40]

Meaning of dividends

United Kingdom domestic law does not generally refer to dividends, but rather, to distributions.[41] The OECD definition of dividends is reflected in art. 10(3) of the Norwegian Treaty, which reads as follows:

> 'The term "dividends" as used in this article means income from shares, or other rights, not being debt-claims, participating in profits, as well as income from other corporate rights which is subjected to the same taxation treatment as income from shares by the laws of the Contracting State of which the company making the distribution is a resident and also includes any other item which, under the laws of the State of which the company paying the dividend is a resident, is treated as a dividend or distribution of the company.'

At present, such dividend articles have limited direct application to distributions made by UK-resident companies other than REITs. They do have an ancillary role in conjunction with the interest article in the context of thin capitalisation. In those treaties that include a reference, the characterisation of the payment under the domestic tax law of state of residence of the dividend paying company, that domestic law will also impact on the characterisation of interest payments under art. 11, where interest is treated as a distribution under that domestic law. This is discussed in detail in relation to interest below.[42] The state of the beneficial owner of the payment is required to adopt the same source state characterisation when eliminating double taxation.[43]

The meaning of the term 'dividend' under the German Treaty was considered in *Memec plc v IRC*.[44] Article 6(4) defined dividends in that article to include the income derived by a sleeping partner from his or her participation as such. The case arose out of distributions by a German silent partnership of dividends it received from German companies to a UK parent. The context in which the issue arose was whether the UK company was entitled to credit for underlying tax pursuant to art. 18(1) of the treaty and s. 792(1) of the Taxes Act 1988 in respect of underlying tax. This would be the case under the treaty if the UK company receiving the dividend controls directly or indirectly at least 25 per cent of the voting power of the German company. The Court of Appeal determined that this wide definition of dividend applied only to the scope of the right to impose withholding tax on such distribution and to ensure that they do not come within the articles relating to business profits or interest. Dividend was undefined in art. 18 providing for UK credit against German tax paid, and in this context the court applied the ordinary meaning of dividend, namely a payment of a part of the profits for a period in respect of a share of a company. This was not the view of Robert Walker J in the High Court. In his dissenting judgement in the Court of Appeal, Sir Christopher Staughton agreed that the definition of dividend in

---

[40] Art. 10(2)(b)(iii).

[41] ICTA 1988, s. 209.

[42] Para. 18-150.

[43] See chapter 14.

[44] [1998] BTC 251; [1998] STC 754, CA.

art. 6 should apply throughout the treaty, citing, in particular a decision of the highest German tax court.

Dividend effectively connected with a permanent establishment

Most treaties following the OECD pattern disapply the rules restricting the taxing rights of the source country where the beneficial owner of the dividends has a permanent establishment with which the holding of shares, in respect of which the dividends are paid, is effectively connected. The common expression of this principle is found in the UK–Poland Treaty:

> '10(4) The provisions of paragraphs (1) and (2) of this Article shall not apply if the beneficial owner of the dividends, being a resident of a Contracting State, carries on business in the other Contracting State of which the company paying the dividends is a resident, through a permanent establishment situated therein, and the holding in respect of which the dividends are paid is effectively connected with such permanent establishment. In such case the provisions of Article 7 of this Convention shall apply.'

In such a case, the business profits rules apply. Under domestic law, a non-resident company will be liable to tax under Sch. D, Case I, as a result of a trade carried on in the UK through a branch or agency. In most cases, this will be limited to share dealers. Taxes Act 1988, s. 95 excludes distribution from Schedule F treatment in the hands of a dealer in shares and requires those amounts to be taken into account in computing profits of the dealer, which are taxed under Sch. D, Case I.[45] This treatment is thus authorised by treaties following art. 10(4). Similar authorisation is found where the dividends are effectively connected with a fixed base through which independent personal services are provided under art. 14. This latter element is present in some treaties[46] but absent in others.[47]

In the Revenue view, a dividend would be 'effectively connected' with a permanent establishment if, for example, a branch of a foreign company bought shares in a UK company out of surplus funds of the branch. If the branch merely invested funds supplied by its head office, any dividend would not be 'effectively connected' with the permanent establishment.[48] The word 'effectively' connotes a strong or real degree of connection as indicated by a full examination of assets deployed in the permanent establishment and functions performed there.[49] More realistically, therefore, this rule is likely to apply only to dealers trading through a properly established branch in the UK in respect of whom distributions fall to be taxed, in the case of companies, under Schedule D Case I pursuant to Taxes Act 1988, s. 95 (see ITTOIA 2005, s. 366(1), for income tax treatment).

---

[45] For non-corporates, see ITTOIA 2005, s. 366(1).

[46] See, for example, the UK–Finland Treaty, art. 11(3).

[47] See, for example, the UK–Morocco Treaty, art. 10(3).

[48] HMRC, *Double Taxation Manual*, para. DT214.

[49] See *Trevor Smallwood Trust v R & C Commrs* (2008) Sp C 669 and chapter 5, para. 14-200 (re POEM).

Foreign dividends and corporate level taxes

The manner in which dividends are taxed is normally further circumscribed by limiting the taxing rights of the contracting state other than where the dividend paying company is resident. The UK–Macedonia Treaty adopts art. 10(5) of the OECD Model in this respect (as shown below):

> '10(6) Where a company which is a resident of a Contracting State derives profits or income from the other Contracting State, that other State may not impose any tax on the dividends paid by the company, except insofar as such dividends are paid to a resident of that other State or insofar as the holding in respect of which the dividends are paid is effectively connected with a permanent establishment situated in that other State, nor subject the company's undistributed profits to a tax on undistributed profits, even if the dividends paid or the undistributed profits consist wholly or partly of profits or income arising in that other State.'

Two principles are reflected in these provisions. First, the contracting state in which a dividend paying company is not resident (the 'source state') may not impose any tax on the dividends. This is the case even if the profits out of which the dividend is paid originated in the source state. This prohibition is broadly expressed. The source state may only tax the dividends if they are paid to a resident of the source state or are paid on a shareholding which is effectively connected with a permanent establishment in the source state. Thus, the source state remains entitled in effect to tax its own residents and permanent establishments within its territory.

Second, the source state may not impose a tax on undistributed profits of a resident of the other state. This is so even if the source of those profits is wholly or partly from within the source state. Undistributed in this sense refers to profits that have not been distributed to shareholders rather than those that have not been transferred within a company from a permanent establishment to the head office. The UK does not impose a tax on undistributed profits, but some of its treaty partners do. Authority to impose a branch profits tax is thus found in several treaties.[50]

Limitations on benefits

A variety of mechanisms are found in dividend articles designed to restrict the application of treaty benefits relating to dividends. These, including the meaning of 'beneficial ownership', are considered in chapter 16.

18-150   Interest

Under domestic law, income tax is to be deducted at the basic rate (20 per cent in 2008–09) source on yearly interest arising in the UK, *inter alia*, where it is paid by any person to another person whose 'usual place of abode is outside the UK'.[51] The relationship between the treaty rules and domestic law relating to interest, and particularly its relationship to distributions is complex and the treatment of any payment, is dependent on the interaction of

---

[50] For example, UK–US, art. 10(7); UK–Canada, arts. 22(3) and (4). See chapter 15, para. 24-200.

[51] ITA 2007, s. 874(1) and (2).

the whole of the interest and dividend articles with the domestic law. Treaty developments have, to some extent, followed developments in domestic law.

The UK negotiating position on interest is to seek to eliminate source country taxing rights entirely. Where this is achieved, treaties use language that appears in the UK–Czechoslovakia Treaty thus:

'11(1) Interest arising in a Contracting State which is derived and beneficially owned by a resident of the other Contracting State shall be taxable only in that other State.'

As a result, some 24 treaties provide that interest arising in one contracting state may only be taxed in the country of residence of a beneficial ownership resident in the other state. United Kingdom Treaty practice in this respect departs from the OECD Model. An example that is close to the OECD Model is found in the UK–Portugal Treaty:

'11(1) Interest arising in a Contracting State and paid to a resident of the other Contracting State may be taxed in that other State.

11(2) However, such interest may be taxed in the Contracting State in which it arises, and according to the law of that State; but where the resident of the other Contracting State is subject to tax there in respect thereof, the tax so charged in the first-mentioned State shall not exceed 10 per cent of the amount of the interest.'

This basic pattern is found in the majority of UK treaties. The rate of tax in the source state in 44 other treaties is limited, insofar as it is below the current UK rate of tax deducted on interest at source of 20 per cent ranging from 5 per cent to 15 per cent. The remaining treaties specify higher rates, but, as a result of the domestic law, these limitations do not have any practical impact on the rate of tax deducted in the UK. As a result of the reductions in UK tax on interest payments, treaties contain a number of detailed rules circumscribing the availability of treaty benefits.

In many cases where treaties permit source state taxation, exemption may be granted in special circumstances. Governmental creditors or debtors may enjoy such treatment as is the case in the UK–Philippines Treaty:

'10(4) Notwithstanding the provisions of paragraphs (2) and (3) of this Article, interest arising in a Contracting State shall be exempt from tax in that State if it is derived and beneficially owned by:

(a)   the Government of the other Contracting State, a political subdivision or local authority thereof or an instrumentality of that other State; or

(b)   a resident of the other Contracting State in respect of a loan made, guaranteed or insured by such instrumentality of that other State as is specified and agreed in letters exchanged between the competent authorities of the Contracting States.

The term "instrumentality" as used in this paragraph means any agency or entity created or organised by either Contracting Government in order to carry out governmental functions.'

Export financing programmes may likewise benefit in similar fashion as illustrated by the UK–Lesotho Treaty:

'11(11) Notwithstanding the provisions of Article 7 of this Convention and of paragraph (2) of this Article, interest arising in Lesotho which is paid to a resident of the United Kingdom shall be exempt from tax in Lesotho if it is paid in respect of a loan made, guaranteed or insured, or any other debt-claim or credit guaranteed or insured by the United Kingdom Export Credits Guarantee Department.'

Financial institutions may also sometimes obtain privileged treatment as in the UK–India Treaty:

'12(3) Notwithstanding the provisions of paragraph (2) of this Article:

(a)   where the interest is paid to a bank carrying on a bona fide banking business which is a resident of the other Contracting State and is the beneficial owner of the interest, the tax charged in the Contracting State in which the interest arises shall not exceed 10 per cent of the gross amount of the interest;

(b)   where the interest is paid to … the Reserve Bank of India, it shall not be subject to tax by the State in which it arises.

The term "instrumentality" as used in this paragraph means any agency or entity created or organised by either Contracting Government in order to carry out governmental functions.'

Meaning of interest

Interest has been held to be a 'payment by time for the use of money'.[52] For domestic tax purposes, certain interest payments, notably those in ICTA 1988, s. 209(2), are deemed to be distributions. This includes interest that represents more than a reasonable commercial return for the use of the loan principal to a company.[53] Also included is any interest on corporate debt or 'securities', which are:

- securities issued otherwise than wholly for new consideration;
- securities convertible directly or indirectly into shares in the company or securities and carrying any right to receive shares in or securities of the company, not being (in either case) securities listed on a recognised stock exchange nor issued on terms which are reasonably comparable with the terms of issue of securities so listed;
- securities under which the consideration for the use of the funds is to any extent dependent on the results of the company's business or any part of it;
- securities which are connected with shares in the company. For this purpose, securities are connected if, in consequence of the nature of the rights attaching to the securities or shares and in particular of any terms or conditions attaching to the right to transfer the shares or securities, it is necessary or advantageous for a person who has, or disposes of or acquires, any of the securities also to have, or to dispose of or to acquire, a proportionate holding of the shares; and
- equity notes issued by the company and held by a company which is associated with the issuer or is a funded company.[54]

Equity notes are generally debt securities with no redemption date or a term exceeding 50 years.[55] Interest on equity notes may be treated as a distribution if they are held by a

---

[52] *Bennett v Ogston* (1930) 15 TC 374, per Rowlatt J, p. 379.

[53] ICTA 1988, s. 209(2)(d).

[54] ICTA 1988, s. 209(2)(e).

[55] *Ibid.*, s. 209(9).

company which is associated or is a 'funded company'.[56] Companies are associated if they are in a 75 per cent group.[57] A funded company is one where there are arrangements involving the company being put in funds directly or indirectly by the issuing company or a company associated with the issuing company.[58]

Following FA 2004, the UK no longer has a mechanism to recharacterise interest payments as distributions in thin capitalisation cases.[59] Thin capitalisation is now addressed through the transfer pricing rules in ICTA 1988, Sch. 28AA.[60] To the extent this is relevant to art. 11 issues, it is considered further in relation to special relationships below.

Where an amount is not interest for treaty purposes, then treaty benefits of the relevant interest article will not apply. In *Bricom Holdings Limited v IRC*,[61] the court concluded that profits of a Netherlands company which were comprised of interest payments were not interest for the purposes of art. 11 of the UK–Netherlands Treaty in the context of a charge under the CFC rules. Article 11 of that treaty provided that 'interest arising in one of the states which is derived and beneficially owned by a resident of the other state shall be taxable only in that other state'. A Netherlands subsidiary of a UK parent company with no other sources of income loaned its funds to the parent company. It was undisputed that the Netherlands company was a CFC, and the Revenue accepted that the effect of the treaty was to exempt the interest both from UK corporation tax and taxation of the interest by deduction at source in the hands of the Netherlands-resident company that received it. However, the interest was not exempt from UK tax under the CFC charge. In determining the chargeable profits for CFC purposes, the Taxes Act 1988, s. 746(6)(a), referred to a purely notional sum equal to the chargeable profits, rather than the profits themselves or any ingredient of the actual profits of the CFC.

The current meaning of interest under art. 11(3) of the OECD Model is set out in art. 10(5) of the Philippines Treaty as follows:

> 'The term "interest" as used in this Article means income from Government securities, bonds or debentures, including premiums and prizes attaching to such securities, whether or not secured by mortgage and whether or not carrying a right to participate in profits, and other debt-claims of every kind as well as all other income assimilated to income from money lent by the taxation law of the State in which the income arises. Penalty charges for late payment shall not be regarded as interest for the purpose of this Article.'

It differs markedly from the definition found in the 1963 Draft Convention as found in art. 11(2) of the Austrian Treaty, which reads as follows:

> 'The term "interest" as used in this Article means income from Government securities, bonds or debentures, whether or not secured by mortgage and whether or not carrying a right to

---

[56] *Ibid.*, s. 209(2)(e)(vii).

[57] *Ibid.*, s. 209(10).

[58] *Ibid.*, s. 209 (11).

[59] FA 2004, s. 34(1)(a) and s. 326, and Sch. 42, Pt. 2(2).

[60] Principally paras. 1A and 1B.

[61] [1997] BTC 471; [1997] STC 1179, CA.

participate in profits, and other debt-claims of every kind as well as all other income assimilated to income from money lent by the taxation law of the State in which the income arises.'

A variety of forms is found in UK treaties. Some (for example, the UK–Iceland Treaty, art. 11(2)) define interest entirely by reference to the domestic law of the contracting state concerned. The treaty definition of dividends will, in many cases, decide whether, and the extent to which, the treatment of interest as a distribution in ICTA 1988, s. 209(2)(d) or (e), is applicable. Where it is not, the interest will be treated as interest for treaty purposes. Those treaties that define dividends by reference to domestic tax law on distributions will in general allow s. 209(2) to operate unimpeded. Treaties with self-contained definitions will typically narrow the application of these rules. Treaties following the OECD Model language do not establish a hierarchy for the classification of payments as between dividends and interest. The UK maintains an observation to the commentary both on the meaning of interest and dividends in light of the treatment of certain interest payments as distributions under the Taxes Act 1988, s. 209(2).[62] It has, therefore, become common to insert wording into UK treaties to the effect that interest does not include any item which is treated as a dividend under the dividend article.[63] The effect of such language is clearly to give priority to the dividend definition, which, where the OECD Model is used, will retain the domestic law characterisation in the source state of the payment.

A small group of treaties specify particular treatment. The Revenue accepts that the treaties with Austria, Fiji, Israel and Sudan allow excessive interest to be characterised as a distribution, but prevent the paying company from being denied a deduction for the distributions (see Israeli Treaty, art. 7(5), for an example). Another example is the treaty with Spain (art. 11(6)), which prevents excessive intra-group interest being treated as a distribution.[64]

Source of interest

If the source of interest is outside the UK, then there is no duty on the payer to deduct income tax on payments to non-residents.[65] The current Revenue view on the location of the source for interest is based on *Westminster Bank Executor and Trust Company (Channel Islands) Limited v National Bank of Greece S.A.*[66] In that case, the obligation in question, a guarantee payment, was made by a foreign corporation with no place of business in the UK. The principal debtor was also a foreign corporation and the obligation was secured on lands and public revenues outside the UK. In addition, funds for payment by the principal debtor would have been provided by a remittance from outside the UK. As a result, the Revenue practice is to regard the residence of the debtor as only one factor. The factors that it regards as important are:

- the residence of the debtor (being the place where the debt will be enforced);

---

[62] OECD Commentary on art. 10, para. 68, and art. 11, para. 37.

[63] See, for example, UK–China Treaty, art. 11(3).

[64] *Tax Bulletin* (June 1998), p.555.

[65] ITA 2007, s. 884, and ITTOIA 2005, s. 830(2)(e).

[66] [1970] 1 QB 251.

- the source from which the interest is paid;
- where the interest is paid; and
- the nature and location of the security for the debt.[67]

Interest must 'arise in a contacting state' in order to fall within the ambit of the interest article. The source of interest for treaty purposes is normally determined by art. 11(5) of the OECD Model. The current version is found in the UK–Poland Treaty:

> '11(6) Interest shall be deemed to arise in a Contracting State when the payer is a resident of that State. Where, however, the person paying the interest, whether he is a resident of a Contracting State or not, has in a Contracting State a permanent establishment in connection with which the indebtedness on which the interest is paid was incurred, and such interest is borne by such permanent establishment, then such interest shall be deemed to arise in the State in which the permanent establishment is situated.'

Interest is deemed to arise in a contracting state. Treaties patterned on pre-1995 versions of the OECD Model include explicitly where the payer is a resident of that state, or the state itself, or a political subdivision, a local authority, or resident of that state. It also applies where the state itself, a political subdivision or local authority, is the payer.[68] A special rule is provided in the case of permanent establishments. Where the payer of the interest has a permanent establishment in a contracting state in connection with which the indebtedness on which the interest is paid was incurred, and the interest is borne by the permanent establishment, then the interest is deemed to arise in the state where the permanent establishment is situated. Treaties adopting the OECD style definition of source have a wider scope than may be the case under UK domestic law. The provision is, however, absent from a number of treaties, such as Oman.[69] In such cases the state in which the interest arises is a matter of construction. The *National Bank of Greece* case is only helpful where all four factors are in or outside a state. There is no clear indication where they are partly in and partly outside a state.

Special relationship

Where there is a special relationship between the payer and the beneficial owner of the interest, or a special relationship between the both of them and some other person, treaty benefits may be limited. In the broadest terms, such rules aim at extending the reduction or elimination of source state taxation only to arm's length amount of interest. The manner in which the amount that qualifies for the treaty benefit is measured varies from treaty to treaty but the mechanism as set out, for example, in art. 11(8) of the Canadian Treaty is consistently adopted:

> 'Where, owing to a special relationship between the payer and the person deriving the interest or between both of them and some other person, the amount of the interest paid exceeds ... the amount which would have been paid in the absence of such relationship, the provisions of this art. shall apply only to the last-mentioned amount. In that case, the excess part of the

---

[67] Inland Revenue, *Tax Bulletin* (November 1993), p. 100.

[68] See, for example, the UK–Ghana Treaty, art. 11(5), and the UK–Papua New Guinea Treaty, art. 12(7).

[69] See art. 11; see also UK–Hungary, art. 11, and UK–Russian Federation, art. 11.

payments shall remain taxable according to the law of each Contracting State, due regard being had to the other provisions of this convention.'

If interest paid exceeds the 'arm's length' amount, the source state must apply any reduction or elimination of tax specified in interest article only to the arm's length amount. Any excess must be treated in accordance with domestic law of the contracting states with due regard to the other provisions of the treaty. Consequently, the source state may, in principle, apply the domestic rates of tax deducted at source and the state of residence of the beneficial owner must give relief for such tax imposed at domestic rates, subject to the operation of other parts of the treaty such as art. 24 (Non-discrimination) and art. 25 (Mutual Agreement Procedure).

Meaning of special relationship

Special relationship is undefined in treaty or domestic law. HMRC takes a very broad view of this expression. The *Double Taxation Relief Manual* states that the phrase 'special relationship' encompasses a wider range of relationships than those identified by 'connected persons' legislation in UK domestic law. A special relationship, it says, exists not only where the parties are associated (parent and subsidary companies or companies under common control) but also where there is any community of interests as distinct from the legal relationship giving rise to the payment.[70] The OECD Commentary on art. 11 refers to circumstances of control, as well as relationships by blood or marriage and any 'other community of interests'.[71]

Effect of special relationship

The special relationship clauses place quantitative limits on the application of the benefits of the interest article. The language used to describe how this limit is to be measured varies and current UK treaty practice does not reflect the OECD Model. A number of early treaties do reflect the approach of the OECD Model, which applies this rule only to the rate of interest and other attributes of the debt, but not to the amount of debt. Article 9(6) of the UK–Israel Treaty is an example:

'7(4) Where, owing to a special relationship between the payer and the recipient or between both of them and some other person, the amount of the interest paid, *having regard to the indebtedness in respect of which it is paid*, exceeds the amount which would have been agreed upon by the payer and the recipient in the absence of such relationship, the provisions of this art. shall apply only to the last-mentioned amount.'

Such provisions require the actual indebtedness or debt claim to be examined but not factors beyond that. Thus, the currency and term of the loan and the existence of security may be relevant but not, for example, whether it should be treated as equity. Finance (No. 2) Act 1992, s. 42, inserted s. 808A into the Taxes Act 1988 in order to override the earlier treaties that contain wording similar to that in art. 7(4) of the UK–Israel Treaty. The effect of this section is to require all treaties which permit the benefit of a reduction in or exemption from UK tax on interest where there was a special relationship clause to permit the special relationship to allow adjustment in respect of both the interest rate and the amount of debt.

---

[70] HMRC, *Double Taxation Manual*, para. DT1917.

[71] At paras. 32-34.

This even applies in relation to those treaties that do not themselves permit adjustment in relation to the level of debt. The amendment at that time was believed to have been introduced as a result of an unpublished Special Commissioner's decision against the Inland Revenue on the point. (The Special Commissioners' decisions were unpublished until 1995.) In these cases, the special relationship provision must be construed as requiring all factors to be taken into account, including, specifically, whether in the absence of the special relationship:

- the loan would have been made at all;
- the amount which the loan would have been; and
- the rate of interest and other terms which would have been agreed.[72]

Taxpayers are required to show either that there is no special relationship or that the amount of interest is what would have been paid in the absence of the special relationship.[73] One concession is given in construing the special relationship: the fact that the lender is not in the business of making loans generally may be ignored.[74] Thus, in principle, comparisons made with banks or other money lending institutions may serve as valid indicators of the amount that would be paid in the absence of a special relationship even if only banks would make a loan on the terms made.

Later treaties permit the examination of both the rate of interest and the amount of debt to which it relates. Article 11(7) of the Latvian Treaty illustrates an alternative formulation that appears in most UK treaties:

> '11(7) Where by reason of a special relationship between the payer and the beneficial owner or between both of them and some other person, the amount of the interest paid exceeds, *for whatever reason*, the amount which would have been agreed upon by the payer and the beneficial owner in the absence of such relationship, the provisions of this Article shall apply only to the last-mentioned amount of interest.'

This wider language requires an examination of all reasons that are relevant to the amount of interest paid exceeding what would have been paid if but for the special relationship.

Transfer pricing adjustments

Where interest is paid in excess of the arm's length amount and an adjustment is made to the profits of the payer under the transfer pricing legislation, then, on making a claim, the excessive interest is not regarded as subject to deduction of income tax at source under of ITA 2007, Part 15.[75] To the extent that a UK borrower is denied a deduction for interest paid in this way, there is no deduction of tax required and the excess interest received will not be taxable in the hands of most non-resident recipients. In such cases, the excess in not taxed in the UK and the special relationship provisions of the applicable treaty will not be engaged in relation to the UK tax system.

---

[72] ICTA 1988, s. 808A(2).

[73] ICTA 1988, s. 808A(3).

[74] ICTA 1988, s. 808A(4).

[75] ICTA 1988, Sch. 28AA, para. 6E.

Interest attributed to a permanent establishment

Reduction or elimination of tax in the source country does not apply where the non-resident has a permanent establishment or fixed base in the source country and the debt claim in respect of which the interest is paid is effectively connected with that permanent establishment. The UK – Ivory Coast Treaty is not untypical:

> '11(5) The provisions of paragraphs (1) and (2) of this Article shall not apply if the beneficial owner of the interest, being a resident of a Contracting State, carries on business in the other Contracting State in which the interest arises, through a permanent establishment situated therein, or performs in that other State independent personal services from a fixed base situated therein, and the debt-claim in respect of which the interest is paid is effectively connected with such permanent establishment or fixed base. In such case, the provisions of Article 7 or Article 15, as the case may be, shall apply.'

Treaty provisions in this respect are similar to those dealing with dividends effectively connected with a permanent establishment. In these cases, either the business profits article (art. 7) or, in appropriate cases, the independent personal services article (art. 14) will apply. This rule should dovetail neatly with two domestic law exceptions from the obligation to deduct tax on interest payments made to a non-resident. First, interest paid to the UK branch of a foreign bank is exempt from the deduction at source rules, where the bank recipient of the interest is within the charge to corporation tax on the interest.[76] In the exceptional joined cases of *IRC v Commerzbank AG* and *IRC v Banco do Brazil SA*,[77] advantage was taken of the unusual wording in the 1945 US Treaty to seek exemption from tax on interest paid by US borrowers to UK branches of a German and Brazilian bank. In that case, it was the branch that sought and obtained exemption. The effect of those articles in the UK was be to permit interest payments to be made gross where the lending bank has a permanent establishment in the UK but was not within the charge to corporation tax on the interest.

Second, attribution of interest to a UK permanent establishment of a non-resident company may also permit a corporate payer to make payments gross to that UK permanent establishment. Deduction of tax at source need not be made by a company if at the time the payment is made, the company reasonably believes that the payment will be an excepted payment.[78] This will be the case where the person beneficially entitled to the income is a non-resident company carrying on a trade through a permanent establishment in the UK and the payment falls to be brought into account in computing the chargeable profits of the non-resident company.[79]

Limitations on benefits

A variety of mechanisms are found in interest articles designed to restrict the application of treaty benefits relating to interest. These, including the meaning of 'beneficial ownership', are considered in chapter 16.

---

[76] ITA 2007, s. 879(1)(a).

[77] [1990] BTC 172; [1990] STC 285.

[78] ITA 2007, s. 930.

[79] ITA 2007, s. 934. See also Inland Revenue, *Tax Bulletin* (No. 54, August 2001), p. 867.

18-200   Royalties

The potential scope for application of royalty provisions to the UK tax system is wide. The domestic and treaty terminology is neither consistent nor coextensive. Although a project of the tax law rewrite project, the current legislation is awkwardly drafted and not entirely consistent. Under the domestic law, in the case of companies within the charge to corporation tax, a largely self-contained code is found in FA 2002, Sch. 29, dealing with 'intangible assets'. The income tax treatment is now divided between ITTOIA 2005[80] as it relates to receipts from 'intellectual property', film and sound recordings as well as certain telecommunication rights, on the one hand, and ITA 2007,[81] which deals with deduction of tax at source on 'annual payments', 'patent royalties' and 'other payments connected with intellectual property', on the other hand. Certain treaties may extend the application of royalty provisions to movable tangible property.

Income tax is charged on royalties and other income from intellectual property.[82] For this purpose 'intellectual property' means any:

(a)   patent, trade mark, registered design, copyright, design right, performer's right or plant breeder's right;

(b)   rights under the law of any part of the UK which are similar to rights within para. (a);

(c)   rights under the law of any territory outside the UK which correspond or are similar to rights within para. (a); and

(d)   idea, information or technique not protected by a right within para. (a), (b) or (c).[83]

Income tax is also charged on profits arising where consideration is received by a person:

- for the disposal of know-how; or
- for giving, or wholly or partly fulfilling, an undertaking which is given in connection with a disposal of know-how, and restricts or is designed to restrict any person's activities in any way.[84] For this purpose, 'know-how' means any industrial information or techniques likely to assist in:

  - manufacturing or processing goods or materials;
  - working a source of mineral deposits (including searching for, discovering or testing mineral deposits or obtaining access to them); or
  - carrying out any agricultural, forestry or fishing operations.[85]

Unusually, income tax is charged on profits from sales of the whole or part of any patent rights granted under the laws of the UK, and the seller is not UK resident and not chargeable

---

[80] Part 5, chapters 2, 3 and 4.

[81] Part 15, chapters 6 and 7.

[82] ITTOIA 2005, s. 579(1).

[83] ITTOIA 2005, s. 579(2).

[84] ITTOIA 2005, s. 583(1).

[85] ITTOIA 2005, s. 583(4).

to corporation tax in respect of the proceeds of the sale.[86] For this purpose, 'patent rights' means the right to do or authorise the doing of anything which, but for the right, would be an infringement of a patent.[87] Income from a business involving the exploitation of films or sound recordings where the activities carried on do not amount to a trade is likewise charged to income tax.[88] Finally, the same is true for on income derived from a relevant telecommunication right that is not used or held for the purposes of a trade, profession or vocation.[89] A 'relevant telecommunication right' means:

- a licence granted under s. 8 of the Wireless Telegraphy Act 2006 in accordance with regulations made under s. 14 of that act (bidding for licences);
- an indefeasible right to use a telecommunications cable system; and
- a right derived (directly or indirectly) from such a licence or indefeasible right.[90]

A general territorial limitation is imposed in the case of non-UK residents by ITTOIA 2005, s. 577. Income arising to a non-UK resident is chargeable to tax under Pt. 5 only if it is from a source in the UK.[91] Income which does not have a source is deemed to be from a source in the UK if it has a comparable connection to the UK.[92] This section is subject to any express or implied provision to the contrary in Pt. 5 (or elsewhere in the Income Tax Acts).[93]

Not all of these payments described in ITTOIA attract deduction of tax at source. Deduction of tax at source is required in relation to 'qualifying annual payments', and royalties or other sums paid in respect of the use of patents[94] and if it is a payment of any royalties, or sums payable periodically, in respect of a 'relevant intellectual property right'.[95]

A payment may be a 'qualifying annual payment' in this context if the recipient it is charged to income tax as royalties etc from intellectual property[96] or in respect of telecommunication rights.[97] A payment may be in respect of 'a relevant intellectual property right' if it is in a copyright (excluding copyright in a cinematographic film or video recording, or the

---

[86] ITTOIA 2005, s. 587.

[87] ITTOIA 2005 s. 587(4).

[88] ITTOIA 2005, s. 609(1).

[89] ITTOIA 2005, s. 614(1).

[90] ITTOIA 2005, s. 614(1) and s. 146.

[91] ITTOIA 2005, s. 577(2).

[92] ITTOIA 2005, s. 577(3).

[93] ITTOIA 2005, s. 577(4).

[94] ITA 2007, s. 898(1).

[95] ITA 2007, s. 906(1).

[96] ITTOIA 2005, s. 579.

[97] ITTOIA 2005, Pt. 5, Ch. 4, and ITA 2007, s. 899(3) and (4).

soundtrack of a cinematographic film or video recording, except so far as it is separately exploited,[98] a right in a design[99] or the public lending right in respect of a book.[100]

In order to attract deduction of tax at source 'qualifying annual payments', and royalties or other sums paid in respect of the use of patents must arise in the UK.[101] The jurisdictional basis for deduction relating to copyright payments and other 'relevant intellectual property rights' is more obscure. Unlike the other categories where the residence of the recipient is irrelevant, copyright and similar rights attract deduction at source on payments only if the usual place of abode of the owner of the right is outside the UK.[102] There is no deduction at source if the payment is made in respect of copies of works, or articles, which have been exported from the UK for distribution outside the UK.[103] Payments in respect of copyright and similar rights also attract deduction of tax if made through UK-resident agents in certain circumstances.[104]

Taxing jurisdiction is ultimately circumscribed in some cases by ITA 2007, Pt. 14, Ch. 1, by limiting non-UK residents to tax deducted at source on disregarded income,[105] which includes annual payments from intellectual property under ITTOIA 2005, s. 579, and telecommunication rights under Pt. 5, Ch. 4, of that act.[106] Where tax is to be deducted it is at the basic rate.[107]

The UK approach to negotiating royalty provisions in treaties is similar to the approach to interest. For example, the elimination of withholding taxes entirely is normally sought, as the OECD Model advocates. Where this is achieved, treaties use language that appears in the UK–Sweden Treaty thus:

> '12(1) Royalties derived and beneficially owned by a resident of a Contracting State shall be taxable only in that State.'

In such cases, the source of the royalty is irrelevant. Royalties are normally only taxable in the country of residence of the beneficial owner in 43 treaties. The UN Model Treaty advocates a positive rate of tax in source states and the majority of treaties that contain royalty articles (a further 62 treaties), including a number with OECD member countries, authorise taxation in the source state, albeit at rates from 5 per cent to 20 per cent and thus typically below the basic UK rate of taxation. The UK–Spain Treaty is representative of this later category:

---

[98] ITA 2007 s 907(2).

[99] A 'right in a design' means the design right in a design, or the right in a registered design – ITA 2007, s. 907(2).

[100] ITA 2007, s. 907.

[101] ITA 2007, s. 899(2).

[102] ITA 2007, s. 906(2).

[103] ITA 2007, s. 906(4).

[104] ITA 2007, s. 908.

[105] ITA 2007, ss. 811 and 815.

[106] ITA 2007, s. 826.

[107] 20 per cent in 2008–09. ITA 2007, s. 901(3), for annual payments, s. 903(5) for patent rights, and s. 906(5) for copyright and similar rights.

'12(1) Royalties arising in a Contracting State which are derived and beneficially owned by a resident of the other Contracting State may be taxed in that other State. 12(2) However, such royalties may also be taxed in the Contracting State in which they arise and according to the law of that State, but the tax charged shall not exceed 10 per cent of the gross amount of the royalties.'

The language in this respect is similar to that found in interest articles. A number of issues that arise in relation to interest also apply to royalties, but there are important differences.

Scope of the royalty article

The definition of royalties as found in the current OECD Model appears in the UK–Moldova Treaty and reads:[108]

'12(3) The term 'royalties' as used in this article means payments of any kind received as a consideration for the use of, or the right to use, any copyright of literary, artistic or scientific work (including cinematograph films, and films or tapes for radio or television broadcasting), any patent, trade mark, design or model, plan, secret formula or process, or other like right or property, or for information (know-how) concerning industrial, commercial or scientific experience.'

In broad terms, such treaties restrict the royalty article to intellectual property related payments. Prior to 1992 the OECD Model expression included payments relating to 'of any kind received as a consideration for the use of, or the right to use industrial, commercial or scientific equipment'.[109]

Modern treaties do not refer to mineral extraction royalties which are within art. 6 (income from immovable property). Some early treaties, such as the Antigua Treaty, which does not contain an article relating to immovable property, specifically exclude royalties or amounts paid in respect of the operation of a mine or quarry or other extraction of natural resources.[110] Despite the change in the OECD Model, a number of treaties particularly with developing countries continue to include payments for the use of or the right to use any industrial, commercial or scientific equipment.[111]

While in the case of interest, the principal classification issue is between treatment as interest under art. 11 or dividends under art. 10, royalty classification issues a principally whether payments relating to intellectual property fall within the royalty provisions of art. 12 or the business profits provisions of art. 7 (and possibly independent personal services of art. 14). In treaties that contain provisions specific to consultancy services, additional boundary issues may arise. Unlike the dividend interest articles, this definition of royalties is not by reference to the classification in the source state, so, in principle, conflicting classifications may be made by the two contracting states.

---

[108] The bracketed expression '(know how)' is not in the OECD Model but appears frequently in UK treaties.

[109] See, for example, the UK–Canada Treaty, art. 12(4).

[110] UK–Antigua, art. 7(2).

[111] See, for example, UK–Latvia, art. 12(3), and UK–Moldova, art. 12(3).

Similar questions arise under domestic law. Income is received from intellectual property must be treated as trading income in priority to non-trading income taxable under ITTOIA 2005, Pt. 5.[112]

For example, copyright royalties paid to an author of a literary, dramatic, musical or artistic work that has been created in the ordinary course of his profession fall into trade profits and not ITTOIA 2005, s. 579(2)(a). Payments that are made to a non-resident author are therefore not subject to deduction of income tax at source.[113] The same is true in relation to payments for other services that give rise to intellectual property rights such as copyright. These include the work of architects in creating plans or professional opinions. The wide reference to 'profits of an enterprise' in art. 7 may mean that payments that are within art. 7 even if there is no trade for UK domestic purposes.

Know-how is recognised in domestic law as 'any idea, information or technique not, in general terms, protected by a statutory intellectual property right'.[114] It is further defined to mean:

'Any industrial information or techniques likely to assist in–

(a) manufacturing or processing goods or materials,
(b) working a source of mineral deposits (including searching for, discovering or testing mineral deposits or obtaining access to them), or
(c) carrying out any agricultural, forestry or fishing operations.[115]'

The OECD Commentary observes that it is undivulged information based on past experience. It is that it represents past experience that distinguishes know-how from the provision of services designed to bring new information into existence.[116]

Purchased software normally includes a licence entitling the purchaser to use the software and authorising limited copying in connection with its use. The supplier's rights include copyright but HMRC usually accepts that the payment for the software is a copyright licence. It is only where the right acquired is to reproduce the software in order to exploit it that the payment may be essentially in respect of the copyright.[117] This should be the case regardless of the delivery medium so that downloaded software is treated in the same way as that supplied on a tangible carrier medium. The division of payments between those that are essentially for the copyright or other intellectual property rights and those where copyright (or another right) is merely a mechanism for the protection of the owners rights is at the heart of the analysis of a wide range of electronic commerce transactions such as viewing databases or use of online software.[118]

---

[112] ITTOIA 2005, s. 575(1).

[113] See HMRC DTM 342590; *Carson v Cheyney's Executor* 38 TC 240; *Hume v Asquith* 45 TC 251.

[114] ITTOIA 2005, s. 579(2)(d).

[115] ITTOIA 2005, s. 583(4).

[116] Commentary to OECD Model, art. 12, para. 7.

[117] See HMRC, *INTM*, para. INTM342630.

[118] See Commentary to OECD Model, art. 12 paras. 14–17.

Source of royalties

Curiously, the OECD Model does not contain rules determining the source of royalties. The HMRC *International Tax Handbook* notes cryptically (at para. INT559) that 'there is, however, no definition of where royalties arise, so the domestic law of each partner determines this'. The UN Model does, however, contain a clause addressing this issue and several UK treaties, including that with Argentina, include such a clause which reads:

> '12(5) Royalties shall be deemed to arise in a Contracting State when the payer is that State itself; a political subdivision, a local authority or a resident of that State. Where, however, the person paying the royalties, whether he is a resident of a Contracting State or not, has in a Contracting State a permanent establishment or a fixed base in connection with which the obligation to pay the royalties was incurred, and such royalties are borne by such permanent establishment or fixed base, then such royalties shall be deemed to arise in the State in which the permanent establishment or fixed base is situated.'

This approach, in the context of limiting taxing jurisdiction, adopts one similar to that taken by the OECD Model, art. 11(5), in relation to interest, namely the location of the payer of the royalty. United Kingdom domestic law, in asserting taxing jurisdiction, is unclear but probably takes a multiple factor approach. The residence of the payer is generally only one factor in relation to the location of source for the purpose of ITTOIA 2005, Pt. 5, and ITA 2007, Pt. 15, others being the location of underlying intellectual property right, the place where payment is to be made and possibly the place where the contract is made. In this respect, a foreign copyright suggests a foreign source royalty, while a UK copyright or other intellectual property right suggests a UK source royalty. HMRC guidance is not systematic in this area, reflecting a variety of rules relating to different kinds of property, but it does accept that unless a patent is a UK patent, the licence cannot be 'for the user of a patent'.[119] It also takes the view that if a copyright is exploited in the UK, the related royalty payment will be regarded as having a UK source irrespective of the law governing the contract.[120] The central feature of intellectual property rights is protection against infringement, which involves the right of the owner to prevent others from undertaking certain activities without his or her permission.[121] This right is territorial in nature by reference to the legal system that establishes the right and as a result, a UK registered patent or trademark, for example, is situated in the UK. Although a European Patent confers in each contracting state the same rights as a national patent, infringement is addressed by national law (see the European Patent Convention art. 64), thereby giving rise to several territorial rights. In the case of Community trade marks, territorial nexus is normally found where the owner has its, domicile, seat or an establishment (see Council Regulation 40/94, arts. 14 and 97).

Concessionary relief may be available for foreign tax credit in circumstances where the payer is foreign, but the payment is for UK purposes treated as having a UK source. The concession reads as follows:

---

[119] HMRC, *Double Tax Relief Manual*, para. DT1912.

[120] HMRC, *INTM*, para. INTM342520.

[121] This approach is reflected in ITTOIA 2005, s. 587(4) thus: 'In this Chapter "patent rights" means the right to do or authorise the doing of anything which, but for the right, would be an infringement of a patent'.

'**ESC B8 Double Taxation Relief: Income Consisting of Royalties and "Know-How" Payments**

Payments made by a person resident in an overseas country to a person carrying on a trade in the United Kingdom as consideration for the use of, or for the privilege of using, in the overseas country any copyright, patent, design, secret process or formula, trade mark or other like property may in law be payments the source of which is in the United Kingdom, but are nevertheless treated for the purpose of credit (whether under double taxation agreements or by way of unilateral relief) as income arising outside the United Kingdom except to the extent that they represent consideration for services (other than merely incidental services) rendered in this country by the recipient to the payer.'

Disposal of intellectual property

Certain disposals of intellectual property are charged to income tax rather than capital gains tax. Thus, where a non-resident sells the whole or part of any UK patent rights, the profit is charged to income tax.[122] Deduction of basic rate tax at source applies to that sum.[123] Assignment of a copyright, a right in a design or the public lending right in respect of a book in consideration of periodical payments by a person whose usual place of abode is outside the UK gives rise to an obligation to deduct tax at source.[124] Similarly, profit on the disposal of know-how is charged to income tax.[125] This includes consideration for giving or fulfilling, an undertaking which is given in connection with a disposal of know-how, and restricts or is designed to restrict any person's activities in any way.

The expression 'royalty' in OECD patterned treaties refers to payments as 'consideration for the use of or the right to use'. This does not in normal language include payment of the purchase price on an outright sale. A payment of this kind is not within the scope of the normal royalty provision but fails to be addressed under art. 13 of the OECD Model (capital gains). Article 12(3)(b) of the US Treaty includes in the definition of 'royalties' gains from the alienation of intellectual property rights which are contingent on the productivity, use, or disposition thereof.

Royalties effectively connected with a permanent establishment

As is the case with dividends and interest, royalties effectively connected to a permanent establishment may be taxed in the state of the permanent establishment in accordance with the business profits rules (art. 12(3) of the OECD Model). The HMRC *International Manual* (para. INTM153130) position is that a royalty may be effectively connected with a permanent establishment if the intellectual property right from which it is derived was acquired out of funds of the branch. A royalty, HMRC says, may also be effectively connected if the branch played an active part in the creation or exploitation of the right in question, notwithstanding that it may not be regarded as an asset of the branch.

---

[122] ITTOIA 2005, ss. 587(1) and (2) (b).

[123] ITA 2007, s. 910.

[124] ITA 2007, s. 906.

[125] ITTOIA 2005, s. 583(1).

Special relationship

United Kingdom treaties deal with the effect of special relationships on royalties (OECD, art. 12) in somewhat similar terms to the way they deal with interest. The treaty benefit may be limited to be restricted where a special relationship exists to the amount which would have been agreed upon by the payer and the beneficial owner in the absence of the special relationship. The Namibian Treaty, art. 9(4), closely follows art. 12(4) of the OECD Model, with the wording thus:

> 'Where, owing to a special relationship between the payer and recipient of a royalty, the amount of the royalty, having regard to the use, right or property for which it is paid, exceeds the amount which would have been agreed upon by the payer and the recipient in the absence of such relationship, the provisions of this Article shall apply only to the last-mentioned amount. In that case, the excess part of the payments shall remain taxable according to the Contracting Parties' own laws, due regard being had to the other provisions of the present Convention.'

It has been UK treaty negotiating policy, however, for some time, to omit from that clause the words 'having regard to the use, right or information for which they are paid'. In most cases those words are replaced by the phrase 'for whatever reason' such as is found in the Maltese Treaty, art. 12(6). Sometimes no alternative wording is included, such as in the Swiss Treaty, art. 12(4). In either event, HMRC has stated that its view of the intention of the special relationship provision is that it should apply not only where the rate at which royalties are paid is excessive but also where, in the absence of the special relationship, the arrangements under which the royalties are paid would not have been entered into at all. Consequently, s. 808B of the Taxes Act 1988 requires treaty provisions relating to royalties to be interpreted in a manner similar to the rules in relation to interest in the Taxes Act 1988, s. 808A. Subsection (2) provides that where a royalty clause refers to the special relationship rule, that it:

> 'Shall be construed as requiring account to be taken of all factors, including:
>
> (a)   the question whether the agreement under which the royalties are paid would have been made at all in the absence of the relationship,
> (b)   the rate or amounts of royalties and other terms which would have been agreed in the absence of the relationship.'

Thus, s. 808B in effect overrides treaties such as the one with Namibia by requiring in such cases that 'the use, right or information for which they are paid' may not be taken into account if independent parties would not have entered into the agreement at all.

Anti-avoidance – special relationship

In relation to the above criteria, the override is much the same as Taxes Act 1988, s. 808A, is with respect to interest. However, s. 808B goes further than that. A detailed anti-avoidance rule has also been tacked on by para. 808B(2)(c) in the guise of interpretation of special relationship. It applies where the asset in respect of which the royalties are paid, or any asset which that asset represents or from which it is derived, has previously been in the beneficial ownership of:

> '(a) the person who is liable to pay the royalties;

(b) a person who is, or has at any time been, an associate of the person who is liable to pay the royalties;

(c) a person who has at any time carried on a business which, at the time when the liability to pay the royalties arises, is being carried on in whole or in part by the person liable to pay those royalties; or

(d) a person who is, or has at any time been, an associate of a person who has at any time carried on such a business as is mentioned in (c) above.[126]'

Where these criteria are fulfilled, the special relationship provision must be construed on the basis of the following factors:

'(a) the amounts which were paid under the transaction, or under each of the transactions in the series of transactions, as a result of which the asset has come to be an asset of the beneficial owner for the time being;

(b) the amounts which would have been so paid in the absence of a special relationship; and

(c) the question whether the transaction or series of transactions would have taken place in the absence of such a relationship.[127]'

For these purposes, a person is an associate of another person at a given time if:

'(a) the first person participates directly or indirectly in the management, control or capital of the other; or

(b) the same person or same persons participate directly or indirectly in the management, control or capital of the first person and the other person within the meaning of Schedule 28AA to Taxes Act 1988.[128]'

It should be noted that the term 'special relationship' remains undefined. Associates in this context are only relevant in relation to the anti-avoidance provisions.

Burden of proof

The burden of proof is placed fully on the taxpayer. The special relationship provision must now be construed as requiring the taxpayer to show:

- the absence of any special relationship; or
- the rate or amount of royalties that would have been payable in the absence of the relationship, as the case may be.[129]

Furthermore, the requirement on the taxpayer to show the absence of any special relationship includes a requirement:

- to show that no person of any of the above descriptions has previously been the beneficial owner of the asset in respect of which the royalties are paid, or of any asset which that asset represents or from which it is derived; or

---

[126] Taxes Act 1988, s. 808B(3).

[127] *Ibid.*, s. 808B(4).

[128] *Ibid.*, s. 808B(9).

[129] *Ibid.*, s. 808B(5).

[130] *Ibid.*, s. 808B(6).

- to show:

  - that the transaction or series of transactions mentioned above would have taken place in the absence of a special relationship; and
  - the amounts which would have been paid under the transaction, or under each of the transactions in the series of transactions, in the absence of such a relationship.[130]

Transfer pricing adjustments

Where royalties are paid in excess of the arm's length amount and an adjustment is made to the profits of the payer under the transfer pricing legislation,[131] there is no equivalent claim to that relating to excessive interest to allow the excessive royalty not to be regarded as subject to deduction of income tax at source under of ITA 2007, Pt. 15. To the extent that a UK borrower is denied a deduction for royalties paid in this way, deduction of tax is required.[132]

Limitations on benefits

A variety of mechanisms are found in royalty articles designed to restrict the application of treaty benefits relating to royalties. These, including the meaning of 'beneficial ownership', are considered in chapter 11.

---

[131] ICTA 1988, Sch. 28AA, para. 1.

[132] Subject to the self-assessment provisions. See chapter 17.

Employment and Pensions

Chapter 10

19-000   Introduction

Income from employment and the treatment of pensions are closely related in UK domestic law. Both are addressed comprehensively in the Taxation (Employment and Pensions) Act 2003, a product of the tax law rewrite project.

19-050   Income from employment

Employment income has traditionally been styled in treaties as 'dependent personal services'. This is now simply referred to as 'Income from employment' in the OECD Model, to make the heading more consistent with the type of activities to which the article relates, and modern UK treaties conform with this language.

The general approach is that residents are normally liable to tax on employment income in their country of residence only, unless the employment is exercised in the other contracting state. The OECD rule is reflected in art. 15(1) of the Hungarian Treaty as follows:

> '[Subject to the provisions of arts. 16, 18, 19, 20 and 21,] salaries, wages and other similar remuneration derived by a resident of a Contracting State in respect of an employment shall be taxable only in that State unless the employment is exercised in the other Contracting State. If the employment is so exercised, such remuneration as is derived there from may be taxed in that other State.'

Article 15 refers to 'salaries, wages, and other similar remuneration' in respect of the employment. The meaning of these expressions and their scope in relation to domestic law is a little contentious. The ordinary meaning of the words 'salary' and 'wages' refer to money. 'Other similar remuneration' must be construed *ejusdem generis* with salary and wages suggesting, if not money, then money's worth. The domestic law adopts a similar classification in relation to 'earnings' in s. 62(2).[1]

ITEPA 2003 adopts a complex hierarchy of classifications. A wide variety of items are assembled for charge to income tax under the expression 'employment income'.[2] It includes 'earnings' as well as amounts 'treated as earnings' and amounts which 'count as

---

[1] 'In those Parts "earnings", in relation to an employment, means–

(a) any salary, wages or fee,

(b) any gratuity or other profit or incidental benefit of any kind obtained by the employee if it is money or money's worth, or

(c) anything else that constitutes an emolument of the employment. [s. 62(2)]'

[2] ITEPA 2003, s. 1(1)(a).

employment income'.[3] These two categories of deemed employment income share common attributes: they are not viewed as wages or salary, or as employment income in the absence of the deeming provisions. That domestic law chooses to deal with them this way does not automatically mean that the same classification applies for treaty purposes. There is thus a cogent argument that art. 15 deals only with earnings as set out in ITEPA 2003, Pt. 3, Ch. 1, and that further amounts taxable under ITEPA 2003 are addressed by other parts of treaties notably art. 21 (Other Income).

In 1997 the OECD Commentary to art. 15 was amended (by the introduction of para. 2.1) to the effect that OECD member countries have 'generally understood' the article to include 'benefits in kind received in respect of employment (for example, stock options, the use of a residence or automobile, health or life insurance coverage and club memberships)'. This view is endorsed by HMRC, which says that the expression 'salaries, wages and other similar remuneration' should be understood in the broadest sense and seen as covering all income from employment, including benefits and share option gains chargeable under the Taxes Act 1988, s. 135 (now ITEPA, Pt. 7, Ch. 5).[4]

The question is uniquely addressed in the UK–Australia Treaty in relation to 'fringe benefits'.[5] Taxing rights are allocated exclusively to the contracting state which would have the primary taxing right over that benefit if the value of the benefit were paid to the employee as ordinary employment income[6] under other provisions of the treaty. However, since this could be either under art. 14 (Employment Income) or art. 20 (Other Income), it sheds little light on the question.

The UK has agreed by means of exchanges of notes or protocol in various terms with three important treaty partners (Australia, Japan and the US) that share option gains are regarded or to be treated as 'other similar remuneration' for these purposes in those treaties.[7] Such agreement does not exist in respect of other contemporary treaties, such as those with Botswana, Canada, France, Jordan, Lithuania and South Africa.

The argument in favour of including both salary as well as various other items treated or counted as employment income in the scope of art. 15 is that it provides consistency of treatment of various forms of consideration for the duties of employment. The argument for treating items other than salary and similar remuneration differently is that while cash remuneration is treated relatively uniformly in different tax systems, and is thus more suitable for concurrent taxing jurisdiction, the treatment of other benefits or amounts deemed to be employment income varies widely and mismatches in treatment are likely.

---

[3] s. 7(1).

[4] HMRC, *Double Taxation Relief Manual*, para. DT1920.

[5] As defined under Australian law; UK–Australia, art. 15(2).

[6] UK–Australia, art. 15(1).

[7] UK–Australia exchange of notes of 21 August 2003, para. 8; UK–Japan Protocol 2 of February 2006, para. 4; UK–US exchange of notes on 24 July 2001.

Such items are thus better dealt with under other parts of the treaty, particularly other income, which typically provides for single taxation in the state of residence only.[8]

United Kingdom domestic law insofar as it taxes 'general earnings' residents on worldwide employment income and non-residents on employment income from UK sources is broadly consistent with this rule. A number of specific jurisdictional rules are found in various parts of ITEPA. Thus, the charge to income tax on general earnings for a tax year in which the employee is UK resident is expressed without any geographic limit in s. 15.[9] General earnings for a year in which an employee is not resident in the UK are only in respect of duties performed in the UK.[10] General earnings are composed of both 'earnings' and amounts 'treated' as earnings.[11]

The domestic charge to income tax on employment income also includes 'specific employment income' which 'counts' as employment income.[12] This covers benefits from employer-financed retirement benefits schemes,[13] payments and benefits on termination of employment[14] and income relating to securities and securities options.[15] The employment related securities regime generally adapts the jurisdictional rules for general earnings.[16] There are no express jurisdictional limits for retirement benefits schemes and the mechanisms for termination payments do not correspond with the taxing jurisdiction allocated in art. 15.[17]

The treaty rule applies generally to employment but is made subject to other parts of the treaty which also deal with specialised aspects of employment income, namely art. 16 (Directors' fees), art. 18 (Pensions) and art. 19 (Government services). In some cases, it is also subject to special rules provided for students and teachers, such as arts. 20 and 21, respectively, for example, in the Hungarian Treaty. Employed artists and sportspeople fall within art. 17 (Artistes and sportsmen).

---

[8] See chapter 12.

[9] In certain circumstances, employees who are resident but not ordinarily resident in the UK may be taxed on the remittance basis on 'foreign earnings' under ITEPA, s. 26, and employees who are resident and ordinarily resident but not domiciled in the UK may be taxed on the remittance basis on 'overseas earnings' under ss. 22 to 25.

[10] ITEPA 2003, s. 27.

[11] See ITEPA 2003, s. 7(3)(b). ITEPA 2003, Pt. 3, sets out what 'earnings' are. Amounts treated as earnings are those under Chs. 7 to 9 of Pt. 2 (agency workers, workers under arrangements made by intermediaries, and workers providing services through managed service companies), Chs. 2 to 11 of Pt. 3 (the benefits code), Ch. 12 of Pt. 3 (payments treated as earnings) and s. 262 of Capital Allowances Act 2001 (CAA 2001) (balancing charges to be given effect by treating them as earnings). See ITEPA 2003, s. 7(5).

[12] ITEPA 2003, s. 6(1).

[13] ITEPA 2003, Pt. 6, Ch. 2.

[14] ITEPA 2003, Pt. 6, Ch. 3.

[15] ITEPA 2003, Pt. 7.

[16] ITEPA 2003, s. 421E and 474.

[17] ITEPA 2003, s. 413 and 414.

19-100 Employment

The source of income within the article is an 'employment'. The expression is not elaborated on in treaties and recourse must be had to domestic law. Under domestic law, the charge under ITEPA 2003 applies to employment, which includes, in particular:

- any employment under a contract of service;
- any employment under a contract of apprenticeship; and
- any employment in the service of the Crown.[18]

This inexhaustive domestic definition relies on the general law relating to employment. The charge to income tax under ITEPA 2003 also extends to any 'office'.[19] 'Office' includes 'in particular any position which has an existence independent of the person who holds it and may be filled by successive holders'.[20] The two notions are not mutually exclusive.[21] In general, the distinction between the two is not material in most cases, but there is no suggestion that an office-holder is necessarily to be within the provisions of art. 15. One exception exists in relation to company directors, who are dealt with under art. 16 of the OECD Model. A company director is regarded as holding an office rather than having an employment.[22]

19-150 Employment versus self-employment

The most important distinction in determining the application of the article will be between employment and self-employment. In addition to the difficulties that may arise in drawing this distinction under domestic law, the possibility of inconsistent categorisation or treatment between the UK and the other contracting state may arise. For example, it is not uncommon for professionals such as lawyers or accountants to hold an office in the course of their professional practice. Directors' fees are, strictly speaking, liable to tax under ITEPA 2003. This would normally be assessable on the individual partners of a firm, but it may be given self-employment treatment under ITTOIA 2005, Pt. 2, pursuant to Extra-Statutory Concession A37, where the directorship is a normal incident of the profession and the particular practice concerned is only a small part of the profits and the fees are pooled for division amongst the partners by agreement.

ESC A37 also may have application in the context of cross-border corporate groups where, for example, a foreign parent company has the right to appoint the director to the board of a UK company and the director nominated is required to hand over any fees or other emoluments received in respect of the directorship to the company appointing him or her.

---

[18] ITEPA 2003, s. 4(1).

[19] ITEPA 2003, s. 5(1).

[20] ITEPA 2003, s. 5(3), which largely codifies the description by Harman LJ in *Mitchell and Edon v Ross* (1961) 40 TC 11, HL, as 'a position or post which goes on without regard to the identity of the holder of it from time to time.'

[21] *Macmillan v CIR* (1942) 24 TC 190.

[22] *Barry v Farrow* [1914] 1 KB 632.

Where the fees are so handed over, the concession will permit these amounts to be included in the nominating company's profits for corporation tax if it agrees to be so taxable. If the company is not within the charge to corporation tax, then it may agree to accept liability in respect of income tax deducted at the basic rate from the fees. This concession only applies to the UK tax treatment.

19-200   Employment income and intermediaries

Potential for mismatching treatment is increased as a result of the increase in rules relating to the provision of workers by intermediaries in ITEPA 2003, Pt. 2, as it applies to 'agency workers',[23] 'arrangements made by intermediaries'[24] and 'managed service companies'.[25] Where the agency workers regime applies, remuneration receivable under or in consequence of the agency contract payments is recharacterised as employment income, including remuneration which the client pays or provides to the agency in relation to the services.[26] It seems doubtful that a payment made to a company in respect of a contract that is not one of employment ought to be regarded as salary in respect of an employment for treaty purposes. Likewise, it seems doubtful that a contract that is not one of employment can be regarded as such for treaty purposes by reason of these domestic provisions.

Further difficult issues arise in the application of treaties to so-called IR35 cases where services are provided through an intermediary.[27] The consequences of an engagement falling within these rules is that if the worker (or an associate of the worker) receives directly or indirectly from the intermediary a payment or other benefit that is not chargeable to tax as employment income, or has rights entitling him or her to receive any such payment or other benefit from the intermediary, the intermediary is treated as making to the worker in that year and the worker is treated as receiving in that year a payment chargeable to income tax as employment income.[28] Similar difficulties in characterising the agreements arise in this context.

In relation to an individual whose services are provided by a managed service company (MSC)[29] and who receives (or whose associate receives) a payment or benefit which can reasonably be taken to be in respect of the services but is not general earnings received by the worker directly from the MSC, that individual is treated as receiving a deemed employment payment from the MSC (ITEPA 2003, s. 61D). There is no requirement to characterise the service agreements to qualify as an MSC.

---

[23] ITEPA 2003, Pt. 2, Ch. 7.

[24] So-called IR35 cases; see ITEPA, Pt. 2, Ch. 8.

[25] ITEPA 2003, Pt. 2, Ch. 9.

[26] ITEPA 2003, s. 44(2).

[27] ITEPA 2003, s. 50(1).

[28] ITEPA 2003, s. 50(1)(b).

[29] Within ITEPA 2003, s. 61B.

Some old colonial style treaties adopt a single article for personal services, whether dependent or independent. In such cases, the distinction between them is irrelevant for treaty purposes. An example of this is found in art. 9(2) of the Antigua Treaty as follows:

'An individual who is a resident of Antigua shall be exempt from United Kingdom tax on profits or remuneration in respect of personal (including professional) services performed within the United Kingdom in any year of assessment if:

(a)   he is present within the United Kingdom for a period or periods not exceeding in the aggregate 183 days during that year; and
(b)   the services are performed for or on behalf of a person resident in Antigua; and
(c)   the profits or remuneration are subject to Antigua tax.'

19-250   Place of performance

The place where an employment is 'exercised' for treaty purposes, and the place where 'duties are performed' under domestic law, are likely to be co-extensive. ITEPA 2003 only provides limited guidance. Section 38 simply associates periods of absence from the office or employment to the place of performance, unless the absence has been in respect of duties performed outside the UK. Similarly, s. 39 associates duties performed in the UK which are merely incidental to the performance of other duties outside the UK with the foreign performance. It states explicitly that it does not affect any question as to where any duties are performed.[30] It would appear that both under treaties and domestic law, the place of performance or exercise of employment is a question of fact. For example, in *Leonard v Blanchard*,[31] a taxpayer sought to have apportioned to emoluments attributable to duties performed outside the UK a part of emoluments attributable to days when he had been absent from his duties. The Court of Appeal held that to show that if the taxpayer on any day on which he was absent from employment, he would have performed duties outside the UK. If he had in reality been present, then evidence to this effect would have had to be presented.

19-300   Short-stay employees

Employees spending short periods of time working outside their country of residence may be exempt from tax in the country of performance of their duties. As a result, non-UK resident employees spending limited amounts of time in the UK for foreign employers may not be subject to UK tax. The OECD approach is reflected in art. 15(2) of the Latvian Treaty as follows:

'Notwithstanding the provisions of paragraph (1) of this Article, remuneration derived by a resident of a Contracting State in respect of an employment exercised in the other Contracting State shall be taxable only in the first-mentioned State if:

(a)   the recipient is present in the other State for a period or periods not exceeding in the aggregate 183 days in any twelve-month period commencing or ending in the fiscal year concerned; and

---

[30] ITEPA 2003, s. 39(3)(a).

[31] [1993] BTC 138; [1993] STC 259.

(b)   the remuneration is paid by, or on behalf of, an employer who is not a resident of the other State; and

(c)   the remuneration is not borne by a permanent establishment or a fixed base which the employer has in the other State.'

Earlier treaties apply the 183-day presence test in relation to any tax year in question rather than a rolling 12-month period, in line with the 1963 and 1977 Model treaties. In determining whether a non-resident employee is present in the UK for the 183-day test, the Revenue practice is to count a part-day as a whole day.[32] This is in accordance with the OECD Commentary on art. 15, para. 5, which says, 'However brief the part of a day counts as a day of presence for this purpose'. This differs from the domestic position in relation to determining residence.[33] In *Hoye v Forsdyke*,[34] it was held that a 'qualifying day' referred to a calendar day ending at midnight. In that case, the legislation specified that 'a person shall not be regarded as absent from the UK on any day, unless he is so absent at the end of it'. The taxpayer had argued that since the meaning of 'day' was ambiguous, a 'normal working day' was a more sensible interpretation than a calendar day ending at midnight. Consequently, in view of the different approaches in counting, presence means that an individual may well escape being resident in a year while exceeding 183 days' presence under this test. The test requires non-working days, such as weekends and holiday, to be included.

Remuneration under such treaties must be paid by or on behalf of an employer who is not a resident of the source state. It is not necessary in such cases that the employer and employee be resident in the same state. The Revenue approach to the application of this rule changed in 1995 in relation to certain short-stay employees. This followed changes to the OECD Commentary to art. 15 in 1992 to address cases of abuse involving the 'international hiring out of labour' through the use of non-resident intermediaries in order to meet the three requirements.[35] This applies where a formal contract of employment remains with an overseas employer, but the employee works in the business of a UK company, which attracts the risks and rewards of the work undertaken by the employee. The overseas employer often recharges the cost of the employee to the UK company in circumstances where the OECD has referred to the UK company as the 'economic employer'.

The OECD Commentary states that in applying the exemption, it is the economic employer, rather than the formal employer, who should be considered as the employer. This approach has been adopted in the UK in respect of employees commencing work after 1 July 1995.[36] A business visitor spending less than 60 days in the UK in a tax year, where that period does not form part of a lengthier presence in the UK, will be regarded by HMRC as insufficiently integrated into the UK business for that business to be regarded as the visitor's employer. In such circumstances, the visitor is viewed by HMRC as satisfying the conditions for the treaty exemption. While some might find the 60-day practice a useful safe harbour in certain

---

[32] HMRC, *Double Taxation Relief Manual*, para. DT1921.

[33] ITA 2007, s. 831(1A).

[34] 55 TC 281; [1981] STC 711, Ch.D.

[35] OECD Commentary to art. 15, para. 8.

[36] Inland Revenue, *Tax Bulletin* (June 1995), p. 220.

circumstances, there is no legal basis, nor support in the commentary, for treating visitors to the UK for more than 60 days as integrated in a local business. HMRC will also seek to apply the 'economic employer' approach in circumstances that it regards as constituting tax avoidance.[37] This, it says, may include cases where the overseas employer is based in a tax haven or the employee is nominally employed by a company which exists to provide his or her services to the UK user of those services; it may be closer to the OECD position. HMRC will not allow a deduction for remuneration paid by a UK company on behalf of an overseas employer if the UK company has not been reimbursed for the expenditure, on the basis of *Robinson v Scott Bader & Co. Ltd*.[38]

The third requirement is that the remuneration is not borne by a permanent establishment or a fixed base which the employer has in the source state. HMRC accepts that a permanent establishment cannot be said to 'bear the remuneration' unless it is charged against its profits without a corresponding credit, for example, by way of a management charge. However, it assumes that in the absence of evidence to the contrary, the cost of remuneration of an employee seconded to the permanent establishment is a deduction in computing the profits of the permanent establishment. This, it says, is the normal basis of allocating costs in accordance with international tax principles. The permanent establishment should therefore be regarded as bearing the cost of the individual's remuneration, unless there is evidence that the overseas head office continues to pay the employee and the cost is not allocated to the UK permanent establishment for UK tax purposes.[39] This is not a matter for presumption but a matter for analysis in accordance with ordinary allocation principles under art. 7.[40] Thus, an employee contributing to the profit-making activity, as a result of which income is allocated to the permanent establishment, will give rise to a deduction in respect of the employee's remuneration. On the other hand, an employee performing stewardship functions on behalf of the head office may not.

19-350   Employment-related securities

The treatment of employment-related securities illustrates difficulties that arise in dealing with non-cash remuneration in the international context. The UK appears to be exceptional in the breadth of the regime in ITEPA 2003, Pt. 7, and, as result, almost all international debate in this area has been in the context of employee share option gains.[41] HMRC views the expression 'salaries, wages and other similar remuneration' as being understood in the broadest sense and covering, among other things, share option gains.[42] In broad terms, the HMRC approach is:

---

[37] HMRC, *Double Taxation Relief Manual*, para. DT1922.

[38] (1984) 54 TC 757.

[39] HMRC, *Double Taxation Relief Manual*, para. DT1923.

[40] See chapter 8, paras. 17-150 to 17-450.

[41] See 'Cross-border income tax issues arising from employee stock-option plans: OECD Committee on Fiscal Affairs', 23 August 2004.

[42] *Ibid.*, para. DT1920. Although the legislation requires the amount of the gain to be taxed under ITEPA 2003, the gain is not 'remuneration'. The benefit of the option contract is a perquisite at the time of grant. See *Abbott v Philbin* (1960) 39 TC 82, HL.

- If the UK is the state of residence when a chargeable event under Pt. 7 occurs, then the UK has the right to tax in full, subject to credit for foreign tax paid on the same income.
- If the other contracting state is not the state of residence when a chargeable occurs, then the employee will be able to make a claim that the UK restrict its taxation to the amount derived from employment in the UK, by way of 'time apportionment'.[43]

Where a resident in a treaty country claimed exemption from tax on the gain, their initial position was that share option gains should be regarded as accruing evenly between the grant and exercise dates. This practice continues for options exercised before 6 April 2005. The commentary to art. 15 was amended in 2005 in line with the 2004 report in terms of which share option gains are apportioned on the basis that the right to exercise an option is earned by service from the date of grant forwards to the date the option vests. Thus, the period between vesting and exercise is not included. The UK now follows this. For options exercised before 6 April 2005, HMRC practice is to apportion the gain over the period from grant to exercise.[44] In general, a similar approach including time apportionment is adopted where shares are acquired other than via an option. Current practice (following FA 2008) in terms of the taxation regime for foreign employees in receipt of employment-related securities is to regard, in general, the period in which a restricted or forfeitable security is earned to be the period between the award of the security and the lifting of the restriction or forfeiture condition.[45] In every case a factual enquiry is necessary.

The 2001 UK–US Treaty, negotiated prior to publication of the OECD Report, was accompanied by an exchange of notes of 24 July 2001, which adopts an interpretation requiring 'any benefits, income or gains enjoyed by employees' under share option plans to be regarded as 'other similar remuneration' for the purposes of art. 14. The effect of this interpretation will commonly give rise to double taxation. The exchange of notes agrees an approach to alleviate this in certain circumstances, where an employee:

- has been granted a share option in the course of an employment in one of the contracting states;
- has exercised that employment in both states during the period between grant and exercise of the option;
- remains in that employment at the date of exercise; and
- under the domestic law of the contracting states would be taxable by both contracting states in respect of the option gain.

Pursuant to the exchange of notes, the contracting state of which the employee is not resident at the time of exercise will only tax that proportion of the option gain which relates to the period or periods between the grant and the exercise of the option during which the individual has exercised the employment in that contracting state. This approach accords with the earlier UK Revenue policy set out in the *Double Taxation Relief Manual*. Recognising that this approach will likely give rise to difficulties, the exchange of notes states:

---

[43] HMRC, *Employment Related Securities Manual*, para. ERSM161310.

[44] HMRC, *ibid.*, para. ERSM161310.

[45] HMRC, *ibid.*, para. ERSM161320.

'With the aim of ensuring that no unrelieved double taxation arises, the competent authorities of the contracting states will resolve by mutual agreement any difficulties or doubts arising as to the interpretation or application of art. 14 and art. 24 (relief from double taxation) in relation to employee share option plans.'

Later treaties that address the question are not consistent. Thus, the UK–Australia Treaty (2003) adopts the OECD view,[46] while the UK–Japan Protocol (2006) treats employment between grant and exercise as the relevant employment.[47]

19-400   Seafarers and aircrew

An exception from the general rule in art. 15 is made in most treaties for seafarers and aircrew employed onboard a ship or aircraft operating in international traffic. There is no direct link to entitlement to deduct the cost of such remuneration, but the rule is designed to match the treatment of profits from shipping and aircraft operations themselves. So under the OECD Model, these employees may be liable to tax in the contracting state where the enterprise has its place of effective management. An example is found in art. 13(2) of the Malaysian Treaty, which reads as follows:

'Notwithstanding the preceding provisions of this Article, remuneration in respect of an employment exercised aboard a ship or aircraft in international traffic may be taxed in the Contracting State in which the place of effective management of the enterprise is situated.'

Thus, aircrew or seafarers who are resident in one of the contracting states may be taxed in the other contracting state only if the transportation enterprise has its place of effective management there. In some treaties, the reference to the place of effective management is replaced with reference to the residence of the enterprise (Korean Treaty, art. 15(3)) or simply a reference to 'an enterprise of a contracting state' (Latvian Treaty, art. 15(3)). These rules only apply to aircrew and seafarers and not, for example, to ground staff.

The UK extends taxing jurisdiction over performance of duties of aircrew and seafarers on aircraft or onboard ships far beyond the actual place of performance. Under UK domestic law, duties performed on an aircraft or a vessel not extending to a port outside the UK, or on a vessel or aircraft engaged on a voyage or journey beginning and ending in the UK, or on a part beginning or ending in the UK of any voyage or journey, are deemed to be performed in the UK.[48] This may be alleviated by the deduction in ITEPA 2003, Pt. 5, Ch. 6, for eligible periods spent performing duties abroad.

19-450   Company directors

Directors' fees are singled out for special treatment. The approach in the OECD Model is reflected in art. 16 of the Singapore Treaty, which reads:

---

[46] UK–Australia, exchange of notes, 21 August 2003, para. 8(c)(i).

[47] UK–Japan Protocol , art. 4(b).

[48] ITEPA 2003, s. 40(1) and (2). An exception is made for seafarers who are resident, ordinarily resident but not domiciled in the UK, for the purpose limiting their earnings from overseas employment under s. 23 (s. 40(3)).

'Directors' fees and other similar payments derived by a resident of a Contracting State in his capacity as a member of the board of directors of a company which is a resident of the other Contracting State may be taxed in that other State.'

Thus, in principle, a contracting state may tax directors' fees in the country of residence of the company on whose board the director serves, even if duties are not performed there. Under domestic law, directors are taxed in the same way as other employees or officers; consequently, non-resident directors will only be taxable in respect of duties performed in the UK. Where this happens, the treaty will permit taxation, notwithstanding that such duties are performed on short visits to the UK. On the other hand, a non-resident director who attends a board meeting or performs some other directors' duty in a state other than where the company is resident is not taxable there on directors' fees. Some treaties refer to other corporate officers consistent with the management structure under the corporate law of the other contracting state (see, for example, the Mexican Treaty, art. 16). Article 16 refers to 'directors' fees and similar payments', unlike art. 15, which refers to 'salaries, wages and other similar remuneration' in respect of employment. The extent to which there are any differences between these expressions is unclear. The OECD Commentary on art. 16, para. 1.1, indicates that the term is generally understood to include benefits in kind.

19-500   Academics

About one-half of treaties contain specific provisions relating to visiting professors and teachers, despite the absence of any model language in either the OECD or UN models. More recent treaties have, however, tended to omit this. The 2003 UK–Australia Treaty and the 2005 UK–Botswana Treaty contain no article dealing with visiting academics, while the 2001 UK–US, 2003 UK–Georgia and 2008 UK–France treaties do contain such provisions. A simple form found in the Antigua Treaty, art. 11, reads as follows:

'The remuneration derived by a professor or teacher who is ordinarily resident in one of the territories, for teaching, during a period of temporary residence not exceeding two years, at a university, college, school or other educational institution in the other territory, shall be exempt from tax in that other territory.'

Implicit in this formulation is that the visiting academic remains ordinarily resident throughout the period in order to benefit from the exemption. This requirement does not appear in later formulations, such as that found in art. 20(1) of the Belgian Treaty, which reads as follows:

'A professor or teacher who is or was formerly a resident of one of the territories, and who receives remuneration for teaching, during a period of temporary residence not exceeding two years, at a university, college, school or other educational institution in the other territory, shall be exempt from tax in that other territory in respect of that remuneration.'

The second format contemplates that visiting academics may become non-resident and indeed not ordinarily resident in their home state during the period of their visit. This may hold out the prospect of tax-free income for those concerned. However, in some cases, the exemption only applies to an academic who is subject to tax in the home territory in respect of the remuneration in question.[49] The exemption is normally limited to remuneration

---

[49] See, for example, Fiji Treaty, art. 21.

derived from teaching. In some cases, the exemption permits research related remuneration to be exempt.[50] This is commonly subject to the limitation in art. 20(2) that the research must be undertaken in the public interest and not 'primarily for the benefit of some other private person or persons'.

Educational institution

Teaching must take place at a university, college, school or other educational institute. In *Barry v Hughes*,[51] it was held in connection with domestic legislation that the words 'other educational establishment' were not to be construed ejusdem generis with 'university, college [or] school' because of the word 'educational'. In that context, education was considered to be devoted exclusively to training of the mind in contradistinction to training in manual skills. In that case, a unit at a hospital for training mentally subnormal individuals was not held to be an educational establishment. Such an interpretation, if applied in the treaty context, could lead to somewhat bizarre results where a visiting physical education teacher to a school might qualify for the exemption, whereas an English language teacher at an institution primarily providing manual training would not.

Two-year limit

The exemption applies in all cases to visits not exceeding two years. The application of this rule has given rise to dispute in two cases, both under the Hungarian Treaty. Article 21(1) of the Hungarian Treaty restricts the exemption to remuneration for teaching or research for a period 'not exceeding two years from the date he first visits that state for such purpose'. In *IRC v Vas*,[52] a Hungarian research associate had three visits to the UK. The first exceeded two years by two days. He accepted that this was not within the exemption, but argued that the two later visits, which were each for fewer than two years, qualified for exemption. The court concluded that the words 'from the date he first visits' were designed to limit the exemption to the period of two years after the first visit to the UK for one of the purposes specified in the treaty. It did not mean that any number of visits limited to two years throughout a taxpayer's working life would be exempt from UK tax provided he or she resumed foreign residence for a period between each of them.

In *Devai v IRC*,[53] a Hungarian academic argued that he had made separate visits within the meaning of art. 21(1) when he came to the UK to take up an appointment at one university and left for a short period before taking up an appointment at another UK university. The Commissioner noted that the purpose of the visit must be to teach (or carry out research), but this is not expressed to tie to a particular establishment. In that case, he had spent a short period of time in Dublin between his appointment in Edinburgh and the second appointment in Belfast. Although he remained a resident of Hungary for tax purposes, it was found that throughout the period his 'home' was in Edinburgh, where he and his family had lived since his initial appointment. The Special Commissioner also concluded that, similarly, a trip to

---

[50] See, for example, UK–Georgia Treaty, art. 20(1).

[51] 48 TC 586; [1973] STC 103, Ch.D.

[52] [1990] BTC 52; [1990] STC 137, Ch.D.

[53] (1996) Sp C 105; [1997] STC SCD 31.

the home does not interrupt the continuity of a visit, provided that it is relatively short, social or recreational in character, and taken with the intention of resuming residence in the UK.

In many cases, visiting professors and teachers will be subject to UK taxation under ITEPA as employees. There may be cases where fees for individual lectures or projects may not be on this basis. Where the treaty provides specific treatment for academics, that specific treatment will apply. In other cases, the normal OECD Model, art. 15, employment income provisions would apply or other articles in the case of non-employment income.

19-550   Diplomats and consular officers

The application of the doctrine of sovereign immunity to the exercise of government functions is extended into the area of remuneration paid to government officials. Treaties addressing these issues usually distinguish between two categories of government employees. Members of diplomatic missions and consular posts represent states and fulfil traditional roles in international relations and law, on the one hand, and state employees more generally, on the other hand.

Diplomats

The treatment of diplomats, as far as tax treaties are concerned, is normally found in the OECD Model, art. 27. An example of this is found in art. 28 of the Spanish Treaty, which reads as follows:

> 'Nothing in this convention shall affect the fiscal privileges of diplomatic or consular officials under the general rules of international law or under the provisions of special agreements.'

This article falls in to the special provisions of Ch. VI of the OECD Model rather than Chs. III (taxation of income) or IV (taxation of capital). Thus, it does not govern the allocation of taxing jurisdiction. The effect of the treaty provision is to preserve the position of diplomats and consular agents under international law and custom. The law and custom relating to diplomats is codified in the Vienna Convention on Diplomatic Relations 1961. Likewise, the taxation of diplomats in domestic law is not dealt with in the tax legislation but under the Diplomatic Privileges Act 1964, which gives effect in UK domestic law to the Vienna Convention. High Commissioners of Commonwealth countries are covered by this act.

Article 34 of the Vienna Convention exempts a diplomatic agent from all dues and taxes, personal or real, national, regional or municipal, subject to specific exceptions. A 'diplomatic agent' is the head of the mission or a member of the diplomatic staff of the mission (art. 1(e)). Other members of the staff of the mission and private servants who are nationals of or permanently resident in the receiving state enjoy privileges and immunities only to the extent admitted by the receiving state. However, the receiving state must exercise its jurisdiction over those persons in such a manner as not to interfere unduly with the performance of the functions of the mission.[54]

---

[54] Vienna Convention on Diplomatic Relations, art. 38 (2).

A diplomatic agent who is a national of or permanently resident in the receiving state enjoys only immunity from jurisdiction, and inviolability, in respect of official acts performed in the exercise of his functions. This is except insofar as additional privileges and immunities may be granted by the receiving state.[55] Article 37(1) of the Vienna Convention extends these privileges to the members of the family of a diplomatic agent forming part of his or her household if they are not nationals of the receiving state. Thus, family members benefit from the exemptions from tax. Service staff are dealt with as follows:

> 'Article 37(3) Members of the service staff of the mission who are not nationals of or permanently resident in the receiving state shall enjoy immunity in respect of acts performed in the course of their duties, exemption from dues and taxes on the emoluments they receive by reason of their employment and the exemption contained in article 33.'

This exemption is strictly applied. In *Jiminez v Inland Revenue Commissioners*,[56] the taxpayer, a national of the Republic of the Philippines, was employed as a cook by the Namibian High Commission in London. Special Commissioner John Walters QC dismissed her claim for exemption from UK income tax on emoluments received by reason of employment as a cook at a diplomatic mission on the basis that she was not a member of the service staff. Moreover, she was permanently resident in the UK within art. 37(3) of the Vienna Convention and for that reason disqualified from exemption from tax under that article. Even if she had not been permanently resident in the UK, she was prevented from enjoying any exemption because there was no notification of her appointment, as required by art. 39(1).

Exceptions to the tax exemption are:

> '(a) Indirect taxes of a kind which are normally incorporated in the price of goods or services;
> (b) Dues and taxes on private immovable property situated in the territory of the receiving State, unless he holds it on behalf of the sending State for the purposes of the mission;
> (c) Estate, succession or inheritance duties levied by the receiving State, subject to [certain exceptions];
> (d) Dues and taxes on private income having its source in the receiving State and capital taxes on investments made in commercial undertakings in the receiving State;
> (e) Charges levied for specific services rendered;
> (f) Registration, court or record fees, mortgage dues and stamp duty, with respect to immovable property, subject to [certain exceptions;[57]'

To the extent that diplomats fall within the exceptions, their tax liability is not governed by the Vienna Convention but may be within the scope of a tax treaty in the normal way.

Consular officers

The position of consular officers and employees is similar under the Vienna Convention on Consular Relations 1962 and given effect by the Consular Relations Act 1968. The convention specifies that:

---

[55] Vienna Convention on Diplomatic Relations, art. 38(1).

[56] (2004) Sp C 419.

[57] Vienna Convention on Diplomatic Relations, art. 34.

'(1) Consular officers and consular employees and members of their families forming part of their households shall be exempt from all dues and taxes, personal or real, national, regional or municipal, except [the same exclusions as apply to diplomats]...

(2) Members of the service staff shall be exempt from dues and taxes on the wages which they receive for their services.

(3) Members of the consular post who employ persons whose wages or salaries are not exempt from income tax in the receiving State shall observe the obligations which the laws and regulations of that State impose upon employers concerning the levying of income tax.[58]'

These international legal requirements are now reflected in domestic law in ITEPA 2003, s. 300, in the case of employment consuls, and in s. 302, in the case of consular employees, and ITEPA 2003, s. 771, in respect of their relevant foreign income. In the case of consular employees, exemption will only apply if it is addressed in a bilateral treaty offering the exemption bilaterally. Official agents are also exempt from income tax if in respect of income from employment as an official agent for a foreign state in the UK if the employee is neither a Commonwealth citizen nor an Irish citizen, and the functions of the employment are not exercised in connection with a trade, business or other undertaking carried on for profit.[59] 'Official agents' are not consuls but are employed on the staff of a consulate, or an official department or agency of a foreign state.[60] In *Caglar & Ors v Billingham (HMIT)*,[61] the taxpayers were 'official agents' of the Turkish Republic of Northern Cyprus, which has not been recognised as a state by Her Majesty's Government. The Special Commissioner concluded that the exemption from income tax was confined to official agents of recognised foreign states.

19-600   Government services

The scope of cross-border activity of modern governments goes beyond the traditional diplomatic roles. The contemporary approach to the tax treatment of individuals engaged in other government service is set out in art. 19(1) of the Norwegian Treaty (2000) which reads:

'(a) Salaries, wages and other similar remuneration, other than a pension, paid by a Contracting State or a political subdivision or a local authority thereof to an individual in respect of services rendered to that State or subdivision or authority shall be taxable only in that State.

(b) Notwithstanding the provisions of subparagraph (a) of this para., such salaries, wages and other similar remuneration shall be taxable only in the other Contracting State if the services are rendered in that State and the individual is a resident of that State who:

(i)   is a national of that State; or

---

[58] Vienna Convention on Consular Relations 1962, art. 49.

[59] ITEPA 2003, s. 301(1).

[60] ITEPA 2003, s. 301(5).

[61] (1996) Sp C 70.

(ii)   did not become a resident of that State solely for the purpose of rendering the services.'

Thus, in most cases, the contracting state or political subdivision thereof employing the individual will have the sole taxing right. Employment income may be taxed in the contracting state where the employment is performed where the individual is either both a resident and a national of that state or a resident but did not become so solely for the purpose of rendering the services in question. Thus, locally hired staff employed by foreign governments will normally be subject to local taxation.

General earnings from overseas Crown employment provided to a person employed in the private sector would either not be within the charge because the employee is non-resident, or taxed on the remittance basis because the employee is not ordinarily resident or non-domiciled, and it is made subject to UK tax by ITEPA 2003, ss. 26(1)(b) and 27(1)(b).

Crown employment is employment under the Crown of a public nature, the earnings from which are payable out of the public revenue of the UK or Northern Ireland.[62] 'General earnings from overseas Crown employment' means general earnings from such employment in respect of duties performed outside the UK.[63] Exemption by order made under ss. 28(5) to (7) removes from the scope of UK income tax locally engaged, low-paid staff employed overseas by the Crown.[64]

Since the role of the state functions vary from one country to another and have varied over time, employment in connection with commercial activities undertaken by a foreign government is taxed under the normal rules. This is illustrated by art. 19(3) of the Norwegian Treaty (2000), which reads:

'The provisions of Articles 15, 16, 17 and 18 of this Convention shall apply to salaries, wages and other similar remuneration, and to pensions, in respect of services rendered in connection with a business carried on by a Contracting State or a political subdivision or a local authority thereof.'

19-650   Pensions

The funding of retirement is a complex issue in the international context because of radically different approaches taken by different countries. The UK treatment has been unified by ITEPA 2003, Pt. 9, which provides for the taxation of pension income, and FA 2004, Pt. 4, which provides for the tax treatment of pension schemes and similar arrangements. The vast majority of treaties and the OECD Model do not deal explicitly with the treatment of contributions to pension schemes or the taxation of those schemes, although occasionally these issues do appear in modern treaties.[65]

---

[62] ITEPA 2003, s. 28(2).

[63] ITEPA 2003, s. 28(2).

[64] See HMRC, *Employment Income Manual*, para. EIM40209.

[65] See, for example, UK–US Treaty, art. 18; UK–South Africa Treaty, art. 17(3); UK–Chile Treaty, art. 17(3); UK–Netherlands Treaty (2008), art. 17.

Pensions are addressed in the OECD Model in very simple terms. This is reflected in only a few UK treaties, one of which is with China. Article 19 reads:

'Subject to the provisions of paragraph (2) of Article 20 (Government Service), pensions and other similar remuneration paid to a resident of a Contracting State in consideration of past employment shall be taxable only in that State.'

The scope of this article is extremely narrow in the sense of being limited to 'pensions' in respect of past employment and did not include retirement annuities for self-employed persons which existed under ICTA 1988, Pt. XIV, Ch. III, prior to FA 2004. As a result, a number of treaties deal with pensions and annuities together, and treat them similarly. Article 18, for example, of the UK–Kazakhstan Treaty reads:

'18(1) Subject to the provisions of paragraph (2) of Article 19 of this Convention, pensions and other similar remuneration paid in consideration of past employment to a resident of a Contracting State and any annuity paid to such a resident shall be taxable only in that State.

18(2) The term "annuity" means a stated sum payable to an individual periodically at stated times during his life or during a specified or ascertainable period of time under an obligation to make the payments in return for adequate and full consideration in money or money's worth.'

There are treaties that permit source state taxation. The UN Model includes an optional art. 18A(2) which permits taxation in the contracting state if the payment is made by a resident of that other state or a permanent establishment situated there, although no UK treaties adopt this. The UK–Nigeria Treaty, art. 18, generally allows source state taxation. As an exception, art. 18(1) of the Swedish Treaty, although permitting taxation in the source state, requires a deduction of one-fifth of the amount to be allowed. On the other hand, art. 19 of the Zambian Treaty permits taxation in the source state only where there is exemption in the residence state. This permission applies where the employment in respect of which the pension is paid was exercised in the source state.

Social security pensions

Social security and old-age pensions are not regarded as paid in consideration of past employment and are therefore not within the pensions article. HMRC treats such pensions as within the other income article.[66] Social security pensions are addressed in a few treaties. Those with Denmark, Finland, Luxembourg, Norway and Sweden and the US authorise taxation in the paying state. In the case of Germany, art. 9(2), provides that remuneration, including pensions paid in respect of present or past services or work out of public funds, is exempt from UK tax, unless the payment is made to a national of the UK who is not also a German national. In *Oppenheimer v Cattermole*,[67] a German-Jewish refugee fled to England in 1939 and became a British national in 1948. After World War II, he received pensions paid out of German public funds in respect of his work in Germany prior to immigration. The taxpayer argued that he was a German national. The House of Lords decided that the reference to nationality was to be determined by the state whose nationality is claimed. Under the basic law of the German Federal Republic enacted in 1949, former German citizens who had been deprived of their nationality for political, racial or religious reasons

---

[66] HMRC, *Double Taxation Relief Manual*, para. DT227.

[67] (1975) 50 TC 159.

were entitled, although still residing abroad, to be renationalised on application. The taxpayer had not taken the appropriate steps to assert his rights under that law. In a related case heard at the same time, *Nothman v Cooper*, the taxpayer also argued that the payments were in the nature of capital compensation. This was rejected. Annuities and pensions payable to victims of Nazi persecution by Germany or Austria are now not subject to income tax in the UK.[68]

Consideration for past employment

It is normally a requirement for source state exemption that pensions and similar remuneration be paid in consideration of past employment. 'Past employment' would appear to refer to employment which has terminated, and any reason for termination should suffice.[69] In relation to other deferred compensation arrangements, the dividing line between items falling within the employment income articles[70] and the pensions articles is unclear but important where exclusive taxing jurisdiction is allocated to the residence state.

The expression 'past employment' does not appear to extend to past self-employment; thus, payments made by a registered pension scheme in respect of self-employed individuals will not fall within pension articles, following the OECD Model. Annuities paid to such individuals within FA 2004, s. 165(2)(a), will likely fall within the annuity provisions. Income withdrawal within s. 165(2)(a) may not. Some treaties do not restrict the treaty benefits to employment-related pensions.[71]

The scope of the article has not been considered by the courts. No comprehensive definition of pension is provided in the treaties. The expression is only partially defined in ITEPA 2003 to include 'a pension which is paid voluntarily or is capable of being discontinued'.[72] The core scope of the expression is now conveniently contained in ITEPA 2003, s. 566, which sets out the meaning of 'pension income' in identifying the items brought into charge under ITEPA 2003, Pt. 9. Pensions and annuities that are exempt under Pt. 9, Chs. 16 to 18, will likewise fall within this treaty expression. Although payments that are authorised to be paid by a registered pension scheme are not in terms charged by FA 2004, Pt. 4, any such payment or benefit within Ch. 3 would likely be a pension or similar remuneration.[73]

---

[68] ITEPA 2003, s. 642.

[69] The circumstances identified in FA 2004, s. 150, are illustrative but not exhaustive:

'150 (1) In this Part "pension scheme" means a scheme or other arrangements, comprised in one or more instruments or agreements, having or capable of having effect so as to provide benefits to or in respect of persons–

(a) on retirement,

(b) on death,

(c) on having reached a particular age,

(d) on the onset of serious ill-health or incapacity, or

(e) in similar circumstances.'

[70] OECD Model, art. 15.

[71] See UK–Canada Treaty, art. 17, and UK–Chile Treaty, art. 17.

[72] ITEPA 2003, ss. 570 and 574(1).

[73] Payments permitted according to FA 2004, s.164(1):

However, in the predecessor legislation, the Taxes Act 1988, s. 612(1), the definition of relevant benefits distinguished a pension (which includes an annuity) from a 'lump sum, gratuity or other like benefit'. In *Johnson v Holleran*,[74] money received from trustees of a pension fund after the cessation of employment in recognition of previous employment and because of disability was a pension. That payments were made on account of disability rather than for past services was immaterial. It was argued that to constitute a pension, the payments must be made after retirement, to a former employee, for past services and must continue for life. The taxpayer argued that he was not retired because if his disability ceased, the payments would cease and he would have to seek employment. It was held that it was sufficient that the particular employment must have ceased, but that this need not have been due to retirement rather than any other cause. The court, noting the absence of a judicial definition of pension, did not attempt one. In *Johnson v Farquhar*,[75] the court confirmed that it was sufficient that the taxpayer became a member of the pension scheme because he was an employee and remained a member until he ceased to be an employee. It was not necessary for the payment to be for past services in the sense of being fully earned and a form of deferred salary. This approach suggests that if past employment is one of the originating causes, this is sufficient. Thus, the expression 'consideration' should not be construed in the English, contract-law sense, but, rather, that the payment is in respect of the employment. On this basis, pensions derived from pension scheme members' contributions qualify for treaty benefits. By the same reasoning, the expression 'other similar remuneration' merely connotes forms of payment other than 'pensions'.

Source of pensions

The *situs* of the payer is the only rule for determining the source of pensions under domestic law. In particular, the underlying reason for the pension is irrelevant. Under domestic law, tax is payable under ITEPA 2003 in respect of any pension which is paid otherwise than by or on behalf of a person in the UK.[76] Foreign pensions are those paid by or on behalf of a person outside the UK to a person resident in the UK.[77] This includes foreign statutory social security pensions.[78]

'The only payments a registered pension scheme is authorised to make to or in respect of a person who is or has been a member of the pension scheme are–

(a) pensions permitted by the pension rules or the pension death benefit rules to be paid to or in respect of a member (see ss. 165 and 167),

(b) lump sums permitted by the lump sum rule or the lump sum death benefit rule to be paid to or in respect of a member (see ss. 166 and 168),

(c) recognised transfers (see s. 169),

(d) scheme administration member payments (see s. 171),

(e) payments pursuant to a pension sharing order or provision, and

(f) payments of a description prescribed by regulations made by the Revenue and Customs Commissioners.'

[74] [1989] BTC 11; [1989] STC 1, Ch.D.

[75] [1992] BTC 3; [1992] STC 11.

[76] ITEPA 2003. s. 569(1).

[77] *Ibid.*, s. 573(1).

[78] *Albon v IRC* [1999] BTC 138; [1998] STC 1181. This is now the subject of statutory rules in ITEPA 2003, Pt. 10, Ch. 6.

19-700 Contributions to pension schemes

Tax relief on contributions to fund pensions is generally only available for contributions meeting the requirements of FA 2004, Pt. 4, Ch. 4. An individual who is an active member of a registered pension scheme is entitled to relief in respect of relievable pension contributions paid during a tax year if, among others, either residence or earnings requirements are satisfied. The residence requirement is met if the individual is resident in the UK at some time during that year, or at some time during the five tax years immediately before that year – and when the individual became a member of the pension scheme. The earnings requirements are met, in particular, if the individual has employment income or income the carrying on or exercise of a trade, profession or vocation (whether individually or as a partner acting personally in a partnership) chargeable to income tax for that year.[79] Thus, broadly speaking, non-resident individuals who carry on personal service activities that the UK is entitled to tax under the treaty provisions considered in Chs. 6 and 7 will be entitled to tax relief on eligible contributions. Relevant UK earnings that are not taxable in the UK by virtue of a treaty are treated as not being chargeable to income tax.[80]

Tax relief on contributions is generally only available for contributions to UK-registered pension schemes. Similar relief may apply in respect of contributions to qualifying overseas pension schemes by individuals moving to the UK.[81] An individual who is a 'relevant migrant member' of a 'qualifying overseas pension scheme'[82] is entitled to tax analogous relief on contributions to that scheme if:

- his or her relevant UK earnings are chargeable to tax for that year;
- he or she is UK resident when contributions are paid; and
- he or she has notified the scheme manager of an intention to claim relief for contributions.[83]

A relevant migrant member is one who was not UK resident when first a member of the overseas pension scheme but was a member when UK residence commenced. Furthermore, the individual must have been entitled to tax relief in respect of contributions paid under the pension scheme under the law of the country in which the individual was resident immediately before the becoming UK resident. Also, the individual must have been notified by the scheme manager that information concerning events that are benefit crystallisation events in relation to the individual will be given to HMRC.[84]

Notwithstanding the limitations placed on cross-border relief for pension contributions, treaty provisions addressing this issue are rare but are increasingly found in modern treaties.

---

[79] See FA 2004, ss. 188(1) and 189.

[80] FA 2004, s. 189(2).

[81] See FA 2004, s. 243 and Sch. 33.

[82] See FA 2004, Sch. 33, para. 5.

[83] FA 2004, Sch. 33, para. 1(1)).

[84] FA 2004, Sch. 33, para. 4.

Treaties with Chile,[85] Denmark,[86] the Irish Republic,[87] the US[88] and Switzerland[89] are examples that provide for relief in respect of contributions to a pension fund established in one contracting state in respect of employment exercised in the other. In each case, relief is subject to detailed conditions which, in general terms, reflect the pattern adopted in FA 2004 in relation to migrant members of overseas schemes. An early example of these provisions is contained in the Irish Treaty, which reads:

'17A(1) Subject to the conditions specified in paragraph (2) of this Article, where an employee ('the employee'), who is a member of a pension scheme which has been approved or is being considered for approval under the legislation of one of the Contracting States, exercises his employment in the other Contracting State:

(a) contributions paid by the employee to that scheme during the period that he exercises his employment in that other State shall be deductible in computing his taxable income in that State within the limits that would apply if the contributions were paid to a pension scheme which has been approved under the legislation of that State; and

(b) payments made to the scheme by or on behalf of his employer during that period:

  (i) shall not be treated as part of the employee's taxable income, and

  (ii) shall be allowed as a deduction in computing the profits of his employer, in that other State.'

As a result, both employer and employee contributions will qualify for relief in that employee contributions will be deductible in computing taxable income within the limits imposed by the state of employment as if they had been paid to a local pension scheme. Likewise, employer contributions are deductible by the employer and not treated as part of the taxable income of the employee. Only employees who are members of a pension scheme approved in one contracting state and exercising employment in the other contracting state qualify for this benefit. In addition, the Irish Treaty, for example, imposes several conditions broadly parallel to the domestic rules which must be met:

'17A(2) The conditions specified in this paragraph are that:

(a) the employee is employed in the other Contracting State by the person who was his employer immediately before he began to exercise his employment in that State or by an associated employer of that employer;

(b) the employee was not a resident of that State immediately before he began to exercise his employment there;

(c) at the time that the contributions referred to in paragraph (1)(a) of this Article are paid, or the payments referred to in paragraph (1)(b) of this Article are made, to the scheme the employee has exercised his employment in that State for:

  (i) less than ten years where he was a resident of the first-mentioned Contracting State immediately before he began to exercise his employment in the other Contracting State, or

  (ii) less than five years in other cases.'

---

[85] Art. 17(3).

[86] Art. 28(3).

[87] Art. 17A.

[88] Art. 18.

[89] Art. 18.

Consequently, these benefits are only available to employees who move in the course of existing employment from one contracting state to the other in order to work in the second state, and were not resident there immediately before starting to work in the state of employment. The benefit is also subject to time limits. Contributions will only qualify if the employment was exercised for less than ten years in the state where the fund is not established, if he or she was resident in the state where the fund is established immediately before starting to work in the other. In other cases, it applies where the employee has exercised his or her employment in the state where the fund is not established for fewer than five years. Employment will qualify with either the same or an associated employer.

These treaties still do not address the problems of cross-border pension arrangements comprehensively. The US Treaty is the first to attempt a more rounded approach to the taxation of pensions and pension payments. The Irish Treaty, while providing for relief for pension contributions only, addressed this issue in the context of occupational pensions. Relief for contributions by self-employed individuals is addressed in the US Treaty. A trend in this direction is indicated in those treaties with Chile and Switzerland.

Apart from the absence of relief for contributions in older treaties, the lack of specific measures also raises questions as to how pension fund investment returns are to be classified where the pension is financed by an individual's own contributions, if they are not specifically recognised under the pensions regime as such. Article 18(2) of the US Treaty extends relief to participants in pension schemes in respect of self-employment along with employment. This applies in both cases only where the employment or self-employment began in the other contracting state. In addition, the pension scheme must 'generally correspond' to a pension scheme established in that other state. General correspondence is a more liberal expression than required under domestic law and as required, for example, under art. 28 of the Danish Treaty. The exchange of notes of 24 July 2001 with respect to the US Treaty lists pension schemes for the purpose of the treaty and includes UK employment-related arrangements and personal pensions.[90] Existing US plans are also included, as well as any 'identical or substantially similar schemes' which are established pursuant to legislation introduced after the date of signature of the treaty. The treaty further provides[91] that where an individual resident in one contracting state is a member or participant in a pension scheme established in the other contracting state, income earned by the pension scheme may only be taxed as the income of the individual – when it is paid to or for the benefit of that individual and, in particular, when it is not transferred to another scheme. Where the individual makes contributions in respect of income or profit which is taxed on the remittance basis, then relief may be reduced in proportion to the amount unremitted.[92] Furthermore, as a boost to the UK pension industry, contributions by US citizens resident in the UK and employed by a UK resident or a permanent establishment in the UK may contribute to UK pension schemes for US tax purposes and contributions are treated as deductible (or excludable) in computing taxable income in the US.[93]

---

[90] See also the memorandum of understanding regarding pension schemes between the UK and Switzerland of 12 February 2008.

[91] See art. 18(1).

[92] See art. 18(4).

[93] See art.5.

Some treaties, such as those with the US[94] and Switzerland,[95] give exclusive taxing jurisdiction in relation to lump sum payments to the state in which the pension is established.

19-750   Government pensions

Government pensions are accorded separate treatment under treaties. They are typically excluded from the pensions article and addressed in the government services article. The OECD Model provisions are contained in art. 19(2) of the Vietnamese Treaty as follows:

'(a)   Any pension paid by, or out of funds created by, a Contracting State or a political subdivision or a local authority thereof to an individual in respect of services rendered to that State or subdivision or authority shall be taxable only in that State.

(b)   Notwithstanding the provisions of sub-paragraph (a) of this paragraph, such pension shall be taxable only in the other Contracting State if the individual is a resident of and a national of that State.'

As with employment income, a distinction is drawn between employees performing a state function and those who do not. The HMRC *Double Taxation Relief Manual* notes that employment with a statutory body set up by a state is not usually regarded as involving payment by or the rendering of services to that state, even if the body is set up and funded by the state. Similarly, employees in nationalised industries are not regarded as coming within government services. HMRC gives the example of members of armed forces or teachers employed by a local authority as paid by the state for services rendered to that state. The widow or dependants of an individual who has rendered services to a state is regarded as being paid by the other state for services rendered to that state.[96]

As with government services, taxing jurisdiction is normally reserved to the paying state. Residents and nationals of the other contracting state are normally to be taxed in that state only, in order to facilitate the hiring of local staff.

---

[94]   Art. 17(2).

[95]   Art. 18(2).

[96]   HMRC, *Double Taxation Relief Manual*, para. DT908.

Capital Gains

Chapter 11

20-000   Introduction

The approach adopted in treaties following the OECD Model to the taxation of capital gains is, in broad terms, similar to that adopted under UK domestic law – the underlying principle being that capital gains are generally only taxable in the contracting state of residence. A typical expression of this treaty rule is found in art. 13(4) of the Bangladesh Treaty, which reads:

'Capital gains from the alienation of any property other than those mentioned in paragraphs (1), (2) and (3) of this Article shall be taxable only in the Contracting State of which the alienator is a resident.'

The balance of the articles constitute exceptions to the general rule. The effect of this general rule was explained by the Special Commissioners in *Trevor Smallwood Trust v R & C Commrs* thus:[1]

'Article 13(4), relating to gains on all other property (including therefore property in a third state), is more general and does not contain any reference to source. It states that if the alienator is Treaty Resident in one state the gains are taxable only in that state . . . The result would be that if the state other than that of Treaty Residence taxed by its domestic law on any basis other than Treaty Residence the Treaty would prevent it. There would be no scope for any basis of taxation in the non-Treaty Residence state to continue. The plain words 'taxable only' in the Treaty Residence state mean what they say.[2]'

No definition of 'alienation' is found in treaties and the term is not used in UK domestic tax law. The charge in respect of capital gains in domestic law is by reference to the disposal of assets,[3] an expression which is undefined and therefore must be given its natural meaning. It is likely a little similar to alienation. In certain cases, a disposal is deemed to occur by domestic law where, according to the natural meaning, there is no disposal. These are also covered by the treaty.

Likewise, no explanation as to what constitutes a capital gain is set out in the treaty. While the distinction between a capital gain and a disposal that falls within the income rules may give rise to very different consequences under domestic law, the need to characterise the proceeds of alienations for treaty purposes, where the OECD pattern is adopted, may be less dramatic. This is because art. 13(4) mirrors, for capital gains purposes, the more general treatment of business profits in art. 7(1) in reserving primary exclusive taxing jurisdiction

---

[1] (2008) Sp C 669.

[2] At para. 103.

[3] TCGA 1992, s. 1(1).

for the state of residence and art. 21 is to the same effect in respect of other income not expressly referred to in the treaty.

Several older treaties do not contain a capital gains article. Most that do not, pre-date the introduction of capital gains tax and are patterned on the colonial model. This is rare in more recent treaties.[4] Capital gains tax may, however, be included in such treaties as a 'substantially similar' tax and its application considered by reference to other treaty provisions.

20-050　Persons chargeable

It is implicit in the scheme of the TCGA 1992 that the person chargeable to tax is the person disposing or deemed to dispose of the asset. In the context of art. 13, such a person is the 'alienator'. There are provisions in domestic law that seek to attribute the gains of the disposer or alienator to others. Of particular significance in the context of art. 13 are those that attribute the gains of non-residents to UK residents. The effect of art. 13(4) is not limited to the alienator. It is the gain that is precluded from tax by reference to the residence of the alienator.

20-100　Gains of non-resident companies

The Taxation of Chargeable Gains Act, s. 13(1), attributes gains of non-resident companies which would be close companies if they were resident in the UK to certain UK-resident individuals. A chargeable gain accruing to such a company is treated as if a proportionate part of the chargeable gain had accrued to any participator with at least a ten per cent participation in the company.[5] HMRC has accepted that these rules may be overridden by treaty.[6]

The effect of treaty provisions on TCGA 1992, s. 13, is expressly overridden by statute where the trustees of a settlement are participators in such a company.[7] Where there are trustees who are such participators, any treaty provisions preventing a charge to tax arising by virtue of the attribution to the trustees under s. 13 are disapplied.[8] Furthermore, if the company is owned by an intermediate company, itself a participator, and that intermediate company is also protected from the UK tax charge by a treaty, then the gain otherwise protected is further attributed to its participators, and so on through any number of companies.[9] This is done to ensure that the gain is deprived of treaty relief. One implication of these provisions is that in their absence, such a treaty precludes TCGA 1992, s. 13, attribution.

---

[4] The UK–Cyprus Treaty is an example.

[5] TCGA 1992, s. 13(2), (3) and (4).

[6] See ICAEW Technical Release, TR 500; see HMRC, *Capital Gains Manual*, para. CGM110411.

[7] TCGA 1992, s. 79B.

[8] TCGA 1992, s. 79B(2).

[9] TCGA 1992, s. 79B(2).

20-150   Gains of non-resident settlements

A settlor who is resident or ordinarily resident in the UK and who is treated as having an interest in a non-resident or dual-resident settlement, may have the chargeable gains accruing to the trustees when they arise attributed to him or her.[10] Similarly, a beneficiary of a non-resident settlement who is either resident or ordinarily resident in the UK, and has received a capital payment from the trustees that is matched with trust gains, will have those gains attributed to him or her to the extent they are not already attributed to a settlor under s. 86.

In *Davies (HM Inspector of Taxes) v Hicks*,[11] it was common ground that although the settlor was interested in the trust and would normally be taxable on the gain on a disposal by the trustees under s. 86, the same provisions of the UK–Mauritius Treaty prevented such a charge. The guidance that exists on this provision is by reference to the identical language contained in the now repealed provisions of TCGA 1992, s. 77, relating to attribution of gains of UK-resident settlements.[12] HMRC administrative practice on application of art. 13(4) to gains attributed to settlors is opaque. Its capital gains manual reads:

> **'Settlor trusts: computations: double taxation relief [34912]**
>
> A settlor may be able to claim exemption on some or all of the attributed trust gains, but this depends on the terms of the particular double taxation agreement. The gain which is chargeable on the settlor is not the same as the gain which accrues to the trustees. Therefore Articles which exempt trustees from UK tax on gains accruing on the disposal of particular property do not necessarily operate to exempt the settlor from liability under Section 77.'

In *Smallwood*, the Special Commissioners made it clear that the effect of art. 13(4) is to preclude the taxation of the settlor where the alienator is resident in the other contracting state.[13] Thus, in that case, had the trustees been found resident in Mauritius and not the UK under the tie-breaker rules in art. 4(3) of the UK–Mauritius Treaty, art. 13(4) would have prevented the charge.

In light of the schemes that formed the subject of both the *Hicks* and *Smallwood* cases, the UK–Mauritius Treaty was amended in 2003 to reserve the right of a contracting state to levy according to its law a tax chargeable in respect of gains from the alienation of any property on a person who is a resident of that state at any time during the fiscal year in which the property is alienated.[14] A similar approach is taken in later treaties.[15] This approach is modified in some treaties. For example, in the UK–Canada Treaty the right to tax residents is restricted to cases where the alienator:

---

[10] TCGA 1992, s. 86.

[11] [2005] BTC 331; [2005] EWHC 847 (Ch), para. 5.

[12] Repealed by FA 2008, s. 8 and Sch. 2, para. 5.

[13] At paras. 103 and 107.

[14] UK–Mauritius Treaty, art. 13(5).

[15] See UK–Australia Treaty, art. 13(6); UK–Botswana Treaty, art. 14(6).

'(a) is a national of the first-mentioned Contracting State or was a resident of that State for 15 years or more prior to the alienation of the property, and

(b) was a resident of the first-mentioned Contracting State at any time during the five years immediately preceding such alienation.[16]'

Following amendment of the UK–Mauritius Treaty, a more draconian treaty override was enacted by FA (No 2) 2005 with respect to disposals made on or after 16 March 2005.[17] Where trustees of a settlement are:

- resident and ordinarily resident in the UK;
- not treaty non-resident during any part of a year of assessment; and
- in the same year neither resident nor ordinarily resident in the UK, or are treaty non-resident,

then no treaty relief is permitted in respect of a disposal by the trustees made during the part of that year that they are non-resident.[18]

20-200   Movable property

Unlike immovable property, which is defined in art. 6 in the case of treaties adopting OECD Model language,[19] movable property is undefined. The distinction between movable and immovable property is not normally drawn in English domestic law, which generally recognises realty and personalty. The distinction is drawn in English private international law.[20]

Capital assets of a permanent establishment

Capital gains are subject to limited taxation in the hands of non-residents. The principal limitation on the charging provision is TCGA 1992, s. 10. Persons who are not resident and not ordinarily resident in the UK are not generally liable to tax in respect of chargeable gains unless they are carrying on a trade in the UK through a branch or agency. Non-residents, who are within the charge, are only liable to tax on gains accruing on the disposal of assets situated in the UK:

- and used in or for the purposes of the trade at or before the time when the capital gain accrued; or
- used or held for the purposes of the branch or agency at or before that time or assets acquired for use by or for the purposes of the branch or agency.[21]

In the case of a non-resident company, liability to corporation tax on chargeable gains under TCGA 1992, s. 8, is restricted in the same way by reference to assets used or held in

---

[16] Art. 13(9).

[17] FA (No 2) 2005, s. 33(2).

[18] TCGA 1992, s. 83A.

[19] See chapter 8, para. 18-050.

[20] Collins, L, *et al.* (eds.), *Dicey, Morris and Collins on the Conflict of Laws* (2008), 14th edn, Sweet & Maxwell, chs. 22–25.

[21] TCGA 1992, s. 10(1).

connection with a trade carried on through a permanent establishment in the UK.[22] Only disposals made at the time when the person is carrying on the trade in the UK through a permanent establishment in the case of a company or otherwise through a branch or agency are taxable.[23] This charge is ring-fenced by deemed disposals in the case of non-residents under s. 25. Where an asset ceases to be a chargeable asset, because it is situated outside the UK, the non-resident owner is deemed to have disposed of it and immediately to have reacquired it at market value.[24] Similarly, where a non-resident ceases to carry on a trade in the UK through a branch or agency, it is deemed to have disposed of the asset at that time and to immediately have reacquired it at its market value.[25] These rules also extend to the assets of a permanent establishment of a non-resident company[26] and to a profession or vocation under ITTOIA 2005.[27]

All treaties with capital gains articles authorise the contracting state where a permanent establishment is located to tax capital gains from the alienation of movable property forming part of the business property of a permanent establishment. Similar rules in earlier treaties also authorise taxation of such capital assets forming part of a fixed base for the purpose of performing professional services. Article 8A(2) of the Israeli Treaty is a typical example:

> 'Capital gains from the alienation of movable property forming part of the business property of a permanent establishment which an enterprise of one of the territories has in the other territory or of movable property pertaining to a fixed base available to a resident of one of the territories in the other territory for the purpose of performing professional services, including such gains from the alienation of such a permanent establishment (alone or together with the whole enterprise) or of such a fixed base, may be taxed in the other territory.'

Treaties negotiated after 2000 that assimilate independent personal services with business profits,[28] delete the reference to professional services.[29] Either form will typically authorise taxation of gains on the disposal of UK branch assets in accordance with TCGA 1992, ss. 10 and 10B.

UK patent rights

The disposal of assets situated in the UK by a non-resident is, as a rule, outside the charge to capital gains tax as a matter of domestic law. Exceptionally, where a non-resident sells all or part of any UK patent rights, the proceeds are chargeable to income tax under ITTOIA 2005.[30] Such rights are not immovable property and disposals should not be liable to UK tax in the absence of a permanent establishment. Source state authority to tax such disposals in

---

[22] TCGA 1992, s. 10B(1).

[23] *Ibid.*, s. 10(2) and s 10B(2).

[24] *Ibid.*, s. 25(1).

[25] *Ibid.*, s. 25(3).

[26] FA 2003, s. 153(2)(b).

[27] TCGA 1992, s. 288(1).

[28] See chapter 8, para. 17-500.

[29] See, for example, the UK–Australia Treaty, art. 13(2), and the UK–Chile Treaty, art. 13(2).

[30] ITTOIA 2005, s. 587(2)(b). See chapter 9, para. 18-200.

the UK–US Treaty is found not in the capital gains article but in art. 12(3)(b), which includes in the definition of 'royalties' gains from the alienation of intellectual property rights which are contingent on the productivity, use, or disposition thereof.

20-250   Immovable property

Under the OECD Model, gains from the alienation of immovable property may be taxed by the state where they are situated.[31] Article 13(1) of the Barbados Treaty contains the customary formulation:

> 'Capital gains from the alienation of immovable property, as defined in paragraph (2) of Article 12, may be taxed in the Contracting State in which such property is situated.'

This authority is broader in certain respects than the scope of the general charge to capital gains on non-residents under domestic law since TCGA 1992, ss. 10 and 10B, requires the immovable property to be included in the assets of a UK permanent establishment or branch or agency. However, by treaty, the immovable property must be situated in the UK to fall within the authority to tax. For the purposes of TCGA 1992, the situation of rights or interests (otherwise than by way of security) in or over immovable property is that of the immovable property.[32]

Development gains relating to land

Gains of a capital nature may give rise to a charge to tax under Sch. D, Case VI, by virtue of the Taxes Act 1988, s. 776, in the case of companies liable to corporation tax, and ITA 2007, Pt. 13, Ch. 3. This occurs when the gains were:

- obtained from the disposal of land acquired with the sole or main object of realising a gain, or which is held as trading stock; or
- developed with the sole or main object of realising a gain from its disposal when developed.

Treaties following the OECD Model will thus allow the charge as it relates to land situated in the UK.

Shares and similar rights

Shares, partnership interests, unit trust participations and the like are not implicitly immovable property. The charge in relation development gains relating to land in the Taxes Act 1988, s. 776, and ITA 2007, Pt. 13, Ch. 3, also applies in relation to a disposal of certain assets deriving their value from land. These assets include:

- any shareholding in a company deriving its value directly or indirectly from land;
- any partnership interest deriving its value directly or indirectly from land;
- any interest in settled property deriving its value directly or indirectly from land; and

---

[31] See chapter 9, para. 18-050 on the meaning of immovable property.

[32] TCGA 1992, s. 275(1)(a). See also s. 275C on the location of co-owners' interests.

[33] ICTA 1988, s. 776(10).

- any option, consent or embargo affecting the disposition of land.[33]

Since immovable property does not normally include shares, a number of treaties authorise the taxation in the *situs* state of shares in companies whose value is based on immovable property. Such provisions are typically inserted at the instance of the other contracting state if that state taxes non-residents on the sale of immovable property under its domestic law. This ranges from a simple formulation found in art. 13(1) of the Egyptian Treaty to gains 'from the alienation of shares in a company, the assets of which consist principally of such [immovable] property' to the complex provisions of art. 13 of the Canadian Treaty. The Canadian Treaty establishes separate rules depending upon whether the alienator and related or connected persons own less than 10 per cent of each class of the share capital of the company and whether the shares are quoted on an approved stock exchange.[34]

20-300   Exploration or exploitation shares

Gains accruing to a non-resident on the disposal of exploration or exploitation rights are treated as gains accruing on the disposal of assets used for the purposes of a trade carried on by that person in the UK through a branch or agency.[35] Exploration or exploitation rights in this context refer to assets used in the exploration or exploitation of the seabed and subsoil, and their natural resources as are situated in the UK or a designated area. Shares deriving their value or the greater part of their value from exploration or exploitation assets are deemed to be such assets. Consequently, a disposal of shares in such a company where the assets are located in the UK may give rise to a charge to capital gains tax.

Several treaties also address rights to explore for or exploit oil and gas. These include treaties with Canada, Sweden and Finland, which treat these rights in the same manner as immovable property. Similarly, shares in companies whose value is based on these rights are typically taxed. See, for example, the Canadian Treaty, art. 13(4)(b). The Canadian Treaty further authorises taxation in the *situs* state in relation to interests in partnerships or trusts, the assets of which consist principally of immovable property, or oil and gas rights.[36] Treaties that have a capital gains article but which do not authorise *situs* taxation of gains on immovable property include the one with Zambia.[37]

20-350   Alienation of ships and aircraft

The normal rule is to give exclusive taxation on the alienation of ships or aircraft operated in international traffic to the country of residence. The rule is expressed in art. 14(4) of the Malaysian Treaty thus:

'Gains derived by a resident of a Contracting State from the alienation of ships or aircraft operated in international traffic by an enterprise of that Contracting State or movable property

---

[34] See arts. 13(2), 13(5)(a) and 13(6).

[35] TCGA 1992, s. 276(7).

[36] Canadian Treaty, art.13(5)(b).

[37] Art. 14.

pertaining to the operation of such ships or aircraft, shall be taxable only in that Contracting State.'

Under domestic law a ship or aircraft is situated in the UK only if the owner is then resident in the UK, and an interest or right in or over a ship or aircraft is situated in the UK if and only if the person entitled to the interest or right is resident in the UK, which dovetails with the treaty rule.[38]

20-400   Exit charges

Where a company ceases to be resident in the UK, it is deemed to have disposed of all of its assets for capital gains purposes and to have immediately acquired them at market value immediately before it ceases to be resident.[39] The assets which remain within the charge to capital gains tax because the company carries on a trade in the UK through a permanent establishment are excluded from this deemed disposal.[40] Since the disposal takes place before the company ceases to be non-resident, the charge will not be within the scope of treaties as the asset will not be owned by a resident of the other contracting state. However, where an election is made under s. 187 to postpone the charge, the position is less obvious. The effect of the election is to deem the gain to accrue to the principal company.[41] The principal company is a 75 per cent shareholder which is resident in the UK.[42] It is submitted that since the actual disposal takes place in a company which is non-resident, gains, which in such circumstances would be protected by suitable treaty provisions, would be exempted by suitable treaty provisions.

A somewhat similar approach is taken in respect of trustees ceasing to be resident in the UK. If trustees of a settlement become neither resident nor ordinarily resident in the UK, they are likewise deemed to have disposed of their assets for capital gains purposes and to have immediately re-acquired them immediately before becoming non-resident.[43] Assets remaining within the charge to capital gains tax are excluded from this.[44] However, if the assets are such that after the trustees have ceased to be resident, gains on the assets concerned would be exempt under the treaty, then they are not excluded from the deemed disposal.[45] Similarly, trustees ceasing to be liable to UK tax while continuing to be resident because of the application of a treaty similarly suffer a deemed disposal.[46]

---

[38] TCGA 1992, s. 275(1)(f).

[39] TCGA 1992, ss. 185(1) and (2).

[40] *Ibid.*, s. 185(4).

[41] *Ibid.*, s. 187(3).

[42] *Ibid.*, s. 187(1)(a).

[43] *Ibid.*, s. 80(2).

[44] *Ibid.*, s. 80(4).

[45] *Ibid.*, s. 80(5).

[46] *Ibid.*, s. 83.

20-450   Foreign exit taxes

A number of jurisdictions also impose an exit charge on individuals ceasing to be resident. The deemed disposal in the foreign jurisdiction is not recognised for UK tax purposes and the tax paid is not allowable as a deduction in computing the gain under TCGA 1992, s. 38. Indeed, s. 38 (4) specifically disallows expenditure in connection with a deemed disposal or acquisition. Thus, the gain in the UK will be computed on the basis of historical cost. Unrelievable double taxation may arise where an individual moving to the UK suffers a deemed disposal and reacquisition abroad and subsequently disposes of the asset while being UK resident. Two treaties contain measures designed to alleviate this problem. Although drafted in bilateral terms, they only apply to individuals moving to the UK, since there is no exit tax for individuals here.

In the case of Australia, the treaty provides for an exemption from capital gains tax in the country of departure if the individual elects to defer taxation until the time of realisation.[47] Thus, an Australian resident moving to the UK who elects to defer the gain and disposes of the asset, while the UK resident will only be liable to tax in the UK on that subsequent alienation.

In the case of Canadian residents moving to the UK, the limitation on taxing jurisdiction in connection with departure from Canada is imposed on the UK under art. 13(10) of the UK–Canada Treaty. In this case, where the individual is treated as having alienated property on ceasing Canadian residence, the UK is only entitled to tax gains in respect of a subsequent disposal of that property to the extent that the gains had not accrued while the individual was resident in Canada. Thus, in effect, the individual may step up the cost of acquisition of the asset to its market value at the time of becoming resident in UK. This relief does not apply to any asset which the UK was entitled to tax under the provisions of art. 13 generally if the asset was disposed of while the individual was still resident in Canada.

20-500   Gains of former residents

A totally different approach is taken in relation to departing individuals. There is no deemed disposal for individuals ceasing to be resident in the UK. Temporary non-residents are individuals who leave the UK and return, where there are fewer than five tax years between the year of departure and return.[48] Subject to the inclusion of gains on the disposal of assets during their period of absence are treated as accruing to such individuals not in the year of disposal but in the year they return.[49] Until 2005, if such individuals qualified for relief from capital gains tax under a suitable treaty, the legislation did not prevent its application.[50]

---

[47] Art.13(5).

[48] *Ibid.*, s. 10A(1).

[49] *Ibid.*, s. 10A(2).

[50] TCGA 1992, s. 10A(10).

Consequently, any exemption specifically given under a treaty was taken into account in arriving at any UK liability.[51] It is implicit in this analysis that in applying a treaty, the actual timing of the disposal is material, rather than the deemed timing. Section 10A(9)(c) now overrides the application of any treaty.

A significant number of treaties authorise contracting states to tax former residents on capital gains for a limited period of time. A current example is art. 13(6) of the Estonian Treaty, which reads:

> 'The provisions of paragraph (5) of this Article shall not affect the right of a Contracting State to levy according to its law a tax on capital gains from the alienation of any property derived by an individual who is a resident of the other Contracting State and has been a resident of the first-mentioned Contracting State at any time during the five years immediately preceding the alienation of the property.'

Since the charge to capital gains tax is levied by reference to both residence and ordinary residence,[52] there may be circumstances in which a departing UK resident is non-resident of the UK both under domestic law and by virtue of a treaty but continues to be ordinarily resident in the UK. This form of wording would allow the UK to tax individuals not resident but ordinarily resident in the UK. The period of residence is less than five years in some treaties (for example, two years in the Bolivian Treaty,[53] three years in the Oman Treaty[54] and three years in the Austrian Treaty) if the gain is not subject to tax in the country of residence at the time the disposal is made.[55]

---

[51] HMRC, *Capital Gains Manual*, para. CGM262290

[52] TCGA 1992, s. 21(1).

[53] Art. 13(6).

[54] Art. 13(7).

[55] Art. 13(5).

Other Income and Miscellaneous Cases

Chapter 12

21-000   Other income

Items of income which are not mentioned in a treaty, by default, fall to be taxed in accordance with the domestic laws of the contracting states. Treaties patterned on the OECD Model attempt to sweep up this residual category through the 'Other Income' article. The simplest form of this article is found in the UK–Sudan Treaty. art. 21, which reads:

> 'Items of income of a resident of a Contracting State being income of a class or from sources not expressly mentioned in the foregoing Articles of this Convention shall be taxable only in that State.'

Consequently, income not expressly dealt with is taxable only in the state of residence. This is broadly in line with the 1963 OECD Draft Convention. A number of older treaties contain no such provision.[1]

However, later treaties patterned on the 1977 OECD Model and later versions contain an exception to this permitting certain income associated with the activity of a permanent establishment to be taxed in that state. This exception is found, for example, in art. 22(2) of the Spanish Treaty, as follows:

> 'The provisions of paragraph (1) of this Article shall not apply if the recipient of the income, being a resident of a Contracting State, carries on business in the other Contracting State through a permanent establishment situated therein, or performs in that other State professional services from a fixed base situated therein, and the right or property in respect of which the income is paid is effectively connected with such permanent establishment or fixed base. In such a case, the provisions of Article 7 or Article 14, as the case may be, shall apply.'

Normally, the other income article covers income from all sources, so that in addition to income from sources in the contracting state where the taxpayer is not resident, income from third countries is also exempt. The UN Model limits the effect on residual income to that from third country sources by the further inclusion of language reflected in the UK–Venezuela Treaty, art. 21(3), as shown here:

> 'Notwithstanding the provisions of paragraphs 1 and 2, items of income of a resident of a Contracting State not dealt with in the foregoing articles of this Convention and arising in the other Contracting State may also be taxed in that other State.'

---

[1] See, for example, UK–Namibia Treaty and UK–Sri Lanka Treaty.

In several treaties, however, other income may be taxed in the country of source. This includes those with Argentina,[2] Singapore[3] and Venezuela.[4]

Since this clause covers all items of income, it may have considerable significance. Items that are recognised by HMRC as commonly within these provisions include alimony, social security pensions, payments under deeds of covenant[5] and payments made to non-resident theatre backers of plays and musicals (also known as 'angels') in return for money put up by them in the finance of a production that are annual payments requiring tax deducted at source.[6] The HMRC view is that capital gains are not covered by the other income article.[7]

It has also become customary for the other income article to be used to attach provisions relating to issues that do not fit neatly within the other parts of the treaty. The result, in many cases, is a specific allocation of taxing jurisdiction for those items otherwise included in the residual other income category.

21-050   Income from trusts and estates

Many treaties deal with payments from trusts and estates in the course of administration by allowing taxing rights under domestic law. Article 20(1) of the Irish Treaty reads:

> 'Items of income of a resident of a Contracting State, wherever arising, being income of a class or from sources not expressly mentioned in the foregoing Articles of this Convention, other than income paid out of trusts or the estates of deceased persons in the course of administration, shall be taxable only in that State.'

This prevents a beneficiary of a discretionary trust who is a resident of the other contracting state from claiming repayment of all the additional and basic rate tax charged on the trustees under ITA 2007, ss. 479 and 493. ESC B18, however, enables such a beneficiary to 'look through' to the income underlying the payments made to him or her and the appropriate article in the treaty will apply to any such income arising in the UK.[8] A number of treaties that do not pick up residual items of income but simply use the article to refer to income from trusts or estates and, indeed in some cases, from trusts only.[9]

An unusual rule is found in the UK–Canada Treaty, specifically authorising Canada to tax UK residents who are beneficial owners of income from trusts or estate resident in Canada. In this case, however, the amount of tax is restricted to 15 per cent of the gross income.[10]

---

[2] Art. 21(5).

[3] Art. 22(3).

[4] Art. 21(3).

[5] HMRC, *International Tax Manual*, para. INTM153240.

[6] *Ibid.*, para. INTM342580.

[7] HMRC, *Double Taxation Relief Manual*, para. DT227.

[8] HMRC, *International Tax Manual*, para. INTM153240.

[9] For example, Falkland Islands, art. 24.

[10] Art. 20(1).

There is no definition of trust or estate, but in this treaty, a trust does not include an arrangement whereby the contributions made to the trust are deductible for Canadian tax purposes.[11]

21-100   Alimony and maintenance payments

Payments made in relation to various family support arrangements are given specific treatment in the UK–Chile Treaty as follows:

'Periodic payments, made pursuant to a written separation agreement or a decree of divorce, separate maintenance or compulsory support, including payments for the support of a child, paid by a resident of a Contracting State to a resident of the other Contracting State, shall be exempt from tax in both Contracting States, except that, if the payer is entitled to relief from tax for such payments in the first-mentioned State, such payments shall be taxable only in the other State.[12]'

This is a rare example of exemption in both contracting states.

21-150   Offshore exploration and exploitation activities

Since the development of the offshore oil and gas industry in the UK from the early 1970s, treaties have contained provisions addressing the manner in which the activities of residents of treaty countries are to be taxed in that context. Jurisdiction to impose income tax, capital gains tax and corporation tax to exploration or exploitation activities in the North Sea under FA 1973, s. 38, applied to the exploration or exploitation of the seabed and subsoil and their natural resources situated both in the UK or a designated area of the Continental shelf. In the absence of such extension, the UK would normally be restricted to the areas of its territorial sea. The breadth of the territorial sea is 12 nautical miles from the coastline.[13] The definition of the UK is also extended in most treaties. For example, the UK is defined in the Canadian Treaty. art. 3(1)(a)(ii), to mean:

'Great Britain and Northern Ireland, including any area outside the territorial sea of the United Kingdom which in accordance with international law has been or may be hereafter designated under the laws of the United Kingdom concerning the Continental shelf, as an area within which the rights of the United Kingdom with respect to the seabed and subsoil and their natural resources may be exercised.'

These provisions extend taxing jurisdiction to the UK areas of the Continental shelf and, in a number of cases, constitute exceptions to the taxing rules found in most treaties. Article 27A of the Canadian Treaty embraces the typical subject matter of these provisions. Pursuant to art. 27A(2), activities in connection with the exploration or exploitation of the seabed and subsoil and their natural resources situated in the other contracting state are generally deemed to be carrying on business in that other contracting state through a permanent

---

[11] Art. 20(3).

[12] See art. 17(2); see also UK–US Treaty, art. 17(5).

[13] Territorial Sea Act 1987, s. 1.

establishment. This is not the case unless these activities are carried on for periods in excess of 30 days in the aggregate in any 12-month period.[14]

Jurisdiction to tax employment income is similarly extended. Salaries and similar remuneration in respect of employment connected with the exploration or exploitation of the seabed may be taxed to the extent that duties are performed offshore in the other contracting state.[15] Thus, the normal exemptions for employment income do not apply in this context.

In art. 28A(4) of the Danish Treaty, profits from the operation in connection with offshore activities of ships or aircraft designed primarily for transporting supplies or personnel, or of tugboats or anchor handling vessels, are only taxable in the state in which effective management of the enterprise is situated. This does not apply to profits during any period in which such a ship or aircraft is contracted to be used mainly for purposes other than transporting supplies or personnel to or between places where offshore activities are being carried out.

Likewise, remuneration in respect of employment exercised on board a ship or aircraft, the profits of which are taxable in this way, are themselves taxable.[16] In several cases, independent personal services are also deemed to be carried on through a fixed base if they are exercised for periods exceeding 30 days in the aggregate in any 12-month period.[17]

Further specific provisions are contained in the Norwegian Treaty dealing with transmedian line oil and gas fields[18] and several specific fields.[19]

21-200   Channel tunnel

In the case of France, a separate article was added to deal with taxation of the Channel Tunnel operations.[20] The principal effect for the operators of the tunnel, is to allocate profits between the UK and French concession holders respectively on an equal basis, subject to detailed conditions.[21] For so long as the shares in the concession holders or their holding companies are required to be stapled to each other, these profits are taxed only in the state in which they are established.[22] If the shares are not stapled, then one-half of the profit is attributed to a permanent establishment in the other contracting state.[23]

---

[14] See art. 27A(3).

[15] See art. 27A(4).

[16] See art. 28A(5)(b).

[17] For example, Norway Treaty, art. 23(5).

[18] Art. 24.

[19] Seatjord field reservoirs, art. 25, Murchison field reservoir, art. 26 and Frigg field reservoir, art. 27.

[20] Art. 7A, by Protocol of 15 October 1987; art. 9 of the 2008 treaty.

[21] 2008 treaty, art. 9(3).

[22] 2008 treaty, art. 9(4).

[23] 2008 treaty, art. 9(5).

An exception is also made for employees of the concession holders. These employees are taxable only in the contracting state in which the concession holder has its place of effective management, and the remuneration is not regarded as being borne by any permanent establishment in the other contracting state.[24]

21-250   Remittance basis taxpayers

Most UK treaties contain provisions limiting benefits in relation to income and gains taxable on the remittance basis. In general, these rules are aimed at individuals who are either resident in but not ordinarily resident, or, resident but not domiciled in, the UK,[25] although some other jurisdictions also tax foreign source income in the hands of individuals and companies on a remittance basis.

Such provisions apply where under the law in the state of residence, a person is subject to tax by reference to the amount of income (or gain) which is 'remitted to or received' in that state and 'not by reference to the full amount thereof'.[26] Thus, where this rule is engaged and the tax of another contracting state is to be relieved, it is decided by the UK on a remittances basis. Where such provisions limit benefits in relation to UK taxation is determined by the remittance basis (if any) of the other contracting state.

Early versions of this rule allow relief under the treaty only to so much of the income as is remitted to or received in the other contracting state.[27] It is apparent that such amounts should qualify for relief in the other contracting state even if they are not taxed in whole or in part for whatever reason under the domestic law of the residence state.

Recent treaties have adopted a much tougher formulation of this principle. For example, art. 24(1) of the Singapore Treaty in common with treaties concluded since the mid-1990s provides that relief in the source state for remittance basis taxpayers is only 'to so much of the income as is taxed in the other contracting state'. This approach does not take into account normal commercial circumstances, such as currency losses, which might eliminate a gain in the country of residence; nor does it take into account personal circumstances, such as persons who do not pay tax because they have low income or other reliefs. It may thus place a remittance base taxpayer who remits an item in a worse position than a taxpayer separate liable on a worldwide basis. Differences in treatment may produce surprising results, particularly for longer-term UK residents required to pay the £30,000 'user fee',[28] with foreign income or gains from different sources with different treaty formulations apply. Nominated income will be treated as taxed although not remitted. On the other hand, nominated income actually remitted by such a person may be treated as not remitted.[29]

---

[24] 2008 treaty, art. 9(6).

[25] See TCGA 1992, s. 12, and ITA 2007, Pt. 14, Ch. A1.

[26] See, for example, UK–Georgia Treaty, art. 24(1).

[27] UK–Thailand Treaty, art. 6.

[28] ITA 2007, s. 809H.

[29] ITA 2007, s. 809H.

The Singapore Treaty does provide some prospect for relief. Article 24(2) provides that the limitation would not apply to any person as may be agreed between the competent authorities of the contracting states. No guidelines are provided as to when such agreement would be appropriate, and nor is there any obligation on the competent authorities to actually agree. None of the other treaties even contemplates exclusions by way of agreement. Similar limitations are imposed on the availability of benefits in UK in respect of income or gains of temporary residents in Australia.[30]

21-300 Students

Payments received by students or business apprentices for the purpose of maintenance, education or training are commonly exempt from tax by treaty in the country of study. Article 20 of the current OECD Model is reflected in art. 19 of the Bulgarian Treaty as follows:

> 'Payments which a student or business apprentice who is or was immediately before visiting a Contracting State a resident of the other Contracting State and who is present in the first-mentioned State solely for the purpose of his education or training receives for the purpose of his maintenance, education or training shall not be taxed in that State, provided that such payments arise from sources outside that State.'

There are numerous variations on this theme. The treaty with Bolivia limits this to the first £3,500 in addition to personal allowances. No time limit is generally expressed, although the words 'who is or was immediately before visiting a contracting state' suggests that this is not open-ended. Others, such as the Belize Treaty, art. 12, simply require that the student be 'from' a contracting state. Those following the 1963 OECD Model apply to students who were 'formerly' a resident of a contracting state. Some treaties, such as those with Bangladesh and China, contain extensive provisions dealing with this issue.

---

[30] UK–Australia Treaty, art. 23(2).

Treaties and European Tax Directives

Chapter 13

22-000 Introduction

The supremacy of the EC Treaty over the bilateral treaties of member states was considered in chapter 2 above. This chapter examines the relationship between tax treaties and other Community legislative instruments. Given the close connection between taxation and sovereignty, the EC Treaty requires unanimous approval of all member states for tax provisions to be enacted, amended or repealed. It is a crucial exception to the principle of majority voting. As a result, progress in the field of harmonisation of company taxation has been extremely slow. The three direct tax measures[1] enacted in 1991 had been in proposal form for over 20 years before becoming law. A second package of direct tax was adopted in 2003.[2] These measures have their legal authority based on art. 94 (ex 100) of the EC Treaty, which provides broad authority for approximation of laws which directly affect the establishment or functioning of the common market. It is clear that subject to the fundamental freedoms granted by Community law, in the absence of harmonising measures, member states are free to tax in accordance with their domestic law.[3] The manner in which this freedom may be limited is determined by the legal instrument chosen for harmonisation.

22-050 Legislative instruments

Briefly, the legislative means available to the EC are:

(1) *regulations.* These are uniform rules and by definition binding in their entirety and directly applicable. They do not have to be adopted in the legislation of member states. They confer rights on individuals which the courts of member states must protect.[4]

(2) *directives.* These are addressed to and binding upon member states. The member states are required to achieve the result described in the directive by legislation into national law. In certain circumstances, directives may be of direct effect if national law is inadequate or if they have not been implemented into national law at all.

(3) *decisions.* These are measures taken in an individual case. A member state or persons

---

[1] Directive 90/434 on the common system of taxation applicable to mergers, divisions, transfer of assets, and exchanges of shares concerning companies of different member states; Directive 90/435 on the common system of taxation applicable in the cases of parent companies and subsidiaries of different member states, and the Convention on the Elimination of Double Taxation in connection with the Adjustment of Profits of Associated Enterprises (90/436).

[2] Directive 03/48 on taxation of savings income in the form of interest payments; Directive 03/49 on a common system of taxation applicable to interest and royalty payments made between associated companies of different member states.

[3] Case C-81/87 *R. v H.M. Treasury and Inland Revenue Commissioners, ex parte Daily Mail and General Trust plc* [1987] BTC 153; [1988] STC 787. See chapter 2.

[4] Case 83/78 *Pigs Marketing Board v Redmond* [1978] ECR 2347.

may be required to perform or refraining from a particular action. These are seldom relevant to taxation.

(4) *opinions*. These are issued by a single Community institution and constitute non-binding legal measures. It allows the institution to express a view on particular events to member states or to persons generally.

22-100   Direct effect

Regulations intrinsically have direct effect. In *Walder v Bestuur der Sociale Verzerkeringsbank,*[5] the ECJ considered the priority of a regulation dealing with social security payments for migrant workers.[6] The ECJ held that the process by which rights and obligations are transferred by member states from their domestic legal systems to the Community cannot be reversed by subsequent unilateral measures that are inconsistent with Community law. Similarly, the same result cannot be achieved by bilateral measures, such as bilateral tax treaties. On this basis, bilateral treaties between member states which are inconsistent with regulations effectively exceed remaining national jurisdiction and, as a result, have no effect.

The position is considerably more complex in relation to directives because of their legal nature. Directives are addressed to member states. The binding force according to art. 249 (ex 189) of the EC Treaty is limited to the result to be achieved upon each member state to which it is addressed, whereas a regulation is binding in its entirety. The result is described in the directive and must be translated within the period specified in the directive into binding provisions of domestic law of member states. Member states remain free to determine the method and form. There is no reason, in principle, why effect might not be given to a directive by means of a treaty. Thus, treaties might contravene the provisions of a directive where it, along with the domestic law of a member state, fails or fails properly to implement a directive.

Directives may be of direct effect in whole or in part. The doctrine of direct effect was first considered in the tax context by the ECJ in the decision of *Becker v Finanzamt Munster-Innenstadt.*[7] The ECJ ruled that wherever the provisions of a directive appear to be unconditional and sufficiently precise as far as the subject matter is concerned, those provisions may in the absence of implementing measures adopted be relied upon against any national provision which is incompatible with the directive insofar as the provisions define rights which individuals are able to assert against that state. As a result, provisions of bilateral treaties between member states which are inconsistent with a directive will in this context have no effect.

---

[5] Case 82/72 [1973] ECR 599.

[6] Reg. 1408/71, art. 3.

[7] Case 8/81 [1982] ECR 53.

22-150   Tax by regulation: the European Economic Interest Grouping

References to taxation are found in certain EC non-tax legislation, such as the European Economic Interest Grouping Regulation.[8]

European Economic Interest Groupings (EEIGs) are a form of statutory joint venture. Article 40 of the regulation requires flow-through tax treatment for EEIGs. It specifies that profits or losses resulting from the activities of a grouping shall be taxable only in the hands of its members. This does not provide a great deal of guidance about the precise treatment. An EEIG has full legal capacity; however, whether it has legal personality is dependent on the domestic law of its country of formation. Thus, whether the members would be liable to corporation tax or income tax is not determined by the Regulation. It would appear that even where an EEIG has legal personality that it is unable to qualify for treaty benefits. While it may be resident in a contracting state, it cannot be liable to tax in that contracting state by virtue of that residence, because profits or losses resulting from its activities are to be taxable only in the hands of its members. Whether one member of an EEIG constitutes a permanent establishment of another will depend on the terms of the EEIG contract and all relevant circumstances.

The official address of an EEIG, under art. 12 of the EEIG Regulation, must be either where the EEIG has its central administration or where one of its members has its principal administration or principal activity. Will this constitute a permanent establishment for treaty purposes? Article 3(1) of the regulation specifies that the purpose of a grouping is to facilitate or develop economic activities of its members, or to improve or increase the results of those activities. Its purpose is not to make profits for itself. The article further specifies that activities must be related to the economic activities of its members and must 'not be more than ancillary to those activities'. Does this mean that the activities of an EEIG can never be more than 'preparatory or auxiliary', as contemplated by art. 5 of the OECD Model Treaty (and therefore never constitute a permanent establishment)? Article 3(2) of the regulation specifies activities which are prohibited as a consequence of these limitations imposed on EEIGs. Unfortunately, despite the fact that the regulation is of direct effect, the EEIG Regulation does not provide sufficient detail to settle these issues.

22-200   Directives and tax treaties

The most important direct tax measures in the corporate context that have a direct correlation with treaty provisions are: the Parent-Subsidiary Directive 90/435, dealing with intra-group cross-border dividends, which occupies the same ground as art. 10; and; the Interest and Royalties Directive 03/49, dealing with cross-border interest and royalty payments between associated companies. Both directives cover the same ground as arts. 11 and 12. The Mergers Directive 90/434 dealing with cross-border mergers, divisions and corporate reorganisations is connected with art. 13. The Arbitration Convention 90/436,

---

[8] 2137/85; [1985] OJL 189/31.

relating to transfer pricing, parallels art. 9, and started life initially as a draft directive. It was finally adopted as a multilateral treaty.

Administrative cooperation among member states is also dealt with by directive. This includes exchange of information and parallels art. 26 of the OECD Model.[9] By contrast, cross-border collection of taxes operates in tandem with art. 27 of the OECD Model.[10]

In the area of personal savings of individuals, the Savings Directive is a hybrid.[11] Although generally a instrument of administrative co-operation for obtaining information on interest income of European residents, it also provides for a tax to be charged in limited circumstances and for the elimination of double taxation arising from the tax so charged.

22-250   The Parent-Subsidiary Directive

The Parent-Subsidiary Directive is aimed at eliminating double taxation on the distribution of profits within corporate groups within the Community. It is of considerable importance in the treaty context since it occupies the same ground in many respects as art. 10 (Dividends) and art. 23 (Elimination of Double Taxation) of the OECD Model.

The main operative provisions of the directive are:

- the exemption from withholding tax in respect of distributions paid on a 10 per cent or larger shareholding to a shareholder in another EC member state;[12] and
- the exemption from or credit for underlying tax for the recipient company by the state of the recipient company in respect of the distribution.[13]

The exemption from withholding tax has been held to be of direct effect in *Denkavit International BV and others v Bundesampt fur Finanzen*[14] on the basis that it is clear and unambiguous.

Qualification

There are a number of requirements that must be complied with in order to fall within the scope of the directive:

---

[9] Directive 77/799 concerning mutual assistance by the competent authorities of the member states in the field of direct taxation and taxation of insurance premiums.

[10] Directive 76/308 on mutual assistance for the recovery of claims relating to certain levies, duties, taxes and other measures with Directive 02/94 laying down detailed rules for implementing certain provisions of Council Directive 76/308.

[11] 03/48 on taxation of savings income in the form of interest payments.

[12] Art. 5(1).

[13] Art. 4(1).

[14] Case C-283/94 [1996] STC 1445.

(1)   Both parent and subsidiary must be forms of entity listed in an appendix to the directive;[15] it does not therefore apply to all entities characterised as corporations for the tax purposes of particular member states.

(2)   Both parent and subsidiary must be resident for tax purposes in a different EC member state[16] and must not be considered as resident outside the Community by virtue of any applicable treaty.[17]

(3)   Both parent and subsidiary must be subject to one of the taxes listed in the directive.[18] These are effectively corporate income taxes levied in the Community.

The 25 per cent equity stake may be replaced by a voting requirement by bilateral treaty.[19] Member states may also unilaterally impose a two-year holding period in order to qualify distributions under the directive.[20] The directive applies to distributions of profits only. Capital gains on the sale of shares of subsidiaries are not covered. It also does not apply to liquidation distributions.[21] The directive permits both domestic or treaty-based provisions to prevent fraud or abuse, but does not impose its own anti-avoidance provisions.[22] It is also not clear whether the directive extends to second or lower-tier subsidiaries, although the general view is that it does not. Article 7(2) is intended to preserve the position of treaties (and domestic law) to some extent. It states that the directive does not lessen the effect of domestic or agreement-based provisions designed to eliminate or lessen economic double taxation of dividends.

Permanent establishments

The benefit of the exemption or credit in the member state of the recipient company is extended to distributions of profits received by permanent establishments of qualifying companies. However, permanent establishments may be situated in a member state other than the one where the dividend-paying subsidiary is located as well as a permanent establishment is situated or in the same member state as the subsidiary.[23] Thus, triangular cases are addressed in a way that bilateral treaties cannot. If, for example, a UK-resident company has a permanent establishment in Germany to which distributions made by a French company are attributed for German tax purposes, the permanent establishment must enjoy the same exemption or credit as to a Germany-resident company on distributions received from the French company. The UK would also be required to provide the same

---

[15] Art. 2(a).

[16] Art. 1(1).

[17] Art. 2(b).

[18] Art. 2(c).

[19] Art. 3(2), first indent.

[20] Art. 3(2), second indent.

[21] Art. 4(1).

[22] Art. 1(2).

[23] Art. 1(1), second and third indents.

double tax relief in such a case.[24] The directive adopts a semi-autonomous definition as follows:

> '2(2) For the purposes of this directive the term "permanent establishment" means a fixed place of business situated in a member state through which the business of a company of another member state is wholly or partly carried on in so far as the profits of that place of business are subject to tax in the member state in which it is situated by virtue of the relevant bilateral tax treaty or, in the absence of such a treaty, by virtue of national law.'

It may be noted that the definition only incorporates art. 5(1) of the OECD Model and therefore agency or service permanent establishments are excluded.[25] Tax treaties are relevant in further narrowing the definition for this purpose to permanent establishments to the extent that their profits are subject to tax under the terms of an applicable treaty.

Implementation

The following subsections discuss the issues surrounding the implementation of the Parent-Subsidiary Directive.

Inward-bound distributions

The UK seeks to comply with the obligation in art. 4(1) of the directive by taxing the dividend and giving credit for underlying tax either by treaty or unilaterally.[26] Although the directive specifies a 25 per cent minimum holding in the capital of the subsidiary, the UK adopts a 10 per cent voting rights test for application of the underlying credit. Strictly however, art. 3 of the directive only permits the substitution of voting rights for capital by means of bilateral agreement. Older treaties made no explicit reference to this. The treaties with Greece and Portugal do not address this issue, although the effect of the domestic law may be as if the directive had been complied with. There is no minimum holding period as a condition of the relief.

Outward-bound distributions

The UK does not, as a matter of domestic law, levy a withholding tax on outward-bound dividends.[27] An exception to this rule is made in relation to distributions by REITs which bear tax deducted at source at the basic rate.[28] While the REIT legislation is designed to discourage REITs from having shareholders who qualify for the benefits of the directive, a REIT that makes a distribution to a person with more than the permitted maximum shareholding is subject to tax on a notional amount treated as income received by the REIT.

This special tax on REITs is likely to constitute a 'withholding tax' under art. 591 of the directive. In *Ministerio Publico and others v Epson Europe BV*,[29] the ECJ considered the

---

[24] Art. 1(1), first indent.

[25] See chapter 6.

[26] See chapter 14, para. 23-450.

[27] See chapter 9, para. 18-100.

[28] See chapter 9, para. 18-100.

[29] Case C-375/98.

legality of a lump-sum tax on successions and donations levied on the income of certain securities (shares and bonds). Under Portuguese domestic law, dividends were subject to a 5 per cent withholding tax on dividends as a substitute for tax under the inheritance and gift tax legislation.

The Advocate General noted that art. 5(1) did not specify any particular tax, and Community law did not operate on the basis of semantic distinctions and theoretical constructions relevant to national law. In any event, the 5 per cent withholding tax was within the directive on a literal or any other method of interpretation. The ECJ adopted a similar approach and ruled that the Portuguese tax was a withholding tax within the directive. The ECJ held that the term 'withholding tax' in art. 5(1) is not limited to specific types of national taxation. The substitute inheritance and gift tax, the court concluded, was a withholding tax for which the chargeable event is the payment of a dividend and the taxable person is the holder of the shares. The substitute inheritance and gift tax has the same effect as a tax on income, and it is immaterial that the tax is called a 'succession and donation tax' and that it is levied in parallel with the income tax. In *Athinaiki Zithopiia AE v Greece* (Case C-294/99) [2001] BTC 451 the ECJ ruled that that where the chargeable event for the tax is the payment of dividends and the amount of tax is directly related to the size of the distribution, then the charge is a withholding tax even if it is borne by the distributing company and not the shareholder.

However, a REIT may not be a 'company of a member state' within art. 2(1) of the directive. In order to qualify, a company must, among other requirements be subject to tax on corporate profits 'without the possibility of an option or of being exempt'.[30] Since the exemption offered to REITs is optional, they may not be within the directive.

Interaction with treaties

The Parent-Subsidiary Directive is relatively narrow in its scope. As a result, it does not fully occupy the field relating to dividends or other profit distributions between member states. Member states are therefore free to agree on the tax treatment of distributions outside the scope of the directive. Treaties or protocols with EU member states negotiated since the entry into force of the directive are not uniform in addressing these issues.[31]

Dividends

Only the Danish Treaty refers explicitly to the directive. In this treaty, a general rate of withholding of 15 per cent on the gross amount of dividends is permitted. This rate is, however, made subject to the provisions of the Parent-Subsidiary Directive and dividends are exempt from tax if the beneficial owner of the dividend is a company which holds at least 25 per cent of the issued share capital of the company paying the dividends.[32] A similar approach is taken in the treaties with France and the Netherlands but exempting from source state tax dividends on a holding of at least 10 per cent of the capital in the company paying

---

[30] Art. 2(1)(c).

[31] For example, see the treaties with Denmark and Finland and the treaties with France and the Netherlands.

[32] Danish Treaty, art. 10(2). At the time the treaty was negotiated, the directive required a 25 per cent participation.

the dividends.[33] The Finnish Treaty, however, provides that dividends may only be taxed in the country of residence of the shareholder.[34]

Elimination of double taxation

In all four treaties, double taxation continues to be relieved in the UK by the credit method.[35] Credit for underlying tax is given where the UK company controls directly or indirectly 10 per cent of the voting power of the Danish company paying the dividend.[36] Denmark however will only give credit for underlying tax where the Danish company owns 25 per cent of the issued share capital of the UK company.[37]

An exchange of notes between the contracting states confirms that by continuing to use the criterion of a holding of voting power in art. 22(1)(b) with respect to the operation of the foreign tax credit in the UK on dividends received by a UK parent from a Danish subsidiary the contracting states note that they are exercising the option provided in art. 3(2) of the Parent-Subsidiary Directive to derogate from art. 3(1) by replacing the criterion of a holding in the capital of a company of another member state by that of a holding of voting rights.

The other three treaties adopt a 10 per cent rule based on ownership of voting power for allowing credit for underlying tax paid by either contracting states on dividends received by a corporate shareholder in the other.[38] An exchange of notes between the UK and Finland confirms the exercise of the option under art. 3(2) of the Parent-Subsidiary Directive to adopt the voting rights criterion. Neither the treaty with France nor the treaty with the Netherlands refers to the exercise of this option.

22-300   Interest and Royalty Directive

The Interest and Royalties Directive also aims at elimination of double taxation. It seeks to achieve this by ensuring that interest and royalty payments are broadly exempt from tax in the source state if the beneficial owner is resident in another member state.[39] It thus occupies the same area as arts. 11 and 12 of the OECD Model. It is given effect in UK law in ITTOIA 2005, Pt. 6, Ch. 9.

The directive specifically declares that it does not affect the application of domestic or agreement-based provisions which go beyond the provisions of this directive and are designed to eliminate or mitigate the double taxation of interest and royalties.[40] As is the

---

[33] French Treaty, art. 11(1)(c); Netherlands, art. 10(2)(b)(i).

[34] Finnish Treaty, art. 11(1).

[35] For example, Danish Treaty, art.22(1).

[36] Art. 10(1)(b).

[37] Art. 22(2)(c).

[38] Finnish Treaty, art. 25(1)(b).

[39] Art. 1(1); ITTOIA 2005, s. 758.

[40] Art. 9.

case with most tax treaties, the benefits of the directive are restricted in cases where there is a special relationship between the payer and the beneficial owner of interest or royalties, or between one of them and some other person. The benefit of the directive is restricted to the amount which would have been agreed by the payer and the beneficial owner in the absence of such a relationship.[41]

Transitional rules for the Czech Republic, Greece, Spain, Latvia, Poland, Portugal and Slovakia permit those member states to impose positive rates of withholding tax which are set to expire on 30 June 2013.[42] These rates are subject to existing bilateral treaty rates. During the transitional period, member states where the payees are situated are required to give credit for the tax permitted to be deducted.[43]

Qualification

The Interest and Royalties Directive adopts the same test to that in the Parent-Subsidiary Directive to determine which entities qualify for benefits.[44] The exemption only applies to payments between associated companies. Under the new regime or where a third company owns at least 25 per cent of the capital of the payer and payee. Companies are associated if, one has a direct holding of at least 25 per cent in the capital of another, or if a company has a direct holding of at least 25 per cent both in the capital of the paying and receiving companies respectively. Holdings must involve only companies resident in the Community. Member states have the option to replace the criterion of a minimum holding in the capital with that of a minimum holding of voting rights.[45] The UK offers the exemption if either the capital or voting rights threshold is reached.[46]

Permanent establishments

The directive has effect in relation to payments to or from a permanent establishment in one member state of a qualifying company in another,[47] but not where interest or royalties are paid by or to a permanent establishment situated in a third state outside the Community and the business of the company is wholly or partly carried on through that permanent establishment.[48] A wholly autonomous definition restricts the term 'permanent establishment' to a fixed place of business situated in a member state through which the business of a company of another member state is wholly or partly carried on.[49]

---

[41] Art. 4(2); ITTOIA 2005, s. 763 and 764; see chapter 9, paras. 18-150 and 18-200.

[42] Art. 6(1).

[43] Art. 6(2).

[44] Art. 3(1)(a).

[45] Art. 3(b).

[46] ITTIOA 2005, s. 761.

[47] Art. 1(1).

[48] Art. 1(8).

[49] Art. 3(c).

The directive adopts its own rules for attribution of the payments. Thus, a permanent establishment is treated as the payer of interest or royalties only insofar as those payments represent a tax-deductible expense for the permanent establishment in the member state in which it is situated.[50] Therefore, the expenditure must first be attributed to the permanent establishment by reference to the tax treaty principles in the OECD Model, art. 7.[51] Two tests must be met for a permanent establishment to be treated as the beneficial owner of interest or royalties:[52] first, the debt-claim – right or use of information in respect of which interest or royalty payments arise must be effectively connected with that permanent establishment. This dovetails with the tax treaty allocation rule in the OECD Model, art. 11(5), in the case of interest, and art. 12(3), in the case of royalties.[53] Second, the interest or royalty must represent income in respect of which the receiving permanent establishment is subject a recognised corporate income tax in the member state in which it is situated. Thus, a 'subject to tax' limitation on benefits is imposed.[54] Where a permanent establishment is treated as the payer, or as the beneficial owner, of interest or royalties, no other part of the company may be treated as the payer, or as the beneficial owner respectively.[55]

Interest

The definition of interest for the purpose of the directive follows art. 11 of the OECD Model Convention. It means income from 'debt-claims of every kind, whether or not secured by mortgage and whether or not carrying a right to participate in the debtor's profits, and in particular, income from securities and income from bonds or debentures, including premiums and prizes attaching to such securities, bonds or debentures.' Penalty charges for late payment are not regarded as interest.[56] Member states are permitted to re-characterise interest as distributions in certain circumstances[57] and the benefits of the directive are restricted to what would have been agreed in the absence of a special relationship by analogy to the OECD Model.[58] The proposal does not deal with the deductibility of interest and royalty payments, or their inclusion in income by the recipient.

Royalties

Royalties similarly follow art. 12 of the OECD Model. They include payment of any kind received as consideration for the use of or the right to use any copyright:

- of literary, artistic or scientific work, including cinematographic films;
- of any patent, trade mark, design or model, secret formula or process;

---

[50] Art. 1(3).

[51] See chapter 8, paras. 17-150 and 17450, and chapter 9, paras. 18-150 and 18-200.

[52] Art. 1(5).

[53] See chapter 8, paras. 18-150 and 18-200.

[54] See chapter 16, para. 25-400.

[55] Art. 1(6).

[56] Art. 2(1)(a).

[57] Art. 4(1).

[58] Art. 4(2).

- for the use of or the right to use industrial, commercial or scientific equipment; or
- for information concerning industrial, commercial or scientific experience.[59]

The definition does not, however, reflect current OECD thinking, which effectively excludes lease payments on industrial, commercial or scientific equipment.

As is the case with the Parent-Subsidiary Directive, the Interest and Royalty Directive does not replace arts. 11 and 12 of the OECD Model. It will occupy the field in certain group and joint venture relationships, but beyond that, treaty rules will continue to apply.

Procedural matters

The directive sets out procedures for its application, including evidentiary and documentary requirements, relief at source and repayment.[60]

22-350   The Mergers Directive

As with the Parent-Subsidiary Directive, the Mergers Directive came into effect on 1 January 1992. The purpose of the directive is to facilitate mergers, divisions, transfers of assets and exchanges of shares between companies established in different member states. The directive is intended to remove tax barriers to such transactions in order to create conditions analogous to those of an internal market.

It will be immediately apparent that the nature of the relief granted under the Mergers Directive does not first obviously within any neat category of treaties based on the OECD Model. Although both the directive and art. 3 of the OECD Model deal with disposals of assets, the principal relief provided for in art. 4 of the directive is deferral of tax on gains. By contrast, art. 13 of the OECD Model generally exempts residents of a contracting state from capital gains in the source state or authorises the source state to tax them. treaty exemptions may be material to transactions involving cash consideration not exceeding 10 per cent, which qualifies for deferral in relation to the non-cash consideration only. Deferral is not contemplated by UK treaties. Reliefs provided in arts. 5 and 6 of the directive dealing with the carry-over of tax attributes in the form of provisions, reserves and losses are not addressed in bilateral treaties in the same coherent way.

Qualifying transactions

There are six forms of qualifying transaction identified by the Mergers Directive. These are:

(1) *merger by absorption:* where one or more companies transfers all of their assets and liabilities to an existing company in exchange for the issue of shares to the shareholders of the transferor company;[61]

(2) *merger by formation:* where two or more companies transfer all of their assets and

---

[59] Draft art. 2(1)(b).

[60] Arts. 1(11) to (16).

liabilities to a company formed by them in exchange for the issue of shares in the new company to the shareholders of the transferor companies;[62]

(3) *merger of wholly-owned subsidiary:* the transfer of all of the assets and liabilities of a wholly-owned subsidiary to its parent company on dissolution;[63]

(4) *exchange of shares:* the transfer of the majority of voting shares of a company to another company in exchange for the issue of shares by the transferee;[64]

(5) *transfer of assets:* transfer of one or more branches of its activity to another company in exchange for the issue of shares to the transferor by the transferee;[65] and

(6) *division:* the transfer by a company of all of the assets and liabilities to two or more new or existing companies in exchange for the pro rata issue to its shareholders of shares of the transferee companies.[66]

22-400   Tax consequences: Mergers Directive

The operational effects of the Mergers Directive are as follows.

Unrealised gains

No tax may be levied on the capital gain arising from a merger or division. In each case, the domestic law of the member state is to be applied in determining the gain or loss in respect of the disposition of the assets.[67] In order to qualify, the assets and liabilities transferred must be effectively connected with a permanent establishment of the receiving company in a member state where the transferring company is located following the transfer. The assets so transferred must also be used in generating income for tax purposes.

Subsequent gains and losses are computed as though the merger or division had not taken place and asset values for capital gains and depreciation purposes are carried over.[68] Where member states operate an elective regime, which permits different base costs for depreciation and capital gains purposes, the roll-over will not apply to assets and liabilities for which such option is exercised.[69]

---

[61] Mergers Directive, art. 2(a), first indent.

[62] Art. 2(a), second indent.

[63] Art. 2(a), third indent.

[64] Art. 2(d).

[65] Art. 2(c).

[66] Art. 2(b).

[67] Art. 4(1).

[68] Art. 4(2).

[69] Art. 4(3).

The roll-over does not apply to assets and liabilities that lie outside such permanent establishments. Special rules are set out for assets forming part of permanent establishments in third countries in the Community.[70]

Losses

The Mergers Directive permits transfer of loss compensation from the transferor company to the permanent establishment of a receiving company only if the member state of the transferor allows the transfer of such losses for domestic reorganisations. The directive does not contain restrictions relating to the carry-forward or carry-back of such losses against income from other sources of the receiving company.[71]

Shareholders' treatment

Shareholders will not be subject to income or capital gains tax on merger, division or exchange of shares provided that the shares received in the exchange carry over the base cost for tax purposes of the securities transferred.[72] Any subsequent transfer of securities so received may be subject to tax in full on any gain rolled over.

Where a company receiving assets has shares in the transferring company, any gain accruing to the receiving company on the cancellation of its holding is not subject to taxation. Individual member states may deviate from this rule where the receiving company's holding in the capital of the transferring company is under 25 per cent.[73]

Cash consideration

In each case, a cash payment not exceeding 10 per cent of the nominal value of the securities received may also be received without the tax free status of the transaction being jeopardised.[74] The cash portion may, however, continue to be taxable.

Permanent establishment

Under the transactions contemplated by the directive, a company incorporated in a member state may effectively be converted into a permanent establishment of a company in another member state. Because in many cases, it will reduce the taxing jurisdiction from a worldwide basis to a local source basis, complex rules have been developed to deal with the problems that arise.

Where the assets transferred include a permanent establishment of the transferring company situated in another member state, that latter state is required to renounce any right to tax the permanent establishment. The state of the transferring company may re-instate losses of the

---

[70] Art. 10.

[71] Art. 6.

[72] Art. 8.

[73] Art. 7.

[74] Art. 2.

permanent establishment that were previously set off against the taxable profits of the company in that state and which have not been recovered.[75]

In all other respects, the state of the permanent establishment must apply the roll-over rule as if it were the state of the transferring company. Where the member state of the transferring company taxes worldwide profits, it will be entitled to tax any profits or gains of the permanent establishment resulting from the merger on condition that it gives relief for tax that would have been charged on the permanent establishment in the same way and in the same amount as if that tax had actually been charged and paid.[76]

22-450   Directive shopping and avoidance

The Parent-Subsidiary Directive and the Interest and Royalty Directive, being analogous to OECD Model arts. 10, 11 and 12 may give rise to what might be called 'directive shopping' or other avoidance that may parallel the issues considered in chapter 16 as they relate to tax treaties. The instruments adopted in the directives are similar to those found in treaties, but the two are not identical. The more recent Interest and Royalty Directive is clearly the more sophisticated. For example, it is worth noting that the Parent-Subsidiary Directive has not adopted the requirement of 'beneficial ownership'.

The Parent-Subsidiary Directive does not contain its own anti-avoidance provisions. Article 1(2) specifies that 'This directive shall not preclude the application of domestic or agreement-based provisions required for the prevention of fraud or abuse'. Thus, in preventing fraud or abuse of the directive, reliance is placed on domestic or treaty provisions. The UK has enacted measures in relation to schemes and arrangements designed to increase credit for foreign tax.[77] The same authorisation of domestic or treaty measures is found in the Interest and Royalty Directive[78] Here the UK has enacted language that tracks the 'purpose' provisions it seeks to include in its treaties.[79] Thus, the benefit of the directive does not apply in relation to a payment if it was the main purpose or one of the main purposes of any person concerned with the creation or assignment of the debt-claim or the right in respect of which the royalty is paid to take advantage of the exemption by means of that creation or assignment.[80] In the *Denkavit* case and related cases[81] the ECJ noted that art. 1(2), which permits a minimum holding period, is aimed in particular at counteracting abuse where holdings are taken in the capital of companies for the sole purpose of benefiting from the tax advantages available and which are not intended to be lasting. But the court rejected an argument of the German Government: that its requirement that a shareholding be held for a minimum of 12 months before a dividend qualified for the withholding tax

---

[75] Art. 10.

[76] Art. 10(2).

[77] ICTA 1988, s. 804ZA.

[78] Art. 5(1).

[79] See chapter 16, para. 25-600.

[80] ITTOIA 2005, s. 765.

[81] Joined Cases C-283/94, C-291/94 and C-292/94, *Denkavit International BV, VITIC Amsterdam BV* and *Vormeer BV v Bundesampt Fur Finanzen* [1996] STC 1445.

exemption could be justified on the basis of art. 1(2). It does not regard this necessary for the prevention of fraud or abuse. The case is not a detailed consideration of the concept of abuse or avoidance under European law. It is perhaps indicative of the fact that a sole or main purpose test reflects European principles.

In addition, the Interest and Royalty Directive contains its own autonomous anti-abuse provision, which specifies that 'member states may, in the case of transactions for which the principal motive or one of the principal motives is tax evasion, tax avoidance or abuse, withdraw the benefits of this Directive or refuse to apply this Directive'.[82]

Similarly, the Mergers Directive contains its own anti-avoidance provision. The benefits of the directive may be refused if a transaction has as one of its principal objectives tax evasion or tax avoidance. In the Mergers Directive it specifies further that: 'if the operations are not carried out for valid commercial reasons such as the restructuring or rationalisation of the activities of the participating companies, this may be held to constitute a presumption of the existence of a tax avoidance purpose'.[83] Thus, it also adopts a form of 'bona fide' test. This wording has been translated into UK enacting legislation as 'bona fide commercial reasons which do not form part of a scheme or arrangements of which the main purpose or one of the main purposes is avoidance of liability to income tax, corporation tax or capital gains tax'.[84] This wording follows the existing expressions relating to corporate reorganisations in TCGA 1992, s. 137(1). The Mergers Directive does not contain a provision, however, authorising domestic or treaty based anti-abuse provisions. In *Hans Markus Kofoed v Skatteministeriet*[85] the ECJ recognised the autonomous nature of art. 11(1)(a), holding that its transposition into the national law of member states is not required.

The ECJ interpreted the requirements of art. 11(1)(a) of the Mergers Directive in the context of a share for share exchange in *Leur-Bloem v Inspecteur der Belastingdienst*.[86] The taxpayer, an individual resident in the Netherlands, was the sole shareholder and director of two Dutch private companies. She planned to contribute the shares in the two companies to a holding company in exchange for the issue of shares in that company. The taxpayer requested a clearance from the tax inspector that the proposed transactions should be treated as a 'merger by exchange of shares' within the meaning of the legislation. This would have allowed her to exclude from tax gains arising on the transfer of shares in the two companies to the third company and the possibility of setting off losses within the corporate group thus created.

The inspector took the view that there was no such merger by exchange of shares and that the purpose of the transaction was not to permanently combine the undertaking of the companies in a large single entity from an economic and financial point of view, as required

---

[82] At. 5(2).

[83] Art. 11(1)(a).

[84] See, for example, TCGA 1992, ss. 140B and 140D.

[85] Case C-321/05.

[86] Case C-28/95 [1997] BTC 504; [1997] STC 1205.

by Netherlands law. Such an entity, he argued, already existed from a financial and economic perspective, since both companies already had the same director and shareholder.

Pursuant to art. 2(d) of the Merger Directive, an exchange of shares is an operation whereby a company acquires a holding in the capital of another company such that it obtains a majority of voting rights in that company in exchange for the issue of securities representing the capital of the acquiring company.

Article 11(1)(a) authorises member states to refuse to apply the benefits of the directive where there is tax avoidance. This is the case where the transaction has as its principal objective, or as one of its principal objectives, tax evasion or avoidance.

The ECJ noted that the requirement that the companies concerned merge their business permanently into a single unit from a financial and economic point of view was inserted into the Netherlands rule pursuant to art. 11 of the Mergers Directive. The court noted that art. 2(d) of the directive laid down clearly that the tax advantages conferred by the directive must apply without distinction to all mergers, divisions, transfers of assets or exchanges of shares, irrespective of the reasons whether they be financial, economic or simply fiscal.

As far as the anti-avoidance provisions of art. 11(1)(a) of the directive are concerned, the court held that it was clear that member states must grant the tax advantages provided for by the directive in respect of exchanges of shares referred to in art. 2(d), unless those transactions have, as their principal objective, or as one of their principal objectives, tax evasion or avoidance. In order to determine whether the proposed transaction has such an objective, the tax authorities cannot confine themselves to apply predetermined general criteria, but must subject each particular case to a general examination.

In framing its questions to the ECJ, the Dutch court asked whether certain specific criteria could limit the scope of application of exchange of share provisions where:

- the acquiring company itself was not carrying on a business;
- the same person is the sole shareholder and director of the acquired company and prior to the exchange the director and sole shareholder in the acquiring company of the exchange;
- the only effect of the exchange is to merge the business of the acquiring company and that of another permanently in a single unit from a financial and economic point of view;
- the only effect of the exchange is to merge the businesses of two or more acquired companies permanently in a single unit from a financial and economic point of view; or
- the exchange is carried out in order to bring about a horizontal set off of tax losses between participant undertakings within a fiscal unity contemplated by Dutch law.

Judicial approaches

The ECJ has had occasion to comment on the question of abuse in relation to interpretation and application of directives which indicate a broad intolerance of abuse. In *Hans Markus Kofoed v Skatteministeriet* it said:[87]

---

[87] Case C-321/05, para. 38.

'Article 11(1)(a) Directive 90/434 reflects the general Community principle that abuse of rights is prohibited. Individuals must not improperly or fraudulently take advantage of provisions of Community law. The application of Community legislation cannot be extended to cover abusive practices, that is to say, transactions carried out not in the context of normal commercial operations, but solely for the purpose of wrongfully obtaining advantages provided for by Community law.'

In that case it was found by the Danish court that the exchange of shares was not carried out for any commercial reason. The court has not, however, been prepared to permit member states to prejudge the existence of abuse, observing in *Leur-Bloem v Inspecteur der Belastingdienst*:[88]

'However, in order to determine whether the planned operation has such an objective, the competent national authorities cannot confine themselves to applying predetermined general criteria but must subject each particular case to a general examination. According to established case-law, such an examination must be open to judicial review.'

The most important statement in this area is not in relation to any direct tax directive but in the context of VAT. The question of abuse of a directive was considered in detail in *Halifax plc v Commissioners of Customs & Excise*[89] where the Court formulated the position in detail as follows:

'69. The application of Community legislation cannot be extended to cover abusive practices by economic operators, that is to say transactions carried out not in the context of normal commercial operations, but solely for the purpose of wrongfully obtaining advantages provided for by Community law (see, to that effect, Case 125/76 *Cremer* [1977] ECR 1593, paragraph 21; Case C-8/92 *General Milk Products* [1993] ECR I-779, paragraph 21; and *Emsland-Stärke*, paragraph 51).

. . .

73. ... a trader's choice between exempt transactions and taxable transactions may be based on a range of factors, including tax considerations relating to the VAT system. Where the taxable person chooses one of two transactions, the Sixth Directive does not require him to choose the one which involves paying the highest amount of VAT. On the contrary, ... taxpayers may choose to structure their business so as to limit their tax liability.

74. In view of the foregoing considerations, ... an abusive practice can be found to exist only if, first, the transactions concerned, notwithstanding formal application of the conditions laid down by the relevant provisions of the Sixth Directive and the national legislation transposing it, result in the accrual of a tax advantage the grant of which would be contrary to the purpose of those provisions.

75. Second, it must also be apparent from a number of objective factors that the essential aim of the transactions concerned is to obtain a tax advantage. ...the prohibition of abuse is not relevant where the economic activity carried out may have some explanation other than the mere attainment of tax advantages.'

---

[88] Case C-28/95, para. 41.

[89] Case C-255/02.

22-500 Associated enterprises

The conclusion of the Convention on the Elimination of Double Taxation in connection with the Adjustment of Profits of Associated Enterprises in effect applies a uniform application of the arm's length principle following art. 9(1) of the OECD Model in relation to transactions between associated enterprises, as well as art. 7(2) in relation to the allocation of profits between a permanent establishment and head office. While this may make similar provisions in bilateral treaties redundant to some extent, it does not enjoy the status of a directive or other legislative instrument under European law. It is simply a treaty entered into among member states which may be amended by agreement between the parties.[90]

22-550 Exchange of information and recovery of taxes

Detailed rules on mutual assistance by the competent authorities of member states in the field of direct and indirect taxation has been dealt with among member states by directive since December 1977. Council Directive 77/799/EEC is considerably more detailed and extensive than those found in art. 26 of the OECD Model. Again, arguably exchange of information provisions in bilateral treaties between member states are redundant.[91]

Arrangements for the competent authorities of one member state to collect taxes on behalf of the authorities in another are found in the directive on mutual assistance for the recovery of claims relating to certain levies, duties, taxes and other measures.[92] It provides wide authority for cross-border collection of taxes in the EU, including in relation to VAT and taxes on income and capital.[93] It is given effect in the UK by FA 2002, s. 134, and Sch. 39, and The Recovery of Duties and Taxes etc. Due in Other Member States (Corresponding UK Claims) Procedure and Supplementary Regulations 2004 (SI 2004/674), which came into force on 1 April 2004. Directive 02/94 lays down detailed rules for implementing certain provisions of the directive.

22-600 The Savings Directive

The Savings Directive[94] is principally an instrument that provides for the automatic exchange of information between member states concerning cross-border interest payments to individuals resident in EU member states to prevent evasion of taxation in their member state of residence on interest they receive in another member state.[95] It does, however,

---

[90] See chapter 19.

[91] See chapter 20.

[92] 76/308.

[93] Art. 2.

[94] Directive 03/48 on taxation of savings income in the form of interest payments.

[95] Art. 1(1).

require the imposition of tax on interest income by payers in Belgium, Luxembourg and Austria during a transitional period.[96]

This ends a year after certain non-EU countries become bound to exchange information with EU member states.[97] During the transitional period, which commenced on 1 July 2005, Belgium, Luxembourg and Austria are required to levy a withholding tax of 15 per cent during the first three years, 20 per cent for the subsequent three years and 35 per cent thereafter where the beneficial owner is resident in a member state other than that in which the paying agent is established.[98] Double taxation which results from the imposition of the withholding tax must be eliminated by the member state of residence of the beneficial owner by way of credit or refund as appropriate.[99]

Beneficial owners may, however, request that no tax be withheld under procedures where the beneficial owner is expressly allowed to authorise the paying agent to report information to the relevant competent authorities covering all interest paid to the beneficial owner by that paying agent, or, where the beneficial owner presents a certificate of residence for tax purposes from the competent authority of his or her member state to the paying agent.[100]

---

[96] Art. 10(1).

[97] Art. 10(1).

[98] Art. 11(1).

[99] Art. 14.

[100] Art. 13(1).

Elimination of Double Taxation: Credit for Foreign Tax

Chapter 14

23-000   Introduction

The principal mechanism traditionally adopted by the UK for avoiding or minimising double taxation on income is the credit method. However, in light of the rulings in Test Claimants in the *FII Group Litigation v Inland Revenue Commissioners* by the ECJ[1] and of the High Court,[2] and to maintain the UK's competitive position, an exemption system is proposed in relation to dividends paid by foreign companies to UK-resident companies.[3] At the time of writing, no change to relieving double taxation from other sources or dividends received except for the purpose of corporation tax is contemplated. Small companies are also proposed to be excluded from the exemption on foreign dividends. Thus, the credit mechanism will continue to be applicable. The credit method is not contemplated in any treaties as a mechanism to relieve double taxation in the UK. This could result in an increase in unrelievable foreign tax for UK-resident companies. A significant number of treaties only reduce dividend withholding taxes if the dividend is subject to tax in the residence state.[4] An alternative credit method is expected to be available for companies.

It is implicit in the credit method approach that income profits or gains are subject to tax twice, once in the country of source and then again in the country of residence. In this respect, the treaty provisions dealing with credit for foreign tax paid should be viewed as a residual clause. The other distributive provisions of the treaty will determine to what extent the source country is entitled to tax the item concerned. If, as a result, the item is subject to tax in a foreign country of source, then, in general terms, UK treaties grant credit for foreign tax paid against UK liability in respect of the same item in the country of residence. Although this approach is generally in line with the policy underlying the OECD Model Treaty, art. 23B, the wording adopted in UK treaties does not follow the OECD Model. The form of wording, which has changed little over the years, usually adopted is typified by the Ugandan Treaty which reads:

'23(1) Subject to the provisions of the law of the United Kingdom regarding the allowance as a credit against United Kingdom tax of tax payable in a territory outside the United Kingdom (which shall not affect the general principle hereof):

(a)   Ugandan tax payable under the laws of Uganda and in accordance with this Convention,

[1] Case C-446/04.

[2] [2008] EWHC 2893 (Ch).

[3] See, for example, HMRC and HM Treasury, 'Taxation of the foreign profits of companies: a discussion document' (June 2007); 'Taxation of the foreign profits of companies: draft provisions' (December 2008).

[4] See chapter 16, para. 25-400.

whether directly or by deduction, on profits, income or chargeable gains from sources within Uganda (excluding in the case of a dividend, tax payable in respect of the profits out of which the dividend is paid) shall be allowed as a credit against any United Kingdom tax computed by reference to the same profits, income or chargeable gains by reference to which the Ugandan tax is computed.'

There are several important differences between the UK approach and that of the OECD Model. UK practice is to set out the UK rules relating to the credit for foreign tax in clauses separate from the equivalent relieving mechanism adopted by the other contracting state, rather than using the bilateral language of the OECD. This facilitates different approaches to the elimination of double taxation by treaty partners, particularly in relation to those countries adopting the exemption method. As will be seen, the key principles adopted in the OECD Model, while not appearing in the text of the article, are generally given effect to in the domestic law. Credit is given 'subject to the provisions of the law of the UK'. This means, in accordance with the provisions of the 'Credit Code'[5] by virtue of the Taxes Act 1988, s. 788(4), and in the case of capital gains, the Credit Code is incorporated by reference.[6] A detailed examination of the rules of the Credit Code is beyond the scope of this work. The interrelationship between treaties and the domestic law is examined in this chapter. Although the credit is expressed to be 'subject to the provisions of the law of the UK', the wording inevitably indicates that this 'shall not affect the general principle hereof'. Following FA 2000, the road to obtaining credit for foreign tax paid has become considerably more tortuous. The extent to which the domestic law may be amended to reduce the availability of the credit thereby affecting the general principle is as yet undetermined.

The difference in relief available under art. 23B of the OECD Model and the typical language found in UK treaties was highlighted in *Legal & General Assurance Society Ltd v Revenue and Customs Commissioners*.[7] In that case, the main issue was the extent to which foreign tax deducted at source, on parts of its investment income from sources in those countries and held as part of its long-term insurance fund was creditable against UK corporation tax. It was held that the taxpayer was entitled to credit the foreign tax against the amount of corporation tax payable in respect of any year of assessment on its profits from its pension business generally. The Revenue had contended that credit was limited to the extent of the corporation tax payable on such proportion of the overall profits of its pension business as the foreign income, gross of foreign tax, bore to the overall income.[8] Evans-Lombe J noted[9] that art. 23B of the OECD Model Convention is an example of how the Revenue's result might have been achieved. However, the words used in UK Treaty practice were held to have a different effect. He said that:

'It is ... article 24 which is crucial: "French tax payable under the laws of France and in accordance with this Convention, whether directly or by deduction, on profits, income or chargeable gains from sources within France (excluding in the case of a dividend, tax payable

---

[5] ICTA 1988, Pt. XVIII, Ch.II, 'Rules governing relief by way of credit'.

[6] TCGA 1992, s. 277(3).

[7] [2006] BTC 713; [2006] EWHC 1770 (Ch)

[8] Other questions of credit for foreign tax of interest only to life assurance companies are not discussed here.

[9] At para. 32.

in respect of profits out of which the dividend is paid) shall be allowed as a credit..." Thus far the sentence indicates no intended limitation of the amount of the French tax which is to be creditable. There then follow the crucial words "shall be allowed as a credit against any [not "the"] United Kingdom tax computed by reference to the same profits, income or chargeable gains by reference to which the French tax is computed ..." It is therefore, again, not to be expected that in the concluding words of this sentence there is to be found a restriction on the amount of creditable foreign tax.'

His conclusion also rested on the purpose of the provision which he explained as follows:

'Where that purpose is apparent, in circumstances where what is in issue is not the purpose of giving relief against foreign tax, but which between two possible ways of conferring that relief was intended by the negotiators or by Parliament, it is more difficult to point with confidence to the objective intended. It is accepted that the Revenue's construction of the relevant provisions results in a substantial part of LGAS' foreign income not qualifying for credit relief. This result must be contrasted with Article 24 of the sample treaty itself, which is headed "elimination of double taxation" and starts with the words "double taxation of income shall be avoided as follows". I read the words of Hoffmann J in the Wimpey case "in my view double taxation relief is intended to ensure that the taxpayer does not suffer tax twice charged upon the same income" in the same sense. If double taxation is to be eliminated in circumstances similar to those of the example, it must follow that the taxpayer should be entitled to credit, against the UK corporation tax thrown up by its computation, for foreign tax paid in the relevant period of assessment, such credit to be limited only so that the foreign tax cannot exceed the UK tax which would have been chargeable on that income.'

Following the decision of the Special Commissioners, also upholding this conclusion,[10] FA 2005 introduced ICTA 1988, s. 798A, and related provisions, overriding the treaty language to require the credit to be calculated in accordance with the HMRC contentions.

23-050   Treaty versus unilateral relief

Credit for foreign tax is available unilaterally where there is no treaty providing for the relief, in circumstances similar to those provided by treaty.[11] The credit mechanism referred to in the treaty is expressed in domestic law in s. 793(1). It makes explicit that foreign tax in this context means only the credit allowed under the treaty in respect of tax chargeable under the law of the other contracting state.[12] Furthermore, no credit may be allowed beyond that authorised by the treaty in question.[13]

Finance Act 2000 inserted s. 793A into the Taxes Act 1988. First, credit may not be given where relief in respect of an amount of tax, which would otherwise be payable under the law of a territory outside the UK, may be allowed by treaty or under the law of the other contracting state as a result of the treaty. This applies regardless of whether the relief has been used or not.[14] Second, credit by way of unilateral relief may not be allowed in respect

---

[10] *Legal & General Assurance Society Ltd v Thomas (HMIT)* (2005) Sp C 461.

[11] ICTA 1988, ss. 790(1), 790(3).

[12] *Ibid.*, s. 792(3).

[13] *Ibid.*, s. 793(2).

[14] *Ibid.*, s. 793A(1).

of tax where credit may be allowed under a treaty in respect of the same amount of tax. This makes clear that credit cannot be claimed under both treaty and unilateral relief. As a result, UK taxpayers seeking to claim credit for foreign tax paid must in the first instance obtain relief available in the other contracting state or under the treaty. These requirements are in addition to the duty to minimise foreign tax by virtue of s. 795A(1).[15] Furthermore, recourse must be had to the tax credit provisions of an applicable treaty, since unilateral relief will not be permitted where credit may be allowed in respect of an amount of tax.[16] These rules have an element of retrospectivity in that they have in effect in relation to claims for credit made on or after 21 March 2000. The legislation also contemplates that treaties may contain express provisions to the effect that relief by way of credit is not to be given in specified cases or circumstances. This will apply in relation to treaties made on or after 21 March 2000. See chapter 12, on time limits for claiming foreign tax credit relief.

There are important differences between credit for foreign tax by treaty and unilateral tax credit relief. Credit for foreign tax under treaties is limited to the taxes which form the subject of the treaty. The single biggest source of difficulties in relation to credit in respect of treaty countries is in federal systems, such as the US and Canada, where treaties are negotiated with the Federal Government, but no constitutional mechanism exists whereby states or provinces are bound by the treaty. Additionally, states or provinces may not have the constitutional right to conclude treaties, leaving unilateral relief as the only option.

23-100   Same income, different person

The OECD Model applies specifically to juridical double taxation, that is, double taxation where the same person is liable to tax irrespective of the same item in both contracting states. The UK Treaty approach is wider, covering, in principle, economic double taxation where the same income or gain is subject to tax in both jurisdictions. This allows for the possibility that the item may be taxed in the hands of one person in one jurisdiction, but in the hands of another in the second, and still qualify for credit.[17] The HMRC *International Tax Handbook* gives examples of the application of this principle. Thus, taxation of income in the hands of a settlor in one jurisdiction and tax in the hands of a beneficiary, say, in the UK, will permit the beneficiary to obtain credit for tax paid by the settlor. Similarly, where directors' fees are treated as income of a partnership or a company under Extra-Statutory Concession A37, tax credit relief is available to the partnership or company despite the fact that the foreign tax may be imposed on the director.[18] The scope of the principle and the relationship between the income or gain to the person claiming credit has not been examined by the courts. In the HMRC view, where the UK charge is made on deemed income or gains, such income or gains are not the same income or gains as charged abroad and, on this basis, they do not accept that income taxable in the hands of a UK resident under ITA 2007, Pt. 13, Ch. 2 (Transfer of assets abroad), would come within the credit rule, because the resident cannot be identified with any particular part of the income which the non-resident

---

[15] See chapter 17, paras. 26-900 to 26-950.

[16] *Ibid.*, s. 593A(2).

[17] HMRC, *Double Taxation Relief Manual*, para. 507; *International Tax Handbook*, para. 618.

[18] HMRC, *Double Taxation Relief Manual*, para. 507.

has received or because the resident is charged by reference to a benefit received out of the assets rather than the income itself.[19] These comments, at least in relation to transferors, are inconsistent with HMRC's other views on attributed income and in the author's view incorrect.

This issue is addressed specifically in the exchange of notes of 24 July 2001 to the UK–US Treaty in the context of fiscally transparent entities and trusts. In that exchange (with respect to art. 24), the contracting parties recognised that in the case of an entity which is fiscally transparent under the laws of either contracting state, there may be a mismatch between the persons taxed in the two countries. In such cases, income is generally treated as accruing to resident of a contracting state for tax credit purposes, even if another person is taxable in the other contracting state. Similar rules are adopted in relation to trusts, where there may be mismatches between contracting states with tax being imposed possibly on the settlor, the trustees or beneficiaries.

23-150   Matching foreign income and tax with UK liability

The wording found in almost all UK treaties refers to credit against UK tax computed by reference to 'the same profits or income by reference to which the [foreign tax] is computed'. This wording was adopted following the decision in *Duckering v Gollan*,[20] which involved the 1947 New Zealand Treaty. In that treaty, credit was given 'in respect of income from sources within New Zealand' and credit allowed 'against any UK tax payable in respect of that income'. The case arose out of a change in New Zealand from taxation on the preceding-year basis to the current-year basis. The UK applied the preceding year basis throughout the years in question. The taxpayer paid New Zealand tax on his income in each year, although in the transitional year it was measured in a different way. This wording referred to as the 'statutory basis' for credit is now only found in very few old treaties.[21] Under the current language credit is applied on the 'root income basis', meaning that it is allowed on foreign tax against any UK tax computed by reference to the same income by reference to which the foreign tax is computed.[22] HMRC permits the root basis to be used even for those treaties where the statutory basis applies.[23]

Some of the more difficult problems arising out of the statutory basis have been resolved by the abolition of the preceding-year basis of taxation. Where foreign tax is levied by way of deduction, there is usually little difficulty in matching the foreign tax paid with the UK tax liability. Where tax is assessed on profits on an annual basis, problems may arise because of differing tax years calling for apportionment. In *Imperial Chemical Industries Ltd v Caro*,[24] the application of UK rules for new sources of income resulted in Australian source income

---

[19] HMRC, *International Tax Handbook*, para. 620.

[20] (1965) 42 TC 333, HL.

[21] See, for example, Myanmar Treaty, art. 14(1).

[22] HMRC, *Double Taxation Relief Manual*, para. 600.

[23] *Ibid.*, para. 603.

[24] (1959) 35 TC 374, CA.

being relevant to UK tax liability in more than one year. Notwithstanding this, it was held that the credit could only be claimed once. Problems relating to relief in respect of income arising in years of commencement is now addressed by the Taxes Act 1988, s. 804.

23-200 Source rules

Source rules may be different under a treaty and domestic law. This may relate to what the appropriate connecting factors are, as well as to the location of the source. Subject to permitted exceptions[25] and HMRC concessions,[26] credit will not be given for foreign tax in respect of UK source income. Apart from individual source rules in the distributive provisions of treaties, most UK treaties adopt the OECD approach in treating income which may be taxed outside the residence state as arising in the other. For example, the Yugoslavian Treaty reads:

> '22(5) For the purposes of the preceding paragraphs of this Article, profits, income and capital gains owned by a resident of a Contracting State which may be taxed in the other Contracting State in accordance with this Convention shall be deemed to arise from sources in that other Contracting State.'

This is of particular importance in relation to trading or professional profits taxed under ITTOIA 2005, Pt. 2, in respect of foreign branches or where, as is the case in some countries involving technical or management fees, tax is deducted in the paying country.[27] HMRC's *Double Taxation Relief Manual*, para. 581, sets out concessionary relaxations of the strict rules.

23-250 Residence

Unlike the OECD Model, the general credit language of the article does not refer to UK residence as a requirement. The Taxes Act 1988, s. 794(1), limits credits for foreign tax allowed by treaty to UK residents only. By contrast, unilateral relief is made available in limited circumstances to non-residents under s. 794(2). It is available for residents of the Isle of Man or of the Channel Islands in respect of tax paid in the Isle of Man or Channel Islands, in addition to UK residents.[28] It is also available for foreign tax computed by reference to employment income where duties are performed wholly or mainly in the same foreign country against income tax charged under ITEPA 2003 and computed by reference to that income, if the person is resident either in the UK or in that other territory.[29] The Finance Act 2000 inserted s. 794(2)(bb) in the Taxes Act 1988 to grant unilateral relief to a branch or agency in the UK in certain circumstances. These provisions were enacted to give effect to the decision of the ECJ in *Compagnie de Saint-Gobain, Zweigniederlassung*

---

[25] Taxes Act 1988, s. 790(5).

[26] Extra-statutory Concession B8.

[27] See *Yates v G.C.A. International Ltd* [1991] BTC 107; [1991] STC 157, Ch.D.

[28] ICTA 1988, s. 794(2)(a).

[29] *Ibid.*, s. 794(2)(b).

Deutschland v Finanzamt Aachen-Innenstadt.[30] However, to the extent that treaties provide more generous treatment than unilateral relief, the UK may still not comply fully with that decision.

23-300   Foreign tax payable

Treaty language typically talks about credit of 'tax payable' in a territory outside the UK. In *Sportsman v IRC*,[31] the taxpayer attempted to argue that he was entitled to credit for French tax in relation to a tax year where no assessment was raised in France, no income tax was paid by him, and no other party made any payment such as by way of withholding on his behalf. He argued that the credit was not confined solely to tax which has been paid, but that it applied to tax that may or should be paid. Inland Revenue attempted to argue that paid and payable were interchangeable in this context, but ultimately the Commissioners appeared to decide that there was no French liability to tax. The Commissioners accepted evidence that in the circumstances, he could not be assessed to tax, nor was there an obligation on his French employer to withhold tax. The Commissioners formed the view that not only had tax not been paid, but there was no basis on which it might be paid, and therefore no credit was allowed.

23-350   Treaty restrictions on credit

Legislation permitting restrictions on foreign tax credits by way of treaty was introduced into the Taxes Act 1988 by FA 2000. Section 793A(3) provides that if a treaty contains express provision to the effect that credit for foreign tax is not to be given under the treaty in specified cases or circumstances, then credit may not be given either by treaty or unilateral relief in those circumstances. This rule has effect in relation to treaties made on or after 21 March 2000. The first treaty made after that was with Norway, signed on 12 October 2000, and the US Treaty, signed on 24 July 2001.

This rule will have particular impact on UK companies claiming credit for tax paid in the UK. Article 24 of the US Treaty contains several limitations on creditability of US tax against UK taxation. Article 24(4)(c) denies the benefit of credit for underlying tax on dividends paid by a US-resident company, and where the UK treats the dividend as beneficially owned by a UK resident, the US treats the dividend as beneficially owned by a resident of the US and the US has allowed a deduction to a US resident in respect of an amount determined by reference to that dividend. This is aimed at certain hybrid financing arrangements, whereby payments may be treated as interest in the US and as dividends in the UK. A second limitation on tax credits is imposed by art. 24(6) in relation to US citizens or former citizens, or long-term residents who are resident of the UK. In such a case, the UK is not 'bound' to give credit to such residents for US tax on profits, income or gains from sources outside the US as determined under UK law. In the case of such items from US sources, the UK will take into account in determining the credit to be allowed only the tax

---

[30] Case C-307/97 [2000] STC 854.

[31] (1998) Sp C 174; [1998] STC SCD 289.

that the US may impose under the treaty on a UK resident who is not a US citizen. The ability to limit tax credits pursuant to s. 793A(3) of the Taxes Act 1988 is bolstered by art. 24(4)(d) of the US Treaty, which excludes art. 1(2) of the treaty from art. 24(4).

23-400   Circular cases

Bayfine UK Products, Bayfine UK v Revenue & Customs[32] had to consider the availability of credit where both contracting states tax a person as a resident by reason of fundamentally different treatment in each respective state. Which country should be entitled to tax and which should then be obliged to give credit for that tax? The taxpayer was an unlimited company incorporated in England and a UK-resident member of the Morgan Stanley group. The taxpayer made a profit which, in principle, was taxable in the UK but it claimed credit for US tax on the same profit paid by its parent, a US corporation against such tax, thus eliminating its UK tax liability. For US tax purposes, the profits of the UK company were treated as profits of the US parent because the UK company was classified as a 'disregarded entity.'

If the same taxpayer is a resident in both states, then the dual-residence provisions of the treaty would resolve residence in favour of one of them for the purpose of applying the treaty. In these circumstances, each state regards a different entity as its resident. The dual residence tie-breaker rules in treaties are silent about what to do when they are different persons. In such cases both states tax their residents and the issue is: who gives credit for the other state's tax? The same issue may arise in relation to CFC-type legislation where income is attributed to a shareholder.

Special Commissioners Avery-Jones and Sadler considered that the way out of the circle in which both states tax on a residence basis and on a literal reading of the treaty both give credit, is to consider who has the stronger taxing right.[33]

This is determined by looking at the treaty as a whole. The UK was taxing a UK resident on UK source income, that is to say, taxing on a residence-plus-source basis. In this case, the US entitlement to tax the parent was by reason of the saving clause in art. 1(4) of the UK–US Treaty, which permits residents to be taxed notwithstanding the treaty. The US, in disregarding the UK taxpayer by treating it as transparent, impliedly acknowledged that the UK has the better right to tax by saying that US taxation of its resident is by virtue of the saving clause.[34] Accordingly, the first taxing right is with the UK. There is no credit to be given because at that stage there is no US tax as the saving clause only comes into operation if the treaty (excluding the saving clause) prevents the US from taxing.

The Special Commissioners held that the fact that art. 1(4) provides that art. 23 (the foreign tax credit) is applicable even though the saving clause allows taxation as if the treaty had not come into effect, demonstrates the secondary nature of taxation by virtue of the saving

---

[32] (2008) Sp C 719.

[33] At para. 64.

[34] Art. 1(4).

clause as a 'secondary' residence state. If the US taxes under the saving clause, one cannot then go back to the beginning of the circle to argue that the UK should give credit first.[35] The saving clause gives a residual taxing right, after giving relief for the first residence state's tax. Thus, the state of the subsidiary as source plus residence state clearly has the stronger taxing right and the state of the parent taxing by virtue of the saving clause gives relief.[36]

23-450   Credit for underlying tax

It is generally UK policy, both under domestic law and treaty, to grant credit for underlying tax paid, where the UK company controls directly or indirectly at least 10 per cent of the voting power in the company paying the dividend. The Ugandan Treaty is, again, a typical example:

> '(b) In the case of a dividend paid by a company which is a resident of Uganda to a company which is a resident of the United Kingdom and which controls directly or indirectly at least ten per cent of the voting power in the company paying the dividend, the credit shall take into account (in addition to any Ugandan tax for which credit may be allowed under the provisions of subparagraph (a) of this paragraph) the Ugandan tax payable by the company in respect of the profits out of which such dividend is paid.'

The treaty rules allowing credit for underlying tax are more specific. The credit is only available for UK-resident companies and the source is only dividends from companies resident in the other contracting state, where the requisite shareholding is present. The vast majority of treaties adopt a 10 per cent voting test in order to qualify for underlying source. Some (see the German Treaty, art. 18(1)(b)) require 25 per cent of the voting power. The domestic law relating to the credit for underlying taxes generally is set out in the Taxes Act 1988, ss. 799–803A. Underlying tax is excluded from the general tax credit provisions, but provided for specifically. The normal form of wording was considered in *Memec plc v IRC*.[37] Credit for underlying tax was denied on the basis that distributions derived by a UK silent partner from its participation in a German silent partnership were not 'dividends' either for the purposes of the tax credit provision of the German Treaty (art. 18), nor for the purposes of the Credit Code. This was despite the fact that in the dividend article of the treaty, the term 'dividends' included income of a silent partner from its participation as such. Peter Gibson LJ for the majority was of the view that in the treaty the ordinary meaning of dividend should be applied, namely, that it is a payment of a part of the profits for a period in respect of a share in a company.[38] It is implicit in the decision that a dividend under the tax credit article of the treaty is also a dividend under the Credit Code.

---

[35] At para. 65.

[36] At para. 66.

[37] [1998] BTC 251; [1998] STC 754, CA.

[38] At 768.

23-500   Tax sparing

Many countries grant different kinds of tax concessions to attract investment, including, in particular, tax exemptions or tax holidays when no tax is paid during a specified period. The benefits of these concessions may be eliminated in relation to UK businesses investing in such countries, because the profits in respect of branch operations in those countries will nonetheless continue to be subject to UK tax. Similarly, dividends from subsidiaries will be taxed in the UK in full, since there will be no underlying tax in respect of which credit could be claimed. Consequently, the UK has agreed with a number of developing countries to treat tax spared (that is not actually paid) as deemed paid for the purposes of enabling UK companies to obtain credit, thus maintaining the efficacy of the foreign incentive. Section 788(5) provides specific authority for tax sparing provisions to be included in treaties. The Indonesian Treaty sets out a modern version of such articles:

> '21(3) For the purposes of paragraph (1) of this Article, the term "Indonesian tax payable" shall be deemed to include any amount which would have been payable as Indonesian tax for any year but for an exemption or reduction of tax granted for the year or any part thereof under Article 15(5) and Article 16(1) and (2) of Law No 1 of 1967 of Indonesia to the extent that these provisions continue in force by virtue of Article 33(2)(a) of Act No 7 of 1983 of Indonesia.

> Provided that relief from United Kingdom tax shall not be given by virtue of this paragraph in respect of income from any source if the income arises in a period starting more than 10 years after the exemption from, or reduction of, Indonesian tax was first granted in respect of that source.'

In line with a change of policy in the OECD generally,[39] UK policy is to seek to eliminate tax sparing from treaties, other than on a selective closely targeted basis and within specific time limits. The Taxes Act 1988, s. 785, was amended by FA 2000, so that tax sparing credit will not generally flow in relation to dividends between related companies but in different jurisdictions under s. 801, unless the treaty in question makes express provision for this relief.

---

[39] See OECD paper, 'Tax sparing: a reconsideration' (1998).

Non-discrimination

Chapter 15

24-000 Introduction

In his influential work *An International Bill of the Rights of Man*,[1] Professor Hersch Lauterpacht wrote:

> 'The claim to equality before the law is in a substantial sense the most fundamental of the rights of man.'

Lord Bingham, in endorsing this statement in *A (FC) and others (FC) v Secretary of State for the Home Department*,[2] observed that:

> 'The Universal Declaration of Human Rights 1948 affirmed, in articles 1 and 2, the general principles of equality and non-discrimination.'

It is not uncommon for domestic tax systems to treat foreigners less favourably than locals. Likewise, it is not unusual for investments made abroad to be more heavily taxed than those made at home. Treaty stipulations against such discrimination need to be seen against both the desire by states to see that their citizens or taxpayers are not treated unequally and the broader context of international legal norms outlawing discrimination that emerged following the Second World War to address abuses of state power by totalitarian and racist regimes. The importance of such stipulations cannot be underestimated. Their inclusion in tax treaties is not to address double taxation but to prevent unfair taxation.

24-050 Tax treaty non-discrimination

The most common prohibitions against tax discrimination found in bilateral treaties appear in art. 24 of the OECD Model, which contains six distinct basic principles:

(1) Nationals of a contracting state may not be subject to any taxation or any requirement connected therewith which is more burdensome than the other contracting state imposes upon its own nationals in the same circumstances. This prohibition applies notwithstanding the fact that the persons are not residents of one or both of the contracting states.

(2) Stateless persons who are residents of one contracting state are similarly to be protected from tax discrimination.

(3) A permanent establishment in a contracting state may not be taxed in a way less favourably than local enterprises of that state.

---

[1] Lauterpacht, H, *An International Bill of the Rights of Man* (1945), Columbia University Press, p. 115.

[2] [2004] UKHL 56 at para. 58.

(4)   Generally, deductions for expenditure made by a resident of one state to a resident of the other are deductible on the same conditions as if they had been paid to a resident of the state in which payment takes place (subject to arm's length provisions).

(5)   Enterprises which are owned by the residents of one contracting state may not be subject to taxation or connected requirements which are more burdensome than similar enterprises in the other contracting state.

(6)   The non-discrimination provisions apply to all taxes and are not limited to those specifically enumerated in the treaty.

These rules are at the heart of an international consensus against discrimination as it relates to tax. The extent to which the article is included in treaties, and its interpretation and application does, however, vary. Other treaty articles may also address equal treatment. The non-discrimination articles operate separately from the allocation of taxing jurisdiction and double tax relief provisions of treaties. Limitations non-discrimination articles place on taxing power are by reference to equality of treatment rather than source of income and gains. They are not a comprehensive ban on all forms of tax discrimination but a series of specific prohibitions only loosely connected and not entirely consistent with each other. In particular, there is no prohibition on discrimination against outward investment. It is only host states that are prohibited from discriminating against foreigners in certain respects.

24-100   Tax treaty non-discrimination and EC law

While the fundamental freedoms of EC law are essentially anti-discriminatory, they may not be identical to the tax treaty prohibitions. Lord Hoffman in *Boake Allen Ltd & Ors (including NEC Semi-Conductors Ltd) v Revenue and Customs Commissioners*[3] regarded the prohibition on discrimination implied in art. 43 of the EC Treaty[4] as having the purpose of preventing a restriction on the freedom of establishment. Tax treaties do not grant such freedoms but simply prohibit discrimination.[5] Nonetheless, where discrimination is found under tax treaty provisions, it is likely to give rise to a breach of Community law as well.[6] The concept of equality is a universal notion. Simply put, like cases ought to be treated alike and different cases ought to be treated differently. In this context, the jurisprudence of the ECJ provides useful analysis of when taxpayers are in comparable circumstances, and the tax consequences that ought to flow from that despite the fact that they may apply in different circumstances. As a practical matter, the elimination of discriminatory tax rules in UK domestic law flowing from decisions of the ECJ has thereby reduced the cases in which such discrimination might otherwise applied to non-EU-based foreign taxpayers.

The article is, however, a general prohibition against the specified forms of discrimination rather than being aimed at particular domestic rules. In *NEC Semi-Conductors Ltd & other*

---

[3] [2007] UKHL 25 at para. 20.

[4] See chapter 2, para. 11-000.

[5] At para. 22.

[6] For example, *R. v Inland Revenue Commissioners, ex parte Commerzbank AG* [1991] BTC 161; 1991 STC 271, QBD.

test cases v Inland Revenue Commissioners,[7] Park J emphasised the general 'precautionary' nature of non-discrimination articles:

'A non-discrimination article by its nature is unlikely to be directed at one or more specific provisions of a contracting state's tax legislation as respects which discrimination was already present in the minds of the negotiators. Rather it is in the nature of a general precautionary provision, meaning that if … it emerges that some provision of the tax law of one of the contracting states … is discriminatory within the terms of the article, the discrimination ought not to be permitted.[8]'

As this chapter shows, the courts in the UK have upheld a number of claims of tax discrimination against foreigners. Taxpayers have, however, failed to obtain redress for these breaches because HMRC has consistently and successfully invoked the non-incorporation of non-discrimination provisions into domestic law in defending claims of discrimination.[9] The extent to which taxpayers rights are given voice in domestic law requires careful attention. In some cases, parallel breaches of EC law by the UK may provide the only practical remedy. HMRC administrative practice does recognise the implications of non-discrimination articles in limited cases. HMRC requires all cases where discrimination is alleged by a taxpayer but is not specifically accepted by HMRC in its manuals to be referred to CT & VAT, International CT.[10] In 2008 the OECD adopted a tendentious revision of the commentary of the article[11] reflected in the public discussion draft on the 'Application and interpretation of Article 24'[12] at odds with much jurisprudence of the ECJ. The cases that concern the UK's troubled former imputation system and its unanticipated cross-border implications have no doubt triggered a defensive response from the administration and much thought by judges as to their proper resolution. As with the construction of ICTA 1988, s. 788, the extent to which the special circumstances these cases ought to inform on the matter of construction of the non-discrimination principles generally is a matter of conjecture.

24-150   Discrimination against foreign nationals and stateless persons

Discrimination against foreign nationals was claimed in *R v IRC ex parte Commerzbank AG*.[13] Under art. 20 of the UK–Germany Treaty (adopting the OECD Model, art. 24(1), language in this respect) and reads in part:

'20(1) The nationals of one of the Contracting States shall not be subject in the other State to any taxation or any requirement connected therewith which is other or more burdensome than

---

[7] [2004] BTC 208; [2003] EWHC 2813 (Ch).

[8] At para 25.

[9] See chapter 1, paras. 10-250. In *Boake Allen Ltd & Ors (including NEC Semi-Conductors Ltd) v Revenue and Customs Commissioners* [2007] BTC 414; [2007] UKHL 25, two of the five law lords relied on this ground.

[10] See HMRC's *Double Taxation Relief Manual*, para. DT1950.

[11] OECD Commentary to art. 24 (2008) revision.

[12] OECD, 3 May 2007.

[13] [1991] BTC 161; (1991) 68 TC 252.

the taxation or connected requirements to which nationals of that other State in the same circumstances are or may not be subjected.'

Commerzbank was incorporated and resident in Germany. It qualified as a national of Germany within the definition in art. 20(2)[14] It operated through a permanent establishment in the UK. Its claim to a repayment supplement, the statutory right to recover interest or its equivalent on the repayment of corporation tax that has been paid in excess of legal liability was refused on the basis that ICTA, s. 825, as it then read only permitted the repayment supplement to be paid to UK residents. By contrast, interest which was charged on overdue payments of tax without making such distinction.

The prohibition is on both taxation which is other or more burdensome and on connected requirements which are other or more burdensome. Nolan LJ agreed that Commerzbank, like a UK national (or resident), had to pay tax on demand, but unlike a UK national, is denied the repayment supplement on proof that it has made an overpayment. It is thus subjected to a requirement connected with taxation which is more burdensome than that imposed on UK nationals. However, the comparison required by art. 20(1) was a comparison between German and UK nationals in the same circumstances. The bank as a German national must be compared with that of a company which is a UK national, that is to say, a company which derives its status as a legal person from the laws in force in the UK. But the comparison was held to be meaningless, because UK tax law in general and corporation tax, in particular, does not depend upon nationality, nor upon the law from which a legal person derives his or her status: it depends upon residence. Thus, a company deriving its status from the laws of the UK, which was resident in the Federal Republic, and which traded through a branch in the UK, would be treated for tax purposes in precisely the same manner as the bank. It is submitted that this reasoning may have been more appropriate prior to FA 1988, s. 66, which adopted incorporation, and thus nationality as a taxing criteria.

It is a curious result, perhaps indicating the lack of coherence and connection between the various sub-articles, that if the comparator was correctly analysed in *Commerzbank*, a stateless person, as a resident of a contracting state, may enjoy better protection than nationals. Stateless persons who are residents of a contracting state shall not be subjected in either contracting state to any taxation or any requirement connected therewith, which is other or more burdensome than the taxation and connected requirements to which nationals of the state concerned in the same circumstances, in particular with respect to residence, are or may be subjected.[15] The 1951 convention relating to the status of refugees and the 1954 convention relating to the status of stateless persons both contain specific references to taxation. These are reflected in art. 24(2) of the OECD Model. 'Other taxation' means different taxation. In *Woodend Rubber v CIR*[16] the Privy Council ruled in the context of a pre-OECD Model Treaty between the UK and Ceylon that income tax other than that to which resident companies were subjected is 'other taxation'. In the same case, the Privy Council upheld the view of the Supreme Court of Ceylon that more burdensome taxation

---

[14] National art. 3(1)(g) means any individual possessing the nationality or citizenship of that contracting state; and any legal person, partnership or association deriving its status as such from the laws in force in a contracting state. See chapter 5, para. 14-050.

[15] OECD Model, art. 24(2).

[16] [1971] AC 321 (PC).

means a higher amount of same tax. The comparison was made by looking at the amount of tax the non-resident would have paid, had it been resident.

24-200   Discrimination against permanent establishments

The prohibition on discrimination against permanent establishments is aimed at business taxation. Article 23(2) of the UK–Switzerland Treaty, tracking art. 24(3) of the OECD Model, reads:

> 'The taxation on a permanent establishment which an enterprise of a Contracting State has in the other Contracting State shall not be less favourably levied in that other State than the taxation levied on enterprises of that other State carrying on the same activities.'

The criteria for differentiation in relation to permanent establishments, is that taxation must not be less favourably levied. In *Commerzbank*, the argument that, irrespective of nationality and residence, the bank was entitled to the repayment supplement because otherwise, taxation would be 'less favourably levied' upon its UK permanent establishment than upon a UK enterprise carrying on the same activities,[17] was rejected because the repayment supplement, although connected with the levy of taxation, does not affect the amount of that levy. This narrow view of 'taxation' and the absence of a prohibition on discrimination relating to 'connected requirements' offers a more restricted scope of protection afforded to permanent establishments.

In *UBS AG v Revenue and Customs Commissioners*,[18] a bank resident in Switzerland, carried on a banking business through a branch in London. It acted as a market maker on the London Stock Exchange, buying and selling securities in the course of a trade. In the course of its activities as a market maker it received dividends from UK-resident companies and received and paid 'manufactured dividends'.[19] The branch had substantial trading losses but a surplus of UK dividends (and manufactured dividends) received by the appellant over manufactured dividends paid. Had the appellant been a UK-resident company, the distributions would have carried with them tax credits.[20]

HMRC argued that the payment of the tax credit is not part of the process of levying of taxation within the treaty article. This was rejected by the Special Commissioners,[21] the High Court[22] and by Moses LJ in the Court of Appeal.[23] In the High Court, Etherton J said:

> 'I reject [the Revenue's] submission on the meaning of "levied on" in Article 23(2) of the Treaty. The levying of tax is a broad concept. As the dictionary definition shows, it encompasses, in its ordinary sense, the imposition of a tax. The imposition of a tax does not

---

[17] UK–Germany Treaty, art. 20(3).

[18] [2006] BTC 232; [2006] EWHC 117 (Ch).

[19] See ICTA 1988, s. 737 and Sch. 23A.

[20] As then provided by ICTA 1988, s. 231.

[21] (2005) Sp C 480, para. 25.

[22] [2006] BTC 232; [2006] EWHC 117 (Ch), para. 20.

[23] [2007] BTC 285; [2007] EWCA 119 (Ch).

denote that a taxpayer will actually be liable to pay an amount of tax after, for example, allowances and reliefs. The tax is imposed, or 'levied', but, in accordance with the tax provisions, there may be nothing to be paid by a particular taxpayer in respect of it. There is nothing in Article 23(2) to restrict it to a narrower meaning. The tax credit payable in consequence of the invocation of s. 243 is part of the levying of corporation tax, notwithstanding that s.243 only operates in circumstances where the company's losses are such that there could never be any question of a liability to make an actual payment of tax.'

In the Court of Appeal, Moses LJ noted that the imposition of a tax comprises the declaration of liability, that is, the part of the statute which determines what persons in respect of what property are liable. The basis of computation must form the first stage of imposition of liability. Only when that basis has been identified can there be any liability. The process of working out a corporation tax computation, and making a return to HMRC follows the basis of computation laid down in the relevant parts of the Taxes Act 1988. The determination of the entitlement of a company resident in the UK to a tax credit was part of the process of computation of its liability. Although a company would only receive a tax credit when it made a claim, the basis of entitlement is logically prior and forms part of the system whereby taxation is imposed.[24]

The only dissenting view was expressed by Arden LJ (Sedley LJ expressed no view.). She noted that the opening words 'the taxation' are not defined in the treaty or domestic law but must be limited to UK tax as defined in the treaty. She observed further that:

> 'Moreover, paras (1) and (5)[25] both refer also to "any requirement connected therewith", but that phrase is absent from para (2). The presence of the words "any requirement connected therewith" in other parts of the articles is an indication that the expression "the taxation" does not cover all aspects of liability to tax. It may therefore be limited to provisions which impose the tax, as distinct from collateral obligations of the taxpayer, such as the obligation to file a return. This approach is supported by the meaning of the word "levied" which on its ordinary meaning means "raised". If that is so, art 23(2) has a more limited field of operation than say art 23(1).[26]'

In her view, it followed that the credits which a UK-resident company received in respect of qualifying distributions were credits against the mainstream corporation tax of the company paying a dividend and not a relief against the income of the recipient of the dividend and did not reduce the liability of the liability of the permanent establishment to account for ACT because it did not do so in any event.[27] The failure to repay tax credits in any year in which the permanent establishment had no liability to pay any tax was not taxation less favourably levied on this basis. While the scope of the prohibition in respect of nationals is different from that relating to permanent establishments, this distinction does not, it is submitted, support the conclusions of Arden LJ in excluding the tax credit from the expression 'taxation'.

---

[24] At paras. 21–27.

[25] Arts. 24(1) and 24(5) of the OECD Model.

[26] At para. 72.

[27] See paras. 70–80.

The comparator in relation to permanent establishments is not the more general 'similar circumstances' as applied to nationals but in relation to local 'enterprises ... carrying on the same activities.' The Special Commissioners considered this aspect in UBS. They concluded that the same activities requirement means that the hypothetical UK-resident company has a market maker. The parties agreed that it should have exactly the same tax losses and receive the same dividends and manufactured dividends as the appellant and should pay the same tax on manufactured dividends. The Revenue argued that profit distribution should also be considered. The Special Commissioners concluded that it is inherent in any comparison between a permanent establishment and a resident company that one must ignore the distribution of profits. The two are different in this respect.[28]

The UK has made concessions in this area to states imposing a branch profits tax.[29] Thus, in the UK – South Africa Treaty, the non-discrimination article does not prevent South Africa from imposing on the profits attributable to a permanent establishment in South Africa of a company, which is resident of the UK, a tax at a rate which does not exceed the rate of a normal tax on companies by more than five percentage points.[30] Similarly, the UK–US Treaty on the discrimination article does not prevent either contracting state from imposing tax a branch profits tax as described in art. 10(7).[31]

HMRC accepts that a permanent establishment will be entitled to the small companies' relief only provided under domestic law to UK-resident companies.[32] In determining what relief is due, the income and the profits of the company as a whole, not only the income and profits of the permanent establishment should be included. The number of any associated companies, wherever resident, should also be taken into account.[33] HMRC does not consider that these provisions permit TCGA 1992, s. 139, to apply to the transfer of assets between permanent establishments in the UK of non-resident companies. The Taxation of Capital Gains Act 1992, s. 139, requires both companies to be resident in the UK to qualify for no gain or loss on the disposal and acquisition.[34]

24-250   Discrimination based on residence of payee

In certain instances, differences in treatment of payments may arise because of the residence of the recipient of a payment. Such difference in treatment is addressed by treaties adopting art. 24(4) of the OECD model, as is the case in the UK–Belgium Treaty, which reads:

> '24(5) Except where the provisions of paragraph (1) of Article 9, paragraph (6) of Article 11, or paragraph (4) of Article 12 of this Convention apply, interest, royalties and other disbursements paid by an enterprise of a Contracting State to a resident of the other Contracting State shall,

---

[28] At paras. 12 and 13.

[29] See *UBS AG v Revenue and Customs Commissioners* (2005) Sp C 480, per Special Commissioner Avery-Jones at para. 13.

[30] Art. 23(6).

[31] Art. 23(6). See also specific US reservation to this effect in the commentary to the OECD Model Convention, art. 24, para. 65.

[32] ICTA 88, s. 13.

[33] HMRC, *Double Taxation Relief Manual*, para. DT1954.

[34] HMRC, *Double Taxation Relief Manual*, para. DT1953.

for the purpose of determining the taxable profits of such enterprise, be deductible under the same conditions as if they had been paid to a resident of the first-mentioned State.'

The prohibition here relates to deduction of such items paid to non-residents on an unequal basis to the same payments made to residents. The extent of the prohibition is limited in the case of interest and royalties to the amount that is not prevented from benefitting from reduced tax by reason of the existence of a special relationship[35] and, generally, where the amount is within the arm's length provisions of art. 9.[36] The unequal treatment is suffered by the enterprise in a contracting state making the payment, but the unequal treatment arises by reason of the residential status of the recipient in the other contracting state.

For example, in the UK, where a company pays interest late on a debt owed to a connected party, and where the full amount of that interest is not brought into account for corporation tax purposes by the creditor, if a 1996, Sch. 9, para. 2 (1A), restriction applies so that the debtor company can only claim relief for the interest when it is paid.[37] This will be the case where a company pays interest late to a non-UK-resident connected company. It is not the case where the creditor is UK resident. HMRC announced on 28 July 2008 its intention to amend the law (in response to rulings from the ECJ), and will not generally seek to apply FA 1996, Sch. 9, para. 2(1A), as it currently stands where the creditor company is not resident in the UK.[38]

24-300   Discrimination based on ownership of enterprises

Virtually all non-discrimination articles confer on enterprises owned by non-residents rights that parallel those granted to nationals. art. 24(4) of the UK–Japan Treaty exemplifies this rule:

'Enterprises of a contracting State the capital of which is wholly or partly owned or controlled, directly or indirectly by one or more residents of the other Contracting State shall not be subjected to any taxation or any requirement in connection therewith which is other or more burdensome than the taxation and connected requirements to which other similar enterprises of the first state may be subjected.'

As in the case of nationals, the prohibition is on any taxation or any requirement in connection therewith which are other or more burdensome. The person protected is an enterprise of one state whose capital is wholly or partly owned or controlled, directly or indirectly by residents of the other state. The comparison must be made with the treatment of other similar enterprises of the host state.

In *Boake Allen Ltd & Ors (including NEC Semi-Conductors Ltd) v Revenue and Customs Commissioners*,[39] the courts considered whether it was contrary to the non-discrimination provisions of the UK–Japan Treaty and other identical treaties to prohibit a UK company

---

[35] See chapter 9, para. 18-150.

[36] See chapter 8, para. 17-700.

[37] FA 1996, Sch. 9, para. 2(1A).

[38] Revenue & Customs Brief 33/08.

[39] [2007] BTC 414; [2007] UKHL 25.

and its Japanese parent company from electing out of the operation of ACT on intra-group dividends paid by a subsidiary to its parent company, when such an election could be made between a UK subsidiary and a UK parent company. This case was inspired by the decision of the ECJ in *Metallgesellschaft v IRC*, where the ECJ concluded that the inability of a European parent company to make such an election with its UK subsidiary was contrary to the right of establishment in EC law.

In the High Court,[40] Park J considered four hypothetical candidates for the comparator 'other similar enterprises':

(1) *UK subsidiaries of other companies resident in the other contracting state.* This was obviously not what was intended, and neither party argued for it in this case.

(2) *UK subsidiaries of other companies resident in third states.* This was the Revenue interpretation up to the hearing but was abandoned at trial. In the judge's view it is extremely difficult to force this interpretation out of the language of the paragraph. It is in effect, a 'most favoured nation' approach rather than discrimination.

(3) *There are no 'other similar enterprises'.* This in the end became the Revenue's position at trial. The Revenue argued that if the hypothetical UK-resident parent would receive (so far as dividends are concerned) the normal tax treatment applicable to UK-resident companies, its UK subsidiary, though an enterprise of the UK, would not be an enterprise 'similar' to the actual enterprise under consideration. because of the UK tax treatment of dividends received and paid, not by the 'enterprises' themselves (NEC and another hypothetical UK subsidiary), but by their parent companies (the Japanese parent company of NEC and the hypothetical UK-resident parent company of the hypothetical UK subsidiary). The Japanese parent company of NEC was not liable to pay ACT if it paid dividends itself; the hypothetical UK parent company of a comparator UK subsidiary would have been liable to pay ACT if it paid dividends itself. The Japanese parent company was not entitled to a UK tax credit if it received dividends from UK sources; the hypothetical UK parent company would have been so entitled. Therefore, because the tax treatments of the parent companies would have been different, the two subsidiaries would not themselves have been 'similar enterprises'. Park J rejected the Revenue argument.[41] In his analysis, the comparison concerned whether the actual Japanese-owned company and another hypothetical UK company are 'similar'. For this it is necessary to assume that if the actual company is a subsidiary of another company, then so is the hypothetical comparator company; but that does not extend to whether the hypothetical UK-resident parent company would have the same a tax treatment on dividends received and paid as if it were not UK resident. The actual company and a hypothetical other UK-resident subsidiary were fairly comparable with each other in this context. They do not cease to be comparable because there would be differences between the UK tax treatment of their respective actual and hypothetical parent companies. The contrary would be difficult to reconcile

---

[40] Under the name *NEC Semi-Conductors Ltd v IRC* [2004] BTC 208; [2003] EWHC 2813 (Ch).

[41] At para. 28.

[42] Art. 24 of the 1977 OECD Model, para. 6.

with the OECD Commentary,[42] which states that the provision 'relates to the taxation only of the enterprises and not of the persons owning or controlling their capital.'

(4) *UK subsidiaries of UK-resident companies.* This was held the correct comparator. Park J concluded that:

> 'The context is a UK subsidiary controlled by a parent company resident in the other contracting state (e.g. Japan) which pays dividends to its parent. In that context ..."other similar enterprises of [the United Kingdom]" means other United Kingdom subsidiaries controlled by parent companies resident, not in the other contracting state, but in the same contracting state (i.e. in the UK) which pay dividends to their parents. In my view it is obvious from the whole scheme and purpose of the non-discrimination article that that is what the particular sub-article is getting at.[43]'

This conclusion was upheld unanimously by the Court of Appeal.[44] Park J also concluded that the ACT paid in consequence of paying the dividends, and inability to make a group income election with its parent to remove the ACT liability was 'taxation or any requirement connected therewith'. He noted that:

> 'It could be regarded as "taxation" in that the result was that ACT (which is certainly taxation of some sort) had to be paid. It could be regarded as a requirement connected with taxation in the sense that, in order to make a group income election, the UK subsidiary needed to have a UK parent company – a requirement with which it could not comply.[45]'

This conclusion and that these were 'other or more burdensome' than the taxation or connected requirements to which the hypothetical UK comparator company would have been subjected was challenged on appeal. The Revenue contended on appeal that the group income election regime is not a taxation or other requirement for the subsidiary, because it relates to the taxation of the group, not of the subsidiary. Lloyd LJ, with the concurrence of Sedley and Mummery LJJ, however, upheld the High Court noting that the ACT regime clearly created different requirements in respect of taxation for the subsidiary of the foreign parent from those which apply to the subsidiary of the UK parent. For the same reason, he said that the provisions concerning ACT are more burdensome for the subsidiary of the foreign parent than for a member of a UK group, because the former does not have the opportunity to avoid having to pay ACT by a group income election.[46]

The House of Lords overturned the decision of the Court of Appeal.[47] Speaking for all five law lords, Lord Hoffmann, rather than considering the treaty language, rephrased the question as 'whether [the ACT regime] discriminates against a UK company on the grounds that its capital is "wholly or partly owned or controlled directly or indirectly" by residents of [the other contracting state].'[48] He drew the comparison between the UK company owned by

---

[43] At para. 29.

[44] [2006] BTC 266; [2006] EWCA Civ 25.

[45] At para. 31.

[46] [2006] BTC 266; [2006] EWCA Civ 25. [2006], para. 43.

[47] [2007] BTC 414; [2007] UKHL 25.

[48] At para. 16.

a foreign resident individual, which, like a UK-resident individual, could not make a group income election with the UK company because neither were within the charge to corporation tax. Since the non-resident parent company was similarly outside the charge to corporation tax. it was not treated unequally by reason of the inability to make a group income election.[49] He further noted that since the election was a group election, it was not possible to decouple of the position of the parent and subsidiary. He concluded that the denial of the right of election was not on the grounds of the company's foreign control but on the grounds that the provisions could not be applied to a case in which the parent company was not liable to ACT.[50] The interpretation of the article by the High Court and Court of Appeal is to be preferred. It is the fact that the UK enterprise is owned or controlled by residents of the other contracting state and not the way in which those residents are taxed that gives rise to the difference in treatment.

24-350   Taxes covered

The OECD Model Convention states that the provisions of the non-discrimination article shall, notwithstanding the provisions of art. 2 (Taxes covered), apply to taxes of every kind and description. Under a specific reservation on this paragraph,[51] the UK reserves the right to restrict the application of the article to the taxes covered by the convention. This was not the case in earlier treaties. Recent treaties demonstrate some inconsistency of approach. For example, the UK–US Treaty adopts the same approach as in OECD Model, while the treaties with Australia and South Africa are consistent with the UK reservation. Lack of incorporation into domestic law is a central problem in this area. The nationality based discrimination in relation to stamp duty reconstruction and acquisition reliefs in FA 1986, ss. 75 to 77, until its repeal by FA 2006 is a case in point.

24-400   Authorisation of discrimination

The OECD Model advocates an exception to the equal treatment rule in relation to personal allowances and reliefs. Typical language in this respect is found in the UK–Russia Treaty:

> '24(5) Nothing contained in this Article shall be construed as obliging either Contracting State to grant to individuals not resident in that State any of the personal allowances, reliefs and reductions for tax purposes which are granted to individuals so resident.'

Thus, contracting states are not obliged to grant to residents of the other contracting state any personal allowances, reliefs and reductions for taxation purposes on account of civil status or family responsibilities which it grants to its own residents.

---

[49] At para. 17.

[50] At para. 22.

[51] Para. 72 of the commentary to the OECD Model Convention on art. 24.

The UK–Australia Treaty,[52] although the first in which Australia has accepted a full non-discrimination article,[53] excludes the benefit of the non-discrimination provisions in relation to any law of a contracting state which:

- is designed to prevent the avoidance or evasion of taxes;
- does not permit the deferral of tax arising on the transfer of an asset where the subsequent transfer of the asset by the transferee would be beyond the taxing jurisdiction of the contracting state under its laws;
- provides for consolidation of group entities for treatment as a single entity for tax purposes *provided that* Australia-resident companies that are owned directly or indirectly by residents of the UK can access such consolidation treatment on the same terms and conditions as other Australia-resident companies;
- provides deductions to eligible taxpayers for expenditure on research and development; or
- is otherwise agreed to be unaffected by this article in an exchange of notes between the Government of Australia and the Government of the UK.[54] The exchange of notes specifies that the non-discrimination article does not oblige a contracting state to allow tax rebates and credits in relation to dividends received by a person who is a resident of the other contracting state.[55]

By contrast, the UK–US Treaty preserves the benefits of the non-discrimination article despite the authority given to contracting states to tax its residents as if the treaty had not come into effect.[56] Article 1(5) requires that 'the provisions of (art. 1(4)) shall not effect … the benefits conferred by a contracting state under … art. 25 (Non-discrimination)'.[57]

Several treaties with the developing countries include exceptions to the non-discrimination rules so as to permit them to offer tax incentives without granting equal access to these incentives to UK residents.[58]

24-450   Most favoured nation treatment

Most favoured nation treatment is not a common feature of UK treaties. although it is not entirely unknown. Most favoured nation treatment is to be distinguished from discrimination. This approach is similar to that found in many commercial and investment treaties[59] as well as the World Trade Organisation.[60] Non-discrimination provisions require

---

[52] 21 August 2003.

[53] Paymaster General before the Eighth Standing Committee on Delegated Legislation, 13 November 2003, column 005.

[54] Art. 25(6).

[55] Exchange of Notes of 21 August 2003.

[56] Art. 1(4).

[57] *Tax Bulletin*, special edition on UK–US Treaty (April 2003), p. 3.

[58] See, for example, UK–Egypt Treaty, art. 23(4)(b) and (c); UK–Philippines Treaty art. 22(6).

[59] See, for example, UK–Singapore Agreement for the Promotion and Protection of Investments, 22 July 1975, art. 3.

[60] See General Agreement on Trade in Services, Pt. II, art. II.

equal treatment in a host state of foreign taxpayers from the other contracting state with its local tax payers. Most favoured nation treatment requires equal treatment in a host state of foreign taxpayers from the other contracting state with foreign taxpayers in a third country. This latter treatment is not found in non-discrimination articles of UK treaties.[61]

An example of a narrowly targeted most favoured nation clause is found in the UK–India Treaty dealing with the deduction of expenses of a permanent establishment:

> '7(6) Where the law of the Contracting State in which the permanent establishment is situated imposes a restriction on the amount of the executive and general administrative expenses which may be allowed, and the restriction is relaxed or overridden by any Convention between that Contracting State and a third State which is a member of the Organisation for Economic Co-operation and Development or a State in a comparable stage of development, and that Convention enters into force after the date of entry into force of this Convention, the competent authority of that Contracting State shall notify the competent authority of the other Contracting State of the terms of the relevant paragraph. in the Convention with that third State immediately after the entry into force of that Convention and, if the competent authority of the other Contracting State so requests, the provisions of this Convention shall be amended by protocol to reflect such terms.'

Under this version, the treaty is not adjusted automatically, but each contracting state is granted an option to require the other to adjust the treaty should the other conclude a more favourable arrangement with a third state.

The UK–Philippines Treaty contains an unusual provision excluding, on the one hand, national treatment, but, on the other hand, providing most favoured nation treatment in relation to access to investment incentives:

> '22(6) Nothing in this Article shall be construed so as to prevent the Philippines from limiting to its nationals the enjoyment of tax incentives granted by law. However, such incentives which are available to nationals of any third State shall likewise be available to nationals of the United Kingdom.'

---

[61] See Canada – South Africa Treaty, art 23(4), below, as an example:

'Taxation is other or more burdensome than the taxation and connected requirements to which other similar enterprises of the first state may be subjected the capital of which is wholly or partly owned or controlled, directly or indirectly by one or more residents of a third State.'

Treaty Shopping and Other Avoidance

Chapter 16

25-000   Introduction

Tax treaty provisions, like their counterparts in domestic tax legislation, are undergoing a fundamental change in perspective. Historically, treaties were entered into in order to avoid double taxation. A second objective was the prevention of evasion by means of exchange of information between tax authorities. In recent times, however, particularly as treaty networks have grown, attention in relation to tax avoidance has spread from the domestic to the treaty area. Historically, several major UK departures from the OECD Model in terms of its negotiating position are addressed almost entirely to avoidance issues. These include the purpose-based test for benefits relating to investment income and the provisions relating to partnership taxation.

25-050   What is avoidance?

A convenient starting point for this topic in the treaty context is the HMRC *International Tax Handbook*, which addresses avoidance in the international context. HMRC's comments on the meaning of the expression are revealing. Paragraph 101 reads as follows:

> 'As our tax code becomes more complex, Inspectors are increasingly called upon to form a judgment whether, on the facts of a particular case, there has been "tax avoidance". The distinction that is drawn is between tax mitigation which may well be considered acceptable and tax avoidance which will not. At one end of the scale, no-one would suggest that moving savings from a bank account into National Savings certificates was objectionable even though the tax payable has been reduced.[1] At the other extreme, when liability is reduced in a wholly artificial way without the taxpayer incurring a loss or expenditure, then that will plainly be avoidance.
>
> Many judges have tried to explain the distinction between mitigation and avoidance – see, for example the judgments of Lords Goff and Templeman in *Craven v White* and of Lord Templeman in *Ensign Tankers*, but these attempts have not been entirely successful. Perhaps the dividing line is impossible to define. In any event, distinctions between the mitigation and tax avoidance are of less concern to the Government than the effect on the yield to the Exchequer.'

This statement is a fair assessment of the issues relating to avoidance in several respects. First, the term 'tax avoidance' is placed in quotation marks suggesting that as a concept with a defined content, it may well not exist in general terms. Second, it recognises that at least some activity is unobjectionable. Third, it appears to acknowledge that while the extremes

---

[1] Despite this, the Inland Revenue argued (unsuccessfully) in *A Beneficiary v IR Commrs* (1999) Sp C 190 that the transfer of funds from a UK bank account to a non-UK account by a non-resident, non-domiciled individual was tax avoidance.

may be easy, the dividing line may be impossible to identify. Fourth, it concedes that this is less an issue of principle, than one of revenue raising.

The *International Tax Handbook* then outlines the Ramsay[2] approach in general terms and turns to the subject of avoidance in the international context. In this regard, it says:

> 'Within the Revenue we do not categorise avoidance in quite the narrow way that the Courts have done. Of course we make a distinction between mitigation and avoidance. However, if a taxpayer takes advantage of the law to get a tax advantage which is not, in our understanding, within the spirit of the legislation, we tend to look on that as avoidance. But unless the prerequisites of the new [Ramsay] approach are present, such avoidance can only be countered by legislation brought in for this purpose.[3]'

It is troubling that tax avoidance is used here in a policy sense to describe inadequacies in the tax base in the same paragraph that includes reference to transactions which may as a matter of law be rendered ineffective by application of the Ramsay doctrine.

The most helpful recent formulation of the statutory meaning of avoidance is that made by Lord Nolan in the House of Lords in *IRC v Willoughby*.[4] In that case, he accepted the argument advanced by the Inland Revenue as to what was meant by 'tax avoidance' for the purposes of the Taxes Act 1988, s. 741.[5] He said:[6]

> 'Tax avoidance was to be distinguished from tax mitigation. The hallmark of tax avoidance is that the taxpayer reduces his liability to tax without incurring the economic consequences that Parliament intended to be suffered by any taxpayer qualifying for such a reduction in his tax liability. The hallmark of tax mitigation on the other hand is that the taxpayer takes advantage of a fiscally attractive option afforded to him by the tax legislation, and genuinely suffers the economic consequences that Parliament intended to be suffered by those taking advantage of the option.'

In referring to investment in personal portfolio bonds, he continued:

> 'In a broad colloquial sense, tax avoidance might be said to have been one of the main purposes of those who took out such policies, because plainly freedom from tax was one of the main attractions. But it would be absurd in the context of section 741 to describe as tax avoidance the acceptance of an offer of freedom from tax which Parliament has deliberately made. Tax avoidance within the meaning of section 741 is a course of action designed to conflict with or defeat the evident intention of Parliament.'

Judges too may use the label 'tax avoidance' as a convenient colloquial expression but do not regard it as a legal rule. In *Westmoreland Investments Ltd v MacNiven (HMIT)*, for example, Lord Hoffmann said:[7]

---

[2] *Ramsay v IRC* (1979-1983) 54 TC 101; [1982] AC 300, HL.

[3] At para. 103.

[4] [1997] BTC 393; [1997] STC 995, HL.

[5] Now contained in ITA 2007, Pt. 13, Ch.3.

[6] At 1003.

[7] [2001] BTC 44 [2001] UKHL 6.

'When the statutory provisions do not contain words like 'avoidance' or 'mitigation', I do not think that it helps to introduce them. The fact that steps taken for the avoidance of tax are acceptable or unacceptable is the conclusion at which one arrives by applying the statutory language to the facts of the case. It is not a test for deciding whether it applies or not.[8]'

'Everyone agrees', he observed, 'that Ramsay is a principle of construction.'[9] Lord Nicholls of Birkenhead agreed, saying:[10]

'Confronted with new and sophisticated tax avoidance devices, the courts' duty is to determine the legal nature of the transactions in question and then relate them to the fiscal legislation.'

This formulation was further refined by the House of Lords' unanimous view in *Barclays Mercantile Business Finance Ltd v Mawson (HM Inspector of Taxes)*, which was:[11]

'The two steps which are necessary in the application of any statutory provision: first, to decide, on a purposive construction, exactly what transaction will answer to the statutory description and secondly, to decide whether the transaction in question does so. As Ribeiro PJ said in *Collector of Stamp Revenue v Arrowtown Assets Ltd* [2003] HKCFA 46, at para. 35:

"The driving principle in the Ramsay line of cases continues to involve a general rule of statutory construction and an unblinkered approach to the analysis of the facts. The ultimate question is whether the relevant statutory provisions, construed purposively, were intended to apply to the transaction, viewed realistically."'

25-100   Treaty interaction with domestic anti-avoidance rules

In an era in which domestic legislation is increasingly laced with anti-avoidance provisions, the relationship between treaties and domestic anti-avoidance rules requires examination. As a general rule, treaties override domestic legislation. In principle, measures labelled as anti-avoidance enjoy no special status. As a result, legislative provisions of any kind, including anti-avoidance rules, are normally overridden by treaties. The OECD commentary following the commentary's amendment in 2003 has attempted to construct an argument[12] (unconvincingly) that domestic anti-avoidance provisions do not, in general, 'conflict' with treaty rules. The question as to whether there is avoidance or not is a conclusion to be drawn by proper analysis of the relevant domestic and treaty rules in the normal way, rather than itself a rule or analytical approach.

25-150   Treaty shopping

The subject of treaty shopping is perhaps one of the key underlying policy issues surrounding the development of treaties. The exact meaning of the term is unclear and is often taken to have a pejorative meaning. It is the major topic identified for analysis under

---

[8] At para. 62.

[9] At para. 28.

[10] At para. 1. See also Lord Hope's view at para. 77.

[11] [2004] BTC 414 [2004] UKHL 51 at para. 36.

[12] Commentary to art. 1, paras. 7.1–9.4 and 22–23.

the heading 'Improper use of the convention' in the commentary to the OECD Model Convention. A variety of other terms have been used, such as treaty abuse and limitation of benefits in the context of the same issue, although these concepts may be wider in scope than treaty shopping, which is now identified by the OECD as a particularly prevalent form of improper use of treaties.[13] (

Problems relating to improper use of treaties were examined in detail by the Committee on Fiscal Affairs of the OECD. In 1987, it published the Conduit Companies Report and the Base Companies Report. The key conclusions of those reports are now included in the official commentary to the OECD Model. The Conduit Companies Report considered improper use of treaties to exist where there is 'a person (whether or not a resident of a Contracting State) acting through a legal entity created in a state with the main or sole purpose of obtaining treaty benefits which would not be available directly to such person'. This chapter will consider opportunities for treaty shopping following this definition in circumstances where the person is neither resident in the same country as the legal entity interposed nor in the country of source.

At a more practical level, all forms of treaty shopping involve a taxpayer selecting from various tax treaties that may be available through the use of intermediate entities in order to produce the least amount of tax. The element in treaty shopping identified by the Conduit Company Report as improper is that treaty shopping involves a claim to the benefit of tax treaties by persons who are viewed as not having the requisite connections with a country whose treaty they seek to benefit from.

A crucial practical element is the interplay between the treaties selected and the domestic tax law of contracting states involved to produce significant overall reductions in tax. In some cases, contracting states deliberately offer such facilities as a matter of policy. In others, it arises as a result of domestic tax laws which permit this without deliberately setting out to do so. This chapter focuses on the treaty aspects. The impact of treaty shopping is principally on the state of source. It may involve tax benefits in the residence country, for example where tax sparing credits are sought.

There are generally considerable incentives for taxpayers to engage in treaty shopping in international transactions. The UK has over 100 treaties covering the whole of the OECD, the majority involve Eastern European countries and a large number of developing and lesser developed countries. A handful of treaties follow the old colonial style, but the vast majority are patterned on various OECD models. More recent treaties with developing countries show some influence of the UN Model. To some extent the fact that there are now so many countries that have relatively standardised treaty provisions with the UK removes some of the incentive for treaty shopping at a fairly rudimentary level. Thus, in many cases, for example, the use of conduit countries to secure reduced rates of withholding tax, permanent establishment benefits or other treaty benefits in straightforward situations is reduced simply because treaties exist with so many countries where investors are located. However, the UK has important trade and investment links with countries where there are no treaties in place, and indeed where there are fundamental differences in tax policy between

---

[13] See the commentary to art. 1, para. 11.

the country where investors or traders are located and the UK. Accordingly, even where treaties exist, there are sufficient variations between them to encourage taxpayers to attempt to choose those that provide the most beneficial treatment.

25-200   Amendments to commentary in 2003

Radical and controversial changes were made to the commentary to the OECD Model in 2003 in pursuit of an anti-avoidance agenda.[14] The changes result from three reports: 'Draft contents of 2002 update to the Model Tax Convention', 2 October 2001, 'Restricting entitlement to treaty benefits', 7 November 2002, and '2003 update of the OECD Model Tax Convention', 28 January 2003. The commentary now asserts that 'a purpose of tax treaties is to prevent tax avoidance'.[15] The significantly expanded discussion on improper use of treaties raises two fundamental questions – namely, whether treaty benefits must be granted when transactions constitute an abuse of those provisions and whether specific provisions and jurisprudential rules of domestic law that are intended to prevent tax abuse conflict with treaty provisions.[16] The commentary now purports to establish a general anti-avoidance rule requiring treaties to be interpreted so as to prevent avoidance. The terms used reflect language commonly used in the UK domestic legislation, that is, where 'a main purpose for entering into certain transactions or arrangements was to secure a more favourable tax position and obtaining that more favourable treatment in those circumstances would be contrary to the object and purpose of the relevant provisions.'[17] The same colloquial use is made of references to tax avoidance in a policy sense to describe inadequacies in treaty provisions, as well as the reference to transactions which may be rendered ineffective by application of legal doctrine, as appears in the UK *International Handbook*, is reflected in the revised commentary.[18]

25-250   Treaty-based anti-abuse measures

This section and the ones that follow focus on treaty provisions aimed at preventing treaty shopping as adopted in UK treaties. It also considers anti-avoidance measures which may be aimed at broader issues than just treaty shopping, but which may also limit treaty shopping. Treaty benefits are normally only available to residents of a contracting state in modern treaties. This issue is examined more fully in chapter 5 above. Residence is thus the normal required connection with a contracting state.

---

[14] See, for example, Arnold, BJ, 'Tax treaties and tax avoidance: the 2003 revisions to the commentary to the OECD Model' *Bulletin for International Taxation* (Vol. 58, No. 6, 2004); Jimenez, A, 'The 2003 revision of the OECD commentaries on the improper use of tax treaties: a case for the declining effect of the OECD commentaries?', *Bulletin for International Taxation* (Vol. 58, No. 6, 2004), p. 17.

[15] Commentary to art. 1, para. 7.

[16] Commentary to art. 1, para. 9.1.

[17] See commentary to art. 1, paras. 9.2–9.5.

[18] Commentary to art. 1, para. 10.

25-300 Beneficial ownership

Articles 10, 11 and 12 of the OECD Model authorise the reduction or elimination of tax in the source state only in respect of the 'beneficial owner'. The OECD Model Commentary[19] suggests that the concept of beneficial ownership does deal with at least some situations of improper use of treaties. Until 2003,[20] the commentary provided modest guidance on the meaning of the term beneficial owner. The only comment in the commentary was the suggestion that treaty benefits are not available when an intermediary such as an agent or nominee is interposed between the beneficiary and the payer.[21]

This commentary incorporates the Conduit Company Report suggestion that treaty benefits would not be available in cases where a person enters into contracts or takes obligations under which he or she has a similar function to those of a nominee or agent. This would suggest that a conduit company can normally not be regarded as the beneficial owner if, although the formal owner of certain assets, it has very narrow powers which render it a mere fiduciary or an administrator acting on account of the interested parties. The Conduit Company Report regards such parties as most likely to be the shareholders of the conduit company. In recognising the difficulties in dealing with this, both the commentary and the Conduit Company Report suggested that contracting states clarify this issue further in the course of their negotiations. Although the beneficial ownership concept is widespread in the dividend, interest and royalty articles of UK treaties, no special definition or elaboration of the concept is to be found in any of them, as advocated by the Conduit Company Report except in the UK–Japan Treaty. The royalty article, for example, includes the following:

> '12(5) A resident of a Contracting State shall not be considered the beneficial owner of royalties in respect of the use of intangible property if such royalties would not have been paid to the resident unless the resident pays royalties in respect of the same intangible property to a person:
>
> (a)   that is not entitled to benefits with respect to royalties arising in the other Contracting State which are equivalent to, or more favourable than, those available under this Convention to a resident of the first-mentioned Contracting State; and
> (b)   that is not a resident of either Contracting State.'

This limitation on benefits is more properly viewed as a look-through rule,[22] despite its formal expression as an elaboration of the meaning of the words. It casts little light on their ordinary meaning other than to suggest that such a resident would be a beneficial owner in the absence of this provision.

The concept of beneficial ownership did not appear in the 1963 OECD Draft Convention. It appeared in the 1977 OECD Model and has been retained in all model treaties, including the UN Model Double Taxation Convention between Developed and Developing Countries, as well as the US Model Treaty. The purpose of the introduction of the beneficial ownership

---

[19] Commentary on art. 1, para. 10.

[20] Discussed in the context of *Indofood*, below.

[21] Commentary on art. 10, para. 12, art. 11, para. 8 and art. 12, para. 4.

[22] See para. 25-650 below.

concept is obscure. The OECD Committee on Fiscal Affairs had apparently originally considered making treaty benefits dependent on payments being liable to tax in the state of residence but opted for the beneficial ownership concept in its place. The subject-to-tax approach would have involved various allocation questions and resultant problems and the 'beneficial ownership' wording was therefore ultimately agreed upon.[23] This earlier view of the OECD has clearly manifested itself in the treaties still in place from the mid-1960s to the early 1970s,[24] which do not have the beneficial ownership requirement but impose a subject-to-tax test.

The majority of the 18 treaties that have dividend, interest or royalty articles with no reference to beneficial ownership are those dating back to the late 1940s and early 1950s involving former colonies. Consequently, it is principally the royalty articles that may have any practical significance in this context.

Another group of treaties which do not include the beneficial ownership concept are those with Germany (1964), Malaysia (1973), Namibia (1962), Portugal (1969) and Singapore (1966). In each case the relevant interest and royalty articles provide that the withholding tax reductions in the country of source are only applicable if those items of income are subject to tax in the country of residence of the recipient. Consequently, as a practical matter, if the beneficial owner of the shares were to be a person not resident in any of those contracting states and not subject to tax in those contracting states, then UK tax benefits would not be available. Thus, every item of income in question must be received by a resident of that contracting state who is subject to tax on that income in the country of residence in question.

If it was found necessary to insert a reference to beneficial ownership in later treaties, presumably this was intended to distinguish between beneficial and legal owners. In relation to those treaties that do not refer to beneficial ownership, for example, art. 7 of the Antigua Treaty, this would permit trustees resident there to claim treaty benefits on royalties even where some or possibly all beneficiaries are resident elsewhere. Vogel suggests further that on the basis of a 'substance over form' approach, the new wording does not in fact introduce a new concept, but simply clarifies the existing position. This conclusion seems inconsistent with the notion that the OECD Committee of Fiscal Affairs considered beneficial ownership as an alternative to the 'subject to tax' approach in dealing with a perceived problem of avoidance arising out of the earlier wording.

The *Indofood* case

There is nothing in arts. 10, 11 or 12 suggesting that as an undefined term, a meaning other than under domestic law by application of art. 3(2) ought to apply where UK tax is concerned. In *Indofood International Finance Ltd v J P Morgan Chase Bank N.A,*[25] the English courts were asked to consider the meaning of 'beneficial owner' in the interest article of the Indonesia–Netherlands Treaty. In doing so, the courts had to decide what an Indonesian tax court would have decided in circumstances where there was no domestic

---

[23] See Vogel, K, p. 456.

[24] Treaties with Germany, Malaysia, Singapore and Portugal.

[25] [2006] BTC 8003 [2006] EWCA Civ 158.

legal meaning of the expression. In such a context, the court had no choice but to rely on international interpretative techniques, as there could be no reference to domestic law. It should be borne in mind that the case involved a commercial dispute in which no tax administration was a party and where commercial rather than tax counsel (let alone tax counsel with experience in treaty issues) argued the case for both parties. The case involved a bond issue by a subsidiary special purpose company (SPV) of an Indonesian company, the proceeds of which were loaned to the parent company.

At the first instance, in the Chancery Division,[26] Evans-Lombe J found that the SPV earned a 0.005 per cent spread between interest earned and paid. He found that the SPV was not a nominee or agent for any other party. Since it was not any sort of trustee or fiduciary, it would have power to dispose of the interest when received as it wishes, although it would be constrained by its contractual obligation to apply the proceeds of the interest payments in performance of those obligations under the bond issue.[27] He concluded:

> 'It is clear to me that in the absence of any trust or fiduciary relationship ... in an insolvency of [SPV] undistributed interest received from the Parent Guarantor would be an asset of [SPV] for distribution amongst its creditors generally, including the [bond holders], pari passu.[28]

> It seems to me that there can be no ambiguity in the application of the concept of beneficial ownership to the loan transaction as proposed to be restructured. The beneficial owner of interest received under a loan transaction must be the lender ... In no sense will [SPV] be acting as nominee or administrator for the ... Noteholders ... The Noteholders will have no claim to be the beneficial owners of the interest. They would be in no position to claim the interest from the Parent Guarantor and for that reason or otherwise to suggest that [SPV] will hold the interest when received on trust for them. ... There will have to be some entity that qualifies as beneficial owner of the interest. It seems to me there will be only one candidate for that, namely, [SPV].[298]'

The Court of Appeal reversed this conclusion, deciding that the SPV was not the beneficial owner of the interest. Observations by the Court of Appeal on the findings of fact, which differed from those found by the trial judge, clearly had an impact on its conclusions. The Court of Appeal found that:[30]

> 'The Parent Guarantor is obliged to pay the interest two business days before the due date to the credit of an account nominated for the purpose by the Issuer [SPV]. The Issuer [SPV] is obliged to pay the interest due to the noteholders one business day before the due date to the account specified by the Principal Paying Agent. The Principal Paying Agent is bound to pay the noteholders on the due date. ... The Issuer [SPV] is bound to pay on to the Principal Paying Agent that which it received from the Parent Guarantor because it is precluded from finding the money from any other source by the Note Conditions.'

Thus, the Court of Appeal found, unlike the trial judge, that there was no spread between interest received and paid. It appeared that the interest was not paid to the SPV. It regarded

---

[26] [2005] BTC 8023 [2005] EWHC 2103 (Ch).

[27] At para. 46.

[28] At para. 49.

[29] Para. 50.

[30] At para. 43.

the fact that neither the SPV was a trustee, agent or nominee for the noteholders or anyone else in relation to the interest receivable as not conclusive. Nor was the absence of any entitlement of a noteholder to security over or right to call for the interest receivable from the Parent Guarantor. In both commercial and practical terms, the SPV was bound to pay on that which it received, and that was what actually happened. The Parent Guarantor was bound to ensure that such an arrangement continue because it could be required to pay again under its guarantee to the noteholders. Sir Andrew Morritt adopted the meaning of beneficial ownership in a circular letter from the Indonesian Tax Inspector as 'the full privilege to directly benefit from the income'. He concluded:

'In practical terms it is impossible to conceive of any circumstances in which the SPV could derive any 'direct benefit' from the interest payable by the Parent Guarantor except by funding its liability to the Principal Paying Agent or Issuer respectively.[31]'

Both courts relied entirely on the 1986 OECD Conduit Company Report and the 2003 OECD Commentary on the Model Convention. The report is more supportive of the decision of the *Indofood* decision at first instance than on appeal.[32] In 2003, the following was added in relation to beneficial ownership a para. 12.1 of the OECD commentary on art. 10, reference to which was made in *Indofood*:

'Where an item of income is received by a resident of a Contracting State acting in the capacity of agent or nominee it would be inconsistent with the object and purpose of the Convention for the State of source to grant relief or exemption merely on account of the status of the immediate recipient of the income as a resident of the other Contracting State. The immediate recipient of the income in this situation qualifies as a resident but no potential double taxation arises as a consequence of that status since the recipient is not treated as the owner of the income for tax purposes in the State of residence. It would be equally inconsistent with the object and purpose of the Convention for the State of source to grant relief or exemption where a resident of a Contracting State, otherwise than through an agency or nominee relationship, simply acts as a conduit for another person who in fact receives the benefit of the income concerned. For these reasons, the [Conduit Companies Report] concludes that a conduit company cannot normally be regarded as the beneficial owner if, though the formal owner, it has, as a practical matter, very narrow powers which render it, in relation to the income concerned, a mere fiduciary or administrator acting on account of the interested parties.'

Thus, on this basis, beneficial ownership would not extend to cases where a person enters into contracts or takes obligations under which he or she has a similar function to those of a nominee or agent or to a conduit company if, although the formal owner of certain assets, it has very narrow powers which render it a mere fiduciary or an administrator acting on account of the interested parties. Both the commentary and the Conduit Company Report suggest that contracting states clarify this issue further if they so desire in the course of their negotiations. There is no such elaboration in the treaties examined in *Indofood* or in any UK Treaty other than that with Japan.[33] HMRC's view is:

'The Indofood decision, is now part of UK law. The decision is also likely to be of persuasive force where related issues for UK DTCs are being considered and that, where it is relevant, HM

---

[31] At para. 44.

[32] In particular, para. 14(b).

[33] See para. 25-750 below.

Revenue & Customs is obliged to follow it. Since the Court of Appeal decision is fully consistent with the UK's existing policy HM Revenue & Customs does not think that, in general, the case will have a significant impact on its current practice.[34]'

The case is not part of UK tax law and the meaning of beneficial ownership is to be taken from domestic law in the case of UK treaties. The High Court's analysis of the treaty language is more consistent with UK domestic law. The case does illustrate the importance of the actual circumstances of the case. Each court found different facts and their conclusions were, as a result, different.

Domestic law

The concept of beneficial ownership is not one that has been exhaustively considered in domestic tax law. The closest parallel is to be found in the Taxes Act 1988, s. 838(3), which prescribes that in the context of share ownership for a group and consortium purposes, ownership means beneficial ownership. However, s. 838 refers generally to ownership of shares, whereas arts. 10 to 12 of the OECD Model refer respectively to beneficial ownership of the dividend, interest or royalty in question. Section 838 does not in any event explain what beneficial ownership is. Domestic law provisions that deal with interest or royalties paid to non-residents do not explicitly refer to beneficial ownership. Where the UK is the source state, the rights in respect of which the income arises will normally be created by UK law. Thus, the underlying rights under the applicable domestic general law must be considered. The cases dealing with beneficial ownership for domestic tax purposes have all involved English law.

A number of cases have considered the question of beneficial ownership in the context of shares. In *Parway Estates Ltd v IRC*,[35] the taxpayer of the company agreed to sell the shares in a subsidiary but before completion of that sale to purchase the assets of the subsidiary. For stamp duty purposes (relief under s. 42 of FA 1930), beneficial ownership of the corporate group is required. The court concluded that where an unconditional sale is executed (of shares in that case), the subject matter of the contract becomes in equity the property of the purchaser. Jenkins LJ equated equitable and beneficial interest in the shares. He agreed with the views of Upjon J in the Chancery Division to the effect that the words 'beneficial owner' in s. 42 of FA 1930 must be construed in 'its ordinary or popular sense'. However, Jenkins LJ found it difficult to understand what an ordinary person would understand from the words 'beneficial owner' in their ordinary sense. He did not think that this had any difference from the legal meaning and effectively equated beneficial with equitable ownership.

In *English Sewing Cotton Company Ltd v IRC*,[36] the taxpayer was the owner of shares in a US company. On 21 July 1941, on the occasion of a loan by the US Government to the UK Government, an agreement was entered into between the American Reconstruction Finance Corporation, as representative of the US Government and the UK Government, under which

---

[34] HMRC, *INTM*, para. INTM332050.

[35] (1958) 45 TC 135.

[36] [1947] 1 All ER 679.

securities owned by persons or companies in Great Britain, including the common shares of the taxpayer's US subsidiary, were mortgaged to the corporation as security for the loan. The UK company argued that for the purposes of excess profits tax that it was not the beneficial owner of the US company. Lord Greene MR noted that there was no special meaning to be extracted from the specific legislation which would result in the words 'beneficial owner' having some meaning other than their ordinary meaning. The court found that the terms of the mortgage were those found in quite ordinary mortgages. It was clear that if the mortgage had been voluntarily given, beneficial ownership in the shares would have unquestionably have remained in the owners. They simply created a relationship of mortgagor and mortgagee. This did not deprive the mortgagor of beneficial ownership. The same was true in relation to an involuntary hypothecation. The impact of the law governing the rights in question was not raised in this case. The shares were in a US company, and there was no indication of the law governing the various arrangements.

In *Wood Preservation Ltd v Prior*,[37] it was held that where a parent company had contracted to sell shares in a subsidiary subject to a condition precedent solely for the benefit of the purchaser that beneficial ownership of the shares had passed to the purchaser even while the contract had remained conditional on the basis that the purchaser could waive the conditions. The case is more important, however, as an illustration of circumstances where beneficial ownership passes, rather than to explain the meaning of the term. The conclusions are, however, based on the application of equitable remedies and are thus by implication supportive of the view that beneficial ownership equates to equitable ownership.

The meaning of beneficial ownership of shares has been most extensively examined in *J Sainsbury plc v O'Connor*.[38] Again, despite lengthy analysis of numerous previous cases, the case is rather more important in describing the circumstances in which beneficial ownership exists rather than attempting any all embracing definition of the term. Clearly as a result of that case, beneficial ownership will not exist without equitable ownership. As Millett J said:[39]

'Beneficial ownership involves more than equitable ownership. It requires more than the ownership of an empty shell bereft of those rights of beneficial enjoyment which normally attach to equitable ownership.'

In the treaty shopping context, it may be worth noting his comments[40] to the effect that beneficial enjoyment of dividends is an important feature of beneficial ownership of shares. He also noted that the right to beneficial receipt of dividends which are declared must be distinguished from the right to cause them to be declared. Consequently, beneficial ownership has nothing to do with control. He noted that in the *Wood Preservation* case, what prevented the taxpayer from being beneficial owner of the shares pending fulfilment of the conditions was not its inability to cause dividends to be declared but its inability to do so for its own benefit. In the context of OECD Model wording, the question is likely to be: for whose benefit may dividends be declared?

---

[37] (1966-1969) 45 TC 112; [1968] 2 All ER 849.

[38] [1990] BTC 363; [1990] STC 516, Ch.D. and [1991] BTC 181; [1991] STC 318, CA.

[39] [1990] BTC 363 at 379; [1990] STC 516, at 530.

[40] At 531.

He also considered that it would be improper to substitute an economic test for a legal one and to confuse the existence of legal rights with their value. He stated that 'beneficial ownership has nothing to do with the value or economic attributes of ownership'. He argued that this was demonstrated by the need for the enactment of what is now the Taxes Act 1988, ss. 413(7) and 413(8).

This particular approach was not commented on by the Court of Appeal. While it is clear that value in the sense of a quantitative view of ownership would not determine beneficial ownership, entitlement to economic attributes is clearly relevant. The reasoning expressed in the Court of Appeal does not put an end to the relationship between beneficial and equitable owners. The Crown argued in that case that they were not the same thing. Although it is still unclear as to how they differ, Lloyd LJ declined to accept the argument of the Crown to form 'a balanced judgment' as to whether the ownership of shares by Sainsbury's was or was not beneficial. He was only prepared to say that where legal ownership was a mere shell, it is relatively easy to draw the inference as a matter of construction that Parliament could not have intended to confer the advantages of group relief. A similar conclusion is likely to result in relation to treaty provisions, although precisely where the dividing line is remains unclear.

Nourse LJ was of the view that beneficial ownership simply means ownership for one's own benefit as opposed to ownership as trustee for another. In his view, it ought not to be difficult to ascertain beneficial ownership, albeit that it may arise in a variety of ways. The question of beneficial ownership in the context of a loan was considered by the Court of Appeal in *Swiss Bank Corporation v Lloyds Bank Limited*.[41] An exchange control notice required Bank of England consent to be obtained to a transfer involving a change of beneficial ownership. In that case an equitable charge and the proprietary equitable interest thereby conferred did not constitute the person with whom the title documents in securities had been deposited as the 'beneficial owner' for that purpose.

In the context of treaty shopping, it may be possible to distinguish several different circumstances where beneficial ownership may be in issue. The first is in relation to dividends where a person other than the legal (registered) owner of the shares is not the beneficial owner by virtue of some contractual arrangement, declaration of trust or other arrangement considered in the cases above. Similarly, ownership may be split between capital beneficiaries (entitled to the proceeds of sale of a share) and income beneficiaries (entitled to the dividends). These cases all involve ownership of the underlying asset which gives rise to the income in question.

25-350 Other specific countermeasures

It was recognised by the Fiscal Affairs Committee in the Conduit Company Report that the fiscal domicile and beneficial ownership provisions may not always provide the requisite connection. That report set out a number of possible approaches that might be adopted in particular bilateral treaties. It also suggested that in the absence of specific safeguards, treaty

---

[41] [1990] 2 All ER 419.

benefits would have to be given even if they were considered to be improper.[42] Although the OECD had noted the growing tendency for the use of conduit companies to obtain treaty benefits not intended by contracting states, it refrained from drafting definitive texts of counter-measures. It also specifically avoided making any strict recommendations as to the circumstances in which such countermeasures should be applied. The OECD was of the view that in dealing with such countermeasures, the treaty negotiators should consider the degree to which tax advantages may actually be obtained by conduit companies, the legal context in both contracting states and the extent to which *bona fide* economic activities might be unintentionally covered by such provisions.

The UK Treaty negotiation appears to follow that OECD thinking on this issue in the sense that it has not sought to include a general anti-abuse or limitation on benefits clause into its treaties. A variety of anti-treaty shopping and limitation-on-benefit techniques are applied to specific items, in particular, treaties where abuse has been identified or feared. The 2003 amendments to the commentary expand the menu of options for contracting states wishing to limit treaty benefits, including model clauses based on the US Model Treaty, general limitation on benefits[43] and the UK purpose-based provisions.[44]

25-400   Subject-to-tax approach

The OECD suggests that treaty benefits may be restricted to circumstances only where the income in question is subject to tax in the state of residence. This is explained on the basis that the aim of treaties is to avoid double taxation. However, for a number of reasons, the OECD Model Convention does not recommend such a general provision. It should be restricted to typical conduit situations, rather than normal international tax relationships.

The use of the subject-to-tax approach in UK is to be found particularly in older treaties. It appears in relation to almost every item of income, such as dividends,[45] interest,[46] royalties,[47] capital gains[48] and personal services.[49] Rules in relation to income and gains taxable on the remittance basis may be viewed as falling into this category.[50]

The distinction between taxed and subject to tax is made clear by HMRC.[51] For example, a person is subject to tax if:

---

[42] At para. 43.

[43] Commentary on art. 1, para. 20.

[44] Commentary on art. 1, para. 21.4; see para. 25-600 below.

[45] UK–Antigua Treaty, art. 6.

[46] UK–Oman Treaty, art. 11(1).

[47] UK–Grenada Treaty, art. 7.

[48] UK–Israel Treaty, art. 8A(4).

[49] UK–Greece Treaty, art. 9.

[50] See chapter 12, para. 21-250.

[51] HMRC, *Double Taxation Relief Manual*, para. 802.

- he or she does not pay UK tax because his or her income is covered by personal allowances or reliefs; or
- income is wholly covered by capital allowances.

The subject-to-tax approach is something of a blunt instrument. It is an 'all or nothing' policy. Thus, an item subject to a very low rate of tax in the residence country may qualify for a large exemption in the source country. Where the item is not taxed in the residence country, it may nonetheless be subject to a high rate of tax in the source country. The switch from a credit to an exemption method of relieving double taxation, as is proposed for the UK,[52] will also produce surprising results. A dividend received by a UK company that is exempt from tax in UK will not qualify for a reduction in withholding tax in the source country. Since no relief is given for either underlying tax or withholding tax on the dividend, the effective rate of tax may be increased as a result of the exemption.

25-450   Exclusion of tax-favoured entities

Another commonly used device is to exclude specific types of companies that enjoy tax privileges in their state of residence. Over 15 treaties contain provisions excluding certain entities from claiming treaty benefits. They focus on entities intended to be foreign-held and exempt from tax either generally or on foreign income. There are four basic forms of clause designed to exclude tax favoured entities, and they are described below.

The Caribbean formula

Article 23 of the Barbados Treaty is a typical example. It excludes from all treaty benefits 'companies entitled to any special tax benefit under the Barbados International Companies (Exemption from Tax) Act 1965 as in effect on July 26, 1965 or any substantially similar law enacted by Barbados after that date'. Similar clauses are found in the treaties with Antigua and Barbuda, and Jamaica. All refer to specific incentive legislation which permits foreign owned companies to either be exempt or enjoy minimal local tax.

The Cypriot formula

Article 24A of the Cypriot Treaty contains a unique limitation rule. Although it refers to tax favoured entities in Cyprus, the limitations only apply in relation to dividends, interest and royalties. In addition, individuals resident in Cyprus who are not Cypriot citizens and enjoy a beneficial tax treatment in Cyprus are also excluded, while the rate of tax charged on them is less than normal Cyprus income tax rates. A *de minimis* exception permits treaty benefits for such individuals on the first £1,500 sterling of UK source income in a year of assessment.

The Channel Islands formula

Amendments were made to the arrangements with each of Guernsey, Jersey and the Isle of Man to take into account new tax favoured entities in each of those jurisdictions. In each case, all treaty benefits are excluded in the case of persons assessed in accordance with or

---

[52] See chapter 14.

who are exempt from assessment by virtue of the incentive legislation unless the person is assessed on the whole of the income or profits at less than the standard rate imposed in that jurisdiction generally.

Article 23 of the Maltese Treaty is somewhat similar. Treaty benefits are not available to companies entitled to benefits under the Malta International Business Activities Act 1988 except those who elect to be subject to the normal provisions of income tax. This option is not available, however, to shipping companies claiming special benefits under the Maltese Merchant Shipping Act 1973.

The CIS formula

A new form of limitation of benefits clause was introduced by the UK in its treaties with the former members of the Soviet Union. For example, art. 23(2) of the Azerbaijan Treaty reads:

> 'A resident of a contracting state who as a consequence of domestic law concerning incentives to promote foreign investment is not subject to tax or is subject to tax at a reduced rate in the contracting state on income or capital gains shall not receive the benefit of any reduction in or exemption from tax provided for in this convention by the other contracting state if the main purpose or one of the main purposes of such resident or a person connected with such resident was to obtain the benefits of this convention.'

Identical provisions are found in the treaties with Belarus, Estonia, Kazakhstan, Latvia, Mongolia, Russia, Ukraine and Uzbekistan. The purpose test is not included in the Russian and Ukrainian treaties.

The precise intent or effect of this clause is not entirely clear. In the case of Estonia and Latvia, exchanges of notes indicate that incentives to promote foreign investment should not be interpreted as including incentives promoting only domestic investment. It is not clear from this clause whether it applies to outward bound investment from either of the contracting states or whether it is intended to cover inward bound investment from outside the contracting states or both. In addition, (apart from Russia and Ukraine) the limitation only applies where one of the main purposes of the resident or a connected person is to obtain the treaty benefits. The motivation in seeking to introduce such a clause is perhaps prophylactic. The tax systems of these countries were very undeveloped at the time the treaties were negotiated and such a clause might assist in limiting benefits if some form of entity which facilitates treaty shopping were to be established under the domestic laws of any of these countries. There was no similar provision in the 1985 treaty with the Soviet Union, and similar clauses have not appeared in other treaties negotiated at around the same time with developing country treaties, such as those with Bolivia and Vietnam.

In a number of cases the exclusion of tax favoured entities has been included by protocol negotiated specifically to deal with that issue. Domestic law in contracting states can clearly be changed more quickly than a treaty renegotiated. Thus, there may be a period during which tax-favoured entities do qualify for treaty benefits. It is perhaps for this reason that HMRC has sought to include the CIS clause even though it may not be entirely effective at eliminating the mischief that it was apparently seeking to prevent. A slightly different approach is seen in relation to Malaysia. For example, companies established in the Labuan tax haven of Malaysia were excluded from treaty benefits under the 1973 treaty. They continue to be excluded under the new treaty. The mechanism has changed, however. The treaty now provides in art. 25(2) for treaty benefits to be denied to persons entitled to any special tax benefit under the law of either contracting state which is identified by exchange of notes. This change in legislative strategy will no doubt enable the tax authorities to easily add to or amend the list of disqualified persons. How far they may be able to go in using such a technique to prevent treaty shopping is unclear.

The OECD commentary relating to residence suggests the use of exchange of information in order to determine the eligibility of entities for treaty benefits. The provisions, which include ineligible entities from treaty benefits, do not exclude the authorisation of exchanges of information or recourse to mutual agreement procedure.

25-500   Channel approach

The channel approach involves a specific and straightforward identification of cases regarded as improper use of a treaty in the treaty itself. No UK treaties adopted this approach until the 2001 UK–US Treaty. Article 11(7) (Interest), art. 12(5) (Royalties) and art. 22(4) (Other income) of the US Treaty (2001) do not apply the benefits of those respective articles in relation to payments made 'under or as part of a conduit arrangement'.[53] A conduit arrangement is defined in art. 3(1)(n) of the treaty to mean the following:

'A transaction or series of transactions:

(1)   which is structured in such a way that a resident of a Contracting State entitled to the benefits of this Convention receives an item of income arising in the other Contracting State but that resident pays, directly or indirectly, all or substantially all of that income (at any time or in any form) to another person who is not a resident of either Contracting State and who, if it received that item of income direct from the other Contracting State, would not be entitled under a convention for the avoidance of double taxation between the state in which that other person is resident and the Contracting State in which the income arises, or otherwise, to benefits with respect to that item of income which are equivalent to, or more favourable than, those available under this Convention to a resident of a Contracting State; and

(2)   which has as its main purpose, or one of its main purposes, obtaining such increased benefits as are available under this Convention.'

Unlike other anti-avoidance measures found in UK treaties, which are expressed in more general terms, this is specifically targeted at treaty shopping. In order to constitute a conduit arrangement, all or substantially all of the income must be paid to a person who is not a resident of either contracting state. The test also retains features of other approaches, namely, the look-through approach and a purpose test.[54]

---

[53] See also the UK–Switzerland Treaty, art. 3(1)(l), inserted by Protocol of 26 June 2007 in relation to royalties and interest.

[54] See HMRC, *Tax Bulletin*, special edition on UK/US Double Taxation Agreement (1 April 2003).

25-550   *Bona fide* provisions

The UK has made extensive use of *bona fide* provisions in treaties for a number of years. The precise wording of the clause has varied over the years. The Conduit Company Report recognised that configurations reflecting treaty shopping structures occur in many normal transactions of enterprises operating internationally. Therefore, it recommended that provisions be included to ensure that treaty benefits are granted in *bona fide* cases. None of the *bona fide* articles found in UK treaties follow the suggested *bona fide* wording in the Conduit Company Report. Rather, they draw on domestic anti-avoidance legislative models.

The most common form of limitation of benefits articles reflecting the *bona fide* approach has generally read:

> 'The provisions of this article shall not apply if the [debt claim] in respect of which the [interest] is paid was created or assigned mainly for the purposes of taking advantage of this article and not for bona fide commercial reasons.'

Clauses of this kind started to appear in the late 1960s and are to be found in numerous interest and royalty articles.

These articles comprise two related tests. The first aim is to deny a treaty benefit where the debt claim, in the case of interest, or a right or property in the case of royalties, is created or assigned to take advantage of the treaty benefit. This wording is similar to that found in domestic anti-avoidance provisions, particularly the Taxes Act 1988, s. 787. In order to apply, the main purpose of the creation or assignment of the right must be the treaty benefit. This is similar to s. 787, which applies only where the sole or main benefit is a reduction in tax liability by means of relief in respect of interest paid. The second test is that the creation or assignment of the rights in question must not be for *bona fide* commercial reasons. It will be necessary for a treaty claimant to satisfy both of the tests in order to qualify for the benefit.[55]

Clauses of this variety appear in some 20 treaties, starting with Germany (1967) and ending with Iceland (1991), despite minor differences in formulation of these provisions. Although the courts have yet to consider these treaty provisions, similar concepts in domestic anti-avoidance rules do give some guidance as to how they might be viewed by the courts. It is far from clear precisely what a 'bona fide commercial transaction' is. In the Court of Appeal, Morritt LJ noted in the context of the defence to the Taxes Act 1988, s. 739, under s. 741(b), that the terms 'bona fide commercial transactions' and 'not designed' for the purpose of tax avoidance could give rise to considerable differences on construction, as had appeared from argument in that case. He declined to consider the issue, as it was not necessary for the purpose of the case.[56]

Other cases involving *bona fide* commercial transactions under the Taxes Act 1988, s. 703, and its predecessors have similarly not sought to define the expression 'bona fide

---

[55] *Hasloch v IRC* (1971) 47 TC 50, a case under the ICTA 1988, s. 703.

[56] *IRC v Willoughby* [1995] BTC 144; [1995] STC 143, CA at 184.

commercial reason'. In *CIR v Brebner*,[57] it was held that determining whether the object of a transaction was a *bona fide* commercial one and that none of the main objects was to gain tax advantages were purely questions of fact. It was therefore for the Special Commissioners to decide upon a consideration of all the relevant evidence before them and the proper inferences to be drawn from that evidence. In the House of Lords, Lord Pearce noted that the object which must be considered is a subjective matter of intention. In the case of a company, this is determined by the directors who govern its policies or the shareholders who are concerned in and vote in favour of the resolution to follow a particular course of action. The purpose of the transaction is therefore a subjective matter determined from the intentions and acts of various members of the group. It may not be narrowed down to a company's objects. It had been argued in that case that a company, being indifferent as to how its assets were distributed, could not have a *bona fide* commercial reason or any reason other than a tax advantage.

A distinction was also drawn between the object of a transaction and ancillary result of that object. If the result was a tax advantage then s. 703 would not apply. In that case, the court considered that it was improper to isolate individual parts of interrelated transactions. It was necessary to consider the main object or objects for which any of them was adopted rather than the effect of each or all of the interrelated transactions.

Most s. 703 circumstances deal with more than one transaction. Treaty bona fide articles, however, focus on only a single transaction in each case. It is necessary to consider only whether the creation or assignment of the rights in question is effected for the purpose of taking advantage of the relevant treaty provision. Consequently, related transactions may only be viewed as part of the evidence in determining whether the relevant transaction has as its main purpose taking advantage of the relevant article.

Lord Upjohn also articulated one of the major difficulties in successfully applying anti-avoidance provisions. He observed[58] that to determine whether a genuine commercial transaction is carried out, there are two ways: one is by paying the maximum amount of tax and the other is by paying no or less tax; as a necessary consequence, it is wrong to draw the inference that in choosing the tax favoured route that one of the main objects, for the purpose of the anti-avoidance provision, is the avoidance of tax. This has been cited frequently in avoidance cases. In the treaty shopping context, this view will impose significant restrictions on successful application of the rules, at least where taxpayers do have a choice. For example, where a non-UK multinational group has subsidiaries in several countries, that an investment into the UK is routed through one which has the most favourable treaty provision will not in itself necessarily infer that the purpose of the creation of the right in question was to gain treaty benefits. In other cases, such as *IRC v Goodwin*,[59] and *Sema Group Pension Scheme Trustees v Inland Revenue Commissioners*,[60] the courts

---

[57] (1966) 43 TC 705, HL. Recent applications include *Snell v R & C Commrs* (2006) Sp C 532 in relation to TCGA 1992, s. 137, paras. 3 and 17; *Snell v R & C Commrs* (2008) Sp C 699 in relation to ICTA 1988, s. 703, para. 21. In each case, the transactions were regarded as *bona fide* but the taxpayers failed to demonstrate that they were not for the purpose of avoiding tax.

[58] At 718.

[59] (1971-1977) 50 TC 583; [1976] STC 28, HL.

[60] [2003] BTC 106 [2002] EWCA Civ 1857.

have similarly either found or not found *bona fide* commercial transactions without analysing the meaning of the words.

The treaty provision is silent as to whose intention is relevant in applying the test. In the *Brebner* case[61] it was clear that it was the intentions of the directors and shareholders of the company who were involved in the transaction that were relevant. However, in *Addy v IRC*,[62] it was held that the test must be applied to those in control of the company in question. Like the concept of beneficial ownership, the courts seem to be able to spot a *bona fide* commercial reason when they see one, although they have some difficulty in describing precisely what the concept embraces.

In *Clark v IRC*,[63] one of the issues that arose was whether the transaction was carried out for 'commercial reasons'. It was not disputed that the transaction in question was 'in every respect bona fide'.[64] This seems to imply that there are two elements of the test, one that it be *bona fide* and, additionally, that it be for commercial reasons; this contrasts with the definition of *bona fide* as qualifying the nature of the commercial reasons. In that case, the Special Commissioners had decided that the commercial reason had to be connected with the vendors' interests in the companies concerned in or affected by the transaction.

However, on appeal Fox J regarded this too narrow an approach. In his view, s. 703 does not contain such a qualification. It merely requires that the transaction be carried out for *bona fide* commercial reasons. That language is entirely at large, and if the taxpayer can prove that the transaction was carried out for *bona fide* commercial reasons, he or she satisfies the requirement of that section.

Carried out in this sense, means carried out by the taxpayer. He went on to rule that the sole question is the nature of the reason for which the transaction was carried out. There is no requirement of nexus with particular parties affected by it or in some way concerned in the transaction.

Section 703 is distinguishable from most formulations of this treaty provision in that the s. 703(1) escape clause includes both transactions carried out for *bona fide* commercial reasons or 'in the ordinary course of making or managing investments'. Only a few treaties contain this wording. They are those with Belgium, Italy, Luxembourg, Norway and Switzerland, and then only in the context of dividends and repayment of the tax credit.

These treaties required the non-UK-resident shareholder claiming the repayment of a credit to show that the shareholding was acquired for *bona fide* commercial reasons. The alternative test, namely, that the share was acquired in the ordinary course of making or managing investments, is not found in any other similar limitation of benefits provision. The non-UK-resident shareholder must also demonstrate that it was not the main object, nor one

---

[61] See above, n. 26.

[62] (1973-1978) 51 TC 71; [1975] STC 610, Ch.D.

[63] (1976-1980) 52 TC 482; [1978] STC 614.

[64] At 624.

of the main objects of the acquisition of shares, to obtain entitlement to repayment of the credit. These provisions were first introduced into the Swiss Treaty by Protocol in 1982. Furthermore, it was the first time that the purpose test was extended to disqualify a payment if one or more of the objects of the transaction was the treaty benefit as compared with where the sole object of the transaction was the benefit (see below).

In *Clark v IRC*, the court found that in the case of one taxpayer, the anti-avoidance provisions did not apply because, looking at the transaction in the context of all of the circumstances, it was for *bona fide* commercial reasons. The overall purpose of the transaction was to purchase a farm adjoining the one that he already owned, and there were good commercial reasons for doing so. The specific transaction which the Special Commissioners had concluded had no commercial reason were simply to finance that purchase. The court rejected the argument of the Crown that the commercial reasons must be intrinsic to the transaction. Instead, the matter must be considered in the context of all the relevant facts and not merely as a part of them.

In that case, another taxpayer was found not to have carried out the transaction for *bona fide* commercial reasons. No commercial reasons entered into his thinking. He was held, however, to have carried out the transactions in the ordinary course of managing investments since he believed that the value of his investment would be threatened, and he accordingly joined in the transaction. The Commissioners ruled that although his transaction was not in the course of making investments, it was in the ordinary course of managing investments. He adopted the most favourable way open to him to protect his investment. This, the Commissioners said, 'is what any prudent investor would do in the ordinary course of managing investments'.

Does the presence of the alternative defence of transactions carried out in the ordinary course of making or managing investments in these treaties mean that in other treaties where only the *bona fide* commercial transaction defence is found, treaty benefits may be denied (because the purpose of the transaction is in the nature of 'investment' rather than 'commercial')? In the Italy and Norway treaties, both defences are found in the dividend articles. The Italy Treaty contains only a commercial reasons defence in relation to interest, while the Norway Treaty contains the commercial reasons defence only in relation to interest and royalties. This issue is not addressed directly in the Conduit Company Report, which refers generally to '*bona fide* transactions'. The examples cited in the report, however, refer to a commercial context in the sense of normal transactions of enterprises operating internationally.

In *IRC v Willoughby*,[65] the Court of Appeal considered the nature of the defences to the application of the anti-avoidance provisions of the Taxes Act 1988, s. 739, contained in s. 741(b). That clause only provides exemption for *bona fide* commercial transactions and makes no reference to the making or managing of investments. The Special Commissioner found that the transfers and associated operations were *bona fide* commercial transactions. Investment in an off-shore single premium personal portfolio bond in order to make provision for a pension by an individual was viewed as a commercial transaction. They were

---

[65] [1995] BTC 144; [1995] STC 143, CA.

designed for the increase of Professor Willoughby's retirement funds taking advantage of a favourable tax regime.

In the Court of Appeal, the Crown argued in relation to s. 741(b) that for a transaction to be commercial, it must be carried out as part of the trade or commerce of both parties. The taxpayer argued that the transfer and associated operations were *bona fide* commercial transactions because they were genuine, for value and at arm's length. Although the decision on s. 741 rested on the application of s. 741(a) (that is, that the transactions were not for the purpose of avoiding tax), Morritt LJ quoted Lord Upjohn in the *Brebner* case in support of his conclusion:

> 'No commercial man in his senses is going to carry out a commercial transaction except upon the footing of paying the smallest amount of tax that he can.'

This seems to suggest a close connection between the two defences. Thus, although the relationship between the two defences remains undefined, the dividing line, if there is one, is likely to be very fine. The same words can mean different things in different parts of the same treaty[66] and thus arguably, the same words may have different meanings in different treaties. A conclusion that both defences meant the same thing in these treaties would of course render the additional wording where it appears otiose. The position is far from clear.

In *Marwood Homes Limited v IRC*,[67] a separation of the two consequences was agreed by the parties. They agreed that for the purposes of s. 703(1), the transactions were not carried out in the ordinary course of making or managing investments. Consequently, the issue to be decided was whether the transactions were carried out for *bona fide* commercial reasons (and that none of the transactions had as their main object or one of their main objects to enable tax advantages to be obtained). The Special Commissioners concluded on the evidence that there was a *bona fide* commercial reason for the transaction. If the directors of the company in question were of the view that the transaction was important for the future prosperity of the business of the company and the group, it could be said that the transaction was carried out for *bona fide* commercial purposes. To determine this, it is necessary to look at the overall position to see what was done for good commercial reasons.

If HMRC seeks to maintain the distinction between the two types of defence in treaties, as argued in the *Willoughby* case, and is successful, the result may be that these clauses will impose significant limitations on the availability of benefits in the treaty articles which do not include the defence in relation to the making of investments. This is because to succeed a taxpayer will have to satisfy both limbs of the test. A non-resident who cannot show both that the source of income in question was not created or assigned mainly for the purpose of taking advantage of the article in question and the existence of *bona fide* commercial reasons will not be entitled to treaty benefits. This would restrict treaty claims only to those claimants engaged in trade or commerce. This would appear to go far beyond the suggestions of the OECD in the Conduit Company Report and on a purposive interpretation, contrary to the general objective of treaties in avoiding double taxation.

---

[66] *IRC v Exxon Corp* [1982] BTC 182; [1982] STC 356; *Memec plc v IRC* [1998] BTC 251; [1998] STC 754, CA.

[67] (1996) Sp C 106; [1997] STC (SCD) 37.

Other interesting comments on the nature of *bona fide* commercial transactions were made in the *Willoughby* case.[68] In particular, a letter from the Inland Revenue to Royal Life (the issuers of the off-shore bond) conceded that the personal portfolio bonds were *bona fide* commercial transactions. The Special Commissioners concluded that in the absence of any reason for impeaching the good faith of either party thereto, it must be a *bona fide* commercial transaction for the purchaser as well. This conclusion was quoted by the Court of Appeal without comment.

If the *bona fide* clause is indeed similar to the Taxes Act 1988, s. 787, then the Inland Revenue may itself have doubts about its effectiveness. The clause is briefly referred to without comment by the Revenue.[69] The *International Tax Handbook* also notes at para. 721 that it is common for parent companies to borrow to fund their subsidiaries, and that in such cases it is difficult to distinguish between routing for tax and purely commercial purposes. At para. 1149, it states that the usefulness of s. 787 is somewhat circumscribed. It is not easily invoked and should only be used for out and out avoidance schemes and not 'judiciously arranged borrowing'.

As a rule, *bona fide* provisions have not been inserted in dividend articles in order to prevent treaty shopping in respect of the repayment of tax credits in relation to dividends paid by UK companies to shareholders in treaty countries. A number of treaties, however, have a limitation-of-benefits provision to prohibit tax credit stripping in relation to dividends earned out of profits by a UK company more than 12 months before a company resident in a treaty country became a 10 per cent owner in the paying UK company. These clauses are typically excluded if it can be shown that the shares were acquired not for the purpose of securing the benefit of the repayment and for *bona fide* commercial reasons. These clauses do not serve any wider anti-treaty shopping purpose.

25-600 Purpose provisions

There have been no cases on the *bona fide* provisions. The Revenue, perhaps believing that it was not achieving what it had hoped, abandoned the *bona fide* wording for the first time in the 1991 Papua New Guinea Treaty.

A wholly new approach emerged in 1992, as reflected in the Guyana Treaty. The now standard provisions found in relation to dividends, interest, royalties and 'other income' typically reads:

'The provisions of this Article shall not apply if it was the main purpose, or one of the main purposes, of any person concerned with the creation or assignment of the rights in respect of which the income is paid to take advantage of this Article by means of that creation or assignment.'

Several observations are appropriate. First, the *bona fide* test was dropped. Second, the purpose test was amended so that it would apply if 'the main purpose or one of the main

---

[68] See above, n. 65.

[69] HMRC, *International Tax Handbook*, para. 709.

purposes' of the creation or assignment of the rights in question was to take advantage of the treaty benefits. This approach echoes wording used in most domestic anti-avoidance provisions, which apply not only where the sole purpose is securing a tax advantage or tax avoidance, but also where merely one of the main purposes is to secure such an advantage. The third change is the identification of the person whose purpose it is to take advantage of the treaty benefits. The new rule applies if it was the purpose of 'any person concerned with the creation or assignment' of the rights in question.

Several issues arise out of this new wording. First, by analogy to the s. 703 cases, the courts have identified a number of persons whose intentions are relevant. If the intentions of the controlling shareholders of a company resident in a contracting state go to making up the purpose for which that company enters into a transaction, does this new wording usefully add anyone not already covered? Second, one of the important issues in the treaty shopping context is whether the intention of a person in a third country would be relevant for this purpose. The difficulty arises out of reading this provision in conjunction with art. 1 of the OECD Model. Article 1 states that 'the convention applies to persons who are residents of one or both of the contracting states'. The plain meaning of the words would seem to suggest that in applying the treaty, any person refers to a person who is a subject of the treaty rather than a resident of a third country. Article 24(1) of the OECD Model shows that express wording is normally required to apply the treaty to persons who are non-residents of both contracting states. On the other hand, the courts have departed from the plain meaning of words in a treaty and adopted different meanings for the same word in different parts of the treaty in *IRC v Exxon*.[70] In that case, the court adopted a different construction of the meaning of resident so that the purpose of the provision in question did not fail in effect. The use of the word 'concerned' may be indicative of a broad intention to cover any person interested, involved or affected.[71]

A further unanswered question is how the drafters of these provisions intended to distinguish the new wording from the earlier form which did not explicitly seek to identify the person whose purpose was relevant in determining the application of the treaty. If the revised wording extends the object to persons unconnected with the taxpayer or residents, of third countries, that may mean that under the earlier *bona fide* provisions, the intentions of a narrower class of persons only are relevant.

Fourth, advantage of the article must be taken 'by means of the creation or assignment' of the rights in question.

At a meeting between representatives of certain professional bodies and the Inland Revenue in May 1994,[72] the Revenue confirmed that the form of anti-treaty shopping article contained in the Guyana Treaty represented the latest thinking on the form of such articles

---

[70] [1982] BTC 182; [1982] STC 356, Ch.D.

[71] See the *Shorter Oxford English Dictionary*, 6th edn (2002), Oxford University Press.

[72] ICAEW Technical Tax Release (Tax 16/94).

and would be the version which it sought to obtain in future negotiations. It has been used consistently since then, and the OECD adopted the language into the Commentary in 2003.[73]

A further significant change in treaty policy on limitation of benefits also took place in the mid-1990s. Until then, these provisions appeared, particularly in interest and royalty articles, in an unsystematic manner. There are some treaties where they do not appear at all and others where they may be restricted, usually to interest articles. Occasionally and more recently, these provisions are also found in clauses relating to management and technical and service fees, presumably at the instance of those governments seeking to follow the UN Model in distinguishing such fees from royalties. Presumably, the inclusion of these provisions in this manner reflected a policy of the Revenue to only seek their inclusion specifically where it believed that a real risk of treaty abuse was an issue. All the most recent treaties now include this provision systematically in all interest and royalty articles without any particular indication as to whether there is perceived to be a real threat of treaty abuse or not. A further development in the more recent treaties has been to seek to include a clause along these lines in the 'other income' article. This appeared for the first time in 1994 in treaties with Kazakhstan and Mexico. It now appears to have become standard practice in later treaties. No reason for this has been given, although it may be as a result of the fact that derivative financial instruments, which can replicate dividends and interests, are normally governed by the 'other income' article. Success in negotiating the inclusion of the provision is uneven. For example, in the Argentina Treaty, this rule is contained in the dividend, interest, royalty and other income articles. In the Singapore Treaty, it does not appear in the 'other income' article.

25-650   Look-through rules

One solution suggested by the OECD is directed at disallowing treaty benefits to a company if it is not owned directly or indirectly by residents of the state in which the company itself is resident. It suggests that this approach may be adequate for treaties with countries which have no or very low taxation and where little substantive business activities would normally be carried on.

A variation of the look-through theory is to exclude companies resident in a contracting state from benefits under a treaty if the company is owned or controlled by residents of a third country who themselves would not qualify for similar treaty benefits.

The OECD acknowledges that the use of look-through provisions is the most radical solution to the problem of conduit companies. The UK has made very limited use of look-through rules.[74] The Icelandic Treaty has such a rule in relation to dividends in art. 10(1)(d) and for interest in art. 11(7) to (9), as well as art. 12(6) to (8), in respect of royalties. The basic structure is similar in all cases. The interest rule in art. 11 reads:

---

[73] Commentary to art. 1, para. 21.4.

[74] One of the first such provisions was art. 10(3)(d) of the 1981 Netherlands Treaty. This treaty was one of the early treaties granting repayment of the tax credit under art. 10(3). The Netherlands was traditionally the major location for conduit companies in relation to reducing source country taxation on dividends. Only three treaties contain classic look-through rules. It is now of historical interest only, since tax credits are no longer repaid.

'11(7) The provisions of paragraph (1) of this Article shall not apply where owner of the interest is a company other than a quoted company, unless the con that it is not controlled by a person, or two or more associated or connected person who or any of whom would not have been entitled to relief under paragraph (1) of the if he had been the beneficial owner of the interest.'

In the case of companies, treaty benefits are denied unless the company concerned satisfies one of two tests:

(1)   Its shares must be officially quoted on a stock exchange in the respective country of residence.[75]

(2)   It can show that they are not controlled by persons who themselves are not entitled to the treaty benefit. If it is controlled by two or more associated or connected persons together, none of those persons would be excluded from the treaty benefit.

For this purpose, a person or two or more associated or connected persons together are treated as having control of a company if, under the laws of the state in which the interest arises, they could be treated as having control of it for any purpose. Similarly, persons are treated as associated or connected if, under those laws, they could be so treated for any purpose.[76] Thus, the widest definition of control or association under the law of the state of source will determine the meaning of these expressions. Where an individual who holds no more than 10 per cent of the total number of shares in a company is treated as having control of it by reason only of the fact that he or she holds ordinary shares in the company carrying full voting and dividend rights, the shares held by him or her are left out of account in determining control except that no more than 25 per cent of the total of such shares in the company may be left out of account in this way.

Treaty benefits are only available if the relevant beneficial owners are themselves able to take advantage of the treaty benefits relating to those items of income under the particular treaty article in question. Therefore, in effect, the elimination of UK tax on interest payments made to unquoted Icelandic companies will only apply where those companies are themselves controlled by residents of Iceland.

These clauses highlight the difficulties identified by the OECD in the Conduit Company Report relating to the use of look-through approach. The report suggests that such provisions are incompatible with the principal of the legal status of corporate bodies as recognised in the legal systems of all OECD member countries, and except in the case of abuse in the OECD Model. The report notes that machinery to apply the clause needs to be simple and secure and that this may require a shift in the burden of proof. In all of these clauses, the burden of demonstrating entitlement to treaty benefits is placed clearly on the claimant. The claimant is required not only to demonstrate *prima facie* entitlement, but also to demonstrate at the same time that the claim does not fall foul of the limitations imposed by the terms of the article.

[75]   Art. 11(8)(a).

[76]   Art. 11(8)(b).

The Conduit Company Report also noted that such provisions require extensive *bona fide* amplifications. None of these provisions in UK treaties contain exceptions in respect of *bona fide* commercial transactions. The severity of the rule is illustrated by the decision of the High Court in *Steele v European Vinyls Corp (Holdings) BV*[77]

A limited exception for minority shareholdings by individuals is contained in art. 11(9). Where an individual is treated as having control of a company only by reason of the fact that he or she holds ordinary shares in the company carrying full voting and dividend rights, the shares held by him or her may be left out of account in determining whether the company is controlled by qualifying persons – if that individual holds not more than 10 per cent of the total number of shares in the company. In addition, no more than 25 per cent of the total of such shares in the company may be excluded on this basis.

This exclusion from the limitation of benefits rules is narrow in scope. Furthermore, disqualification applies to a person, or two or more associated or connected persons, who would not have been entitled to the treaty benefit in question if he or she, or they, controlled the Icelandic company. Control for this purpose means control for any purpose of UK tax law. One of the circumstances in which these provisions have significant impact is where there are a number of shareholders, one or more of whom is not entitled to treaty benefits, as illustrated in the *Euro Vinyls* case. There, the very wide application of the meaning of control and of connection resulting from the provisions of a shareholders agreement excluded the Dutch company in question from treaty benefits as a result of a small holding by an Italian company, which itself was not entitled to a tax credit.

In recommending the look-through approach, the Conduit Company Report regards such rules as relatively simple and straightforward. While the success in limiting treaty benefits for third country residents as illustrated in the *Euro Vinyls* case is possible, it clearly does not apply in all circumstances. In addition, it may still not entirely eliminate treaty shopping, except by use of the most stringent tests, such as those found in the Danish Treaty. This would also have adverse effects in non-tax avoidance circumstances. At a meeting in May 1996 between representatives of certain professional bodies and the Inland Revenue,[78] the Revenue announced that discussions had taken place on the anti-abuse provisions in the interest and royalty articles in the Denmark and Iceland treaties. The Revenue confirmed at that meeting that the particular wording is not in any other treaty currently being negotiated. It would have appeared that the look-through approach was likely to be consigned to the history books of UK treaty policy, until the signing of the US Treaty (2001).

25-700   US Treaty (2001)

The US has gone to extraordinary lengths in drafting a 'foolproof' look-through limitation of benefits provision contained in art. 26 of its Model Treaty. The UK agreed to the inclusion of a modified form of this clause in the 2001 treaty signed on 24 July 2001. In addition to the adoption of a look-through approach, the treaty departs from existing UK treaty policy

---

[77] [1995] BTC 32; [1995] STC 31, Ch.D.; [1996] BTC 425; [1996] STC 785, CA. See para. 25-750 below.

[78] ICAEW Technical Tax Release (Tax 14/96).

by applying to benefits under the treaty generally. Unlike other treaties, where limitations of benefits apply to specific articles only and are targeted at specific abuses, art. 23(1) of the US Treaty only grants benefits to residents of a contracting state who are 'qualified persons'. The article is lengthy and complex. The main categories of qualifying residents are:[79]

- individuals;
- certain governmental entities;
- certain unit trusts;
- certain companies,
    - with shares listed on a recognised Stock Exchange;
    - which are direct or indirect subsidiaries owned through a chain of resident companies; or
    - which are principally owned by 'equivalent beneficiaries' and less than half the company's gross income is deductible on payment to non-equivalent beneficiaries (Equivalent beneficiaries are essentially residents of the EU, the EEA or North American Free Trade Area, where there are broadly equivalent limitations of benefit rules and comparable treaty benefits under a treaty with the source state.);[80]
- pension plans principally for the benefit of resident individuals; and
- certain trusts where the beneficiaries are qualifying residents or equivalent beneficiaries.

Treaty benefits may, however, be granted to a resident who is not otherwise entitled to benefits if the competent authority determines that the establishment, acquisition or maintenance of such resident, and the conduct of its operations, did not have as one of its principal purposes the obtaining of benefits under the treaty.[81]

This style of limitation is now included among the options in the OECD commentary.[82] A comprehensive look-through provision patterned on the US Model also appears in the UK–Japan Treaty.[83] Only a resident of a state that meets the requirements of art. 22 qualifies for benefits under art. 7 (Business profits) arts. 12 (Royalties), 13 (Capital gains) or 21 (Other income), and the zero rate on tax on dividends (art. 10(3)) and interest (art. 10(3)).

25-750   Other approaches

Article 11(6) of the former Japanese Treaty (1969) contained a unique limitation clause as far as UK treaties are concerned. It simply stated that in the context of dividends, relief from tax of a contracting state was subject to the same limitations as those imposed in respect of relief or exemption from tax under the laws of the contracting state by any provision enacted in order to maintain the proper incidence of liability to tax and to prevent the obtaining of undue tax advantages. The article was particularly curious because the treaty applied a *bona*

---

[79] Art. 23(2).

[80] Art. 23(7)(d).

[81] Art. 23(6).

[82] Commentary to art. 1, para. 20.

[83] Art. 22.

fide provision of the kind described above in the case of interest and royalties. The effect of art. 11(6) was to preserve domestic anti-avoidance enactments such as the Taxes Act 1988, s. 703. The current treaty (2006) prefers to place reliance on the limitations on benefits set out in the treaty itself.

The UK–Australia Treaty contains unusual provisions addressing the application of domestic anti-avoidance legislation. Article 25(6) saves certain domestic rules from the non-discrimination article.[84]

25-800   Procedural methods

The UK has recently attempted to use procedural rules in order to combat avoidance. An exchange of notes in connection with the amending protocol of 15 October 1996 to the treaty with Denmark contains an unusual arrangement. The arrangement states that where a contracting state seeks to invoke the anti-avoidance provisions relating to dividends, interest or royalties, it should notify the other contracting state of that. This curious provision is also found in other more recent treaties, such as those with Singapore. Article 11(10) of the Singapore Treaty, for example, reads as follows:

> 'In the event that a resident of a contracting state is denied relief from taxation in the other contracting state by reason of the provisions of paragraph (9) of this Article, the competent authority of that other contracting state shall notify the competent authority of the first mentioned contracting state.'

The treaties where this wording has appeared all contain exchange of information provisions to cover this in any event. Why then is this wording inserted into these treaties? No public explanation of it has been given by HMRC to date. The reason is therefore a matter of speculation. It may be simply viewed as a warning to those who might use the treaty in a manner that one tax authority regards as impermissible, that this will not remain a unilateral issue. The other contracting state will become involved if treaty relief is denied as a result of these provisions.

25-850   Judicial approaches √

This section examines the few judicial statements that might be viewed as expressing opinions on treaty shopping, as well as the potential application of domestic law anti-avoidance doctrines to the question.

Commerzbank

The high water mark of judicial tolerance towards treaty shopping is perhaps the decision in *IRC v Commerzbank*.[85] The court sanctioned benefits under the US Treaty being conferred on residents of Brazil and Germany. The basis on which this was allowed involved two simple propositions. The first, which the Inland Revenue conceded in the High Court, is that

---

[84] See chapter 15, para. 24-400.

[85] [1990] BTC 172; [1990] STC 285.

there is no legal reason why a treaty cannot deal with rights and obligations of persons other than citizens, residents and corporations of the contracting parties. The second was that the words of art. XV of the US Treaty were clear. Their natural and ordinary meaning was to exempt from UK tax interest which had been paid by US corporations except for certain specified UK recipients. The treaty could not be construed as expanding the exception beyond the category of recipients described in the article.

Padmore

Another case that may be viewed as judicial authorisation of treaty shopping is *Padmore v IRC*.[86] In that case, a UK-resident partner in a partnership managed in Jersey claimed exemption on his share of the partnership profits by virtue of the Jersey Treaty on the basis that the partnership was a Jersey enterprise carrying on business in Jersey without a permanent establishment in the UK.

The Inland Revenue argued that a business carried on in partnership between, for example, Jersey residents, UK residents and third-country residents should be treated under the treaty as:

- a Jersey enterprise, insofar as it is carried on and its profits belong to the Jersey residents;
- a UK enterprise, insofar as it is carried on by and its profits belong to UK residents; or
- neither a Jersey enterprise nor a UK enterprise, insofar as it is carried on by and its profits belong to third country residents.

This argument was dismissed on the basis that partnership income is assessed for UK and Jersey purposes on an artificial basis (in the name of the partnership) on the partners who are jointly liable for the whole of any tax which may be payable. Thereafter, there is an apportionment of the income between the partners so as to arrive at each individual's liability.

The Crown, however, argued that this approach was not consistent with the general scheme of the treaty. It was argued that the scope and purpose of para. 3(2) (the business profits provision) was to remove UK tax liability from the profits of a Jersey enterprise trading in the UK but not through a permanent establishment, and that it was not directed at and did not apply to the UK tax liability of a partner receiving his or her share of the profits.

Again, Peter Gibson J determined the matter on the basis of the plain meaning of the words of the treaty. The effect of the treaty was that all industrial or commercial profits of a Jersey enterprise are not subject to UK tax whether earned in Jersey, the UK or elsewhere, except to the extent that they are attributable to a permanent establishment in the UK. That left Jersey alone as between itself and the UK free to tax those profits. He concluded that in order to achieve the result the Crown argued for, extra wording was needed in the treaty such as that found in the Swiss Treaty. It provides that in the case of a partnership, the UK's right to tax UK-resident partners on their share of partnership income is not restricted. The Crown's argument that the treaty should not be read so as to produce an adventitious or

---

[86] [1987] BTC 3; [1987] STC 36 Ch.D.

anomalous benefit to the taxpayer was not accepted. There was no basis to imply any additional provisions into the clear wording of the treaty.

In addition to the changes in UK domestic law in the Finance (No. 2) Act 1987, s. 62, effectively overriding treaty provisions, the UK then adopted wording found in recent treaties. An example is art. 24 of the Ukraine Treaty, which authorises the UK to tax UK resident partners of Ukrainian partnerships. That wording would not appear, however, to have ended the ability of partners resident in third countries to claim treaty benefits through the partnership where it is taxed as a separate entity. *Padmore* would appear to support the proposition that as long as a foreign partnership qualifies as an enterprise of another contracting state, partners not resident in that contracting state may be able to claim treaty benefits.

European Vinyl

If the *Commerzbank* case represents the high water mark of judicial permissiveness toward treaty shopping, then *Steele v European Vinyl Corp (Holdings) BV*[87] is the low water mark. In that case, a joint venture was established between Imperial Chemical Industries plc, a UK resident and EniChem SpA, an Italian resident. The joint-venture vehicle was a Netherlands resident company effectively owned 50 per cent by the ICI Group and 50 per cent by EniChem. The Netherlands company claimed payment of tax credits pursuant to art. 10 of the 1981 Netherlands Treaty. Under art. 10(3)(d)(i), payment only applied if the Netherlands company could show that it was not controlled by a person, or two or more associated or connected persons together who, or any of whom, would not have been entitled to a tax credit if he or she had been the beneficial owner of the dividends paid. EniChem would not have been entitled to a tax credit under the Italy Treaty at that time. It was accepted that the shareholders were not associated and the only question was whether they were connected persons.

Article 10(3)(d)(ii) required the question as to whether they were connected to be determined for this purpose by UK domestic law. Lightman J held that under the relevant domestic law,[88] they were connected with each other.

It was argued by the taxpayer in the Chancery Division that the mischief at which these provisions were aimed was the prevention of 'treaty shopping'. This would be sufficiently achieved if it applied only to persons who are genuinely connected. By that it was meant otherwise than through the mere coincidence of their exercising joint control of a company. It was argued that it would be arbitrary and unjust to deny tax credits to a company merely because its shareholders, otherwise unconnected, and acting together to exercise control over its affairs, should be denied the tax credit. It was therefore suggested that in the circumstances the 'connection' contemplated in the treaty should be restricted to 'real and free standing connections'. Connections should only therefore refer to subsections (2) to (6) of s. 839 of the Taxes Act 1988 – not the more extensive factors in subsection (7).

---

[87] [1995] BTC 32; [1995] STC 31, Ch.D.; [1996] BTC 425; [1996] STC 785, CA.

[88] ICTA 1988, ss. 839(7) and 416.

The Court, however, rejected this argument on the basis that the reference to domestic law in art. 10(3)(d) referred to persons connected under the laws of the UK 'for any purpose'. These words required adoption of the full test, rather than a more limited test argued for by the taxpayer.

On appeal to the Court of Appeal, the taxpayer argued that unless and until s. 839 is applied for some substantive tax purpose arising between the Inland Revenue and the taxpayer, the definition in s. 839(7) cannot come within art. 10(3)(d)(ii) of the treaty. It argued that the analysis of Lightman J was incorrect upon a 'true construction of the convention which is in origin a treaty between the United Kingdom and the Kingdom of the Netherlands'. It was argued that the principles expressed in the *Commerzbank* case should apply.

Morritt J noted, however, that under the treaty it was sufficient if the shareholders of the Netherlands company 'could' be treated as connected under UK domestic law.

Consequently, the essential issue was the true meaning and purpose of the additional words in the treaty requiring connection 'for any purpose'. He ruled that the use of the word 'could' in conjunction with 'any purpose' excluded any requirement that there be some substantive issue between the Revenue and the taxpayer, other than the availability of the tax credit for the purpose of which the connection arises or is relevant. If there was no other issue, then s. 839 as a whole ought to apply, and there is no basis for implying a condition that subsection (7) should be excluded.

The second argument was that the provisions of s. 839 generally could not have been intended to apply in a case where there was no suggestion that the intermediate company had been set up for the purpose of obtaining a tax credit to which its members were not entitled. Plus, the application of the article would remove the entitlement to the tax credit from all the members, not merely from that member who by an historical accident was not entitled to it.

This argument was similarly rejected by the Court of Appeal. It was held that the requirement was that the persons in question could be treated as connected for any purpose, not for all purposes. Any purpose would include a limited purpose such as that contemplated by subsection (7) by the words 'in relation to the company', as well as the unlimited purposes contemplated by subsection (1).

Morritt LJ said that these conclusions did not arise from an unduly literal construction of the treaty. He said that the provision in question is an anti-avoidance measure designed to prevent the artificial creation of entitlement to tax credits under the law of the UK. That law had several provisions dealing with control, connection and association. He said it was fanciful to suppose that the draftsperson of the treaty intended to restrict the application of those provisions to cases where they already applied or to limit it to those which did not apply.

The Court accepted that the shareholders' agreement and the interposition of EVC between its shareholders and its UK subsidiary were not parts of a scheme designed for the purpose of creating an entitlement to a tax credit where none would otherwise exist. The absence of such a purpose did not render the anti-avoidance provision inapplicable.[89]

The taxpayer argued that even if the definition in s. 839(7) would apply, the limitation in it that members were to be treated as connected 'in relation to that company' took it out of the scope of art. 10(3)(d) of the treaty. The requirement in that provision of the treaty, it was argued, was that the persons in question could be treated as connected for any purpose not for all purposes. It was, however, held that any purpose would include a limited purpose, such as that stipulated in subsection 839(7).

It was also argued by the taxpayer that the treaty provision should be construed as an anti-avoidance provision. In addition, the taxpayer argued that it should therefore not apply on the basis that the shareholders agreement and the interposition of the Netherlands company between the members of the joint venture and the UK subsidiary were not part of a scheme designed for the purpose of creating an entitlement to tax credit when none would otherwise exist. The Court of Appeal concluded that art. 10(3)(d) was of general application and could not be limited to cases of 'avoidance' only. Such a construction would confine the general application of the provision to an area smaller than that which the draftsperson must have had in mind. This statement, in particular, confirms that limitation of benefit provisions merely form part of the text of the treaty and are integral conditions to be fulfilled in order to qualify for treaty benefits. No special rules of construction apply by virtue of the fact that they are 'anti-avoidance' provisions.

The common feature of these cases is that no general anti-treaty shopping doctrine appears to exist under UK law. A number of theories about the application of treaties in this area have been argued by both the Revenue and taxpayers in these cases. The courts have, however, relied largely on the plain meaning of words in coming to their conclusions about whether they favoured allowing treaty benefits or not. In the *Euro Vinyls* case, the courts were concerned with construing a limitation of benefits provision. In the *Commerzbank* case, they were concerned with construing a treaty provision which was not limited to residents of contracting states. A further feature in common is that the courts relied on the natural and ordinary meaning of the words. The application of a more purposive approach, as adopted in *IRC v Exxon Corporation*,[90] for example, may well have produced different results.

Indofood

In *Indofood* the question of treaty shopping (from an Indonesian perspective) was raised explicitly. In the Court of Appeal, Sir Andrew Morritt observed:[91]

> 'As I have mentioned, on 24 May 2004, the Republic of Indonesia terminated the Mauritian DTA with effect from 1 January 2005. It issued a lengthy statement explaining the problems to

---

[89] It is noteworthy that the joint venture vehicle was a Netherlands company. Its shareholders were Italian, German, Swiss and UK companies. There was no other obvious connection with the Netherlands. Indeed, its co-ordination centre or administrative headquarters were in Brussels. Clearly some attention was paid to the tax planning aspects.

[90] See above, n. 66.

[91] At para. 15.

which the Mauritian DTA had given rise. In essence, they arose from the decision of the Government of Mauritius in 2001 to allow non-residents in Mauritius to use the Companies Act to set up various business agencies including special purpose vehicles and thereby enabled: ... "non resident parties in Mauritius to commit treaty shopping and treaty tax abuse by exploiting the Double Tax Avoidance Agreement for tax evasion in the country where tax rate is higher (in Indonesia)".

Without the benefit of Article 11.2 of the Mauritian DTA the rate of withholding tax for which the Parent Guarantor was liable in respect of the interest payable to the Issuer under the Loan Agreement would go up to the standard rate of 20 per cent from 1 January 2005.'

In examining the Indonesian law on the subject, he noted that 'there is no free-standing principle of Indonesian law which requires an advantage apparently obtained under a tax avoidance scheme to be denied to a participant in that scheme, though the existence of a tax avoidance scheme may be relevant to questions of legislative interpretation'.[92] In order to determine if the interposed company was the beneficial owner, it was necessary to test whether the legal, commercial and practical structure behind the loan notes was consistent with the concept that it could enjoy the benefit of the income.[93] He ruled that it was not and concluded that this result was consistent with the evident purpose and object of the treaties. While the English court was called upon to decide what an Indonesian court would have done in circumstances, the approach of Sir Andrew Morritt echoes that of the House of Lords in *Barclays Mercantile v Mawson* in relation to domestic law.

HMRC has given some indication that it will seek to apply the Ramsay doctrine to treaty shopping.[94] Perhaps the final words should be those of Lord Hoffman, when he said in *MacNiven v Westmoreland Investments Ltd*[95] in relation to domestic statute:

'There is ultimately only one principle of construction, namely to ascertain what Parliament meant by using the language of the statute. All other "principles of construction" can be no more than guides to which past judges have put forward, some more helpful and insightful than others, to assist in the task of interpretation.'

---

[92] At para. 24.

[93] At para. 43.

[94] See HMRC, *International Tax Handbook*, para. 708.

[95] [2001] BTC 44; [2001] STC 237, HL, at para. 29.

Practical Application

Chapter 17

26-000   Introduction

Taxpayers seeking to benefit from the application of treaties are faced with a range of procedures which vary according to the nature of the income or gain, the benefit sought and, in some cases, the treaty in question.

Lord Dunedin famously explained the tripartite elements of the tax system in *Whitney v IRC*, where he said:[1]

> 'There are three stages in the imposition of a tax: there is the declaration of liability, that is the part of the statute which determines what persons in respect of what property are liable. Next, there is the assessment. Liability does not depend on assessment. That, ex hypothesi, has already been fixed ... Lastly, come the methods of recovery, if the person taxed does not voluntarily pay.'

As a rule, the mechanisms for relieving double taxation by allocating taxing jurisdiction and eliminating double taxation (examined in chapters 5 to 14) address the first (determination of liability) stage only. With few exceptions, the second assessment stage is a matter of domestic law and practice.

26-050   Treaty-based procedures

A few treaties contain procedural rules for their application. Thus, art. 23 of the UK–Austria Treaty provides that:

> 'Where tax has been deducted at the source from dividends, interest or royalties in excess of the amount of tax chargeable in accordance with the provisions of Article 10, 11 or 12 the excess amount of tax shall be refunded upon application being made to the competent authority concerned within three years of the end of the calendar year in which the dividends, interest or royalties were payable.'

Under such arrangements, refunds of amounts withheld in excess of treaty rates are guaranteed by treaty if the application is made within the time limit. Others, such as the UK–Italy Treaty, while guaranteeing refunds, adopt domestic time limits set out other procedural requirements, such as that the residence state certifying that the taxpayer has fulfilled conditions the required for entitlement to the refund.[2]

---

[1] [1926] AC 37 at 52.

[2] UK–Italy Treaty, arts. 29(1) and 29(2).

The second and third stages give rise to special considerations in the context of international activity, given the historical inability of tax administrations to extend their reach beyond national boundaries.[3] These considerations have generally given rise to the need for mechanisms for assessment and collection that are within the jurisdiction of the UK courts. The assessment and collection stages are, as a result, frequently combined into a single process, in the context of non-residents. Thus, the UK system of assessment of direct taxes, which is generally divided between self-assessment and deduction at source, relies particularly on deduction at source in relation to the income, profits and gains of non-residents.

26-100 Self-assessment

Any person who is chargeable to income tax or capital gains tax for a year of assessment is required by notice either to complete a return or to give notice of chargeability.[4] Similarly, a company which is chargeable to corporation tax for an accounting period is likewise required by notice to complete a return or notify that it is chargeable to tax.[5] In each case, the return must include a self-assessment of the taxpayer's liability.[6] Self-assessment requires a tax return to be filed by a fixed date and payment of all income and capital gains tax or profits in the case of companies for the year by fixed dates. More importantly, self-assessment requires taxpayers to form their own conclusions about their liability to tax and to report those conclusions in the form of reported income and gains on the tax return. Compliance is monitored by enquiries into returns and taxpayers will have to retain records and information in order to support the basis on which income and gains are returned.

Deduction at source

Deduction of tax at source on certain items is provided generally in the Income Tax Act 2007, Pt. 15, and, specifically in relation to employment and pension income, in ITEPA 2003, Pt. 11. A person whose sources of income are taxed entirely by way of deduction at source is not required to notify chargeability.[7]

26-150 Claim or self-assessment of treaty benefits

The precise manner in which treaties have effect varies depending upon the particular income or gain in question. The obscure language of the Taxes Act 1988, s. 788(3), gives rise to questions about the assessment mechanisms compounded by its considerably predating the modern self-assessment legislation. Pursuant to Taxes Act 1988, s. 788(3), treaties have effect insofar as they provide (among others):

---

[3] See chapter 20, para. 29-000.

[4] Taxes Management Act 1970 (TMA 1970), s. 7(1).

[5] FA 1998, Sch. 18, para. 2(1).

[6] TMA 1970, s. 9, and, in the case of companies, FA 1998, Sch. 18, para. 7(1).

[7] TMA 1970, s. 7 (3).

- for charging UK income or chargeable gains of non-residents;[8] or
- for determining the income or chargeable gains to be attributed to:

  - non-residents and their agencies, branches or establishments in the United UK; or
  - residents who have special relationships with non-residents.[9]

This carries with it the implication that treaties modify the domestic law by displacing the relevant domestic law provisions with the relevant treaty provisions, thereby declaring the tax liability to be as expressed in the treaty. In such cases, the full implication of self-assessment of tax liability taken to its logical conclusion is particularly noticeable in relation to non-residents who, but for the provisions of a treaty, would be liable to tax under domestic law and where no tax is deducted at source on payments to them. Where the relevant provisions of a treaty can be said to provide for the 'charging' or determining the income or chargeable gains of non-residents and exclude all liability to UK tax, then no obligation to notify chargeability should arise. The most important and acute illustration of this arises in relation to the question as to whether a non-resident trading in the UK, but who by virtue of a treaty does not have a permanent establishment, is required to notify chargeability to tax and to file a tax return. On this approach, the non-resident it is not within the charge to income tax or corporation tax on this account and need not notify chargeability and need not file a return.

Section 788(3)(a) gives effect to treaties which provide for 'relief from income tax or from corporation tax in respect of income or chargeable gains'. Section 788(6) adds a procedural appendage to this, specifying that 'except in the case of a claim for an allowance by way of credit in accordance with Chapter II of this Part, a claim for relief under subs. (3)(a) above shall be made to the Board'. In such a case, does a 'claim' need to be made in order to benefit from a treaty? The word 'relief' is not a term of art but has been used in tax legislation to refer to a provision which reduces the tax which would otherwise be payable.[10] Although, as has been seen, treaties are generally relieving in nature, where the treaty declares the tax liability to be in accordance with its terms, calling the treaty provision a relief in this sense is somewhat circular.

Much of the difficulty is as a result of the use of a handful of expressions that are used in more than one sense and whose meaning may have changed over time. The Taxes Act 1988, Pt. XVIII (Double taxation relief), is not consistent as to where a claim needs to be made and in some places assumes rather than mandates a claim is appropriate.[11] Such assumptions may be relics of the pre–self-assessment system. The better view of s. 788(6) is that where a claim is appropriate, it merely sets out to whom the claim should be made.[12]

---

[8] S. 788(3)(b).

[9] S. 788(3)(c).

[10] Lord Hoffmann in *Taylor (HMIT) v MEPC Holdings Ltd* [2004] BTC 20, at para. 10. See also *Sheppard and another (Trustees of the Woodland Trust) v IRC (No. 2)* [1993] BTC 113; [1993] STC 240 at para. 254, and *IRC v Universities Superannuation Scheme Ltd* [1997] BTC 3; [1997] STC 1 at para. 17-18.

[11] See also FA 1994, s. 249, which makes the same assumption.

[12] HMRC, *International Tax Manual*, para. INTM157030.

The argument for saying that the existence or non-existence of a permanent establishment is a provision for 'charging UK income' of non-residents under s. 788(3)(b) and that the non-existence of a permanent establishment negates chargeability to tax is compelling. The Revenue's *International Tax Handbook* (which predates self-assessment) may provide some implicit support for this. It explains that the expressions 'charged' and 'chargeable' are used in two ways in the Taxes Acts. The first is in the sense of 'liable' or 'within the charge' to tax as in tax charged on income under Sch. D. The second is in the sense of 'assessable', as when tax under Sch. D is charged on the person receiving or entitled to the income. Since, for example, in the permanent establishment context, treaty provisions typically do not impact on the assessment machinery, the existence or non-existence of a permanent establishment does appear to go to the meaning of chargeable in the first sense referred to by the Revenue.[13] The Revenue handbook also refers to the existence of permanent establishments as 'the treaty charge'.[14] On the other hand, Help Sheet HS 304 (Non-residents relief under double taxation agreements) is written on the basis that a claim is necessary.

Current HMRC practice is to require the following non-resident individuals to complete a self-assessment return:

- Lloyds underwriters;
- partners in a UK partnership and trading in the UK; and
- those who have a UK property business.

In the employment area, directors of a UK company or employees performing duties in the UK may be required (as well as anyone realising capital gains or liable to a higher rate tax) or may be entitled to reduced age relief.

26-200   Claims

Where a claim is to be made it must be in accordance with the procedure for claims generally contained in Taxes Management Act (TMA) 1970, s. 42, and FA 1998, Sch. 18, paras. 9 and 10, and Pt. VII, for corporation tax. Generally, a claim for a relief or repayment of tax must be for an amount which is quantified at the time when the claim is made.[15] A separate code of rules is provided for claims which are not included in returns.[16]

Time limits

Time limits for making claims are prescribed generally by TMA 1970, s. 43. In the case of income tax, a claim must be made within five years from 31 January next following the year of assessment to which it relates. In the case of corporation tax, a claim must be made within six years from the end of the accounting period to which it relates.[17] Similar time limits are

[13] HMRC, *International Tax Handbook*, para. 902.

[14] *Ibid.*, para. 849.

[15] TMA 1970, s. 42(1A) and FA 1998, Sch. 18, para. 54, for corporation tax.

[16] TMA 1970, Sch. 1, s. 42(11).

[17] FA 1998, Sch. 18, para. 55.

imposed specifically in relation to claims for foreign tax credits provided by treaties under Taxes Act 1988, s. 806(1). For claims made after 21 March 2000, claims for credit for foreign tax in respect of income or chargeable gain which falls to be charged for a year of assessment must be made before the fifth anniversary of 31 January next following that year of assessment or, if later, 31 January next following the year of assessment in which the foreign tax is paid. In the case of corporation tax, the claim must be made not more than six years after the end of the accounting period or, if later, one year after the end of the accounting period in which the foreign tax is paid. These changes were made as a result of representations dealing with unusual circumstances in which the foreign tax may be paid too late for credit relief to be claimed within the normal six-year limit. For example, where interest is received on a loan, the loan agreement may specify that interest is paid eight years after the loan is made. It is only then that the foreign tax is paid by means of withholding from the interest payment. Tax may have been charged in the UK on the interest on an accruals basis from the start of the loan. When the foreign tax is ultimately paid in year eight, a claim for credit relief in relation to that part of the interest in the earliest years would have been outside the normal six-year limit.[18]

Documentation

There are no non-tax procedures, such as registration with other authorities, as a precondition to entitlement to treaty relief. Generally, limited documentation or evidence is required to support a claim. However, unlike the approach to self-assessment in relation to domestic law, supporting evidence is required in some cases.

Published Revenue materials, including claim forms, indicate the documentation required for normal claims in relation to dividends, interest and royalties. Wide power to call for documents for the purpose of enquiries exists.[19] Where a claim is made which is not included in a return in respect of residence, ordinary residence or domicile, evidence may be required on affidavit.[20]

Where HMRC questions the validity of the claim, further evidence may be required to demonstrate the claimant's fulfilment of the treaty requirements. If the matter is disputed on appeal to the Special Commissioners, the rules of evidence may apply.[21] In *Forth Investments Ltd v IRC*,[22] the Inland Revenue rejected a claim under the Barbados Treaty for repayment of the dividend tax credit on the basis that it was not satisfied that the claimant company was a resident of Barbados. When the matter came before the Special Commissioners, the claimant sought to rely on statements made by the secretary of the company as to the residence of the company and a certificate of residence signed by the Deputy Commissioner for the Inland Revenue in Barbados. The Special Commissioners

---

[18] The effect of the wording of s. 806(1) before FA 2000 was considered by the Court of Appeal in *Commercial Union Assurance Co. v Shaw* [1999] BTC 12; [1999] STC 109 at 117.

[19] TMA 1970, s. 19A, in relation to returns, and Sch. 1A, para. 6, in relation to claims not included in returns. From 6 April 2009, these powers are contained in FA 2008, Sch. 36.

[20] TMA 1970, Sch. 1A, para. 2(6).

[21] *Special Commissioners (Jurisdiction and Procedure) Regulations* 1994 (SI 1994/1811), reg. 17(4) and 17(17).

[22] (1971-1977) 50 TC 617; [1976] STC 399 Ch.D.

held that both documents were hearsay and thus inadmissible as evidence of the residence of the company. They further declined to exercise their discretion under the rules of court[23] to admit them in evidence because of the company's long delay in prosecuting its appeal and failure to comply with procedural rules which permitted the admission of hearsay evidence on a discretionary basis. The High Court upheld the Commissioners' decision and ruled that the exercise of discretion not to admit the documents under the rules of court was not unreasonable in the circumstances.

The Special Commissioners, in their decision, noted with surprise the argument of the Inland Revenue that a certificate of residence provided by the tax administration of a contracting state, the form of which the Inland Revenue itself prescribed, should be excluded as hearsay. They found it incongruous that such a certificate should be available as evidence to the Inland Revenue but denied to the appellate body whose function it was to review the Inland Revenue decisions. Nonetheless, they concluded that the certificate was hearsay under existing law. The rule against hearsay was abolished by the Civil Evidence Act 1995, although the act continues to impose procedural requirements in respect of such evidence. The rules of evidence before the Special Commissioners are less formal, and the Revenue will find it more difficult to exclude such evidence. Other challenges on the basis of the weight of foreign official certification may also be difficult. In *Trevor Smallwood Trust v R & C Commrs*,[24] a certificate of residence of by the Mauritius tax authorities was accepted without dispute.

Where documents may be subject to UK stamp duty if they are brought into the UK,[25] liability to stamp duty would arise in circumstances where the original document is required by the Inland Revenue. Copies are stated to be sufficient for this purpose where documents are required in relation on claim forms.[26] The Inland Revenue has said that if documents are to be relied upon by a person in support of any claim to relief, or otherwise used in evidence in relation to any liability to tax, or the amount thereof, the Revenue cannot be compelled to accept in support of such claim or as evidence unstamped originals or conformed unstamped copies of documents.[27]

26-250   Deduction at source

The withholding of tax by a payer on payments to non-residents is found in a variety of different circumstances under domestic law. The obligation to deduct tax imposed on a payer is a separate issue from the liability of the payee to tax thereon. Consequently, in UK practice, the treaty benefit in relation to a non-resident payee is that of the payee only and not that of the payer. Qualifying non-residents are able to benefit from treaties in two ways:

(1)   Where tax is deducted at source giving rise to a tax liability on the part of the payee in

---

[23] *Rules of the Supreme Court* (SI 1965/1776), Ord. 38, r. 29.

[24] (2008) Sp C 669.

[25] Stamp Act 1891, s. 14.

[26] See Form DT/Individual, for example.

[27] *Tax Bulletin* (No. 30, August 1997), p. 459.

excess of that authorised by treaty, a claim may be made by the payee for repayment of the excess as described above.

(2)   A variety of rules and arrangements permit payees either to make payments without deduction of tax or at rates authorised by treaty. These rules vary according to the source of income.

From a day-to-day perspective, the procedure for obtaining treaty benefits is generally the same in each case, the difference being simply whether the relief is given at the time of payment or by subsequent refund. The legal basis is, however, different and rights of the taxpayer differ accordingly. A claim for repayment is normally a claim under TMA 1970, s. 42, and Sch. 1A, with its inbuilt self-assessment mechanisms. The commissioners for HMRC are authorised to make regulations generally for carrying out the provisions of Taxes Act 1988, s. 788, and treaties.[28] The regulations do not include any right to apply or rules to regulate applications to pay at treaty rates, so that an exercise of powers under the regulations is an exercise of administrative power.[29] Specific authority is given to provide in regulations for securing that relief from taxation does not enure for the benefit of persons not entitled to such relief. Regulations may also be made to address circumstances where tax deductible from any payment has not been deducted in order to purportedly comply with any treaty, and where it is discovered that the treaty did not apply to that payment. The recovery of tax by assessment on the person entitled to the payment or by deduction from subsequent payments may be authorised by regulation.

General regulations made pursuant to this power deal with exemption from or reduction in the rate at which tax is deducted at source on certain income.[30] The regulations apply to treaty residents who are entitled to exemption or partial relief from UK income tax deducted at source. It only applies in respect of persons who are beneficially entitled to the income.

26-300   Notice to pay at treaty rates

Where an application has been made by the beneficial owner of the item, the payer of such income may be directed by notice in writing given by the board that he or she shall:

- not deduct tax;
- not deduct tax at a higher rate than is specified in the notice; or
- deduct tax at a rate specified in the notice instead of at the lower or basic rate otherwise appropriate.

Where notice is given, any income paid after the date of the notice for a year for which the treaty has effect must be paid as directed in the notice. The effect of such a notice is to substitute the treaty rate for the domestic law rate of deduction for all domestic law purposes in relation to the payer as well as the non-resident.

---

[28] ICTA 1988, s. 791.

[29] See chapter 18, para. 27-050.

[30] *Double Taxation Relief (Taxes on Income) (General) Regulations* 1970 (SI 1970/488).

A notice may be expressed to become ineffective if certain specified events happen. If to the knowledge of the payer any of the specified events happens, any payment made to the non-resident after that event becomes known to the payer must be subject to deduction of tax at domestic rates, in accordance with domestic law. Any notice may be cancelled by notice by or on behalf of HMRC. After the receipt of a cancellation notice, deduction of tax must be at domestic rates, in accordance with domestic law.

If, after a notice has been given, it is discovered that the non-resident is not entitled to the treaty benefit referred to in the notice, any tax which, but for the notice, would have been deductible from any payment made to the non-resident by the payer but in compliance with the notice has not been so deducted may be assessed on the non-resident under Case VI of Sch. D by an inspector. Alternatively, on the direction of HMRC, tax may be deducted by the payer out of so much of the first payment made to the non-resident after the date of the direction as remains after the deduction of any tax deductible in the absence of the treaty. Any balance which cannot be deducted out of the first payment must be deducted, subject to the same limitation, out of subsequent payments until the whole of the tax has been deducted.

26-350 Manufactured overseas dividends

Specific regulations[31] authorise the making of arrangements with payers of manufactured overseas dividends to enable the payment to be made without deduction of UK tax. This applies to recipients who are resident in a treaty country where the treaty contains an 'other income' article which exempts such payments from tax. These arrangements made pursuant to the regulations are published in the form of guidance notes. As an important international financial centre, the UK has developed a variety of arrangements involving claims and payments made through intermediaries or custodians. For example, arrangements have been made with a number of UK banks that act as global custodians for large numbers of non-residents and manage UK investment portfolios. These aim at streamlining the handling of claims using agreed and defined criteria. Such banks send blocks of claims at a time to a dedicated section at the CNR. In return, they receive single aggregate payments for each such block.

26-400 Forms

The same forms are used to seek authorisation to pay at the treaty rate as are used for repayment; the same evidence of entitlement must be submitted in support of the application. In most cases, a standard form[32] may be used, although there are also forms tailored to specific treaties and specific forms of income. Forms are generally available in English, although many are also available in the language of the other contracting state and from the tax authorities of such state. Questions on the form are designed to determine eligibility for treaty benefits and generally follow the criteria set out in the relevant treaty

---

[31] *Income Tax (General) (Manufactured Overseas Dividends) Regulations* 1993 (SI 1993/2004).

[32] Forms DT/Individual and DT/Company.

provision. These include questions relating to the residence of the claimant, the presence of a permanent establishment in the UK and beneficial ownership. Other conditions, such as whether the recipient is subject to tax where the treaty so requires, are included. Forms also ask questions that go beyond the criteria for eligibility under the treaty, notably in relation to former residence in the UK.

26-450   Beneficial ownership

Claims for benefits in relation to dividend, interest or royalty payments must be made by the beneficial owner of the dividend and all forms require a declaration of beneficial ownership by the claimant. Consequently, if shares are registered in the name of any person who is not the beneficial owner, it is the beneficial owner and not the registered owner who is entitled to claim. Additional information may be required where the registered owner, as appears on dividend vouchers, is not the same as the declared beneficial owner. Where beneficial ownership of dividends is questioned and the relevant treaty contains a beneficial ownership provision, then the claimant will have to prove this element to receive the payment. Several forms of limitation of benefit provisions appear in the relevant articles of UK treaties. Most claim forms do not solicit specific information relating to all these provisions. There are certain exceptions. For example, in relation to the US Treaty, questions are designed to consider the application of the conduit arrangements defined in art. 1(3) to dividends, interest and royalties.

26-500   Procedure

The claim must be certified by the tax authority of the claimant's state of residence. Certification must include the residence of the claimant and in certain cases that the claimant is subject to tax on the income in question. In some cases the taxpayer identification number (TIN) must also be certified by the foreign tax authority. Some forms may demand information that is beyond that required by the treaty in question.

The procedure for filing claims varies. All require submission to the foreign tax authorities for certification. Thereafter, some are filed in the UK (for example, Canada), while in others the claim is simply submitted through the foreign tax authority (for example, Switzerland). In some cases, a distinction is drawn between the first claim and subsequent claims. Thus, in a number of cases a first claim must be submitted to the tax authorities in the other contracting state, with subsequent claims being submitted to the UK authorities[33] (for example, Japan).

The treaty claim forms included in the individual self-assessment tax return (used by resident and non-resident individuals alike) are more general and depart from the claim forms in relation to specific treaties in that they do not solicit information corresponding to specific treaty provisions. In the case of the claim on Help Sheet HS302, the taxpayer simply claims the benefit by reference to the type of income, the relevant treaty article and the

---

[33] The Centre for Non-Residents.

domestic and treaty rates of tax. By comparison, a separate tax return (SA700) is used by non-resident companies and makes no reference to treaty questions.

26-550   Dividends

The UK does not generally impose a tax on distributions paid to non-residents. Deduction of income tax at source on distributions by REITs is governed by regulations authorised under ITA 2007, ss. 973 and 974.[34] HMRC will not issue a notice to pay at treaty rates under the terms of SI 1970/488.[35] Thus, treaty non-residents may only claim repayment of some or all of the tax that is deducted from PIDs that are paid by UK REITs. Specific claim forms are required[36] and some treaties have country specific REIT claim forms.

26-600   Interest and royalties

As noted in chapter 9[37] tax must be deducted on certain interest payments by the UK payer at source. Although the position is not unarguable, the long standing HMRC practice and the assumption on which related legislation is based is that this means deduction at the domestic rate and not the treaty rate. The HMRC position is that the obligation on the part of UK payers to deduct tax is separate from the non-resident's entitlement to treaty benefits. Where tax is not deducted or is deducted at the treaty rate in the absence of HMRC authorisation, interest on unpaid tax will be sought on the difference between the full domestic rate and the tax actually deducted from the time of payment of the interest or royalty concerned, even if the beneficial owner subsequently claims relief.[38]

Directions are not made to payments in respect of coupons for any interest, but, under arrangements approved by the Revenue, any such payments may be made without deduction of tax or with tax deducted at treaty rates – if the non-resident or any person acting on his behalf makes a claim to the payer in prescribed form. In that case, payments may be generally made at treaty rates on the same basis as if a notice were given.

Qualifying non-residents may claim repayment of tax deducted at source. HMRC requires underlying documentation in addition support of the claim forms. Thus, a copy of the text of any agreement or exchange of correspondence regulating the terms on which interest is paid is required for a claim relating to interest. In the case of royalties, a copy of the licence agreement or contract must be submitted in support of the claim. Application may also be made for relief at source. However, there is recognition that delays may occur because of the need to obtain foreign tax authority certification of residence combined with HMRC examination of the particular circumstances of the payment. There are mechanisms that

---

[34] *Real Estate Investment Trusts (Assessment and Recovery of Tax) Regulations* 2006 (SI 2006/2867). See chapter 9, para. 18-100.

[35] HMRC, DT guidance note 9.

[36] UK-REIT DT Individual and UK-REIT DT Company.

[37] Paras. 18-150 and 18-200.

[38] HMRC, *INTM*, paras. INTM574030 and INTM574040.

permit an element of self-assessment to the application of treaties. In the case of royalties, a statutory framework applies. In the case of interest, it is by way of administrative practice.

Royalties

A company may calculate the amount of tax to be deducted by reference to the treaty rate on a royalty if, at the time the payment is made, the company reasonably believes that, the payee is entitled to treaty relief in respect of the payment.[39] For this purpose, 'royalty' includes a payment received as consideration for the use of, or the right to use, a copyright, patent, trade mark, design, process or information, as well as the proceeds of the sale of the whole or part of any patent rights.[40] The ability to self-assess treaty application is limited to corporate payers.

This self-assessment is subject to administrative supervision. If an officer of HMRC is not satisfied that the payee will be entitled to relief under a treaty in respect of one or more payments of royalties that a company is to make, the officer may direct the company is not to self-assess the application of the treaty to the payment or payments.[41] This power applies to prospective payments only. However, a company operating under these provisions remains at risk if, in fact, the recipient is not entitled to treaty relief. In such a case, the right to pay at the treaty rate is treated as never having existed.[42]

Interest

Although HMRC is understood not to be unwilling to move to an entirely self-certification system, it does apply a more relaxed administrative approach to authorising deduction of tax at source at treaty rates in cases it regards as low risk in relation to interest.

First, a practice of informal clearance may provisionally allow payment at treaty rates from between the date of receipt of a certified treaty claim by CNR and the date of final determination of the claim, but not from the date the loan is made to the date of receipt of the treaty claim.[43]

Second, the Provisional Treaty Relief Scheme[44] is a voluntary scheme that applies to two types of loans where HMRC regards there as being only a 'negligible risk' that an application for treaty relief would fail. They are:

- 'one to one' company loans where there is no shareholding relationship or common ownership between the parties involved, for example, where the lender is an overseas lending institution; and
- syndicated loans where there is a syndicate manager.

---

[39] ITA 2007, ss. 911(1) and 911(2).

[40] ITA 2007, s. 913(1).

[41] ITA 2007, s. 912.

[42] ITA 2007, s. 911(3).

[43] HMRC, *INTM*, para. INTM574040.

[44] HMRC, *INTM*, para. INTM574040, and see the HMRC publications referred to there.

In these cases, provisional authority may be given until superseded by a notice to pay at treaty relief under SI 1970/488 is given. The provisional authority will be invalidated if a formal application for treaty clearance is not made within three months of the provisional authority. The risk is effectively with the payer who will be liable for both tax and other consequences if a successful treaty claim is not made.

EC Interest and Royalties Directive

The Interest and Royalties Directive recognises that the application of treaty provisions often entails burdensome administrative formalities and cash-flow problems for the companies concerned which itself is incompatible with the notion of a single market.[45] The directive accordingly contains procedural rules in order to specify the standards required in the administration of its provisions.[46] These include the right of member states to require evidence that taxpayers meet the criteria for eligibility as a precondition to the elimination of withholding,[47] the need for a direction by the tax administration that tax need not be deducted,[48] as well as the standards to be observed for the operation of the exemption.[49]

In the UK, the procedural elements are addressed in a manner that parallels the approach taken for tax treaty purposes. Thus, royalty payments may be self-assessed by the payer if it reasonably believes that the payment is exempt,[50] but it is under a duty to deduct the if it is not so exempt.[51] HMRC has the power to not apply the self-assessment by notice where it is satisfied that the exemption does not apply.[52] Payees are under an obligation to notify both HMRC and the payer of change in circumstances that cause the exemption to not apply.[53] Interest payments on the other hand are exempt pursuant to the directive only if HMRC has issued an exemption notice.[54] Section 762 of ITTOIA 2005 authorises the commissioners for HMRC to make regulations about exemption notices.[55] The essential difference between the details relating to exemption notices and those issued under SI 1970/488 to pay at treaty rates is the right of appeal[56] in recognition of the rights granted under Community law.

---

[45] Interest and Royalties Directive 03/49, Recital 2.

[46] Art. 1(11) to (16).

[47] Art. 1(11).

[48] Art. 1(12).

[49] Art. 1(13).

[50] ITA 2007, s. 914 (1)(a).

[51] ITA 2007, s. 914(1)(b).

[52] ITA 2007, s. 915.

[53] ITA 2007, s. 916.

[54] ITTOIA 2005, s. 758(5).

[55] Exemption From Tax For Certain Interest Payments Regulations 2004 (SI 2004/2622).

[56] SI 2004/2622, reg. 9.

26-650 Business profits

The mechanism adopted is to impose all compliance obligations in respect of trading in the UK jointly on the UK representative of a non-resident and the non-resident. The UK representative is defined for the purposes of income tax as the branch or agency through which the non-resident carries on any trade, profession or vocation[57] and for corporation tax it is the permanent establishment.[58] The UK representative is jointly responsible with the non-resident for all tax obligations and liabilities in relation to the trade, profession or vocation carried on through the branch or agency. This extends to all matters relating to self-assessment of tax, and to the collection and recovery of tax and covers notification of chargeability, the obligation to make a return and self-assessment, liability to make interim and final payments of tax and liability to surcharges, and interest and penalties in connection with these obligations and liabilities.[59] The UK does not generally require deduction of tax at source on payments to non-residents under this heading.[60] Unlike persons making payments under deduction of tax, the UK representative is able to make a treaty claim in that capacity on behalf of the non-resident it represents.

Non-residents and their agents, it would appear, are entitled to self-assess the existence of a permanent establishment. Such a view would be based on the proposition that permanent establishment provisions of treaties provide for charging UK source income or gains of non-residents pursuant to the Taxes Act 1988, s. 788(3)(b). By so doing, they define taxing jurisdiction and do not provide for 'relief' from income tax or corporation tax under s. 788(3)(a) for which a claim is required.[61]

The stringent interest and penalty regimes applicable to self-assessment and pay-and-file (in the case of companies) create considerable incentive for non-residents and UK representatives to make accurate assessments in this respect. This is particularly so in the case of UK representatives who, as a practical matter, will be within the jurisdiction of the UK courts. Consequently, where a non-resident forms the view that its activities constitute trading in the UK through a branch or agency for domestic law purposes, but falls short of those constituting a permanent establishment for treaty purposes, there is a premium on coming to the correct conclusion. Where the HMRC interpretation is sought on this, a positive answer will put the matter at an end. A negative reply with which the non-resident disagrees may mean that the matter would ultimately need to be resolved through formal dispute resolution mechanisms.

---

[57] FA 1995, s. 126(2).

[58] FA 2003, s. 150(2).

[59] FA 1995, s. 126, Sch. 23, for income tax, and FA 2003, s. 150.

[60] Payments to entertainers or sportsmen are an important exception: ITA 2007, ss. 966 to 970. See para. 26-750 below.

[61] See para. 26-100 above.

26-700 Employment income

Most employment income is taxed by deduction at source under the PAYE rules in such cases where the employee has no other reason to notify chargeability then no such obligation will arise.[62] If a repayment of tax is sought, HMRC practice is to require a self-assessment return. Where the employee is non-resident (or if resident, not ordinarily resident) also performs duties outside the UK, a direction may be sought for PAYE to be operated only in relation to the proportion taxable in the UK.[63] Application for such a direction must provide 'such information as is available and is relevant to the giving of the direction'. Where a treaty (typically following art. 15 of the OECD Model) precludes UK taxation, this route may be used to restrict PAYE to income taxable in accordance with the treaty. Other reporting obligations are not limited by treaty and therefore continue to apply.

26-750 Entertainers and sportspeople

Where non-resident entertainers or sportspeople perform in the UK, deduction of tax at source may be required.[64] It is possible under regulations to apply for a reduction in the withholding payments.[65] The regulations make no reference to treaties. The HMRC approach is that the tax must be withheld, even if the income is not subject to UK tax as a result of the application of a treaty.[66] This is on the basis that the withholding is merely on account of the final tax liability, and that whether or not a particular treaty is applicable cannot be considered fully at the withholding stage. Thus, non-residents subject to withholding under these rules can only make a claim for repayment of the tax withheld on submission of a claim with a return.

26-800 Residence: individual

An assertion of the appropriate residence is an essential element for the application of treaty benefits. Neither the forms completed in connection with arriving in or departure from the UK[67] nor the domicile questionnaire[68] address residence for treaty purposes, although the information they contain may be material to the question. These forms would not normally, however, provide sufficient information to address the tie-breaker provisions of the OECD Model article.

The self-assessment tax return specifically raises the question of dual residence. The individual self-assessment tax return requires individuals who are resident in a country other

---

[62] TMA 1997, s. 7(2).

[63] ITEPA 2003, s. 690.

[64] ITA 2007, ss. 966 to 970.

[65] *Income Tax (Entertainers, etc.) Regulations* 1987 (SI 1987/530), reg. 5.

[66] FEUSO, para. 8A.

[67] Forms P85 on departure or form P86 on arrival.

[68] From Dom 1.

than the UK under a treaty and at the same time resident in the UK to indicate that fact on the return (that is, the non-resident pages) and the country in which treaty residence is claimed.

Individuals who are non-resident or resident in another country for the purpose of a treaty and are claiming relief under a treaty are required to indicate the amount of relief that they are claiming. Moreover, material published by HMRC to assist with individual tax return preparation now deals with the question of dual residence and the application of treaty tie-breaker provisions.[69] It contains a summary of the tie-breaker rules under the OECD Model. Also included is specific information in relation to the US Treaty. This comprises an explanation of the main US domestic rules on residence, as well as the treaty fiscal residence provisions. A separate form to accompany the self-assessment return is also provided to claim treaty benefits where the tie-breaker is not in issue.[70]

A certificate of residence from the tax administration of the other contracting state is required under both forms. This is modified in the case of the US. United States citizens are required to self-certify the application of the US 'substantial presence' test. United States resident aliens must produce either a copy of their Green Card or, if they are not Green Card holders, a certificate of residence from the IRS. Thus, although taxpayers are generally required to self-assess or self-certify the facts relevant to their tax position, this is not the case in relation to assertions of residence of a contracting state where treaty benefits are claimed. In this case, a certificate of residence is required to be submitted with the return. The certificate of residence is an annual requirement. In addition, where the treaty so requires, the certificate must confirm that the individual is subject to tax in whole or part in the country of residence. Where only part of the income is taxed in the country of residence, that part must be shown in the certificate. HMRC will normally refuse a treaty claim if a certificate is not forthcoming.[71]

HMRC will normally certify residence to enable individuals to obtain relief from foreign tax under a treaty, for example, by certifying a foreign claim form.[72]

Other conditions for individuals

The self-assessment forms require non-residents to satisfy themselves that all of the conditions of the relevant treaty are met in making a treaty claim.[73] Where UK residents only qualify for foreign treaty benefits if they are subject to tax in the UK, then this may also be the subject of certification.

---

[69] Helpsheet IR302. See also HMRC, *INTM*, para. INTM154020.

[70] Helpsheet IR304.

[71] HMRC, *INTM*, para. INTM154040.

[72] *Tax Bulletin*, (No. 29, June 1997). See also HMRC, *INTM*, para. INTM162031.

[73] Helpsheet IR304.

26-850 Residence: company

HMRC practice in relation to certifying the residence of companies for foreign treaty claim purposes is more circumspect. The *International Manual* states:

'HM Revenue & Customs will support companies that are UK resident in their legitimate claims to relief from foreign tax where a DTC is in place, just as companies that are residents of a foreign State will expect the tax authorities of that State to support them in their legitimate claims to relief from UK tax under a DTC.

. HM Revenue & Customs must take reasonable precautions against any statements made by it being used to obtain relief from foreign tax if that relief is not due. It is important that we do not jeopardise our relations with other States as we have a responsibility to the generality of UK taxpayers to maintain the UK's reputation in this area.[74]'

As a result, HMRC may refuse a certificate in circumstances where it regards it as improper, such as if the company is an agent in relation to income in respect of which the foreign claim is made. Detailed requirements are therefore imposed.[75]

Where it is sought to demonstrate that the effect of the tie-breaker is to make a dual-resident company resident outside the UK, an assertion will need to be made to this effect, even though a claim is deemed made. No formal procedure is provided. In the context of a company ceasing to be resident in the UK, the pre-migration notification procedure required in FA 1988, s. 130,[76] is also required.

26-900 Minimising foreign tax

UK treaty provisions normally permit a credit against UK tax, tax payable under the laws of the other contracting state and in accordance with the treaty in question. (See, for example, the Netherlands Treaty, art. 21(5).) The Revenue practice will permit credit to be given only for foreign tax which is payable in accordance with the treaty. Consequently, the claimant must take all necessary steps to reduce foreign liability to the level permitted by the treaty.

This general limitation of credit to that payable under the treaty has been elevated to an obligation to minimise foreign tax in the FA 2000. Paragraph 6 of Sch. 30[77] restricts credit for foreign tax under any treaty to the tax which would be allowed:

'had all reasonable steps been taken:

(a) under the law of the territory concerned; and

(b) under any arrangements made with the government of that territory to minimise the amount of tax payable in that territory.'

---

[74] HMRC, *INTM*, para. INTM162031.

[75] See HMRC, *INTM*, paras. INTM162031 and INTM162031.

[76] See also Statement of Practice SP2/90.

[77] ICTA 1988, s. 795A(1).

There a general obligation not only to minimise the amount of tax payable in the other contracting state, but also to take specific steps (including claiming or otherwise securing the benefit of reliefs, deductions or allowances, and making elections for tax purposes). For this purpose, any question as to whether it would have been reasonable for a person to take these steps is determined on the basis of 'what might reasonably be expected to have been done in the absence of double taxation relief'. The application of such a rule in practice can give rise to considerable difficulties.

The HMRC *International Manual* (at para. INTM164140) gives examples previously given by the Inland Revenue in the March 2000 paper 'Double taxation relief for companies: outcome of the review' and by Parliament at the committee stage for the Finance Bill 2000.

These include acceptance of an estimated tax assessment in the other country which is likely to be excessive, not claiming an allowance or relief (for example expenses, capital allowances or losses) that is generally known to be available; and, where the other country's domestic law or the relevant treaty provides for alternative bases of taxation, not choosing the basis which would produce the lowest tax bill.

Examples where, in the view of HMRC, the provision would not apply are not claiming a relief, the availability of which is uncertain, and where disproportionate expenditure would have to be incurred in researching the other country's law and pursuing the claim; claiming that a loss incurred in the other country should be carried forward rather than backwards or vice versa; and the case of underlying tax paid by a subsidiary company where the UK company which claims relief for that tax is not in the position to influence the amount of tax paid.[78] The manual also notes that the foreign tax which is allowable for credit is the tax which represents the final liability and not tax paid on account. Similarly, interest or penalties which may be paid in the other country are excluded.

In *Bayfine UK Products v Revenue & Customs*,[79] HMRC sought to probe the outer limits of this rule. In order to do so, it argued, a comparison is to be made between the actual situation and the result if there had been no UK credit. But, it argued, the hypothesis of there being no UK credit should not feed through to affect the foreign tax analysis. The Special Commissioners were of the view, however, that the hypothesis is required to be taken only as a test of the reasonableness of the steps, and that this excluded the possibility that foreign anti abuse doctrine might treat a transaction as not having happened. They held that it is the person claiming credit who is expected to take the relevant steps and that the steps must be confined to those which the taxpayer claiming credit is in a position to take (as the HMRC manual states). They rejected the argument that a different standard applies in dealing with tax avoidance. In that case, the company claiming credit was, unusually, at the bottom of a chain of companies and thus not in a position itself to take the steps to reduce the foreign tax that HMRC argued it should have.[80]

---

[78] See HMRC, *INTM*, para. INTM161250, on minimising withholding taxes.

[79] (2008) Sp C 719

[80] See also *Hill Samuel Investments Ltd v R&C Comm* [(2009) Sp C 738

26-950   Administration of treaties

Claims for treaty relief are administered by the Centre for Non-Residents (CNR). It administers the tax affairs of non-resident individuals, trusts and intermediaries in the financial sector and is responsible for deduction and relief at source schemes. Certain issues involving the application of treaties are dealt with by the HMRC Business International.[81] Forms and explanatory material is available online, as is electronic submission of certain returns.[82]

Extensive information is published in the context of the application of treaties. The extent to which HMRC is bound by published guidance is an evolving area of administrative law. Most official publications contain caveats indicating, typically, that the information is 'guidance only'. The courts have indicated that a statement formally published to the world by the Revenue might safely be regarded as binding, subject to its terms in any case falling clearly within them.[83]

There is no general statutory advance ruling procedure. HMRC will advise on its interpretation of the law in relation to a specific transaction, including where the application of treaties is in issue, in accordance with HMRC Code of Practice (No. 10). Taxpayers are entitled to rely on such guidance only in accordance with administrative law principles.[84]

---

[81] Frequent internal reorganisations in recent years have resulted in name changes and some changes in function. HMRC manuals and other publications in recent years may, depending on their vintage, refer to the Inland Revenue International Division, Revenue Policy (International) and, most recently, CT and VAT International CT.

[82] See http://www.hmrc.gov.uk.

[83] *R. v Inland Revenue Commissioners, ex parte MFK Underwriting Agencies Ltd. & Ors. and related applications* [1989] BTC 561; [1989] STC 1873, QBD at 892.

[84] See, particularly, *R v Inland Revenue Commissioners, ex parte Matrix Securities Ltd* [1994] BTC 85; [1994] STC 272, HL.

Disputes and Mutual Agreement Procedure (MAP)

Chapter 18

27-000 Substantive disputes

Historically, disputes with the Revenue at a substantive level have generally been dealt with by way of appeal. All appeals in respect of double taxation relief were dealt with before the Special Commissioners.[1] Specific provision for appeal to the Special Commissioners in relation to questions of domicile or ordinary residence was provided in the Taxes Act 1988, s. 207, and, for income tax, in TCGA 1992, s. 9(2). Further appeals from determinations of the Special Commissioners could be made to the High Court on a point of law.[2] Such appeals were heard in the Chancery Division of the High Court. An appeal from the Special Commissioners could also be made direct to the Court of Appeal, if all the parties so consented. This occurred only if the Special Commissioners certified that the decision involved a point of law relating wholly or mainly to the construction of legislation which had been fully argued before them and fully considered by them, and if the leave of the Court of Appeal had been obtained.[3]

Under powers granted by the Tribunals, Courts and Enforcement Act 2007, s. 30, the Lord Chancellor has ordered the transfer the functions of the Special Commissioners to the new First-tier Tribunal or the new Upper Tribunal of the Tax Chamber set up under that Act with effect from 1 April 2009 (see Transfer of Tribunal Functions and Revenue and Customs Appeals Order SI 2009/56). The Special Commissioners are abolished with effect from that date. Simultaneously, an optional statutory review by HMRC of appealable decisions is introduced.[4] The appeal process will operate in two distinct stages. The first stage will be for the taxpayer to notify HMRC of an appeal. The taxpayer may ask for an internal review by HMRC; HMRC may offer such a review; or the taxpayer may appeal to the tribunal.[5] If the review does not resolve the dispute, then the second stage is for the taxpayer to notify the appeal to the tribunal.[6]

---

[1] Tax tribunal of first instance. See also TMA 1970, s. 46C(3).

[2] *Ibid.*, s. 56A(1).

[3] *Ibid.*, s. 56A(2).

[4] TMA 1970, s. 49B and following sections.

[5] TMA 1970, s. 49A.

[6] TMA 1970, s. 49B.

All appeals will commence in the Lower Tier Tribunal. The tribunal rules[7] contemplate that cases in the Tax Chamber may be dealt with in one of four procedural tracks: paper, basic, standard or complex (reg. 23). When proceedings are started, a case will fall into either the paper, basic or standard track as provided in the relevant practice direction. The tribunal may give a direction allocating a case to a different track at any time, whether on the application of a party or on its own initiative. The tribunal may give a direction allocating a case to the complex track if the tribunal considers that the case:

- will require lengthy or complex evidence or proceedings;
- involves an important principle of law or an unusually complex issue; or
- involves an unusually large financial sum.

Cases, and particularly complex cases, may be transferred to, and determined by, the Upper Tribunal (reg. 28).

The new appeal system eliminates the right to appeal decisions of either the Lower Tier or Upper Tribunal. In each case, permission to appeal must be obtained.[8] Where an appeal from the Upper Tribunal lies, it will be to the Court of Appeal. The Lower Tier or Upper Tribunal both have powers to review their respective decisions.[9]

27-050 Judicial review

Additional remedies may be available as a matter of administrative law in certain circumstances. Where there is no statutory right of appeal, judicial review may be obtained of the manner in which HMRC made the decision complained of. The new system established under the Tribunals, Courts and Enforcement Act 2007 will give the Upper Tribunal of the Tax Chamber jurisdiction to hear certain tax related applications for judicial review that were previously heard in the High Court.[10]

Judicial review is generally available where the decision complained of was such that no authority properly directing itself on the relevant law and acting reasonably could have reached it, a failure to comply with the rules of natural justice, a want or excess of jurisdiction or error of law on the face of the record. Recent cases of judicial review in the tax field have focused particularly on the extent to which HMRC may depart from a guidance it has given on the tax consequences of particular transactions.

Few reported applications for judicial review have involved treaty issues. Those that have, illustrate difficulties that have arisen in the applications of treaties. In *R v IRC, ex parte Commerzbank AG*,[11] the taxpayer, Commerzbank AG, was incorporated and resident in

---

[7] *Tribunal Procedure (First-Tier Tribunal) (Tax Chamber) Rules* 2009 (SI 2009/196).

[8] Tribunals, Courts and Enforcement Act 2007 (TCEA 2007), s. 11 and 13.

[9] TCEA 2007, ss. 9 and 10.

[10] TCEA 2007, s. 15.

[11] [1991] BTC 161; [1991] STC 271, QBD.

Germany. After protracted litigation[12] the taxpayer succeeded in recovering tax paid in respect of interest under art. 15 of the US Treaty. The taxpayer then sought to obtain the repayment supplement (interest) in respect of the tax overpaid. This was refused by the Inland Revenue on the basis that under domestic law, the repayment supplement was only payable to UK residents. The taxpayer applied to the High Court for judicial review. One of its arguments was that the residence requirement was inconsistent with the non-discrimination provisions of art. 20 of the German Treaty since it resulted in treatment in connection with taxation that was more burdensome than that imposed on UK nationals. The claim under the treaty was nor upheld by the court, although similar arguments on non-discrimination under the EC Treaty were ultimately upheld by the ECJ.[13]

In *R v IRC, ex parte Opman International UK*,[14] a company applied for a determination that they were not liable to tax on certain royalties paid to them in the UK pursuant to the Netherlands Treaty. Internal difficulties at the Inland Revenue over a long period of time caused the applicant's accountant to believe that the application would be refused. Without informing the Inland Revenue, the applicant applied for leave to seek judicial review, which was granted. Within a month, the Inland Revenue determined the matter in the applicant's favour. The applicant then sought to discontinue the judicial review proceedings and claim payment of their costs. No order for costs was made on the grounds that the applicant did not inform the Inland Revenue of the intention to seek judicial review. If an indication of that sort had been given, the court believed that the matter would have been dealt with at a higher level and would likely have been more promptly resolved.

Woolf J (as he then was) also noted that although an appeal procedure was available on the substance of the dispute, this did not exclude the possibility of judicial review. He noted that even though a judicial review is a procedure of last resort, it may be appropriate where the alternative procedure does not achieve a just resolution of the applicant's claim.[15]

In *R v IRC, ex parte Howmet Corp.*,[16] the applicant sought leave to apply for judicial review of a decision of the Inland Revenue to revoke a ruling that the UK subsidiary of a US parent company should be regarded as UK resident for tax purposes.

The ruling arose out of a proposed restructuring of the UK subsidiary which would involve payment of a dividend to the US parent, which would qualify for a half-credit under art. 10 of the US Treaty. The applicants claimed that they had made clear that the ruling was required in connection with the restructuring of the company and that they were not seeking clearance for the overall effect of the reconstruction, but only the residence of the company. The applicants argued that details of the capitalisation and the declaration and payment of the dividends were not relevant to the test of residency. The Crown argued that the utmost candour was required and that all the facts were not disclosed, including the intention to

---

[12] Case C-330/91, *IRC v Commerzbank* [1990] STC 285.

[13] Case C-1330/91 [1993] BTC 299; [1993] STC 605.

[14] [1985] BTC 606; [1986] STC 18, QBD.

[15] See, however, *O'Neil and Others v C.I.R* [2001] UKPC 17; [2001] STC 742 PC, where it was held that judicial review would only be granted in exceptional cases where appeals could be made by the statutory procedure.

[16] [1994] STC 413, QBD.

make a claim under art. 10 of the treaty. The court held that there was an arguable case and that consequently leave to seek judicial review was granted.

In *R. v I.R. Commrs., ex parte Camacq Corporation and Cambrian & General Securities plc*[17] an application for judicial review was sought in regards to a decision by the Inland Revenue to revoke a direction given to a UK company to pay a dividend gross. A US escrow agent held shares for the benefit of the US Treasury as part of a civil penalty levied against Mr Ivan Boesky. In the course of attempting to sell the shares of the company, it was proposed to pay a dividend on the shares and consent was sought for the tax credit to be repaid on the basis that the beneficial owner was the US Government and entitled to repayment of the credit by virtue of sovereign immunity. Without repayment of the tax credit, the transaction would not have gone ahead, because the sale price would not have been acceptable to the seller.

As soon as authorisation to repay the tax credit was given, the Inspector of Foreign Dividends (now the Centre for Non-Residents (CNR)) reported the authorisation to the International Division. The latter had doubts about whether, in the particular circumstances, it was appropriate to pay the tax credit. Consequently, the authorisation to pay gross was revoked. The Inland Revenue view was that the dividend seemed to have been artificially arranged in order to take advantage of the UK tax rules in circumstances in which it would appear that under the Taxes Act 1988, s. 235, and art. 10 of the US Treaty, the tax credit would not be available to other shareholders. Although the case did not deal specifically with the application of the treaty, it was analogous to a claim for a reduction of tax at source. In the course of his judgement, Lloyd LJ indicated, obiter, that although the Double Taxation Relief Regulations[18] permitted the making of arrangements in relation to dividends, there is no obligation on the Inland Revenue to enter into any such arrangement. If the Tax Inspector had never given his or her original authorisation, he or she could not have been compelled to do so by way of a judicial review. He concluded that the actions of the Inspector were not unreasonable in the circumstances and that the original direction to pay gross did not produce a legitimate expectation that the credit would be paid. The case is indicative of the fact that although the court has jurisdiction to review the accuracy in law of the Revenue's reason for revoking a decision to pay dividends gross, in appropriate circumstances such decisions are justified.

27-100 Complaints

HMRC has established procedures for dealing with complaints. Where taxpayers believe that they have been badly treated, they may ask for the case to be reviewed by the complaints manager for the office in which the matter arose.

If the complaints manager does not settle the complaint to the taxpayer's satisfaction, the matter may be referred to the director with overall responsibility to take a fresh look at it. The complaint may also be put to the adjudicator to consider the matter and recommend

---

[17] [1989] BTC 480; [1989] STC 785, QBD; [1989] STC 796, CA.

[18] SI 197/317.

appropriate action. The adjudicator is an impartial referee whose recommendations are independent.

Complaints dealt with by the adjudicator are limited to the way in which the HMRC has handled a taxpayer's affairs, such as mistakes, delays, behaviour of staff, departmental procedures or the use of discretion in making an individual decision.

The adjudicator's mandate does not cover ministerial decisions or appeals on substantive matters that are handled by way of appeal. It does not cover complaints already investigated by the Parliamentary Ombudsman or those on which a court has already ruled or which are already subject to court proceedings.

In certain circumstances, complaints may be made to the parliamentary ombudsman where administrative failure has led to injustice. All complaints must be referred to the ombudsman by a Member of Parliament. No investigation may be made into any action for which the person aggrieved has entitlement to apply to a tribunal or to a remedy in a court of law. However, investigations may be made if, in the circumstances, it is not reasonable to expect the person aggrieved to resort to such a right or remedy.[19]

By way of example, in the international context, delay in refunding tax to a Canadian company and delay in adjusting the PAYE code number of a research fellow at a Swiss University resulted in financial loss to these taxpayers because of an official currency devaluation in 1967. The ombudsman considered that the only adequate remedy in these cases would be an *ex gratia* payment of compensation equal to the financial loss suffered as a result of the maladministration. This approach was agreed by the Inland Revenue.[20]

27-150   MAP

Mutual agreement procedure (MAP) is provided for in most UK treaties other than those following the colonial model. The precise terms on which the MAP operates needs to be considered by reference to each individual treaty. Although the vast majority follow the OECD Model, they are not all identical. Since the MAP exists by virtue of treaties only, the starting point must be the relevant treaty. A modern example is found in the Czech Treaty. Article 24 reads as follows:

'(1)   Where a resident of a Contracting State considers that the actions of one or both of the Contracting States result or will result for him in taxation not in accordance with this Convention, he may, notwithstanding the remedies provided by the national laws of those States, present his case to the competent authority of the Contracting State of which he is a resident.

(2)   The competent authority shall endeavour, if the objection appears to it to be justified and if it is not itself able to arrive at an appropriate solution, to resolve the case by mutual agreement with the competent authority of the other Contracting State, with a view to the avoidance of taxation not in accordance with the Convention.

---

[19]   Parliamentary Commissioner Act 1967, s. 6(4).

[20]   'Second report of the parliamentary commissioner for administration'; annual report for 1968 Cases C-230/68 and C-258/68.

(3)   The competent authorities of the Contracting States shall endeavour to resolve by mutual agreement any difficulties or doubts arising as to the interpretation or application of the Convention.

(4)   The competent authorities of the Contracting States may communicate with each other directly for the purpose of reaching an agreement in the sense of the preceding paragraphs.'

Both the OECD and the EC have been active in improving the quality of the mutual agreement process and in resolving longstanding questions about its operation.[21] Much of this now appears in the commentary on art. 25 of the 2008 Model Treaty. The European dimension is discussed in chapter 19.

27-200   MAP: taxation not in accordance with the treaty

Mutual agreement procedure normally fulfils two dispute resolution roles. The first is to address cases raised by taxpayers that the terms of a treaty have not been adhered to by one of the tax administrations. Entitlement to invoke MAP by a taxpayer is not dependent on double taxation but by taxation that is not permitted by the treaty. Recourse to the MAP is most commonly found in relation to application of the arm's length principle, both between associated enterprises under art. 9 and in determining the attribution of profits to permanent establishments under art. 7, as well as the special relationship provisions of arts. 11 and 12. Where this occurs in the context of differing views between contracting states on the application of a treaty, most treaties that follow the OECD Model allow taxpayers to submit the issue for discussion between the competent authorities to see if they can agree a resolution.

Typically, a resident of a contracting state must present the case to the competent authorities in its state of residence. Thus, other than in the case of art. 9, which may involve residents of both contracting states and the tie-breaker rules in art. 4, the MAP cannot be validly invoked by presenting a case in the source state.

Mutual agreement procedure was operated in the UK entirely by administrative practice until it was put on a statutory basis in FA 2000. ICTA 1988, s. 815AA, provides a mechanism for giving effect to a case presented either to the commissioners of HMRC or the competent authority of the other contracting state that he or she is taxed otherwise than in accordance with the treaty.

In the UK, there is no set form of claim to initiate the MAP. Applications should be made in writing specifying the years concerned, the nature of the action giving rise to taxation not in accordance with the treaty, as well as the names and addresses of the parties to which the procedure relates, including UK taxpayers' tax district and reference numbers.[22] Mutual

---

[21] 'OECD: improving the resolution of tax treaty disputes', report adopted by the Committee on Fiscal Affairs on 30 January 2007.

[22] Inland Revenue, *Tax Bulletin* (No. 25, October 1996), p. 346; HMRC, *INTM*, para. INTM153270; HMRC's *Double Taxation Relief Manual*, para. 232, specifies that the position of the foreign revenue authorities together with copies of correspondence with those authorities should be provided.

agreement procedure is dealt with by HMRC Business International, except in the case of the petroleum industry, which is dealt with by the Oil Taxation Office.

The legislation clarifies that invoking the MAP under a treaty does not constitute a claim for relief and is accordingly not subject to s. 42 of TMA 1970 or other enactments relating to the making of claims.

27-250   MAP: time limits

Care should be exercised particularly in relation to time limits for presenting a case. The time limits in relation to treaties must be considered in the context of domestic limitations in each country and in the treaty.

Income and Corporation Taxes Act 1988, s. 815AA(6), requires any case for the MAP to be presented within six years of the end of the chargeable period to which the case relates, or such longer period as may be specified by treaty. The presentation of a case under the new legislation does not constitute a claim for relief, and, accordingly, TMA 1970, s. 43, and other statutes relating to time limits are inapplicable. It also resolves the problem which exists under other self-assessment legislation relating to claims, namely, that the claim should be quantified at the time that it is made. In addition, careful attention will need to be paid to time limits in other contracting states.

United Kingdom treaty practice is to rely on domestic time limits but, not infrequently, treaties include time limits in line with art. 25(1) of the OECD Model. Thus, art. 25(1) of the UK–Belgium Treaty specifies that:

'The case must be presented within three years from the first notification of the action resulting in taxation not in accordance with the provisions of the Convention.'

Most recently, extended time limits have started to appear which more closely reflect the UK domestic law, such as in art. 25(1) of the UK–Japan Treaty, which reads:

'The case must be presented within three years from the first notification of the action resulting in taxation not in accordance with the provisions of the Convention or, if later, within six years from the end of the taxable year or chargeable period in respect of which that taxation is imposed or proposed.'

In the UK, HMRC has agreed that this will be either the date of issue of a statutory notice required to conclude an assessment or any related appeal procedures for the period of assessment in question, or a letter of acceptance by an officer of the board of HMRC to settlement terms for the period in question.[23]

---

[23] See the competent authority agreement regarding the definition of 'first notification' under para. 1 of art. 26 (Mutual Agreement Procedure) of the Convention between the United States of America and the United Kingdom of Great Britain and Northern Ireland for the avoidance of double taxation with respect to taxes on income, signed at London on 24 July 2001; EU Code of Conduct on the Arbitration Convention; see also OJ C176 of 28 July, p. 8; see also Annex to the draft code of conduct Communication from the Commission to the Council, the European Parliament and the European Economic and Social Committee on the work of the EU Joint Transfer Pricing Forum in the field of business taxation from October 2002 to December 2003 and on a proposal for a Code of Conduct for the effective implementation of the Arbitration Convention (90/436/EEC of 23 July 1990) COM/2004/0297 final.

27-300   MAP: appeal versus MAP

Entitlement to invoke the MAP is expressed to be 'notwithstanding the remedies provided by the national laws' of the contracting states. It is, in consequence and additional process available to taxpayers and not a substitute for the appeal process or any other domestic law mechanisms. The practice adopted by HMRC in this respect is explained in the *International Tax Manual*:

> 'Companies can present their case to the UK competent authority whenever they feel double taxation is likely to be in point and protective presentations can be made to comply with the time limits. However a resolution under the mutual agreement procedure will not, other than in exceptional circumstances, be actively pursued until the amount of tax at stake has been finalised. This means that appeal rights must have been exhausted either through reaching an agreement with a taxpayer or through the litigation process.[24]'

Dilemmas in this respect are highlighted by the practice in relation to transfer pricing: Where an adjustment is made in relation to an issue raised in the UK and settled either by determination of an appeal under TMA 1970, s. 54, or by the courts, the UK would take the matter up under the MAP with the treaty partner to obtain that country's agreement to a corresponding adjustment. The precise implications of this approach have given rise to some controversy. TMA 1970, s. 54, provides for the settling of appeals by agreement. The effect of the section is that a settlement by agreement is deemed to be a determination by the Tribunal. The effect of this would be to limit MAPs to seeking corresponding relief in the other contracting state, where the dispute has been settled by agreement between HMRC and the taxpayer. As a result of discussions between HMRC and professional bodies, HMRC has indicated that it may be willing to discuss the scope for entering into competent authority discussions before an assessment is settled. It also welcomes early notification of disputes with overseas authorities. A claim for corresponding adjustment in respect of action by an overseas authority must be made within six years and a claim may be made within six years even if an appeal has been settled by agreement under s. 54 or earlier.[25] The UK competent authorities recognise that investigations may take many years to resolve and will therefore accept protective claims.

This may arise in other areas as illustrated by the Special Commissioners' decision in *Financial Institution v Inland Revenue Commissioners*.[26] The decision involved an application in 2002 by the Revenue to have appeal listed for hearing. The taxpayer had appealed in 1996 against refusal of tax credit claims in tax years 1991–93. The taxpayer was at the same time in dispute with the foreign revenue authority for the same period, and resolution of the foreign dispute might have removed the need for the UK appeal. Special Commissioner Avery-Jones noted that there could be two further appeals from the first instance court in the foreign appeal. He directed that the appeal stand over until determination by the first instance foreign court so long as it took place during the first half of 2003.

---

[24] HMRC, INTM, para. INTM470010.

[25] Chartered Institute of Taxation, 'Notes of meeting between Inland Revenue International Division and representatives of professional bodies held on December 10, 1996', 10 April 1997.

[26] (2002) Sp C 346.

27-350   MAP: methods of giving relief

Mutual agreement procedure is an imperfect remedy in that contracting states are only required to 'endeavour' to resolve difficulty, rather than actually to solve them. UK experience would indicate that most problems are ultimately resolved, although in many cases, this can take a considerable amount of time.

In relation to the US Treaty, the competent authorities have agreed to endeavour to deliver a position paper to the other party within 120 days of receipt of the presentation of a case. The objective of the two competent authorities is generally to resolve cases by concluding a mutual agreement within 18 months from transmittal of the position paper by one contracting state to the other. In the context of transfer pricing and advanced pricing agreements, they will endeavour to agree a joint timetable for dealing with the various stages of the application with the aim of securing mutual agreements within a similar time-frame, taking into account the complexities of the particular cases involved. There are no other published statements involving other contracting states. In some cases, delays may be extended, for example, because of language difficulties where both underlying documentation and the position papers of each contracting state are required to be translated. In relation to the US, where negotiations continue beyond a time-frame agreed upon, senior officials will undertake a review of the case to ensure that all appropriate action is taken to facilitate a resolution of the matter. In addition, the UK and US have undertaken not to withdraw from MAPs without meeting face to face to discuss specifically the problems or concerns that give rise to the consideration of withdrawal.

Mutual agreement procedure is a government to government activity and taxpayers have no legal entitlement to participate in or observe the negotiations. The process is one of consultation between the two competent authorities. As a practical matter, the UK recognises the interest of the taxpayer and does endeavour to keep taxpayers informed about progress and will invite taxpayers to make further submissions as may be helpful in reaching a resolution. The extent to which the taxpayer is invited to participate informally by providing and presenting information is at the discretion of the competent authorities. Mutual agreement procedure is an administrative process. It is in essence a request to the UK and its treaty partner to act reasonably in resolving a dispute.

The domestic legislation contemplates two ways in which a case may be resolved where a person is taxed in the UK or the other contracting state other than in accordance with the relevant treaty. Section 815AA(1)(b) permits HMRC either to arrive at a solution to the case or to make a mutual agreement with the competent authorities of the other contracting state. Where this is done, HMRC must give effect to the solution or mutual agreement 'notwithstanding anything in any enactment' – this gives broad powers to HMRC to adapt the tax rules to give effect to a treaty, either unilaterally or by mutual agreement. Any adjustment as is appropriate in consequence may be made whether by way of discharge or repayment of tax, the allowance of credit against tax payable in the UK, the making of an assessment or otherwise.[27]

---

[27] ICTA 1988, s. 815AA(2).

Following agreement between the competent authorities, the UK company will normally be invited to submit revised tax computations reflecting the agreed relief. This will need to be implemented in the form of a claim as contemplated by s. 815AA(3). A further time limit is imposed for claiming relief. Where a case is resolved through this procedure, a claim for relief under any provision of the Taxes Acts 1988 may be made pursuant to the resolution at any time within 12 months after notification of the resolution to the person affected. This applies notwithstanding any other time limits for making claims.[28]

27-400 MAP: treaty interpretation or application

Typical mutual agreement articles provide not only for the invoking of the procedure to resolve individual cases of the application of a treaty, but also authority for the contracting states to 'resolve by mutual agreement any difficulties or doubts arising as to the interpretation or application of the Convention'. This second authority does not require to be invoked by taxpayers but is the mechanism for maintaining the sound operation of the treaty. It may facilitate practical issues, such as the operation of procedures for relief at source, or the application of the treaty to changed domestic circumstances. There are also specific issues that are to be resolved by mutual agreement. The most common is the resolution of dual residence under art. 4(2)(d) of the OECD Model, where other tie-breaker tests have failed to produce a result. In the UK–US Treaty, a list of items suitable for agreement on the interpretation or application of the treaty are identified. The competent authorities may agree:

'(a) to the same attribution of income, deductions, credits, or allowances of an enterprise of a Contracting State to its permanent establishment situated in the other Contracting State;

(b) to the same allocation of income, deductions, credits, or allowances between persons;

(c) to the same characterization of particular items of income, including the same characterization of income that is assimilated to income from shares by the taxation law of one of the Contracting States and that is treated as a different class of income in the other Contracting State;

(d) to the same characterization of persons;

(e) to the same application of source rules with respect to particular items of income;

(f) to a common meaning of a term;

(g) that the conditions for the application of the second sentence of paragraph 5 of Article 7 (Business Profits), paragraph 9 of Article 10 (Dividends), paragraph 7 of Article 11 (Interest), paragraph 5 of Article 12 (Royalties), or paragraph 4 of Article 22 (Other Income) of this Convention are met; and

(h) to the application of the provisions of domestic law regarding penalties, fines, and interest in a manner consistent with the purposes of this Convention.[29]'

In the exchange of notes of 24 July 2001 to the US–US Treaty, the competent authorities agreed to publish any principle of general application established by agreement between

---

[28] ICTA 1988, s. 815AA(3).

[29] US Treaty, art. 26(3).

them. This authority is not infrequently used.[30] Any unpublished agreement would not have any binding effect in legal proceedings.

27-450   MAP: communication between competent authorities

The treaty article normally authorises the competent authorities to 'communicate with each other'. Although the precise scope of this authority is undefined, MAP articles are always found in conjunction with exchange of information provisions. This supports the mutual agreement process which necessarily involves the sharing of information. Communication for the purpose of MAP may not be used for any other purpose.

27-500   MAP: arbitration

The limits to MAP are highlighted by HMRC in the *International Manual*:

> 'It is very important to realise that the mutual agreement procedure does not guarantee the elimination of double taxation. The treaty says that the competent authorities will 'endeavour' to do so. In the vast majority of cases this is achieved but there is no guarantee. It is perfectly possible that each competent authority will believe (and have very good reasons for believing) that the arm's length price is different and this will result in unrelieved double taxation. This can happen only in extremis.[31]'

Despite the high success rate claimed, the process can be drawn out over many years, particularly in transfer pricing cases. The inability of MAP to ensure a final resolution of issues arising under treaties has been seen as one of the principal obstacles to ensuring an effective MAP. Accordingly, the EU and, more recently, the OECD[32] have endorsed compulsory binding arbitration as a mechanism to achieve certainty. Apart from the EC Arbitration Convention,[33] the earliest reference to this in a UK Treaty is in the exchange of notes to the UK–Azerbaijan Treaty with reference to art. 26(2) (Mutual agreement procedure) in which the competent authority of the UK agreed to notify the competent authority of Azerbaijan if a change in the domestic law of the UK to permit binding arbitration with a view to the negotiation of a protocol to provide for such a procedure. The existing domestic legislation in ICTA 1988, s. 815AA, could accommodate arbitration, except that no provision is made for disclosure of information to the arbitrators.

The 2008 treaties with France and the Netherlands are the first UK treaties to include a binding arbitration mechanism patterned on the OECD Model. The basic right to arbitration in the French Treaty reads:

---

[30] See, for example, the competent authority agreement regarding the definition of 'first notification' under para. 1 of art. 26 (Mutual Agreement Procedure) of the Convention between the US of America and the UK of Great Britain and Northern Ireland for the avoidance of double taxation with respect to taxes on income, signed at London on 24 July 2001; Memorandum of Understanding regarding pension schemes based on art. 24 of the convention between the UK of Great Britain and Northern Ireland ('UK') and the Swiss Confederation for the avoidance of double taxation with respect to taxes on income of 8 December 1977, signed at London on 12 February 2008.

[31] HMRC, *INTM*, para. INTM470010.

[32] OECD Model Treaty art. 25(5) inserted in 2008.

[33] Discussed in chapter 19.

'26(5) Where,

(a) under paragraph 1, a person has presented a case to the competent authority of a Contracting State on the basis that the actions of one or both of the Contracting States have resulted for that person in taxation not in accordance with the provisions of this Convention; and

(b) the competent authorities are unable to reach an agreement to resolve that case pursuant to paragraph 2 within two years from the presentation of the case to the competent authority of the other Contracting State;

any unresolved issues arising from the case shall be submitted to arbitration if the person so requests.'

The OECD adopts a liberal view as to when actions have resulted in taxation not in accordance with the treaty as including an official notification by a tax authority of its intention to impose tax in a particular manner.[34] Arbitration is not an alternative to resolution by agreement between the competent authorities. If they are agreed, then there can be no arbitration. The OECD also raised the possibility of alternative dispute resolution methods, such as mediation[35] or experts.[36] The benefit of such provisions even with other EU member states who are parties to the Arbitration Convention is that arbitration under these rules covers all unresolved questions under the respective treaties, not only the arm's length principle.[37] Taxpayers are offered the choice to accept the arbitrators' decision, but the binding nature of the arbitration, if the affected taxpayers do agree, is expressed as follows:

'Unless a person directly affected by the case does not accept the mutual agreement that implements the arbitration decision, that decision shall be binding on both Contracting States and shall be implemented notwithstanding any time limits in the domestic law of these States.'

The OECD recommends exclusion of domestic remedies if arbitration is elected.[38] This is reflected in the UK France Treaty thus:

'These unresolved issues shall not, however, be submitted to arbitration if a decision on these issues has already been rendered by a court or administrative tribunal of either State or if the case has been presented to either competent authority under the European Convention on the elimination of double taxation in connection with the adjustment of profits of associated enterprises, signed on 23rd July 1990.'

No priority is expressed in relation to the EU Arbitration Convention, but arbitration is excluded if a case has been presented under that convention. This exclusion does not appear in the UK–Netherlands Treaty. Thus, the general interaction between domestic remedies and the MAP will apply in relation to the Netherlands. Treaty provisions do not address the detailed procedural mechanisms to give effect to these rights, leaving the competent authorities of the contracting states to settle the mode of application of these provisions by mutual agreement. The OECD has proposed a model form of agreement that the competent

---

[34] Commentary on the OECD Model, art. 25, para. 72.

[35] Commentary on the OECD Model, art. 25, para. 86.

[36] *Ibid.*

[37] See chapter 19.

[38] Commentary on the OECD Model, art. 25, para. 76.

authorities may use as a basis to implement the arbitration process.[39] The model agreement is intended to stand as a framework for all arbitrations rather than for a particular dispute.

27-550   MAP and GATS dispute resolution

The OECD has identified problems that have arisen out of the application of the General Agreement of Trade in Services (GATS) which entered into force on 1 January 1995 and to which the UK is a party.

Articles XXII(3) of GATS provides that a dispute on the application of art. XVII of the agreement in national treatment rule may not be dealt with under the dispute resolution mechanisms of arts. XXII and XXIII if the disputed measure falls within the scope of an international agreement relating to double taxation. Where there is a dispute as to whether the measure is within the scope of a tax treaty, either state may refer the matter to the Council on Trade in Services, which must refer the matter for binding arbitration.

Difficult legal interpretations have arisen in relation to this. A footnote states that if the dispute relates to a treaty which exists at the time of entry into force of GATS, then the matter may only be brought to the Council on Trade in Services if both states agree. There is some debate about the legal status of a footnote.

The implication of this footnote is that tax treaties would be treated differently depending on whether they were concluded before or after the entry into force of GATS. The OECD considers this inappropriate, particularly where a treaty in force on 1 January 1995 is subsequently re-negotiated, or where a protocol is included after that time.

The OECD regards the expression 'falls within the scope' as inherently ambiguous. This is demonstrated by the inclusion of both an arbitration clause and a clause exempting pre-existing conventions from its application in order to deal with disagreements related to its meaning. In the view of the OECD, a country could not argue in good faith that a measure relating to tax to which no provision of a tax treaty applied fell with the scope of that convention. It argues that it is unclear whether the phrase covers all measures that relate to taxes covered by all or only some of the provisions of the tax treaty.

In order to avoid these difficulties, the OECD suggests a clause for inclusion in the treaty which statew that, for the purpose of art. XXII (3)3 of GATS, any dispute as to the application of the tax treaty in question will only be brought before the Council for Trade in Services with the consent of both contracting parties. It recommends that the interpretation of the paragraph should be resolved by MAP in the event of any doubt or any other procedure that the contracting states may adopt. The first treaty to address this issue is the UK–US Treaty. Article 1(2) specifies that the treaty does not restrict in any manner any benefit presently or in the future accorded by any other agreement between the contracting states. Furthermore, the application of art. XVII of GATS is specifically not applied, and any question arising as to the interpretation or application of the treaty and, in particular,

---

[39] Annex to the commentary to the OECD Model, art. 25.

whether a tax measure is within its scope, is to be determined exclusively in accordance with the MAP.[40] For this purpose, a 'measure' is a law, regulation, rule, procedure, decision, administrative action or any similar provision or action.[41] In the exchange of notes, the UK and the US identified the (non-tax) treaties between them that may impose national treatment or most favoured nation obligations. They have undertaken to ensure the proper interpretation of the tax treaty and other agreements with respect to tax measures, if further treaties come into force creating such obligations.

---

[40] US Treaty, art.1(3).

[41] Art. 1(3)(b).

Arbitration Convention

Chapter 19

28-000   Introduction

European Community member states executed a unique multilateral treaty on the elimination of double taxation in connection with the adjustment of profits of associated enterprises on 23 July 1990. Austria, Finland and Sweden acceded to the convention when they joined the EC in 1994. It is based on a draft directive first presented by the EC to the Council on 25 November 1976 and adopts some elements of the arbitration system originally proposed in the draft directive. The convention was drawn up in a single original in the Danish, Dutch, English, French, German, Greek, Italian, Irish, Portuguese and Spanish languages – all ten texts being equally authentic.[1] Although a treaty, rather than another EC instrument, the approach of the ECJ in reconciling different language versions is likely to be followed.[2]

The process of signature and ratification has been tortuous. Briefly, the convention came into force on 1 January 1995 for a five-year period.[3] It was supplemented by an additional convention signed on 21 December 1995 and provided for the accession of Austria, Finland and Sweden to the Arbitration Convention.[4]

By a protocol dated 25 May 1999,[5] the convention was extended for further five-year periods of five years at a time. This extension is automatic unless a contracting state informs the Secretary-General of the Council of the EU at least six months before the expiry of any five-year period. The protocol entered into force on 1 November 2004 and took effect as from 1 January 2000.

A convention to extend the scope of the Arbitration Convention to the EU member states that joined the EU on 1 May 2004[6] requires signature and ratification by each of the 25 EU member states at the time. It allows bilateral application of the convention between those member states that have ratified it, which will allow the convention to become partially applicable. The only member state which has not is Italy.

---

[1] The related conventions and protocols have also expanded the languages to match those of new member states.

[2] See, for example, Case C-420/98: *W.N. v Staatssecretaris van Financien* [2001] BTC 366; [2001] STC 974.

[3] Art. 20, first sentence.

[4] Convention of 21 December 1995 concerning the accession of the Republic of Austria, the Republic of Finland and the Kingdom of Sweden to the Convention on the Elimination of Double Taxation in Connection with the Adjustment of Profits of Associated Enterprises (OJ C 26 of 31 January 1996).

[5] OJ 1999 C 202.

[6] OJ C160 of 30 June 2005, pp. 1–22.

The Council of Ministers adopted a decision extending the scope of the Arbitration Convention to Bulgaria and Romania from 1 July 2008.[7]

The convention represents a remarkable development in dealing with double taxation within the EU. First, because it is a multilateral treaty on the subject, and, second, because it has acted as a model for arbitration between tax authorities. It is the first UK treaty to deal with dispute resolution between competent authorities by arbitration. It offers an alternative to bilateral treaties in some cases, although both may in some instances be invoked at the same time. In cases where there is no bilateral tax treaty, or where the treaty does not provide for a MAP,[8] this convention offers the only possibility for such arrangements.

The EU Joint Transfer Pricing Forum, which was aimed at finding pragmatic, non-legislative solutions to the practical problems posed by transfer pricing practices in the EU, produced the code of conduct[9] adopted by the Council of Ministers in November 2004, a political commitment to ensuring a more effective and uniform application by all member states. It also produced a code of conduct on transfer pricing documentation for associated enterprises in the EU adopted by the Council on 27 June 2006[10] to will standardise 'transfer pricing' documentation requirements.

28-050   Scope of convention

The convention does not make specific reference to its personal scope in the same way as the OECD Model. Article 1(1) of the convention specifies that the convention applies to 'an enterprise of a contracting state'. No further explanation of the term is provided, although art. 3(2) adopts a variant of the OECD Model in specifying that any term not defined in the convention is to have the meaning it has under the applicable treaty between the member states concerned, unless the context requires otherwise.[11] This will mean that the precise application will vary from treaty to treaty somewhat uneven depending on the countries concerned, particularly in relation to partnerships and joint ventures. The position is particularly uncertain where more than two countries are involved or where there is no treaty between the countries concerned. Plainly, the convention will not apply to cases where one party to a transaction is not an 'enterprise'.

Article 1(2) states that a permanent establishment of an enterprise of a contracting state situated in another contracting state is deemed to be an enterprise of the state in which it is situated. The definition thus excludes the application of the convention to residents of third states. Permanent establishments of non EC enterprises in two or more EC countries would not be able to rely on the provisions of the convention.

---

[7] OJ L 174 of 3 July 2008, pp. 1–5.

[8] For example, UK–Greece Treaty.

[9] OJ C176 of 28 July 2006, p. 8.

[10] OJ C176 of 28 July 2006, p. 1.

[11] See chapter 8, para. 17-050, on the meaning of enterprise.

The territorial scope of the convention is restricted to that defined in art. 227(1) EC of the treaty establishing the EEC but excludes the French overseas territories, the Faroe Islands and Greenland.[12]

28-100 Taxes covered

The convention applies generally to taxes on income.[13] It covers, in particular, direct tax on individuals and companies that are imposed by member states (income tax and corporation tax in the UK) and where adjustments are made to profits of an enterprise in a contracting state, either under its domestic law or under the transfer pricing principles established in the convention. The convention is applicable only to taxes on income as specifically set out[14] and any identical or similar taxes that may be imposed by member states after the date of signature. Thus, the CFC charge[15] appears excluded by reason of the decision in *Bricom Holdings Ltd v IRC*.[16] Therefore, transfer pricing disputes involving controlled foreign companies as it applies to the CFC charge will be outside the convention.

Likewise, the taxes covered in the convention do not always correspond precisely with the taxes referred to in bilateral treaties between member states. For example, in the case of Germany, it excludes the capital tax (Vermagensteuer) covered in the Germany–UK Treaty. The trade tax (Gewerbesteuer) is covered only in the convention insofar as it is based on trading profits. By comparison, the trade tax in the Germany–UK Treaty is covered in relation to the tax as it applies both to income and to capital. There is also some inconsistency between the various member states. For example, the Danish church tax is covered by the convention, but the German church tax is not.

28-150 Arm's length standard

The convention is engaged where:

> 'Profits which are included in the profits of an enterprise of a contracting state are also included or are also likely to be included in the profits of an enterprise of another contracting state on the grounds that the principles set out in article 4 and applied either directly or in corresponding provisions of the law of the state concerned have not been observed.'

The arm's length standard set out in art. 4 of the convention adopts precisely the wording developed in art. 9(1) of the OECD Model in connection with related party dealings. It also reproduces art. 7(2) of the OECD Model, which requires the profits of a permanent establishment to be determined on a separate enterprise basis.[17] Thus, the convention covers both cases where a transaction is carried out directly between two legally distinct enterprises

---

[12] Art. 16.

[13] Art. 2(1).

[14] The taxes are listed in art. 2(2).

[15] ICTA 1988, s. 747.

[16] [1997] BTC 471; [1997] STC 1179 CA.

[17] See chapter 8, para. 17-150ff.

and cases where a transaction is carried out between one of the enterprises and the permanent establishment of the other enterprise situated in a third country.[18] By adopting these well-established standards, the contracting parties avoid any new controversy on the subject. No explicit reference is made to the OECD Transfer Pricing Guidelines. Adoption of OECD language means that interpretation is facilitated by reference to the OECD Commentary on these articles, and the various OECD studies on transfer pricing are implicitly recognised. In furtherance of this, the Code of Conduct requires the arm's length principle 'as promulgated by the OECD' to be applied, 'without regard to the immediate tax consequences for any particular Contracting State'.[19] However, any source of double taxation arising for reasons other than the application of the arm's length principle is outside the scope of the convention.

28-200   Participation in management, control or capital

The convention applies the OECD Model test as to when profits of associated enterprises are subject to adjustment. It thus applies where an enterprise of a contracting state participates directly or indirectly in the management, control or capital of an enterprise in another contracting state. Alternatively, it applies where the same persons participate directly or indirectly in the management, control or capital of an enterprise in two different contracting states.[20] The convention does not explicitly address the application of bilateral treaties to interest and royalties where amounts are affected by 'a special relationship between the payer and the beneficial owner of the interest or the royalties, or between both of them and some other person'.[21] However, the broad scope of the convention by reference to the principles in art. 4 means that the effect of the application of the royalty or interest articles on double taxation will need to be taken into account.

28-250   Elimination of double taxation

The central distinguishing feature of the convention from the mutual agreement provisions of bilateral treaties is that its purpose is to guarantee the elimination of double taxation. For this purpose, the convention establishes its own standard as to when double taxation is deemed to be eliminated. Double taxation of profits is treated as having been eliminated if either the profits are included in the computation of taxable profits in one state only, or the tax chargeable on those profits in one state is reduced by the tax chargeable on them in another.[22] Relief from double taxation in the form of corresponding adjustments where profit that has been taxed in one state is increased in another state, as specified in art. 9(2) of the OECD Model Convention, is not included. This is, however, built in to the interpretation of the elimination of double taxation. No provision is made for so-called secondary

---

[18] Joint Declaration on art. 4(1).

[19] Code of Conduct, para. 3.1(a).

[20] See chapter 8, para. 17-700.

[21] See chapter 9, para. 18-150.

[22] Art. 14.

adjustments to restore the overall relationship of the parties after adjustments have been made.

28-300   Time limits

The EC Arbitration Convention adopts the same three-year limitation rule for presenting a case to the competent authorities found in the OECD Model.[23] Where the mutual agreement is sought with competent authorities in an EU member state, there will be a choice as to whether the MAPs of a bilateral treaty are invoked or whether the equivalent provisions under art. 6 of the Arbitration Convention are used (although bilateral treaty MAP in most cases cannot lead to arbitration). The time limits in relation to other bilateral treaties must still be viewed in the context of domestic limitations or those specified in the relevant treaty. In the UK, where the general time limit for invoking MAP is six years, if the convention is not evoked within the three-year convention limit, arbitration will not be possible.

The three-year time limit starts to run upon the first notification of the action which results or is likely to result in double taxation.[24] The meaning of this expression is addressed in the Code of Conduct under which all member states agreed that the date of the first tax assessment notice or equivalent which results or is likely to result in double taxation is considered as the starting point for the three-year period. The precise application of this in the domestic law of each member state is set out in the Annex to the Code of Conduct.[25] In the UK, HMRC has agreed that this will be either the date of issue of a statutory notice required to conclude an assessment and/or any related appeal procedures for the period of assessment in question, or a letter of acceptance by an officer of the board of HMRC to settlement terms for the period in question.

28-350   Adjustment procedure

Details of the mutual agreement and arbitration procedures comprise the bulk of the convention and constitute its most innovative features. Unlike most bilateral treaties, the procedures for seeking mutual agreement are set out at length.

Initial resolution

An opportunity for quick resolution of adjustments is initially provided by art. 5, which requires a contracting state intending to adjust the profits of an enterprise to inform the enterprise of its intended action and to provide it the opportunity to inform the other enterprise. This is intended to give that other enterprise the opportunity in turn to inform the other contracting state. Sufficient time must be given to the taxpayer to notify relevant related parties and the other contracting state. If, after this has been done, both the enterprises and the contracting states agree to the adjustment, the matter is concluded.

---

[23] Art. 6(1).

[24] Art. 6(1).

[25] Code of Conduct, para. 1.

MAP

If either enterprise considers that the arm's length principle has not been properly applied, it may invoke the MAP irrespective of any other remedy provided under domestic law.[26] In the UK, this is done under the same statutory provisions as bilateral MAP.[27] The right differs from the OECD Model in that the case may be presented either to the competent authority of the state of residence or in which its permanent establishment is situated.[28] Furthermore, if other states may be concerned in the case, the competent authority to whom the case is presented must, without delay, notify the competent authorities of those other states.

If the complaint appears to be well-founded and if the competent authority receiving the case is not itself able to arrive at a satisfactory solution, then the competent authority receiving the case must endeavour to resolve the case by mutual agreement with the competent authority of any other contracting state concerned, even if time limits under domestic laws have expired.[29] Detailed procedures for the conduct of the MAP is set out in the code to resolve cases as quickly as possible having regard to the complexity of the issues in the particular case.[30] This resolution is given effect to in the UK by ICTA 1988, s. 815AA.

Arbitration

If the competent authorities jointly fail to resolve the matter by agreement that eliminates double taxation within two years of the case first having been submitted, they must establish an advisory commission in accordance with the convention's procedures.[31] Thus, arbitration is not an option offered to the taxpayer. The competent authorities are bound to resort to this automatically if the case is not resolved within the time limit.

The Code of Conduct sets out detailed requirements as to when a case will be regarded as having been submitted according to art. 6(1) in order to determine the commencement of the two-year period. Thus, a case is submitted when the taxpayer provides the following:

- identification (such as name, address, tax identification number) of the enterprise of the contracting state that presents its request and of the other parties to the relevant transactions;
- details of the relevant facts and circumstances of the case (including details of the relations between the enterprise and the other parties to the relevant transactions);
- identification of the tax periods concerned;
- copies of the tax assessment notices, tax audit report or equivalent leading to the alleged double taxation;

---

[26] Art. 6(1).

[27] ICTA 1988, s. 815AA. See chapter 18, para. 27-150.

[28] See chapter 18, para. 27-150.

[29] Art. 6(2).

[30] Code of Conduct, para. 3.

[31] Art. 7(1).

- details of any appeals and litigation procedures initiated by the enterprise or the other parties to the relevant transactions and any court decisions concerning the case;
- an explanation by the enterprise of why it thinks that the principles set out in art. 4 of the Arbitration convention have not been observed;
- an undertaking that the enterprise shall respond as completely and quickly as possible to all reasonable and appropriate requests made by a competent authority and have documentation at the disposal of the competent authorities; and
- any specific additional information requested by the competent authority within two months upon receipt of the taxpayer's request.[32]

The code treats the two-year period as starting when this information and the request are received by the competent authority or, if later, the date of the tax assessment notice or equivalent notifying a final decision on the additional income.[33]

Advisory Commission

The term arbitration does not appear in the convention. The Advisory Commission is the panel established on an ad hoc basis to hear disputes under the convention.[34] It consists of a chairperson plus two representatives of each competent authority and an even number of independent persons of standing (to be appointed by agreement or by the drawing of lots by the competent authorities concerned).[35] A list of independent persons of standing is maintained by the Secretary General of the Council of the EC, with five persons nominated from each member state.[36] It specifies in detail the qualifications for nomination. The chairperson must be either qualified to hold the highest judicial office in his or her country or a jurisconsult of recognised competence.[37] Taxpayers have no participation in the selection of the panel. The competent authorities may object to independent panel members if they work for the tax administration concerned, or if they are owners, employers, or advisers of one of the parties, or where adequate objectivity is not assured.

The arbitration process is between the contracting states concerned and not between the taxpayer and the authorities. This is also one of its disadvantages – in principle, the taxpayer is not involved in the process. The Code of Conduct amplifies the procedures for the functioning of the Commission.[38] However, art. 10(2) of the convention permits the associated enterprises in question to appear or be represented before the Advisory Commission on request. The enterprises concerned must appear before the commission if requested by the commission to do so.

---

[32] Code of Conduct, para. 2(i).

[33] Code of Conduct, para. 2(ii).

[34] Art. 9(1).

[35] Art. 9(3).

[36] Art. 9(4).

[37] Art. 9(5).

[38] Code of Conduct, para. 2(i).

Information

The taxpayers concerned may provide any information, evidence or documents that they consider likely to be of use to the commission. Taxpayers and the competent authorities must give effect to any request for information from the commission. However, contracting states are not required to carry out administrative measures at variance with their domestic law or normal administrative practice, or to supply information not obtainable under domestic law or normal administrative practice. Similarly, competent authorities are not obliged to supply information that would disclose any trade secret or be contrary to public policy.[39] Disclosure of information by HMRC to the commission is authorised by Taxes Act 1988, s. 816(2A). The commission itself is also subject to security obligations. The UK enforces this with criminal sanctions under FA 1989, s. 182A.

Costs

The taxpayer is entitled to representation and must bear its own costs in connection with the proceedings. The other costs of the procedure are borne equally by the contracting states concerned. Participation by the enterprise, whether at its request or at the request of the commission, will be at its own cost. Article 11 (3) of the convention provides that the costs of the arbitration procedure are to be borne by the contracting states concerned equally, other than those of the associated enterprises. The convention is silent on the taxpayers' costs; therefore, it would appear that no award of costs is possible in that regard.

Opinion of Advisory Commission

The opinion of the Advisory Commission is to be adopted by simple majority and must be delivered not more than six months from the date on which the matter was referred to it.[40] A decision that will eliminate double taxation must be taken within six months of the date on which the Advisory Commission delivers its opinion.[41] The Code of Conduct sets out the expected contents of the opinion.[42] The competent authorities may take a decision that deviates from the Advisory Commission's opinion, but if they fail to reach agreement, they are required to act in accordance with that opinion.[43] In the UK, opinions of the Advisory Commission are to be given effect to pursuant to s. 815B(1)(b) of the Taxes Act 1988 and s. 815B(3) of the Taxes Act 1988 in relation to the extension of time limits.

Where transfer pricing disputes arise in the context of other EU member states, there are advantages in invoking the Arbitration Convention rather than simply the bilateral treaty. The availability of arbitration does provide an incentive for the tax authorities to resolve the question.

---

[39] Art. 10(1).

[40] Art. 11(1).

[41] Art. 12(1).

[42] Code of Conduct, para. 4.4.

[43] Art. 12(1).

28-400   Choice of forum

The Arbitration Convention permits the arbitration procedures to operate, even where the matter is before the courts of a member state. In this setting, taxpayers are not precluded from appealing transfer pricing assessments while proceeding with competent authority proceedings In such a case, the two-year limitation period will only start to run when the judgement of the final court of appeal is given. The establishment of the Advisory Commission charged with addressing the double taxation question need only be established either when the time for appeal has expired or any appeal has been withdrawn before a decision is delivered.[44] The extent to which these remedies are independent in practical terms is limited by the extension of the time taken to progress through the various stages set out in the convention.

A further dimension is added by the consequences in domestic law of judicial decisions. This is addressed in the convention as follows:

> '7(3) Where the domestic law of a contracting state does not permit the competent authorities of that state to derogate from the decisions of their judicial bodies, paragraph 1 shall not apply unless the associated enterprise of that state has allowed the time provided for appeal to expire, or has withdrawn any such appeal before a decision has been delivered. This provision shall not affect the appeal if and in so far as it relates to matters other than those referred to in article 6.'

The UK has recorded a declaration that it regards this as applicable to the decisions of UK courts. The HMRC position is that before the arbitration stage can commence, the time for appeal must have expired without an appeal having been made or the taxpayer must have withdrawn the appeal or settled it by agreement. As a result, UK taxpayers are put to the choice, in effect, of choosing arbitration or the domestic appeals process. Since the convention only applies to transfer pricing, appeals may relate to issues of double taxation not addressed by the convention. In this context, HMRC will agree that taxpayers will not be denied access to arbitration, purely because of the outstanding appeal or appeal rights, as long as suitable undertakings are given by the taxpayer acknowledging that the appeal's process will not extend to the transfer pricing issue which is the subject of arbitration.[45] The EU Transfer Pricing Forum noted that this practice is widely adopted in member states and has simply recommended that tax collection procedures be suspended during the dispute resolution process.[46]

The convention applies strictly to transfer pricing disputes and not to any other matters that may be the subject of mutual agreement proceedings. Presentation of a case under the convention involves the same procedure in the UK as under bilateral treaties. The remedy for a failure to carry out the provisions of the convention would be by way of judicial review.

---

[44] Art. 7(1).

[45] Inland Revenue, *Tax Bulletin* (October 1997), p. A67.

[46] Code of Conduct, para. 5.

28-450   Penalty proceedings

The competent authorities are not required to initiate mutual agreement arbitration proceedings if domestic, legal or administrative proceedings against the taxpayer have resulted in a final ruling that one of the enterprises is liable for a serious penalty by virtue of an action giving rise to an adjustment or transfer of profits.[47] A schedule to the convention details what each member state regards as a serious penalty. Typically, these relate to fraudulent or criminal conduct. In the UK, 'serious penalty' means criminal and administrative sanctions in respect of the fraudulent or negligent delivery of incorrect accounts, claims or returns for tax purposes. A mere allegation that serious penalty proceedings will commence will not eliminate competent authority proceedings which may be stayed until the judicial or administrative proceedings have been concluded.[48]

28-500   Conclusion

The convention is a significant step forward in solving increasingly difficult transfer pricing issues. Since the convention entered into force on 1 January 1995, it is understood that there is only one decided arbitration. This has led some to conclude that the convention is of little practical significance. A number of practitioners, both in the private sector and in tax authorities have, however, commented that even if there were not to be a single arbitration, the convention has a helpful role to play by encouraging revenue authorities to take a reasonable approach to transfer pricing within the EU, rather than risk the arbitration procedure. The success of the convention is therefore in the absence of cases, rather than in their presence. The convention provides that the rulings of the commission may be published subject to the consent of the taxpayer concerned.[49] It would undoubtedly be an important contribution to learning on the subject if they are, particularly if detailed reasons for decisions are provided.

The original draft directive proposed that existing treaty arrangements with respect to transfer pricing would remain intact. The convention is silent on this point. A single standard and a single procedural approach for all transfer pricing issues within the Community are clearly desirable and the Code of Conduct proposes its time limit recommendations and conduct of MAP should be extended to bilateral treaty procedures.[50] The adoption of binding arbitration in bilateral treaties between member states[51] offers further choices for taxpayers.

Rules for ensuring procedural safeguards and due process in the proceedings of the Advisory Commission are not addressed in the convention, although the Code of Conduct had added flesh to the bones in this respect. The convention does not specify any judicial authority for

---

[47] Art. 8(1).

[48] Art. 8(2).

[49] Art. 12(2).

[50] Code of Conduct, para. 3.4.

[51] Chapter 18, para. 27-500.

supervision of the Advisory Commission, nor are any standards of fairness set out. The result is that a taxpayer who claims a lack of fairness will have to resort to domestic law remedies within the jurisdiction in which the proceedings might take place. It would have been preferable for the convention to deal with this both by stating a set of guidelines on procedural fairness, such as the 1977 Resolution of the Council of Europe on the 'Protection of the Individual in Relation to Acts of Administrative Authorities', and by providing an appeal process, preferably to the ECJ, as recommended by the European Commission.

International Administrative Cooperation

Chapter 20

29-000 Introduction

The rule that the courts of one country will not enforce the penal and revenue laws of another country has been described by Dicey[1] as well established and almost universal. Two explanations for the rule were set out by Lord Keith in Government of India, *Ministry of Finance (Revenue Division) v Taylor* [1955] AC 491. One is that enforcement of a claim for taxes is an extension of sovereign power. The second is that a court will not recognise liabilities running in a foreign state, if they run counter to the 'settled public policy' of its own. A court should not pass upon the provisions for the public order of another state.

Indirect enforcement of foreign revenue laws, indicates in particular, where a foreign company in liquidation seeks to recover from one of its directors assets under his or her control and where the liquidator is appointed by a foreign tax authority only for the purpose of satisfying the foreign authority's unsatisfied claim for taxes due.[2]

The last airing of the question of enforcement of the revenue laws of one state in another (and its implications under European law) occurred before the Court of Appeal in England at the end of the 20th century in *QRS1 Aps and Others v Frandsen*.[3] The case involved an attempt by the Danish tax authorities to collect unpaid taxes in England. The respondent (Mr Frandsen) was resident in the UK and domiciled in England within the meaning of the Brussels Convention on Jurisdiction and the Enforcement of Judgements in Civil and Commercial matters. He was therefore within the jurisdiction of the English courts. Until 1992, the respondent owned several Danish companies directly or indirectly. In November 1992, all of the assets of the companies were disposed of for cash. This cash was then used by the companies to purchase the respondent's shares. In 1994, the companies were put into liquidation on the ground that they had been engaged in asset stripping. In March 1995, the Danish tax authorities claimed corporation taxes of DKr 30 million plus DKr 10 million in interest against the companies. At that stage, the companies had no assets and their only creditor was the Danish tax authorities. The Danish tax authorities appointed a liquidator and agreed to fund an action by the companies against the respondent based on Danish law prohibiting companies from providing financial assistance for the acquisition of their own shares.

Claims were commenced both in England and Denmark for restitution of the value of the assets which were disposed of to finance the purchase of Mr Frandsen's shares. The

---

[1] Collins, L, *et al.*, p. 97.

[2] See *Peter Buchanan Limited v McVey* [1955] AC 516.

[3] [1999] BTC 8023; [1999] STC 616 CA.

companies also claimed, as an alternative, damages arising out of the respondent's negligence or reckless default in allowing the companies to suffer loss as a result of the asset stripping in which he had been involved. Mr Frandsen applied to strike out the action in the English courts on the basis that it was for the enforcement of a foreign revenue law.

29-050   What are the Revenue matters?

In the High Court, it was argued that although the principle on the indirect enforcement of foreign revenue laws still applied, the issue should be approached from the point of view of the Brussels Convention. In particular, art. 1 provides:

> 'This Convention shall apply in civil and commercial matters whatever the nature of the Court or tribunal. It shall not extend, in particular, to revenue, customs or administrative matters.'

It was argued that proceedings by a liquidator to realise a company's assets are 'civil and commercial matters' for the purposes of art. 1. Furthermore, indirect enforcement of a claim at the behest of a revenue authority is not a revenue matter. There is no definition of 'revenue matters' in the convention and no decision of the ECJ as to what the words mean. Sullivan J saw no reason to restrict 'revenue matters' in the context of the convention to direct as opposed to indirect enforcement of revenue claims. It was necessary to look at the substance and not merely the form of the claim.

In the Court of Appeal, Simon Brown LJ noted that the facts were in all material respects indistinguishable from those in the *Buchanan* case. In the absence of a definition in the convention or any ECJ decisions on the meaning of the term, the test was to ask what the original member states would have regarded as revenue matters for the purposes of the convention. After reviewing both foreign jurisprudence and commentary, it was held, therefore, that a claim of this kind plainly fell within the compass of revenue matters as that expression would be understood by all member states for the purposes of art. 1 of the convention.

29-100   Is the rule against enforcing foreign revenue judgements contrary to the EC Treaty?

The companies argued that the rule against indirect enforcement of revenue laws is incompatible with Community law. It was based on the assumption that the Brussels Convention does not extend to the claim (because it is a revenue matter), and therefore national rules on jurisdiction and enforcement apply. Those rules are subject to the rules of the EC Treaty, which is not altered or reduced by the Brussels Convention. The liquidator, it is argued, was seeking to provide a cross-border service protected by art. 49[4] of the treaty. That service was the recovery in England of monies owed to Danish companies for which the liquidator is remunerated by the Danish tax authorities. The rule against enforcing foreign tax judgements has the effect of restricting the liquidator's rights under art. 49. Any restriction on these rights must be objectively justified.

---

[4] Formerly art. 59.

For the purpose of this argument, the court only addressed the question of objective justification, assuming for this purpose the correctness of the earlier aspects of the argument. The question of justification was to be determined by examining the reasoning underlying the rule against enforcing foreign tax claims. The two explanations for the rule as set out by Lord Keith in *Government of India, Ministry of Finance (Revenue Division) v Taylor* [1955] AC 491. One is that enforcement of a claim for taxes is an extension of sovereign power. The second is that a court will not recognise liabilities running in a foreign state if they run counter to the 'settled public policy' of its own. A court should not pass upon the provisions for the public order of another state. It was argued by the companies that the first explanation is a justification for the exclusion of direct enforcement claims. However, in the case of indirect claims, it was agreed that there is no need to scrutinise the Danish tax law, and therefore the second explanation does not apply. These arguments were rejected by the court on the basis that once it is recognised that an indirect claim is caught by the rule, simply because in substance it is a claim brought by a nominee for a foreign state to give extra-territorial effect to that state's revenue law, both explanations apply equally to justify a bar on indirect claims as on direct claims. If the claim that this is a private law claim is rejected, there can be no better reason for allowing indirect claims than direct ones. The court had no doubt on the interpretation of the relevant Community law and therefore felt it unnecessary to make a reference to the ECJ.

Although the courts had no difficulty in dismissing the claim and, in particular, rejecting the suggestion that the longstanding rule was amended by the EC Treaty or by the Brussels Convention. Simon Brown LJ acknowledged that within the EU, there may be good arguments for disapplying the rule with regard to both direct and indirect claims, while rejecting the idea that the law currently permitted this. He noted the words of Lord Templeman in *Williams and Humbert Limited v W & H Trademarks (Jersey) Limited* [1986] AC 368, in which he said:

'This rule with regard to revenue laws may in the future be modified by international conventions or by the laws of the European Economic Community in order to prevent fraudulent practices which damage all states and benefit no state.'

The most dramatic development in 21st century treaty practice has been the rapid expansion of international cooperation among tax administrations and the development of international instruments to facilitate this. The UK is at the forefront of this.

29-150   Authority for administrative cooperation

While historically, sovereign states did not cooperate with each other in the administration of taxation, an important exception over the last 60 years (at least) is in the area of exchange of information. This has been viewed as the single route whereby contracting states gave effect to the purpose stated in the heading of model treaties in relation to the prevention of tax evasion.

Exchange of information with foreign tax administrations has long been associated with UK tax treaties. The domestic authority for such exchange has undergone significant change in the first years of the 21st century. Historically, domestic authority to exchange information was linked to the authority to relive double taxation by treaty.[5] Until 2000, exchange of information with treaty partners was only possible within the framework of a tax treaty generally. However, as part of the UK's participation in the OECD Programme against Harmful Tax Practices, Taxes Act 1988, s. 815C, was inserted by FA 2000, s. 146(1). It contemplated the conclusion of agreements between the UK and any territory with a view to the exchange of information necessary for carrying out the domestic laws of the UK concerning income tax, capital gains tax and corporation tax in respect of income and chargeable gains; and those of the other territory. This was to give effect in domestic law to tax information exchange agreements entered in to with tax havens pursuant to the OECD programme. The second legislative change was expansion of the domestic authority to disclose information to foreign tax administrations; in the relevant legislation, the terms 'necessary for carrying out' in relation to this expansion were changed to 'foreseeably relevant to the administration or enforcement of' by FA 2003, s. 198(1). Any treaty made before that date was required to be read as including this wider language, thus overriding the treaties with retrospective effect.[6]

The current regime is found in FA 2006, ss. 173 to 175, which set out a code that deals with all forms of administrative cooperation between HMRC and foreign tax administrations.[7] The central direction to give effect to treaties that cover this area is s. 173, which reads:

'(1) If Her Majesty by Order in Council declares that–

    (a)   arrangements relating to international tax enforcement which are specified in the Order have been made in relation to any territory or territories outside the UK, and

    (b)   it is expedient that those arrangements have effect,

those arrangements have effect (and do so in spite of anything in any enactment or instrument).

(2)   For the purposes of subs. (1) arrangements relate to international tax enforcement if they relate to any or all of the following–

    (a)   the exchange of information foreseeably relevant to the administration, enforcement or recovery of any UK tax or foreign tax;

    (b)   the recovery of debts relating to any UK tax or foreign tax;

    (c)   the service of documents relating to any UK tax or foreign tax.'

The authority thus now applies to all taxes or duties imposed by the UK. In the case of foreign taxes, it is restricted to tax or duty imposed under the law of the territory, or any of the territories, in relation to which the treaty has been made.[8]

---

[5] See, for example, former ICTA 1988, s. 788(2), and TCGA 1992, s. 277(4).

[6] FA 2003, s. 198(3).

[7] The previous legislative provisions were repealed by FA 2006, s. 178 and Sch. 26.

[8] See FA 2006, s. 173(3).

29-200   Exchange of information: duty of confidentiality

At common law, there appears to have been no duty of confidentiality, although there is apparently a convention that the Revenue does not supply the Treasury or other government departments with confidential information relating to individual taxpayers.

Since 2005, direct taxation is under the management of the Commissioners for Revenue and Customs.[9] The Revenue and Customs officials may not disclose information which is held by the Revenue and Customs in connection with a function of the Revenue and Customs.[10] Under domestic law, Each person who is appointed as a Commissioner or officer of the Revenue and Customs must make a declaration acknowledging this obligation of confidentiality.[11] In addition, a person who discloses revenue and customs information relating to a person whose identity is specified in the disclosure, or whose identity can be deduced from it, is guilty of an offence.[12] Article 8 of the European Convention of Human Rights has the effect of imposing a duty of confidentiality.

Under UK domestic law, HMRC may disclose personal information to other government departments under a variety of statutes. As will be seen in this chapter, the extent to which HMRC is able to disclose information under domestic law, impacts on the breadth of disclosure to foreign tax administrations. Statutes authorising domestic disclosure include:

- Land Registration Act 1925, s. 129;
- Parliamentary Commissioner Act 1967, s. 8;
- FA 1972, s. 127;
- Social Security Pensions Act 1975, s. 59K(6);[13]
- FA 1978, s. 77;
- Tenant's Rights etc. (Scotland) Act 1980, s. 1;
- Social Security and Housing Benefit Act 1982, s. 25;
- National Audit Act 1983, s. 8;
- Data Protection Act 1984, s. 17;
- Housing Associations Act 1985, s. 62;
- Social Security Act 1986, s. 59;
- Taxes Act 1988, ss. 375(9), (10), 816;
- Social Security Administration Act 1992, s. 122;
- Charities Act 1993, s. 10(2).

HMRC may also disclose personal information to the police under:

- Drug Trafficking Offences Act 1986, s. 30;
- Prevention of Terrorism (Temporary Provisions) Act 1989, s. 17, Sch. 17.

---

[9] Commissioners For Revenue And Customs Act 2005 (CRCA 2005), s. 5.

[10] CRCA 2005, s. 18(1).

[11] CRCA 2005, s. 3(1).

[12] CRCA 2005, s. 19(1).

[13] From July 18, 1990 by virtue of SI 1990/1446.

29-250   Exchange of information: authority to exchange of information

Authority to give effect to exchange of information treaty provisions does not itself relieve the obligations of confidentiality. Specific authority is provided. Accordingly, no obligation of secrecy (whether imposed by statute or otherwise) prevents the Commissioners for Her Majesty's Revenue and Customs or any authorised Revenue and Customs official from disclosing to any authorised foreign tax official any information which is permitted to be so disclosed in accordance with the treaty.[14] Exoneration from the obligation of secrecy is similarly given in relation to information required to be disclosed under the Arbitration Convention in pursuance of a request made by an Advisory Commission set up under that convention.[15]

29-300   Exchange of information: sources of information

The information that HMRC is required to provide may be broken down into three categories. The first is information that it already holds. The second is information from other government sources. In relation to this second category, FA 2006, s. 173(4)(a), specifies that no obligation of secrecy (whether imposed by statute or otherwise) prevents any Minister of the Crown, or person with responsibilities in any government department, from disclosing to the Commissioners for Her Majesty's Revenue and Customs or any authorised Revenue and Customs official any information which is authorised to be disclosed under a treaty. Thus, information held by any part of the UK government is available to be provided to foreign tax administrations.

The third source of information is that available to HMRC by exercise of its information gathering powers. FA 2006, s. 174, codified the extension of the use of HMRC powers under s. 20 of TMA 1970 to call for information relevant to liability to income tax, corporation tax or capital gains tax for the benefit of foreign tax administrations in relation to taxes which are the subject of treaties. HMRC powers have themselves been consolidated by FA 2008, Sch. 36, to apply across the board to all taxes administered by HMRC. These replace those in FA 2006 and were expanded on 1 April 2009.

A number of provisions enhance the ability of the HMRC to provide information to tax authorities in other contracting states by requiring this information to be available. An example of this is the special powers to obtain information related to income from securities, particularly from intermediaries, under TMA 1970, s. 24. Subparagraph 24(3) excludes banks from the obligation to disclose any particulars relating to income from securities in cases where the person beneficially entitled to the income is not resident in the UK. However, where the beneficial owner of the income from such securities is resident in a country where a double taxation treaty under s. 788 is in effect, this exemption is inapplicable. Thus, banks are required to provide information where the beneficial owners are resident in treaty countries.

---

[14] FA 2006, s. 173(4)(b).

[15] *Ibid.*, s. 816(2A).

Parliament has given further significant powers to the Inland Revenue to assist foreign countries in carrying out the tax laws of those foreign countries. As a result of FA 2000, information returns made by financial institutions under TMA 1970, s. 17, have to include amounts paid or credited to individuals and the estates of persons who are not ordinarily resident in the UK and to trustees of discretionary and accumulation trusts where the trustees and beneficiaries are not UK resident. Provision is made for regulations to specify the form of return together with additional information to be furnished, including, in prescribed cases, the name and address of persons beneficially entitled to interest paid or credited. Although the audit power under Taxes Act 1988, s. 482, is abolished, the regulations may provide for a similar audit power.

The information powers contained in TMA 1970, s. 18, relating to returns of interest paid or received are amended to apply to paying and collecting agents, as well as banks. This is to replace the paying and collecting agent schemes, which are abolished. The effect of these rules is to put HMRC in a position to provide information on savings income to authorities of other countries by way of treaty.

The commentary to art. 26 of the OECD Model highlights that it is not only taxpayer specific information that may be exchanged. Other information relating to tax administration may also be exchanged.[16]

A narrower exception to the secrecy obligation is also made in relation to shipping and air transportation agreements. This permits disclosure of 'such facts as may be necessary to enable relief to be duly given in accordance with the arrangements specified'.[17]

29-350   Exchange of information: treaty provisions

Every bilateral double tax treaty that the UK has entered into contains an article dealing with exchange of information. UK practice is broadly in line with the OECD Model, the most recent version of which is reflected, for example, in the current UK – Saudi Arabia Treaty as follows:

> '26(1) The competent authorities of the contracting states shall exchange such information as is foreseeably relevant for carrying out the provisions of this Convention or to the administration or enforcement of the domestic laws of the contracting states concerning taxes of every kind and description imposed on behalf of the contracting states, or of their political subdivisions or local authorities, insofar as the taxation thereunder is not contrary to this Convention, *in particular, to prevent fraud and to facilitate the administration of statutory provisions against legal avoidance*. The exchange of information is not restricted by arts. 1 and 2 of this Convention.'

Treaties in this form provide for information exchanged to a very wide extent. The OECD adopted the wide 'foreseeably relevant' threshold for disclosure in the 2005 model. Information falls within this article if:

---

[16] Commentary to OECD Model, art. 26, para. 5.1.

[17] *Ibid.*, s. 816(4).

- it is for carrying out the provisions of the treaty; or
- it is for carrying out the provisions of the domestic law of either contracting state concerning taxes covered by the treaty insofar as taxation thereunder is not contrary to the treaty.

This gives broad authority to exchange information. Information is neither limited to the taxes that form the subject matter of the treaty nor to persons who are within the scope of the treaty. Thus, information may be exchanged about persons who are not residents of either contracting state. The wording in italics is not found in the OECD Model but is found frequently in recent UK treaties. Given the breadth authority, it is unclear what this additional language adds.

Earlier treaties do not authorise such extensive exchange. Many are patterned on earlier OECD language, such as the Korean Treaty, art. 27(1), the relevant part of which reads as follows:

> 'The competent authorities of the contracting states shall exchange such information as is necessary for carrying out the provisions of this Convention or of the domestic laws of the contracting states concerning taxes covered by the Convention insofar as the taxation thereunder is not contrary to the Convention.'

Information falls within this form of article if it is necessary for carrying out the provisions of the treaty; or the provisions of the domestic law of either contracting states concerning only taxes covered by the treaty. A number of treaties limit the exchange to information necessary for carrying out the provisions of the treaty, or for the prevention of fraud, or the administration of statutory provisions against legal avoidance in relation to taxes which are the subject of the agreement. Examples of this are to be found in the Seychelles Treaty, art. 14(1), and the UK–Namibia Treaty, art. 21. These narrower, exchange of information provisions, were also contained in the Swiss Treaty. Article 25(1) of the Swiss Treaty, as amended by the 2007 Protocol, limits exchange of information other than in connection with the application of the treaty to domestic law issues relating to holding companies and to domestic law 'in cases of tax fraud or the like'. In these treaties, where neither the application of the treaty itself, nor tax evasion or statutory anti-avoidance provisions are in issue, no exchange of information is authorised. Since residents of third countries will not generally be able to benefit from such treaties, information relating to them can only be exchanged in cases involving tax fraud or the application of statutory anti-avoidance provisions in one of the contracting states.

The scope of authority to supply information is further limited. Article 27(2) of the Korean Treaty (adopting OECD Model, art. 26(3)), for example, reads:

> 'In no case shall the provisions of paragraph 1 be construed so as to impose on a contracting state the obligation:
>
> (a) to carry out administrative measures at variance with the laws and administrative practice of that or of the other contracting state;
>
> (b) to supply information which is not obtainable under the laws or in the normal course of the administration of that or of the other contracting state;
>
> (c) to supply information which would disclose any trade, business, industrial, commercial or

professional secret or trade process, or information, the disclosure of which would be
contrary to public policy (ordre public).'

In modern treaties, a contracting state is not under an obligation to take administrative steps
beyond those of both states. Thus, the UK may not use its information powers on behalf of a
foreign tax administration not themselves able to use such information powers nor to use
information powers the other state has but which the UK does not. Similarly, a contracting
state is not under an obligation to supply information which is not obtainable under the laws
or in the normal course of the administration of that or the other contracting state. This
means, for example, if the other contracting state does not permit information to be
communicated between government departments, the UK competent authority may not
provide information obtained in this way. It may be noted that the article uses the word
'shall', implying that the exchange of information is mandatory, rather than discretionary.
Some limits on the obligation are contained in the article. The wording of the current model
is important. It relieves a contracting state from the obligation. The fact that there is no
discretion to provide information has the effect of a prohibition on providing information
that falls within this article, on the basis that the tax authorities are under a general duty of
confidentiality. Some other older treaties do not contain these limitations at all,[18] with the
result that, for example the UK may use information powers in FA 2008, Sch. 36, to obtain
information on behalf of such states even if the tax authorities there had no such powers.

Second, there is no obligation to supply information which would disclose any trade,
business, industrial, commercial or professional secret, or trade process, or information, the
disclosure of which would be contrary to public policy. Some treaties such as that with
Germany do not contain the public policy exclusion.

Another innovation of the 2003 OECD Model is reflected in art. 26(4) UK – Saudi Arabia
Treaty:

> 'If information is requested by a contracting state in accordance with this art., the other
> contracting state shall use its information gathering measures to obtain the requested
> information, even though that other State may not need such information for its own tax
> purposes. The obligation contained in the preceding sentence is subject to the limitations of
> paragraph (3) of this art. but in no case shall such limitations be construed to permit a
> contracting state to decline to supply information solely because it has no domestic interest in
> such information.'

Thus, each contracting state makes its information machinery available to the other, purely
as an extension of the machinery of that other state. Neither FA 2006, s. 174, nor its
successor provisions require any UK interest in a matter relating to the exercise of powers in
respect of a relevant foreign tax. The second sentence of this treaty provision would
preclude such a rule and any argument that to do so would be contrary to public policy.

The UK–France Treaty also reflects in part a new development in the 2005 OECD Model:

> '27(5) In no case shall the provisions of paragraph 3 be construed to permit a contracting state
> to decline to supply information solely because the information is held by a bank, other

---

[18] For example, UK–Burma (Myanamar), art. 15; UK–Nigeria, art. 25.

financial institution, nominee or person acting in an agency or a fiduciary capacity or because it relates to ownership interests in a person.'

Use of exchanged information

Early treaties imposed a simple and strict obligation on secrecy and disclosure as illustrated by art. 25 of the UK–Nigeria Treaty:

'Any information so exchanged shall be treated as secret and shall not be disclosed to any persons other than those (including a court or administrative body) concerned with the assessment, collection, enforcement or prosecution in respect of taxes which are the subject of this Agreement. No information shall be exchanged which would disclose any trade, business, industrial or professional secret or trade process.'

More recently, treaties have adopted a more permissive approach for the receiving state. 2007 Protocol to the UK–Swiss Treaty describes the duties of the receiving state as follows:

'25(2) Any information received under paragraph 1 by a contracting state shall be treated as secret in the same manner as information obtained under the domestic laws of that State and shall be disclosed only to persons or authorities (including courts and administrative bodies) concerned with the assessment or collection of, the enforcement or prosecution in respect of, the determination of appeals in relation to the taxes covered by this Convention, or the oversight of the above. Such persons or authorities shall use the information only for such purposes. They may disclose the information in public court proceedings or in judicial decisions.'

Under such treaties, the receiving state is required to do no more than treat it in the same way as locally obtained information. Disclosure is also permitted to persons or authorities concerned with the oversight of the administration and appeals. Both rules permit the receiving state latitude in how they deal with taxpayers' information and do not seek to impose an internationally recognized standard. The use of information obtained from foreign tax administrations has been evident in recent decisions of the Special Commissioners.[19]

A limitation under domestic law is imposed on the Commissioners for HMRC, and authorised Revenue and Customs officials not to disclose any information under a treaty, unless they are satisfied that the authorities of the territory concerned are bound by, or have undertaken to observe, rules of confidentiality with respect to the information which are not less strict than those applying to it in the UK and parallels these treaty obligations.[20] The exact basis for this in the treaties is unclear but it appears to be a legal limitation of the kind contemplated by art. 26(2)(a) of the OECD Model.

HMRC states that no information from an overseas tax authority can be disclosed to any other government department or to the police or used by HM Revenue and Customs for other purposes, such as national minimum wage or tax credits.[21] As already noted, a number of exceptions to the general rule apply to confidentiality in the domestic context which serve to permit the supply of potentially sensitive information to foreign tax administrations which

---

[19] See *Shepherd v R & C Commrs* (2005) Sp C 484, para. 30; *R and R v Holden (HMIT)* (2004) Sp C 422, at para. 85.

[20] FA 2006, s. 173(5).

[21] HMRC, *IHT*, para. INTM156050.

may then be passed on to other parts of the foreign government in cases where treaties only require exchanged information to be treated in the same way as locally obtained information. In the context of international exchanges of information, authority under the Prevention of Terrorism (Temporary Provisions) Act 1989 is perhaps the most troublesome. The legitimacy of the label of 'terrorist' varies enormously depending on political perspective. Furthermore, anti-terrorist legislation is notoriously used by undemocratic regimes in order to suppress opposition that falls far short of the notion in democratic societies.

Furthermore, it would be fair to note that in some of the UK's treaty partners, respect for the rule of law by those in power is weak. This may be accompanied by a disregard of international legal obligations and consequently domestic international and legal rights may be more theoretical than practical. If information is used for improper means, particularly in a covert manner, local legal remedies are unlikely to be of much use.

Other treaty provisions involving exchange of information

Certain procedures under bilateral double tax treaties implicitly involve exchange of information. Treaties that include art. 9(2) of the OECD Model in relation to transfer pricing adjustments require the competent authorities to consult each other if necessary in determining adjustments. Similarly, resort to the MAP in art. 25(1) requires communication with each other. It would, however, appear that in these cases, information on taxpayers needs to be handled in accordance with the exchange of information requirements of those relevant treaty articles.

Article 10(1) of the Arbitration Convention also contains information provisions. Apart from enabling the affected enterprises to submit information, the convention requires the competent authorities of contracting states to effect any requests made by the Advisory Commission for information, evidence or documents. This authority is subject to the limitations commonly found in double tax treaties, namely, that states are not under any obligation:

- to carry out administrative measures at variance with domestic law or normal administrative practice;
- to supply information which is not obtainable under domestic law or normal administrative practice; or
- to supply information which would disclose any trade, business, industrial or professional secret, or trade process or information, the disclosure of which would be contrary to public policy.

An exchange of notes of 15 December in connection with the 1996 Protocol to the treaty with Denmark contains an unusual specific obligation to exchange information in relation to the application of limitation of benefit provisions connected with dividend, interest and royalty payments. The exchange of notes requires the competent authority of each contracting state to notify the other where the limitation of benefit provisions of the treaty as amended by the Protocol in relation to dividends, interest and royalties are applied to deny relief from taxation. This is a somewhat curious item. The reason for it is far from clear. It does not appear to impose any particular additional obligation on the contracting states beyond the existing exchange of information provisions contained in both the treaty and in the EC Mutual Assistance Directive.[22] Similar wording appears in the text of the treaty itself in art. 11(10) of the Singapore Treaty.

In particular, art. 4(1) of the EC Mutual Assistance Directive provides for spontaneous exchange of information in a number of circumstances particularly where tax avoidance may be suspected, should cover the circumstances referred to in the exchange of notes completely. One may speculate that the contracting states have concerns that the limitation of benefits provision may give rise to difficulties under European law, particularly if they are applied in a discriminatory manner, and they would wish to be seen to be collaborating with each other in order to avoid this. Both contracting states might be defendants in an action attacking the provision even if it was applied only by one of them.

29-400 Exchange of information agreements

Until 2000, exchange of information with treaty partners was only possible within the framework of a tax treaty generally. However, as part of the UK's participation in the OECD Programme against Harmful Tax Practices, Taxes Act 1988, s. 815C was inserted by FA 2000, s. 146(1). It contemplated the conclusion of agreements between the UK and governments of any territory simply with a view to the exchange of information. The purpose of such agreements is not so much to exchange information, but to obtain information from tax haven jurisdictions, although the legislation contemplates the supply of information to the other contracting state.

The UK has entered into such an agreement with Bermuda which does not impose any tax. Although drafted in reciprocal terms, it is plain that the intent is to require Bermuda to provide information to the UK. It provides for exchange of information relating to all existing taxes imposed by the contracting states and future similar taxes.[23] Information may be exchanged on request only.[24] If the information in the possession of the requested competent authority is not sufficient to enable it to comply with the request, it must use all relevant information gathering measures to provide the applicant competent authority with the information requested, even if the requested authority does not need the information for its own tax purposes.[25] Both territories must ensure that their respective competent authorities have the authority to obtain and provide information held by banks and trustees and on the ownership of companies subject to limits[26] and the necessity of the requesting authority to demonstrate the relevance of the information sought.[27] Tax examinations to interview individuals and examine records with the written consent of the persons concerned may be held by HMRC in Bermuda (see art. 6).

---

[22] 77/799/EEC.

[23] Art. 3.

[24] Art. 5(1).

[25] Art. 5(2).

[26] Art. 5(4).

[27] Art. 5(7).

29-450 EC Mutual Assistance Directive

Bilateral treaties between EC Member States invariably provide for exchanges of information. In addition, the subject of exchange of information is also dealt with by Community law. The first Exchange of Information Directive in 1976 did not deal with direct taxation. It only covered customs duties, agricultural levies and certain claims under the common agricultural policy, with VAT added in 1979. It also differed from other Directives in that it provides for mutual assistance for the recovery of claims in respect of certain indirect taxes.

Council Directive 77/799/EEC[28] covers mutual assistance by competent authorities in the field of direct taxation and VAT. It is considerably more detailed than the provisions of art. 26 of the OECD Model. It specifies all of the taxes to which it applies in each member state and the competent authorities. It provides for specific authorisation of exchanges on request, automatic exchanges of information and spontaneous exchanges of information.

In relation to exchanges on request, the competent authority of the requested state need not comply with the request if it appears that the requesting authority has not exhausted its own usual sources of information (which it could have utilised according to the circumstances without running the risk of endangering the attainment of the sought-after result).[29] The requested member state must arrange for the conduct of appropriate enquiries necessary to obtain such information.[30] The directive is explicit that in exercising information gathering powers on request, member states must act as if proceeding on their own account.

In relation to automatic exchanges of information, once the competent authorities of member states have agreed under the consultation procedure on the categories of information to be exchanged, it must be exchanged without prior request. There is no option of refusing to supply the information.[31]

Spontaneous exchanges of information may be made in the following circumstances:[32]

(1) the competent authority of one member state has grounds for supposing that there may be a loss of tax in another member state;

(2) a person liable to tax obtains a reduction in or an exemption from tax in the one member state which would give rise to an increase in tax or to liability to tax in the other member state;

(3) business dealings between a person liable to tax in a member state and a person liable in another are conducted through one or more countries in such a way that a saving in tax may result in one or the other member state or both;

---

[28] 19 December 1977.

[29] Art. 2(1).

[30] Art. 2(2).

[31] Art. 3.

[32] Mutual Assistance Directive, art. 4(1).

(4)   the competent authority of a member state has grounds for supposing that a saving of tax may result from artificial transfers of profits within groups of enterprises; or

(5)   information forwarded to the one member state by the competent authority of another has enabled information to be obtained, which may be relevant in assessing liability to tax in the latter member state.

The application of art. 4(1) in relation to spontaneous obligations to provide information has been considered by the ECJ in *W.N. v Staatssecretaris van Financien*.[33] In that case, a taxpayer resident in the Netherlands deducted maintenance payments which he made to his estranged wife in computing his taxable income in the Netherlands. His wife lived in Spain. The Netherlands tax authorities took the view that the payments might affect the levying of tax in Spain. They proposed to send information on the payments to the Spanish authorities. The taxpayer objected that they were not entitled to under art. 4(1)(a) of the Mutual Assistance Directive. He complained that it was not established that the payments would give rise to taxation in Spain.

The court, however, held that for the purposes of this article in the directive, it was sufficient for the tax lost to be supposed by the informer state. It was not necessary to have to be proved or to be referred to in an express measure by the recipient state. That interpretation was in accordance with both the literal terms of the provision and the purpose of the directive which was to enable the correct assessment of income and capital taxes in various states and to combat evasion.

In the context of the directive's purpose, the information would only be of any use to the recipient's state tax authorities if it arrived before the relevant assessment to tax was made. It was not to be expected that the informer state had extensive knowledge of the legal and factual framework in the other state which would have to be implied by a requirement that an assessment to tax had already to have been made. The article meant that a state was to forward information to another where the former had grounds for supposing that without that information, an unjustified saving in tax might be going to arise in the latter state. It is implicit in the judgement that a payment of any kind to a recipient of another member state may have tax consequences in that state and that this alone justifies the provision of the information.

The directive provides for consultations to be held if necessary in order to deal with exchange of information issues both under the directive and pursuant to any bilateral arrangement. Authorisation is given for designated authorities to communicate directly with each other in specified cases or in certain categories of cases.[34]

Member states are not required to take any steps which are at variance with their own law or administrative practice and may refuse disclosure of commercial, industrial or professional secrets, or of a commercial process or where disclosure would be contrary to public policy.[35]

---

[33] Case C-420/98 [2001] BTC 366; [2001] STC 974.

[34] Art. 9.

[35] Art. 8(1) and (2).

Where for practical or legal reasons the information cannot be provided, this is also a limit to disclosure.[36]

The secrecy provision requires information to be made available only to persons directly involved in the assessment of tax or in administrative control of the assessment, as well as in connection with judicial proceedings. The information may not be used other than for tax purposes.[37] Where a member state has information requirements narrower than those of the directive, they may refuse information if the recipient state does not undertake to respect those narrower limits. If the informing state could, however, use the information for other purposes, then it may be sent to other states for similar purposes.[38] Provision is also made for information to be passed on to third member states if this is considered appropriate (see art. 7(4)).

Other administrative assistance

Administrative assistance beyond the simple exchange of information is envisaged by the directive. Thus specific rules provide for simultaneous examination of taxpayers[39] and for the pooling of experience with a view to improving cooperation.[40] Provision is also made for collaboration by state officials in accordance with procedures as may be laid down.[41] The directive does not restrict the wide application of other exchange of information obligations.[42]

Service of notices

Member states are obliged, on receipt of a request from another member state, to deliver instruments and decisions of the requesting tax administration on their behalf to any person residing within their jurisdiction.[43] The member state receiving such a notification request need only use the same method to notify the taxpayer as its domestic law allows in relation to similar documents originating from its tax administration.[44] The date of delivery and responses from the recipient of the notification must be communicated to the requesting state.[45]

---

[36] Art. 8(3).

[37] Art. 7(1).

[38] Art. 7(2).

[39] Art. 8b.

[40] Art. 10.

[41] Art. 6.

[42] Art. 11.

[43] These obligations are given effect in domestic law by F(No. 2)A 2005, s. 68.

[44] Art. 8a(1).

[45] Art. 8a(3).

UK implementation

In giving effect to the EC Mutual Assistance Directive, Finance Act 2003, s. 197(1), simply authorises disclosure to the competent authorities of another member state any information required to be so disclosed by virtue of the Mutual Assistance Directive. Unlike the treaty provisions in FA 2006[46] does not seek to establish its own independent standard. Section 197(2) authorises disclosure of information to tax authorities in other member states, subject to the same exceptions found in the case of treaty exchanges of information, namely that HMRC is satisfied that the competent authorities of the other state are bound by or have undertaken to observe rules of confidentiality which are no less strict than those applying in the UK. Second, they may not authorise the use of information disclosed under the directive other than for the purpose of taxation or to facilitate legal proceedings for the failure to observe the tax laws of the receiving state.[47]

Finance Act 1990, s. 125, extended the information-gathering powers of the Inland Revenue under s. 20 of the Taxes Management Act (TMA) 1970 to include exercising powers on behalf of other member states, in relation to their taxes on income and capital.[48]

HMRC powers contained in FA 2008, Sch. 36, apply across the board to all taxes administered by HMRC. These replace those in FA 1990, s. 125, in relation to all taxes and duties covered by the provisions for the exchange of information under the directive (as amended from time to time)[49] from 1 April 2009.

Procedure

Only authorised HMRC officers can disclose information to an authorised officer of the government of the country concerned.[50]

The Commissioners of Revenue and Customs have delegated responsibility for exchanges of information to the Centre for Exchange of Intelligence (CEI), part of HM Revenue & Customs Intelligence.[51] The CEI is responsible for passing the information to the overseas tax authorities and will decide whether it is within the scope of the relevant agreement and appropriate to send. It is therefore important that any matters of a potentially sensitive nature are brought to the attention of the CEI.[52] Requests for information – both inward and outward – relating to aggressive or abusive tax avoidance schemes with an Australian, Japanese, Canadian or American connection are dealt with by the Joint International Tax Shelter Information Centre (JITSIC). UK delegates to JITSIC are part of the HMRC Anti-

---

[46] See para. 29-250 above.

[47] FA 2003, s. 197(3).

[48] FA 1990, s. 125(2).

[49] FA 2008, Sch. 36, para. 63(4)(a).

[50] HMRC, *IHT*, para. INTM153280.

[51] HMRC, *IHT*, para. INTM156010.

[52] HMRC, *IHT*, para. INTM156030.

Avoidance Group (AAG).[53] The Revenue internal manuals give some indication of procedures and suitable cases for exchange of information.

Although the mechanisms for exchange of information are set out as a matter of law, the process is conducted entirely in secret. No provision is made for notification or consultation with taxpayers. The HMRC *Double Taxation Relief Manual*[54] does refer to 'matters of a potentially sensitive nature (for example, a 'trade secret')', which should be brought to the attention of the liaison group responsible for exchanges of information. Indication to HMRC that there is information which should not be exchanged is a delicate matter. There are obvious problems related with the lack of transparency in the process. In this context, the rules relating to sharing information with other government departments in the UK are varied and may require interpretation. Giving effect to the limitations contained in s. 816(2ZA), for example, may be a legally complex issue requiring detailed knowledge of the legal system of the other contracting state. This places a heavy burden on those responsible for administering the exchange of information. Officials who are beyond reproach, hardworking and diligent will find proper compliance with the existing rules extremely demanding. The secrecy of the process undermines confidence in it when viewed from the outside in the same way that tax administrators view taxpayer secrecy as undermining confidence in compliance with tax rules.

The Keith Committee[55] recommended that procedures should be introduced to enable taxpayers to be informed of requests for commercially sensitive information and that an opportunity to challenge exchanges of information before an independent tribunal should be established. The Inland Revenue resisted this.[56] No attention to this appeared to have been given in framing the powers in FA 2008, Sch. 36, either. Such a right is likely to exist under the Human Rights Act 1998, and a failure on the part of HMRC officials to respect it may give rise to a claim for damages.[57]

29-500 Savings Directive

The Savings Directive[58] is the first measure by the EU to coordinate national tax systems relating to personal taxation. It applies to the taxation of savings income in the form of interest payments. Free movement of capital guaranteed by arts. 56 to 60 of the EC Treaty gave some member states concern that this freedom would result in evasion of tax by residents not declaring interest earned outside their state of residence. It is thus justified by art. 58(1) of the EC Treaty under which member states have the right to take all requisite measures to prevent infringements of national law and regulations, in particular in the field

---

[53] HMRC, *IHT*, para. INTM156020.

[54] At para. 351.

[55] Report of the Committee on Enforcement Powers of Revenue Departments (CMND 8822), paras. 23, 4.1-3.

[56] Inland Revenue and the Taxpayer (December 1986), para. 6.5.5.

[57] Human Rights Act 1998, s. 8.

[58] Directive 03/48 on taxation of savings income in the form of interest payments as amended by Council Decision 2004/587/EC.

of taxation.[59] The directive is implemented in UK law by regulations authorised under FA 2003, s. 199.[60]

The stated aim of the directive is to enable interest income of individuals resident in member states to be made subject to effective taxation there where the interest is paid in another member state.[61] The real effect is broader since the application is conditional on treaties or other arrangements being in place with certain third countries to apply the same measures.[62] The third countries are: Switzerland, Liechtenstein, San Marino, Monaco, Andorra and all relevant dependent or associated territories (the Channel Islands, the Isle of Man and the dependent or associated territories in the Caribbean).

The directive requires member states to establish an elaborate mechanism for the gathering and exchange of information on cross-border interest payments in the EU. Member states are required to ensure that 'paying agents' are able to identify 'beneficial owners' of 'interest' and their tax residence in accordance with minimum specified standards.[63] Paying agents are required to report the identity of such individuals who are not resident in the member state where the paying agent is established, along with bank account details and interest payments to the competent authorities.[64] The competent authority of the member state of the paying agent must regularly and automatically communicate this information to the competent authority of the member state of residence of the beneficial owner.[65] The operation of a withholding tax in accordance with arts. 10 to 13 of the Directive is considered in chapter 13. The provisions of the Mutual Assistance Directive 77/799 apply generally to information exchanged but the operation of art. 8 of that directive, which limits the obligations to exchange information, are excluded.[66] Thus, under this directive, information cannot be refused to be exchanged by reason of public policy. A member state believing that the tax administration of another had been infiltrated by organised criminals would nonetheless be required to provide the information.

Interest

Broad meaning is given to the term 'interest' beyond its ordinary linguistic usage. The starting point is the meaning found in art. 11(2) of the OECD Model, namely, interest paid or credited to an account, relating to debt claims of every kind, whether or not secured by mortgage and whether or not carrying a right to participate in the debtor's profits. This also includes income from government securities and income from bonds or debentures, including premiums and prizes attaching to such securities, bonds or debentures but

---

[59] See chapter 2.

[60] *Reporting of Savings Income Information Regulations* 2003 (SI 200/3297) as amended by SI 2005/1539, SI 2006/3286 and SI 2008/2682).

[61] Art.1(1).

[62] Art. 17(2).

[63] Directive, art. 3; SI 2003/3297, reg. 9.

[64] Directive, art. 8; SI 2003/3297, regs. 10 to 15.

[65] Art. 9.

[66] Art. 9(3). See para. 29-400 above.

excluding penalty charges for late payment.[67] It also includes interest accrued or capitalised at the sale, refund or redemption of debt claims.[68] Income distributions of certain collective investment vehicles that invest in debt instruments and the income on the sale, refund or redemption of interests in such vehicles are likewise included in the term.[69] The scope of the expression is not uniform and the directive gives the member state of the paying agent options so that, for example the interest may be annualise over a period of time up to one year, and such annualised interest may be treated as an interest payment even if no sale, redemption or refund occurs during that period.[70]

Beneficial ownership

Similarly, beneficial ownership is broadly defined. Unlike the use of the expression in bilateral treaties, where it is designed to narrow the availability of treaty benefits, the expression is used expansively and includes evidentiary requirements. Thus, 'beneficial owner' means any individual who receives an interest payment or any individual for whom an interest payment is secured, unless he or she provides evidence that it was not received or secured for his own benefit.[71] Interest is not received or secured for own benefit only if the recipient acts as a 'paying agent' or acts on behalf of a legal person which is generally liable to tax on business profits, or on behalf of certain collective investment vehicles, or acts on behalf of another individual who is the beneficial owner and whose identity and residence is disclosed in accordance with the requirements of the directive.

Where a paying agent has information that suggests that the individual recipient is not the beneficial owner, reasonable steps must be taken to determine who the beneficial owner is, failing which the individual recipient must be treated as the beneficial owner.[72]

Paying agent

A 'paying agent' is generally any economic operator who pays interest to or secures the payment of interest for the immediate benefit of the beneficial owner, whether the operator is the debtor of the debt claim or the operator charged by the debtor or the beneficial owner with paying interest or securing the payment of interest.[73] Although bank interest is clearly the most important application of the directive, its scope thus includes all payers of interest, as well as financial intermediaries who make interest payments on behalf of debtors.

---

[67] Directive, art. 6(1)(a); SI 2003/3297, reg. 8.

[68] Art. 6(1)(b).

[69] Art. 6(1)(c) and (d).

[70] Art. 6(5); see SI 2003/3297, reg. 8.

[71] Art. 2(1).

[72] Art. 2(2).

[73] Art. 4(1); SI 2003/3297, reg. 3.

29-550 EC savings income treaties

The UK, along with other EU member states, has entered into multilateral treaties with the each of the states mentioned in the Savings Directive, art. 17(2)(i), in 2004.[74] These treaties replicate broadly the terms of the Savings Directive. In the case of dependent and associated territories, bilateral treaties have been entered into with the Channel Islands, the Isle of Man and certain territories in the Caribbean on similar terms.

29-600 EC mutual assistance in the recovery of taxes

Within the EC, limited ability to recover taxes and duties of one member state by another has existed since the 15 March 1976 Directive on Mutual Assistance for the Recovery of Community Related Duties.[75] It is only in the early years of the 21st century, however, that both Community law mechanisms and tax treaties have significantly expanded the ability of countries to collect taxes outside their home jurisdictions with the assistance of foreign tax administrations. In 2001 the scope of the directive was expanded to include, in particular, excise duties, VAT, taxes on income and capital, as well as on insurance premiums and related penalties and interest.[76] The present legislative implementation into UK law is through FA 2003, s. 134 and Sch. 39. These authorise proceedings to be taken by or on behalf of HMRC to enforce the tax claims of other member states, by way of legal proceedings, distress, diligence or otherwise, as might be taken to enforce a the equivalent UK tax claim.[77] Procedural and other implementing measures are addressed by regulation.[78] The directive merely enables one tax administration to act as a collection agency. The forum for disputing liability is the member state whose tax is in issue and collection proceedings in the UK may be taken against a person who shows that liability is or is about to be contested before a court, tribunal or other competent body in the member state in question with reasonable expedition.[79] It will be a defence to collection proceedings in the UK that a final decision on the foreign claim has been given in favour of the taxpayer by a court, tribunal or other competent body in the member state in question.[80]

29-650 Bilateral tax treaty assistance in recovery of taxes

In the 2005 version of its model treaty, the OECD introduced a new art. 27 to authorise contracting states to recover taxes on behalf of each other. While membership of the EU carries with it, requirements to uphold administrative and judicial standards and the rule of

---

[74] Andorra, 15 November 2004; Liechtenstein, 15 November 2004; Monaco, 7 December 2004; San Marino, 7 December 2004; Switzerland, 26 October 2004.

[75] 76/308 arts. 2(2)(b), 2(2)(c) and 2(2)(d).

[76] See art. 2(2).

[77] FA 2002, Sch. 39, para. 2(1).

[78] FA 2002, Sch. 39, para. 2(1); *Recovery of Duties and Taxes Etc. Due in Other Member States (Corresponding UK Claims, Procedure And Supplementary) Regulations* 2004 (SI 2004/674).

[79] FA 2002, Sch. 39, para. 4.

[80] FA 2002, Sch. 39, para. 5.

law, the OECD, in recognising the possibly uneven adherence to such standards of governance, recommends a cautious approach in considering the inclusion of such measures in bilateral treaties.[81] The first agreement of this kind in a bilateral treaty is in the 2007 Protocol to the New Zealand treaty, which affords comprehensive assistance as proposed by the OECD Model:

> '25A(1) The contracting states shall lend assistance to each other in the collection of revenue claims. This assistance is not restricted by articles 1 and 2 of this Convention. The competent authorities of the contracting states may by mutual agreement settle the mode of application of this article.
>
> 25A(2) The term "revenue claim" as used in this article means an amount owed in respect of taxes of every kind and description imposed on behalf of the contracting states insofar as the taxation thereunder is not contrary to this Convention or any other instrument to which the contracting states are parties, as well as interest, administrative penalties and costs of collection or conservancy related to such amount.'

As with the modern exchange of information provisions, cross-border connection is not limited either to the taxes that form the subject of the treaty or to persons who are resident in one or both states. The term 'revenue claim' is the same as that used in the Brussels Convention[82] and, although it is intended to cover all taxes, the use of the expression 'taxes' itself is unexplained. Contracting states are required, on request, to collect taxes on behalf of each other that are enforceable under the laws of the requesting state and owed by a person who, at that time, cannot, under the laws of the requesting state, prevent their collection. Such claims must be collected by the requested state in accordance with its tax enforcement and collection laws as if it were its own revenue claim.[83] This includes conservancy measures.[84] It is not possible to contest the existence, validity or the amount of a revenue claim of the state requesting collection before the courts or administrative bodies of the other requested state.[85] Limitations on the obligation to collect tax analogous to the limitations to exchange information as follows:

> 'In no case shall the provisions of this art. be construed so as to impose on a contracting state the obligation:
>
> (a) to carry out administrative measures at variance with the laws and administrative practice of that or of the other contracting state;
>
> (b) to carry out measures which would be contrary to public policy;
>
> (c) to provide assistance if the other contracting state has not pursued all reasonable measures of collection or conservancy, as the case may be, available under its laws or administrative practice;
>
> (d) to provide assistance in those cases where the administrative burden for that State is clearly disproportionate to the benefit to be derived by the other contracting state;
>
> (e) to provide assistance if that State considers that the taxes with respect to which assistance is requested are imposed contrary to generally accepted taxation principles.'

---

[81] Commentary to art. 27, para. 1.

[82] See para. 29-050 above.

[83] Art. 25A(3).

[84] Art. 25A(4).

[85] Art. 25A(6).

Such arrangements are given effect in domestic law by order made pursuant to FA 2006, s. 173(1)(b). Their implementation is by regulation made under the powers granted under FA 2006, s. 175.[86] The regulations adopt the same mechanism as found in the case of EU member state taxes – that is, where a foreign administration requests recovery of tax on their behalf, it is to be treated as if it was an amount of UK income tax for the purpose of powers of collection laid down in the Taxes Acts are applicable.[87]

29-700   Convention for mutual administrative assistance in tax matters

One of the most comprehensive endeavours to enable cross-border cooperation is the Multilateral Convention on Administrative Assistance in the Assessment and Collection of Tax, which was opened for signature for members of the Council of Europe and OECD on 25 January 1988. Current parties are Azerbaijan, Belgium, Denmark, Finland, France, Iceland, Italy, the Netherlands, Norway, Poland, Sweden and the US. It has also been signed by Canada and the Ukraine but not yet ratified there. While UK policy from 1998 was not to sign the convention, a change in approach gave rise to signature by the UK in 2008.

The Convention contemplates wide-ranging cooperation between tax administrations. The forms of assistance available for contracting states include exchange of information,[88] participation in foreign tax examinations,[89] service of documents[90] and assistance in the recovery of taxes.[91] The taxes potentially covered are also intended to be comprehensive including motor vehicle tax, estate duty taxes and social security contributions apart from taxes on income and capital, and VAT.[92] States may sign with reservations, either as to the taxes covered, or as to certain types of assistance which they will not provide.[93] Thus, it is not homogenous in its application.

In the UK the convention applies effectively to all taxes except customs duties, taxes imposed by or on behalf of political subdivisions or local authorities of contracting states and social security contributions.[94]

---

[86] *Recovery of Foreign Taxes Regulations* 2007 (SI 2007/3507).

[87] SI 2007/3507, reg. 3.

[88] Ch. III, s. II.

[89] Art. 9.

[90] Ch. III, s. III.

[91] Ch. III, s. II.

[92] Art. 2.

[93] Art. 30.

[94] Declaration contained in a letter from Ambassador of the UK to the OECD, deposited with the instrument of ratification on 24 January 2008, and transmitted by the Director of Legal Affairs of the OECD by a letter dated 6 February 2008, registered by the Secretariat General on 11 February 2008.

Double Taxation Treaties

Appendix

1-000   UK Tax Treaties at 31 March 2009

The table below lists UK tax treaties, arranged alphabetically. All current and pending agreements are reproduced in CCH's *Blue Book* (Annotated UK Double Tax Treaties). Certain historic treaties are included for reference and completeness. Where the UK has concluded a treaty with a particular country the table provides the following information:

(1)   the date of the agreement;

(2)   the number of the statutory instrument (or, if before 1948, the number of the statutory rules and orders) to which the provisions of the agreement are appended;

(3)   the status of the agreement i.e. 'current' or 'terminated'.

Where an agreement has been signed but has not yet entered into force this is indicated by the word 'pending'.

All agreements are comprehensive agreements, unless otherwise indicated, and apply in respect of income, capital gains and capital. It should be noted that, as a result of political developments, certain treaties may be of limited or revised application. The status of these treaties is discussed in Chapter 1, paragraph 10-500.

Bilateral treaties

COUNTRY	SI (SR & O) No.	STATUS
Afars and Issas – see Djibouti		
Alderney – see Guernsey		
Algeria		
Air Transport Agreement of 27 May 1981	1984/362	Current
Andorra		
EC Savings Agreement of 15 November 2004		Current
Anguilla (formerly part of		
St. Christopher, Nevis & Anguilla)		
Tax Information Exchange Agreement of 28 September 2004		Current
Antigua & Barbuda		
Agreement of 19 December 1947	1947/2865	Current
Amending Agreement of 15 March 1968	1968/1096	Current
Argentina		
Convention of 3 January 1996	1997/1777	Current
Amending protocol of 3 January 1996	1997/1777	Current

COUNTRY	SI (SR & O) No.	STATUS
Armenia		
Note – See SP 4/01 for the status of the Convention of 31 July 1985 with the former USSR.		
Aruba		
Tax Information Exchange Agreement of 11 April 2005	2005/1458	Current
Australia		
Agreement of 7 December 1967	1968/305	Terminated
Amending Protocol of 29 January 1980	1980/707	Terminated
Convention of 21 August 2003	2003/3199	Current
Austria		
Convention of 29 July 1956	1957/598	Terminated
Convention of 30 April 1969	1970/1947	Current
Amending Protocol of 17 November 1977	1979/117	Current
Amending Protocol of 18 May 1993	1994/768	Current
Azerbaijan (formerly part of the USSR)		
Convention of 23 February 1994 (as modified by Exchange of Notes of 9 September 1994)	1995/762	Current
Bangladesh (formerly part of Pakistan)		
Convention of 8 August 1979	1980/708	Current
Barbados		
Agreement of 26 March 1970	1970/952	Current
Amending Protocol of 18 September 1973	1973/2096	Current
Barbuda – see Antigua & Barbuda		
Basutoland – see Lesotho		
Bechuanaland – see Botswana		
Belarus		
Convention of 7 March 1995	1995/2706	Pending
Note – see SP 4/01 for the status of the Convention of 31 July 1985 with the former USSR.		
Belgium		
Convention of 1 June 1987	1987/2053	Current
Belize (formerly British Honduras)		
Arrangement of 19 December 1947	1947/2866	Current
Amending Arrangement of 8 April 1968	1968/573	Current
Amending Arrangement of 12 December 1973	1973/2097	Current
Bermuda		
Tax Information Exchange Agreement of 4 December 2007	2008/1789	Current
Bolivia		
Convention of 3 November 1994	1995/2707	Current
Bosnia-Herzegovina (formerly part of Yugoslavia)		
Convention of 6 November 1981	1981/1815	Current
Note – For the status of the Convention of 6 November 1981 with the former Yugoslavia, see SP 3/07.		
Botswana		
Agreement of 5 October 1977	1978/183	Terminated
Agreement of 9 September 2005	2006/1925	Current
Brazil		
Shipping and Air Transport Agreement of 29 December 1967	1968/572	Current
British Guiana – see Guyana		
British Honduras – see Belize		
British Solomon Islands – see Solomon Islands		

COUNTRY	SI (SR & O) No.	STATUS
British Virgin Islands		
Tax Information Exchange Agreement of 11 April 2005	2005/1457	Current
Convention of 29 October 2008		Pending
Tax Information Exchange Agreement of 29 October 2008		Pending
Brunei		
Arrangement of 8 December 1950	1950/1977	Current
Amending Arrangement of 4 March 1968	1968/306	Current
Amending Arrangement of 12 December 1973	1973/2098	Current
Bulgaria	1987/2054	Current
Burma (Myanmar)		
Agreement of 13 March 1950	1952/751	Current
Amending Protocol of 4 April 1951	1952/751	Current
Cameroon		
Air Transport Agreement of 22 April 1982	1982/1841	Current
Canada		
Convention of 8 September 1978	1980/709	Current
Amending Protocol of 15 April 1980	1980/1528	Current
Amending Protocol of 16 October 1985	1985/1996	Current
Amending protocol of 7 May 2003	2003/2619	Current
Cayman Islands		
Tax Information Exchange Agreement of 17 March 2005		Current
Ceylon – see Sri Lanka		
Chile		
Convention of 12 July 2003	2003/3200	Current
China		
Air Transport Agreement of 10 March 1981	1981/1119	Current
Agreement of 26 July 1984	1984/1826	Current
Amending Protocol of 2 September 1996	1996/3164	Current

Note – The agreement dated 26 July 1984 does not apply to the Hong Kong Special Administrative Region (Inland Revenue *Tax Bulletin*, Issue 25, October 1996, p. 357. See separate note under Hong Kong for details of agreements specific to the region).

Croatia (formerly part of Yugoslavia)		
Convention of 6 November 1981	1981/1815	Current

Note – For the status of the Convention of 6 November 1981 with the former Yugoslavia, see SP 3/07.

Curaçao – see Netherlands Antilles		
Cyprus		
Convention of 20 June 1974	1975/425	Current
Amending Protocol of 2 April 1980	1980/1529	Current
Czechoslovakia (see Czech Republic; Slovak Republic)		
Czech Republic (formerly part of Czechoslovakia)		
Convention of 5 November 1990	1991/2876	Current

Note – For the status of the Convention of 5 November 1990 with the former Czechoslovakia, see SP 5/93.

Dahomey – see Benin		
Denmark		
Convention of 11 November 1980	1980/1960	Current
Amending Protocol of 1 July 1991	1991/2877	Current
Amending Protocol of 15 October 1996	1996/3165	Current
Dominica		
Arrangement of 4 March 1949	1949/359	Terminated

COUNTRY	SI (SR & O) No.	STATUS
Amending Agreement of 7 March 1968	1968/1098	Terminated
Egypt		
Convention of 25 April 1977	1980/1091	Current
Eire – see Ireland		
Ellice Islands (now Tuvalu) – see Kiribati and Tuvalu		
Estonia		
Convention of 12 May 1994	1994/3207	Current
Exchange of Notes of 12 May 1994	1994/3207	Current
Ethiopia		
Air Transport Agreement of 1 February 1977	1977/1297	Current
Falkland Islands		
Arrangement of 25 June 1997	1997/2985	Current
Faroes		
Convention of 20 June 2007	2007/3469	Pending
Fiji		
Convention of 21 November 1975	1976/1342	Current
Finland		
Convention of 17 July 1969	1970/153	Current
Amending Protocol of 17 May 1973	1973/1327	Current
Amending Protocol of 16 November 1979	1980/710	Current
Amending Protocol of 1 October 1985	1985/1997	Current
Amending Protocol of 26 September 1991	1991/2878	Current
Amending Protocol of 31 July 1996	1996/3166	Current
France		
Estate, Inheritance and Gift Agreement of 21 June 1963	1963/1319	Current
Convention of 22 May 1968	1968/1869	Current
Amending Protocol of 10 February 1971	1971/718	Current
Amending Protocol of 14 May 1973	1973/1328	Current
Amending Protocol of 12 June 1986	1987/466	Current
Amending Protocol of 15 October 1987	1987/2055	Current
Convention of 28 January 2004		Withdrawn
Convention of 19 June 2008	2009/226	Pending
French Guiana– see France		
Gambia		
Convention of 20 May 1980	1980/1963	Current
Georgia		
Agreement of 13 July 2004	2004/3325	Current
Germany		
Convention of 26 November 1964	1967/25	Current
Amending Protocol of 23 March 1970	1971/874	Current
Ghana		
Convention of 20 January 1993	1993/1800	Current
Gibraltar		
Tax Information Exchange Agreement of 19 December 2005	2006/1453	Current
Gilbert Islands – see Kiribati		
Greece		
Convention of 25 June 1953	1954/142	Current
Grenada		
Arrangement of 4 March 1949	1949/361	Current
Amending Agreement of 25 July 1968	1968/1867	Current

COUNTRY	SI (SR & O) No.	STATUS
Guadeloupe – see France		
Guernsey		
Arrangement of 24 June 1952	1952/1215	Current
Amending Arrangement	1994/3209	Current
Tax Information Exchange Agreement of 19 November 2004	2005/1262	Current
Amendments of 20 January 2009		Pending
Tax Information Exchange Agreement of 20 January 2009		Pending
Guyana (formerly British Guiana)		
Convention of 17 December 1992	1992/3207	Current
Guyane – see France		
Holland – see Netherlands		
Hong Kong (Special Administrative Region)		
Article 14 (relief from double taxation)		
Air Transport Agreement of 2 June 1998	1998/2566	Current
Shipping Transport Agreement of 13 December 2000	2000/3248	Current
Hungary		
Convention of 28 November 1977	1978/1056	Current
Iceland		
Convention of 30 September 1991	1991/2879	Current
India		
Estate, Inheritance and Gift Agreement of 3 April 1956	1956/998	Current
Convention of 25 January 1993	1993/1801	Current
Indonesia		
Convention of 5 April 1993	1994/769	Current
Iran		
Air Transport Agreement of 21 December 1960	1960/2419	Current
Ireland		
Convention of 2 June 1976	1976/2151	Current
Amending Protocol of 28 October 1976	1976/2152	Current
Estate, Inheritance and Gift Agreement of 7 December 1977	1978/1107	Current
Amending Protocol of 7 November 1994	1995/764	Current
Amending protocol of 4 November 1998	1998/3151	Current
Isle of Man		
Arrangement of 29 July 1955	1955/1205	Current
Amending Arrangement	1991/2880	Current
Amending Arrangement	1994/3208	Current
Tax Information Exchange Agreement of 19 November2004	2004/1263	Current
Amendments of 29 September 2008	2009/228	Pending
Tax Information Exchange Agreement of 29 September 2008	2009/228	Pending
Israel		
Convention of 26 September 1962	1963/616	Current
Amending Protocol of 20 April 1970	1971/391	Current
Italy		
Estate, Inheritance and Gift Agreement of 15 February 1966	1968/304	Current
Convention of 21 October 1988	1990/2590	Current
Ivory Coast (Côte d' Ivoire)		
Convention of 26 June 1985	1987/169	Current
Jamaica		
Agreement of 16 March 1973	1973/1329	Current

COUNTRY	SI (SR & O) No.	STATUS
Japan		
Convention of 10 February 1969		
Exchange of Notes of 10 February 1969 }	1970/1948	Terminated
Amending Protocol of 14 February 1980	1980/1530	Terminated
Convention of 2 February 2006		
Protocol of 2 February 2006		
Exchange of Notes of 2 February 2006 }	2006/1924	Current
Jersey		
Arrangement of 24 June 1952	1952/1216	Current
Amending Arrangement	1994/3210	Current
Tax Information Exchange Agreement of 19 November 2004	2005/1261	Current
Amendments of 10 March 2009		Pending
Tax Information Exchange Agreement of 10 March 2009		Pending
Jordan		
Shipping and Air Transport Agreement of 6 March 1978	1979/300	Terminated
Convention of 22 July 2001	2001/3924	Current
Kampuchea – see Cambodia		
Kazakhstan		
Convention of 19 April 1994	1994/3211	Current
Amending protocol of 18 September 1998	1998/2567	Current
Kenya		
Agreement of 31 July 1973		
Amending Protocol of 20 January 1976 }	1977/1299	Current
Exchange of Notes of 8 February 1977		
Kiribati and Tuvalu (formerly Gilbert and Ellice Islands)		
Arrangement of 10 May 1950	1950/750	Current
Amending Arrangement of 4 March 1968	1968/309	Current
Amending Arrangement of 25 July 1974	1974/1271	Current
Korea		
Convention of 25 October 1996	1996/3168	Current
Kuwait		
Air Transport Agreement of 25 September 1984	1984/1825	Terminated
Agreement of 23 February 1999	1999/2036	Current
Protocol of 23 February 1999	1999/2036	Current
Kyrgystan (formerly part of the USSR)		
Note – See SP 4/01 for the status of the Convention of 31 July 1985 with the former USSR.		
Latvia		
Convention of 8 May 1996	1996/3167	Current
Lebanon		
Shipping and Air Transport Agreement of 26 February 1964	1964/278	Current
Lesotho (formerly Basutholand)		
Convention of 29 January 1997	1997/2986	Current
Libya		
Convention of 17 November 2008		Pending
Liechtenstein		
EC Savings Income Agreement of 15 November 2004		Current
Lithuania		
Convention of 19 March 2001	2001/3925	Terminated
Convention of 21 May 2002	2002/2847	Current
Luxembourg		
Convention of 24 May 1967	1968/1100	Current

COUNTRY	SI (SR & O) No.	STATUS
Amending Protocol of 18 July 1978	1980/567	Current
Amending Protocol of 28 January 1983	1984/364	Current
Macedonia (formerly part of Yugoslavia)		
Convention of 6 November 1981	1981/815	Terminated
Convention of 8 November 2006	2007/2127	Current
Malawi		
Agreement of 25 November 1955	1956/619	Current
Amending Agreement of 1 April 1964	1964/1401	Current
Amending Agreement of 2 April 1968	1968/1101	Current
Amending Agreement of 10 February 1978	1979/302	Current
Malaysia		
Agreement of 10 December 1996	1997/2987	Current
Malta		
Convention of 12 May 1994	1995/763	Current
Martinique – see France		
Mauritius		
Convention of 11 February 1981	1981/1121	Current
Amending Protocol of 23 October 1986	1987/467	Current
Amending Protocol of 27 March 2003	2003/2620	Current
Mexico		
Convention of 2 June 1994	1994/3212	Current
Moldova (formerly part of the USSR)		
Convention of 8 November 2007	2008/1795	Current
Monaco		
EC Savings Income Agreement of 7 December 2004		Current
Mongolia		
Convention of 23 April 1996	1996/2598	Current
Montenegro		
Convention of 6 November 1981	1981/1815	Current

Note – For the status of the Convention of 6 November 1981 with the former Yugoslavia, see SP3/07.

COUNTRY	SI (SR & O) No.	STATUS
Montserrat		
Arrangement of 19 December 1947	1947/2869	Current
Amending Arrangement of 8 April 1968	1968/576	Current
Tax Information exchange Agreement of 16 December 2004	2005/1459	Current
Morocco		
Convention of 8 September 1981	1991/2881	Current
Namibia (formerly South West Africa)		
South African Convention of 28 May 1962	1962/2352	Current
Extension of 8 August 1962	1962/2788	Current
South African Amending Protocol of 14 June 1967	1967/1489	Current
Extension of 14 June 1967	1967/1490	Current
Netherlands		
Estate, Inheritance and Gift Agreement of 15 October 1948	1950/1197	Terminated
Estate, Inheritance and Gift Agreement of 11 December 1979	1980/706	Current
Convention of 7 November 1980	1980/1961	Current
Amending Protocol of 12 July 1983	1983/1902	Current
Amending Protocol of 24 August 1989	1990/2152	Current
Amending Protocol of 7 September 1995	1996/730	Current

COUNTRY	SI (SR & O) No.	STATUS
Convention of 26 September 2008	2009/227	Pending
Netherlands Antilles		
Convention of 31 October 1967	1968/577	Terminated
Tax Information Exchange Agreement of 12 Apri 2005	2005/1460	Current
New Hebrides – see Vanuatu		
New Zealand		
Convention of 4 August 1983	1984/365	Current
Protocol of 4 November 2003	2004/1274	Current
Protocol of 7 November 2007	2008/1793	Current
Nigeria		
Agreement of 9 June 1987	1987/2057	Current
Northern Rhodesia – see Zambia		
Norway		
Convention of 3 October 1985	1985/1998	Terminated
Convention of 13 December 2000	2000/3247	Current
Nyasaland – see Malawi		
Oman		
Agreement of 23 February 1998	1998/2568	Current
Pakistan		
Estate, Inheritance and Gift Agreement of 8 June 1957	1957/1522	Current
Convention of 24 November 1986	1987/2058	Current
Papua New Guinea		
Convention of 17 September 1991	1991/2882	Current
Philippines		
Convention of 10 June 1976	1978/184	Current
Poland		
Convention of 16 December 1976	1978/282	Terminated
Convention of 20 July 2006	2006/3323	Current
Portugal		
Convention of 27 March 1968	1969/599	Current
Réunion – see France		
Rhodesia – see Zimbabwe		
Romania		
Convention of 18 September 1975 ⎫	1977/57	Current
Exchange of Notes of 3 February 1976 ⎭		
Russia		
Convention of 15 February 1994	1994/3213	Current
St. Christopher (St. Kitts) & Nevis		
Arrangement of 19 December 1947	1947/2872	Current
St Lucia		
Arrangement of 4 March 1949	1949/366	Terminated
Amending agreement of 5 April 1968	1968/1102	Terminated
St Vincent		
Arrangement of 4 March 1949	1949/367	Terminated
Amending agreement of 1 April 1968	1968/1103	Terminated
San Marino		
EC Savings Income Agreement of 7 December 2004		Current
Sarawak – see Malaysia		
Saudi Arabia		
Air Transport Agreement of 10 March 1993	1994/767	Current
Convention of 31 October 2007	2008/1770	Current
Senegambia – see Gambia and Senegal		

COUNTRY	SI (SR & O) No.	STATUS
Serbia (formerly part of Yugoslavia)		
Convention of 6 November 1981	1981/1815	Current

Note – For the status of the Convention of 6 November 1981 with the former Yugoslavia, see SP 3/07.

Seychelles		
Arrangement of 8 August 1947	1947/1778	Terminated
Amending agreement of 18 March 1969	1969/379	Terminated
Sierra Leone		
Arrangement of 19 December 1947	1947/2873	Current
Amending Agreement of 18 March 1968	1968/1104	Current
Singapore		
Convention of 12 February 1997	1997/2988	Current
Slovak Republic (formerly part of Czechoslovakia)		
Convention of 5 November 1990	1991/2876	Current

Note – For the status of the Convention of 5 November 1990 with the former Czechoslovakia, see SP 5/93.

Slovenia (formerly part of Yugoslavia)		
Convention of 13 November 2007	2998/1796	Current
Solomon Islands		
Arrangement of 10 May 1950	1950/748	Current
Amending Arrangement of 8 April 1968	1968/574	Current
Amending Arrangement of 25 July 1974	1974/1270	Current
South Africa		
Convention of 21 November 1968	1969/864	Terminated
Estate, Inheritance and Gift Agreement of 13 July 1978	1979/576	Current
Convention of 4 July 2002	2002/3138	Current
Southern Rhodesia – *see Zimbabwe*		
South Korea – see Korea		
South West Africa – see Namibia		
Soviet Union – see Union of Soviet Socialist Republics		
Spain		
Convention of 21 October 1975	1976/1919	Current
Exchange of Notes of 13 December 1993	1995/765	Current
Sri Lanka		
Convention of 21 June 1979		
Exchange of Notes of 13 February 1980	1980/713	Current
Sudan		
Convention of 8 March 1975	1977/1719	Current
Swaziland		
Agreement of 26 November 1968	1969/380	Current
Sweden		
Convention of 30 August 1983	1984/366	Current
Estate, Inheritance and Gift Agreement of 8 October 1980	1981/840	Current
Amending Protocol of 13 June 1989	1989/986	Current
Switzerland		
Estate, Inheritance and Gift Agreement of 12 June 1956	1957/426	Terminated
Convention of 8 December 1977	1978/1408	Current
Amending Protocol of 5 March 1981	1982/714	Current
Amending Protocol of 17 December 1993	1994/3215	Current
Estate, Inheritance and Gift Agreement of 17 December 1993	1994/3214	Current
EC Savings Income Agreement of 26 October 2004		Current

COUNTRY	SI (SR & O) No.	STATUS
Amending Protocol of 26 June 2007	2007/3465	Current
Taiwan		
Agreement of 8 April 2002	2002/3137	Current
Tajikistan		

Note – See SP 4/01 for the status of the Convention of 31 July 1985 with the former USSR.

Thailand		
Convention of 18 February 1981	1981/1546	Current
Trinidad & Tobago		
Convention of 31 December 1982	1983/1903	Current
Tunisia		
Convention of 15 December 1982	1984/133	Current
Turkey		
Agreement of 19 December 1986	1988/932	Current
Turkmenistan		

Note – See SP 4/01 for the status of the Convention of 31 July 1985 with the former USSR.

Turks and Caicos		
Tax Information Exchange Agreement of 16 December 2004		Current
Tuvalu – see Kiribati & Tuvalu		
Uganda		
Convention of 23 December 1992	1993/1802	Current
Ukraine		
Convention of 10 February 1993	1993/1803	Current
Union of Soviet Socialist Republics		
Air Transport Agreement of 3 May 1974	1974/1269	Current
Convention of 31 July 1985	1986/224	Current
United States of America		
Estate, Inheritance and Gift Agreement of 16 April 1945	1946/1351	Terminated
Estate, Inheritance and Gift Agreement of 19 October 1978	1979/1454	Current
Convention of 31 December 1975		
Protocol of 26 August 1976		
Protocol of 31 March 1977 ⎫		
Protocol of 15 March 1979 ⎭	1980/568	Terminated
Convention of 24 July 2001⎫		
Protocol of 19 July 2002 ⎭	2002/2848	Current
Uzbekistan		
Convention of 15 October 1993	1994/770	Current
Venezuela		
Convention of 11 March 1996	1996/2599	Current
Vietnam		
Convention of 9 April 1994	1994/3216	Current
Zaire		
Shipping and Air Transport Agreement of 11 October 1976	1977/1298	Current
Zambia		
Convention of 22 March 1972	1972/1721	Current
Amending Protocol of 30 April 1981	1981/1816	Current
Zanzibar – see Tanzania		
Zimbabwe		
Convention of 19 October 1982	1982/1842	Current

Multilateral conventions

- EC Convention of 23 July 1990 on the elimination of double taxation in connection with the adjustment of profits of associated enterprises (90/436/EEC) (the Arbitration Convention); and
- OECD/COE Convention on Administrative Assistance in the Assessment and Collection of Tax.

Table of Cases

(References are to paragraph numbers)

Cam

Table of Legislation and Statutory Instruments

(References are to paragraph numbers)

Table of Bilateral Treaties

(References are to paragraph numbers)

Table of Other Treaties and Conventions

(References are to paragraph numbers)

Index

(References are to paragraph numbers)